The Double Eagle Guide to

CAMPING *in*

WESTERN

PARKS *and* FORESTS

VOLUME VI

SOUTHWEST PLAINS

TEXAS
OKLAHOMA

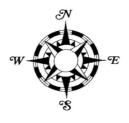

A DOUBLE EAGLE GUIDE™

DISCOVERY PUBLISHING
BILLINGS, YELLOWSTONE COUNTY, MONTANA USA

The Double Eagle Guide to Camping in Western Parks and Forests
Volume VI Southwest Plains

PUBLISHED BY
Discovery Publishing
Editorial Offices
Post Office Box 50545
Billings, Montana 59105 USA

Discovery Publishing is an independent, private enterprise. The information contained herein should not be construed as reflecting the publisher's approval of the policies or practices of the public agencies listed.

Information in this book is subject to change without notice.

Cover Photos (clockwise from the top):
        Humboldt National Forest, Nevada
        Lake Owyhee State Park, Oregon
        Memphis Lake State Recreation Area, Nebraska
        Big Bend National Park, Texas

Frontispiece: Monahans Sandhills State Park, Texas

10 9 8 7 6 5 4 3 2 1

June 16, 1994   8:18 AM Mountain Time

Produced, printed, and bound in the United States of America.

ISBN 0-929760-26-3

TABLE OF CONTENTS

(Page intentionally left blank)

8

INTRODUCTION TO THE *Double Eagle*™ SERIES

Whether you're a veteran of many Western camps or are planning your first visit, this series is for you.

In the six volumes of *The Double Eagle Guide to Camping in Western Parks and Forests*, we've described most public campgrounds along or conveniently near the highways and byways of the 17 contiguous Western United States. Also included is basic information about jackcamping and backpacking on the millions of acres of undeveloped public lands in the West. Our goal is to provide you with accurate, detailed, and yet concise, *first-hand* information about literally thousands of camping areas you're most likely to want to know about.

The volumes which comprise the *Double Eagle*™ series constitute a significant departure from the sketchy, plain vanilla approach to campground information provided by other guidebooks. Here, for the first time, is the most *useful* information about the West's most *useable* public camping areas. We've included a broad assortment of campgrounds from which you can choose: From simple, free camps, to sites in deluxe, landscaped surroundings.

The name for this critically acclaimed series was suggested by the celebrated United States twenty-dollar gold piece--most often called the *"Double Eagle"*--the largest and finest denomination of coinage ever issued by the U.S. Mint. The *Double Eagle* has long been associated with the history of the West, as a symbol of traditional Western values, prosperity, and excellence.

So, too, the *Double Eagle*™ series seeks to provide you with information about what are perhaps the finest of all the West's treasures--its public recreational lands owned, operated, and overseen by the citizens of the Western United States.

We hope you'll enjoy reading these pages, and come to use the information in the volumes to enhance your own appreciation for the outstanding camping opportunities available in the West.

Live long and prosper.

Thomas and *Elizabeth Preston*
Publishers

CONVENTIONS USED IN THIS SERIES

The following conventions or standards are used throughout the *Double Eagle*™ series as a means of providing a sense of continuity between one park or forest and other public lands, and between one campground and the next.

State Identifier: The state name and number combination in the upper left corner of each campground description provides an easy means of cross-referencing the written information to the numbered locations on the maps in the Appendix.

Whenever possible, the campgrounds have been arranged in what we have determined to be a reasonable progression, and based on *typical travel patterns* within a region. Generally speaking, a north to south, west to east pattern has been followed. In certain cases, particularly those involving one-way-in, same-way-out roads, we have arranged the camps in the order in which they would be encountered on the way into the area, so the standard plan occasionally may be reversed.

Campground Name: The officially designated name for the campground is listed, followed by the park, forest, or other public recreation area in which it is located.

Location: This section allows you to obtain a quick approximation of a campground's location in relation to nearby major communities.

Access: Our *Accurate Access* system makes extensive use of highway mileposts in order to pinpoint the location of access roads, intersections, and other major terminal points. (Mileposts are about 98 percent reliable--but occasionally they are mowed by a snowplow or an errant motorist, and may be missing; or, worse yet, the mileposts were replaced in the wrong spot!) In some instances, locations are noted primarily utilizing mileages between two or more nearby locations--usually communities, but occasionally key junctions or prominent structures or landmarks.

Since everyone won't be approaching a campground from the same direction, we've provided access information from two, sometimes three, points. In all cases, we've chosen the access points for their likelihood of use. Distances from communities are listed from the approximate **midtown** point, unless otherwise specified. Mileages from Interstate highways and other freeway exits are usually given from the approximate center of the interchange. Mileages from access points have been rounded to the nearest mile, unless the exact mileage is critical. All instructions are given using the current official highway map available free from each state.

Directions are given using a combination of compass and hand headings, i.e., "turn north (left)" or "swing west (right)". This isn't a bonehead navigation system, by any means. When the sun is shining or you're in a region where moss grows on tree trunks, it's easy enough to figure out which way is north. But anyone can become temporarily disoriented on an overcast day or a moonless night while looking for an inconspicuous campground turnoff, or while being buzzed by heavy traffic at a key intersection, so we built this redundancy into the system.

Facilities: The items in this section have been listed in the approximate order in which a visitor might observe them during a typical swing through a campground. Following the total number of individual camp units, items pertinent to the campsites themselves are listed, then information related to 'community' facilities. It has been assumed that each campsite has a picnic table.

Site types: (1) Standard--no hookup; (2) Partial hookup--water, electricity; (3) Full hookup--water, electricity, sewer.

We have extensively employed the use of *general* and *relative* terms in describing the size, separation, and levelness of the campsites ("medium to large", "fairly well separated", "basically level", etc.). Please note that "separation" is a measure of relative privacy and is a composite of both natural visual screens and spacing between campsites. The information is presented as an *estimate* by highly experienced observers. Please allow for variations in perception between yourself and the reporters.

Parking Pads: (1) Straight-ins, (sometimes called "back-ins")-- the most common type, are just that--straight strips angled off the driveway; (2) Pull-throughs--usually the most convenient type for large rv's, they provide an in-one-end-and-out-the-other parking space; pull-throughs may be either arc-shaped and separated from the main driveway by some sort of barrier or 'island' (usually vegetation), or arranged in parallel rows; (3) Pull-offs--essentially just wide spots adjacent to the driveway. Pad lengths have been categorized as: (1) Short-- a single, large vehicle up to about the size of a standard pickup truck; (2) Medium--a single vehicle or combination up to the length of a pickup towing a single-axle trailer; Long--a single vehicle or combo as long as a crew cab pickup towing a double-axle trailer. Normally, any overhang out the back of the pad has been ignored in the estimate, so it might be possible to slip a crew cab pickup hauling a fifth-wheel trailer in tandem with a ski boat into some pads, but we'll leave that to your discretion.

Fire appliances have been categorized in three basic forms: (1) Fireplaces--angular, steel or concrete, ground-level; (2) Fire rings--circular, steel or concrete, ground-level or below ground-level; (3) Barbecue grills--angular steel box, supported by a steel post about 36 inches high. (The trend is toward installing steel fire rings, since they're durable, relatively inexpensive--50 to 80 dollars apiece--and easy to install and maintain. Barbecue grills are often used in areas where ground fires are a problem, as when charcoal-only fires are permitted.)

Toilet facilities have been listed thusly: (1) Restrooms--"modern", i.e., flush toilets and usually a wash basin; (2) Vault facilities--"simple", i.e., outhouses, pit toilets, call them what you like, (a rose by any other name.....).

Campers' supply points have been described at five levels: (1) Camper Supplies--buns, beans and beverages; (2) Gas and Groceries--a 'convenience' stop; (3) Limited--at least one store which approximates a small supermarket, more than one fuel station, a general merchandise store, hardware store, and other basic services; (4) Adequate--more than one supermarket, (including something that resembles an IGA or a Safeway), a choice of fuel brands, and several general and specialty stores and services; (5) Complete--they have a major discount store.

Campground managers, attendants and hosts are not specifically listed since their presence can be expected during the regular camping season in more than 85 percent of the campgrounds listed in this volume.

Activities & Attractions: As is mentioned a number of times throughout this series, the local scenery may be the principal attraction of the campground (and, indeed, may be the *only* one you'll need). Other nearby attractions/activities have been listed if they are low-cost or free, and are available to the general public. An important item: *Swimming and boating areas usually do not have lifeguards.*

Natural Features: Here we've drawn a word picture of the natural environment in and around each campground. Please remember that seasonal, even daily, conditions will affect the appearance of the area. A normally "sparkling stream" can be a muddy torrent for a couple of weeks in late spring; a "deep blue lake" might be a nearly empty hole in a drought year; "lush vegetation" may have lost all its greenery by the time you arrive in late October. Elevations above 500′ are rounded to the nearest 100′; lower elevations are rounded to the nearest 50′. (Some elevations are estimated, but no one should develop a nosebleed or a headache because of a 100′ difference in altitude.)

Season, Fees & Phone: Seasons listed are approximate, since weather conditions, particularly in mountainous/hilly regions, may require adjustments in opening/closing dates. Campground gates are usually unlocked from 6:00 a.m. to 10:00 p.m. Fee information listed here was obtained directly from the responsible agencies just a few hours before press time. Fees should be considered **minimum** fees *per camping vehicle*, since they are always subject to adjustment by agencies or legislatures. Discounts and special passes are usually available for seniors and disabled persons. The listed telephone number can be called to obtain information about current conditions in or near that campground.

Camp Notes: Consider this section to be somewhat more subjective in nature than the others. In order to provide our readers with a well-rounded report, we have listed personal comments related to our field observations. (Our enthusiasm for the West is, at times, unabashedly proclaimed. So if the prose sometimes sounds like a tourist promotion booklet, please bear with us--there's a lot to be enthusiastic about!)

Editorial remarks (Ed.) occasionally have been included.

A Word About Style...

Throughout the *Double Eagle*™ series, we've utilized a free-form writing concept which we call "Notation Format". Complete sentences, phrases, and single words have been incorporated into the camp descriptions as appropriate under the circumstances. We've adopted this style in order to provide our readers with detailed information about each item, while maintaining conciseness, clarity, and conversationality.

A Word About Print...

Another departure from the norm is our use of print sizes which are 10 to 20 percent larger (or more) than ordinary guides. (We also use narrower margins for less paper waste.) It's one thing to read a guidebook in the convenience and comfort of your well-lit living room. It's another matter to peruse the pages while you're bounding and bouncing along in your car or camper as the sun is setting; or by a flickering flashlight inside a breeze-buffeted dome tent. We hope *this* works for you, too.

A Word About Maps...

After extensive tests of the state maps by seasoned campers, both at home and in the field, we decided to localize all of the maps in one place in the book. Campers felt that, since pages must be flipped regardless of where the maps are located, it would be more desirable to have them all in one place. We're confident that you'll also find this to be a convenient feature.

A Word About 'Regs'...

Although this series is about public campgrounds, you'll find comparatively few mentions of rules, regulations, policies, ordinances, statutes, decrees or dictates. Our editorial policy is this: (1) It's the duty of a citizen or a visitor to know his legal responsibilities (and, of course, his corresponding *rights*); (2) Virtually every campground has the appropriate regulations publicly posted for all to study; and (3) If you're reading this *Double Eagle*™ Guide, chances are you're in the upper ten percent of the conscientious citizens of the United States or some other civilized country and you probably don't need to be constantly reminded of these matters.

And a Final Word...

We've tried very, very hard to provide you with accurate information about the West's great camping opportunities But occasionally, things aren't as they're supposed to be .....

If a campground's access, facilities or fees have been recently changed, please let us know. We'll try to pass along the news to other campers.

If the persons in the next campsite keep their generator poppety-popping past midnight so they can cook a turkey in the microwave, blame the bozos, not the book.

If the beasties are a bit bothersome in that beautiful spot down by the bog, note the day's delights and not the difficulties.

Thank you for buying our book. We hope that you'll have many terrific camping trips!

Texas

Public Campgrounds

The Texas map is located in the Appendix on page 175.

TEXAS
Panhandle
Please refer to the Texas map in the Appendix

Texas 1

HARBOR BAY
Lake Meredith Recreation Area/NPS

Location: Texas Panhandle northeast of Amarillo.

Access: From Texas State Highway 136 (West Broadway) at the west edge of the city of Fritch, turn northwest onto a paved local road (should be signed for Harbor Bay) and proceed 1.5 miles to the campground.

Facilities: Approximately 30 camp/picnic sites; sites are essentially small and closely spaced; parking areas are on sandy soil, any-size, any-way; adequate space for large tents; a few barbecue grills; b-y-o firewood; no drinking water; vault facilities; paved main driveway; limited+ supplies and services are available in Fritch.

Activities & Attractions: Fishing (generally good for walleye and catfish, so-so for bass); fishing pier; boating; boat launch and dock; Alibates National Monument, with its ancient flint quarries, is a few miles west of here.

Natural Features: Located along the edge of Harbor Bay on the south-east shore of Lake Meredith; vegetation consists of sparse grass, small bushes, and a few large hardwoods; most sites are unshaded, some are wind-sheltered; bordered by boulder-dotted bluffs; elevation 3000'.

Season, Fees & Phone: Available all year, with limited services October to April; no fee (subject to change); 14 day limit; Lake Meredith Recreation Area Headquarters, National Park Service, Fritch, (806) 857-3151.

Camp Notes: From the foregoing description, you may have visualized a place that doesn't have much to offer. Well, strictly from a facilities standpoint, it doesn't. But then why is it filled to (and beyond) capacity on nearly every summer weekend? Most of the campers at Lake Meredith are locals--from 100 to 150 miles away--and most are repeat customers. Most come to fish and boat, and this spot allows them to participate with relative ease. A boat can be beached right alongside a camp/picnic site. (Technically, all of the sites at Lake Meredith are picnic sites--hence no fee--but Park Service officials say it's OK to camp, as long as you don't exceed the 14 day limit.)

Texas 2

SANFORD-YAKE
Lake Meredith Recreation Area/NPS

Location: Texas Panhandle northeast of Amarillo.

Access: From Texas State Highway 136 at the southeast city limits of the city of Fritch, turn north onto a paved local road and proceed (if you pass a stadium on the left, you're on the right road) 2.7 miles to a 3-way intersection; turn east/northeast (right) and continue for 2.6 miles (past the ranger station); turn west (left) into the camp area.

Facilities: Approximately 50 camp/picnic sites; sites are small to medium-sized, with minimal to fair separation; parking pads are gravel, generally medium to long straight-ins or pull-offs which may require some additional leveling; adequate, though generally sloped, space for medium to large tents on a grassy/stoney surface; ramadas (sun shelters) for most sites; barbecue grills; b-y-o firewood; water at a central faucet; restrooms; holding tank disposal station; gravel driveways; limited+ supplies and services are available in Fritch.

Activities & Attractions: Fishing; boating; boat launch; (a swimming pond/lagoon with a large sandy beach is located below the dam, a couple of miles northeast of here).

Natural Features: Located on a bluff above the south-east shore of Lake Meredith, a reservoir on the Canadian River; vegetation principally consists of sparse grass, sage, yucca and medium to large hardwoods which provide very light shade for some sites; encircled by semi-arid, windswept High Plains; elevation 3000'.

Season, Fees & Phone: Available all year, with limited services October to April; no fee (subject to change); 14 day limit; Lake Meredith Recreation Area Headquarters, National Park Service, Fritch, (806) 857-3151.

Camp Notes: Just west of here are two other small camping areas worth considering: Cedar Canyon, which is popular because of its lakeshore location; and Fritch Fortress, on a high, unprotected blufftop, which might appeal to some campers because it *isn't* popular. Both have drinking water; Cedar Canyon has vaults, Fritch Fortress has restrooms. Lake Meredith is one of two federal recreation areas in Texas that are operated by the National Park Service. (The other is Amistad Recreation Area on the Rio Grande near Del Rio.) However, unlike most other recreation areas operated by the Park Service, they're not called "*National* Recreation Areas". Lake Meredith was created by a Bureau of Reclamation dam and the Park Service was found to be a (willing) caretaker of the substantial piece of property. It does seem that universal appeal in terms of location, geography, potential activities, attractions, and especially funding for development, were deficient. Since most of the visitors come from Amarillo and other nearby environs, it might have very well been called a "Lake Meredith *Regional* Recreation Area", but then the feds couldn't have gotten involved. The lake is named for A.A. Meredith, the principal advocate of the water project.

Texas 3

BUFFALO LAKE
Buffalo Lake National Wildlife Refuge

Location: Texas Panhandle southwest of Amarillo.

Access: From U.S. Highway 60 in Umbarger (12 miles southwest of Canyon, 20 miles northeast of Hereford), turn south onto Farm Road 168 and proceed 2 miles; at a point where the road turns sharply east, drive south on a gravel access road for 0.6 mile to the entrance station; continue for 0.1 mile beyond the entrance, swing west (right) for 0.8 mile, then south for a final 0.2 mile to the campground.

Facilities: 25 campsites; sites are medium-sized, essentially level, with fair separation; parking pads are gravel, medium+ straight-ins; adequate space for large tents on a grassy surface; barbecue grills; b-y-o firewood is recommended; water at central faucets; restrooms; gravel driveways; gas and groceries in Umbarger; adequate+ supplies and services are available in Canyon.

Activities & Attractions: Hiking trails; self-guiding auto tours; wildlife observation; managed hunting.

Natural Features: Located on a grassy flat in a narrow valley (or a wide, shallow canyon) above Buffalo Lake on the *Llano Estacado*; sites are light-to-moderately shaded/sheltered by large hardwoods; surrounding plains are covered with tall grass and wildflowers; in a good year, up to a million ducks may winter in this area; elevation 3000'.

Season, Fees & Phone: Available all year, with reduced services in winter; $3.00 per day entrance/use fee (Golden Eagle Passports are accepted); 7 day limit; Buffalo Lake National Wildlife Refuge Headquarters (806) 499-3382.

Camp Notes: Because the shallow, 1600-acre lake is subject to the caprices of climate and season, you may encounter little more than a damp marsh. If you come here spring to fall, you'll probably find a nice, very quiet campground in a pleasantly green setting. The West's NWR's usually aren't highly regarded for their camping facilities, but unless you insist on a campground with all the fixin's, this little spot should prove to be quite agreeable. *Llano Estacado*, the famed 'Staked Plains' of West Texas and Eastern New Mexico have been traveled by Europeans since Coronado first explored this vast region in 1542, and for untold prior centuries by Indians. The name refers to the Plains' great isolated escarpments which, when viewed from a distance, resemble fortresses or stockades with outer walls made of tall pickets or stakes sunk into the earth.

Texas 4

PALO DURO CANYON
Palo Duro Canyon State Park

Location: Texas Panhandle southeast of Amarillo.

Access: From Interstate 27 at the Canyon exit (14 miles south of Amarillo), travel east on Texas State Highway 217 for 10 miles to the park entrance; proceed down a winding, steep grade for 3 miles to the canyon floor; continue for 1.5 miles to 5 miles to the 6 camp loops (in the order listed): *Hackberry*, *Fortress Cliff*, *Sunflower*, *Cactus*, *Juniper*, *Mesquite*.

Facilities: *Hackberry*: 33 campsites with partial hookups; *Fortress Cliff*: 18 standard campsites; *Sunflower*: 18 standard campsites; *Cactus*: 7 standard campsites; *Juniper*: 20 campsites with partial hookups, designated for trailers; *Mesquite*: 20 campsites with partial hookups; sites vary from small to medium+, most are reasonably level, with fairly good to excellent separation; parking pads are paved or packed gravel, mostly medium-length straight-ins; Juniper loop has long pull-throughs; tent spaces vary from small to large; many sites have ramadas (sun shelters); barbecue grills and fireplaces; b-y-o firewood; water at faucets throughout; restrooms with showers; holding tank disposal station; paved driveways; adequate+ supplies and services are available in the city of Canyon.

Activities & Attractions: Interpretive center; historical exhibits; hiking trails; trail rides, train rides, historical performances in an outdoor amphitheater (extra charge for the last 3).

Natural Features: Located in miles-long, mile-wide Palo Duro Canyon along Prairie Dog Town Fork of the Red River; sites receive minimal to medium shade/shelter from medium to large hardwoods and junipers; bordered by 800', brilliant red canyon walls; elevation 3000'.

Season, Fees & Phone: Open all year, subject to weather and road conditions; 14 day limit; reservations recommended for spring through fall weekends; please see Appendix for additional reservation information and standard Texas state park fees; park office (806) 488-2227.

Camp Notes: Best bets? For a tent site, the Sunflower Loop; for hookups, Mesquite lacks natural shade but provides the best views, Juniper has the largest and most private sites, and Hackberry is a good compromise. *Palo Duro* means "hardwood", and the canyon is colorful in both geology, botany and history. Aboriginals hunted mammoths and other animals in the canyon nearly 12,000 years ago. Coronado may have camped here in 1541 while searching for the Seven Cities of Cibola. By the early 1800's the canyon had become a Comanche stronghold. In 1874, troops led by Colonel Ranald Mackenzie (also see Mackenzie Lake Campground) attacked a large gathering of Comanches and Kiowas camped near the southeast corner of the present-day state park. Mackenzie's men won the battle--the last great encounter in the Texas Indian Wars. Two years later, Charles Goodnight established a large cattle ranch here, using an earthen dugout hut as his headquarters. (The site of the dugout is near the Hackberry camp loop). Several years earlier, Goodnight and his partner Oliver Loving had blazed the famous Goodnight-Loving cattle trail from North Texas to Cheyenne. Considering all of the park's history and geography, it would be worth going out of your way to camp in this emerald-fringed, cardinal-colored chasm.

Texas 5

PIONEERS
Collingsworth County Park

Location: Texas Panhandle east of Amarillo.

Access: From U.S. Highway 83 at a point 7 miles north of Wellington, at the north end of the bridge which spans the Salt Fork of the Red River, 18 miles south of Shamrock, turn west into the park entrance; the camping area is at the southwest corner of the park. (Note: U.S. 83 is a 4-lane, divided highway in this area; a crossover is provided for northbound traffic at this point.)

Facilities: 12 campsites with partial hookups, plus additional room for several standard/tent campers; sites are small+, level and closely spaced; parking surfaces are paved, long pull-throughs or short straight-ins (depending upon another camper's use of the pad); ample space for large tents on a grassy surface; ramadas and barbecue grills close-by; b-y-o firewood; water at sites and at central faucets; restrooms (shared with the day use area); mostly paved driveways; limited+ supplies and services are available in Wellington.

Activities & Attractions: Good highwayside stop.

Natural Features: Located on a grassy flat along the north bank of the Salt Fork of the Red River; sites receive light-medium shade from large hardwoods; elevation 2100'.

Season, Fees & Phone: Available all year, subject to weather conditions; $4.00; 3 day limit; Collingsworth County Parks and Recreation Department, Wellington, (806) 447-5408.

Camp Notes: Some sources claim that there are 24 sites here vs the 12 stated above. OK, but don't forget to tuck-in all the sideview mirrors when the last dozen vehicles are squeezed through the parking pads. Small, local parks rarely deserve more than a mention--typically because they're in considerably less-than-useable condition. But this one has well-built restrooms and picnic ramadas, plus spacious, nicely landscaped grounds, which might make it a handy and pleasant roadside stop for you some night.

Texas 6

MACKENZIE LAKE
Mackenzie Water Authority

Location: Texas Panhandle southwest of Amarillo.

Access: From Texas State Highway 207 at a point 7 mile north of its junction with Texas State Highway 86 west of Silverton, 41 miles south of Claude, turn west into the recreation area entrance station; proceed south across the dam on a paved road for 0.8 mile, then on gravel for another 0.4 mile to the camping areas.

Facilities: 63 campsites, including 38 with partial hookups; sites vary from very small to large, with minimal to fairly good separation; parking surfaces are gravel/grass, short to medium-length straight-ins, many of which will require a little additional leveling; tent space varies from small to large; (only some sites have tables, more tables are planned); central shelters; barbecue barrels; b-y-o firewood; water at sites and at several faucets; central restrooms with showers; holding tank disposal stations; gravel driveways; gas and groceries in Silverton.

Activities & Attractions: Fishing for bass, walleye, crappie, perch, stripers and assorted catfish; boating; boat launches and docks; windsurfing; nature trail.

Natural Features: Located around the rim of what formerly was Tule Canyon, above the south shore of Mackenzie Lake; some hookup sites are situated along the top of a point of land, remaining sites are on flats and slopes above the main shore; rocky outcroppings, unusual rock formations and sheer rock walls constitute much of the lake's shoreline; elevation 3100'.

Season, Fees & Phone: Available all year, subject to weather conditions; $3.00 for a standard site, $8.00 for a hookup site, plus daily entrance fee of $3.00 per person 13 or older; 14 day limit; (no phone).

Camp Notes: The lake was named for Colonel Ranald S. Mackenzie who led U.S. troops against hostile Indians and desperados who roamed the High Plains in the 1870's. Mackenzie's forces tackled the toughest taming jobs as far north as Central Wyoming and as far south as the Rio Grande.

Texas 7

CAPROCK CANYONS
Caprock Canyons State Park

Location: Texas Panhandle southeast of Amarillo.

Access: From Texas State Highway 86 at the west edge of the town of Quitaque (16 miles southeast of Silverton, 10 miles west of Turkey), turn north onto Ranch Road 1065 and proceed 3 miles to a fork; bear left at the fork for 1 mile to the park entrance; continue northwest (past the lake) for 0.3 mile, then northeast for a quarter-mile to the *Honey Flat* area; or continue for an additional 4 miles north, then west, to the *South Prong* walk-in area).

Facilities: *Honey Flat*: 35 campsites, including 25 with partial hookups, in a single large loop; sites are medium-sized, level, with fair to good separation; parking pads are paved, medium-length straight-ins; ample space for large tents on a grassy surface; ramadas (sun/partial wind shelters) for all sites; fire rings; b-y-o firewood; water at faucets throughout; restrooms with showers; holding tank disposal station; paved driveway; *South Prong*: 20 simple walk-in tent campsites, accessible via short trails; (a backpack camping area in North Prong is accessible via a 1-mile trail); sites are large, with excellent separation; sites are within 300 yards of a designated parking lot; no drinking water; vault facilities; gas and groceries are available in Quitaque.

Activities & Attractions: 16 miles of hiking and equestrian trails; swimming, fishing and limited boating; interpretive displays.

Natural Features: Located on a plain at the base of the Caprock Escarpment; vegetation principally consists of tall grass and large brush, plus some hardwoods and junipers; Honey Flat is out on the open plain; sites in South Prong are nestled up against the base of the cliff near the streambed of the South Prong of the Little Red River; 100-acre Lake Theo is the park's water feature; elevation 2400'.

Season, Fees & Phone: Open all year; 14 day limit; reservations recommended for spring through fall weekends; please see Appendix for additional reservation information and standard Texas state park fees; park office (806) 455-1492.

Camp Notes: The Caprock Escarpment is a several-hundred-mile-long, redrock cliff which serves as the geological boundary between the High Plains to the west and the Rolling Plains to the east. The 'scarp rises a thousand feet above the tablelands below, and its multi-faceted, rough-hewn rocks and canyons are absolutely fiery in the vibrant, angled light of a.m. and p.m. There's also quite a lot of wildlife in the park, including some exotic species that have been transplanted from locations around the world. (Smile, if you see an *aoudad*.)

BUFFALO SPRINGS LAKE
Lubbock County Water District 1

Location: West Texas southeast of Lubbock.

Access: From any major highway entering Lubbock (i.e., I-27, U.S. 84, U.S. 87, U.S. 62/82), pick up Loop 289 and travel toward the southeast corner of the city to near milepost 16; take the exit for Farm Road 835/East 50th Street/Buffalo Springs Lake; proceed east then south on Farm Road 835 for 4 miles; turn east (left) onto a 4-lane access road for 0.3 mile to the park entrance/office; continuing ahead, then down the hill and around to the west end of the lake will put you in the campground.

Facilities: Approximately 100 campsites, about half with full or partial hookups; sites are small to small+, with nominal to fair separation; parking surfaces are gravel/earth, medium to medium+ straight-ins or pull-throughs; a little additional leveling may be required in some sites; water at sites and at central faucets; restrooms with showers; disposal station; paved main roadway, gravel/earth sub-drives; gas and groceries on the Farm Road; complete supplies and services are available in Lubbock.

Activities & Attractions: Mason-Audubon Society Interpretive Center; nature trail; fishing; boating; waterskiing.

Natural Features: Located in Yellowhouse Canyon on the south-west shore of Buffalo Springs Lake, a long, thin, winding impoundment on the North Fork & Double Mountain Fork of the Brazos River; sites receive light to medium shade/shelter from large hardwoods on a grassy surface; bordered by nearly treeless bluffs; elevation 3200'.

Season, Fees & Phone: Open all year; $9.00 for a standard site, $10.00 for a partial hookup site, $11.00 for a full hookup site; (prices include admission for 2 adults); 14 day limit; park office (806) 747-3353.

Camp Notes: Few other full-service public camps in Texas are handier to a major city than this one. The local Audubon people clearly have put forth a lot of effort into enhancing the nature study opportunities here.

OLD FLOREY
Florey County Park

Location: West Texas north of Odessa.

Access: From U.S. Highway 385 at a point 9.5 miles north of Andrews and 19 miles south of Seminole, turn east onto County Park Road and proceed 1.2 miles; turn south into the park.

Facilities: Approximately 125 campsites, most with partial hookups; sites are very small to small, level, with nil separation; parking surfaces are sandy gravel, mostly short straight-ins; adequate space for large tents; a few tables and barbecue barrels are nearby; water at most sites; holding tank disposal station; paved main driveway; adequate+ supplies and services are available in Andrews.

Activities & Attractions: Tennis and volleyball courts; pavilion; playground; campfire circle.

Natural Features: Located on and around a large, tree-and-grass-covered infield; most sites are unshaded; surrounded by plains, agricultural land and oil fields; (you may want to inquire about the "Poisonous Gas" signs posted by everyone's' favorite oil company); elevation 3200'.

Season, Fees & Phone: Open most of the year; $3.50 for a standard site, $6.00 for a hookup site; 7 day limit; park office (915) 523-4812.

Camp Notes: Some sources claim there are as many as 250 sites here. In actuality (and practicality), to jam that many campers on these rather nicely kept grounds would be to establish a feedlot packed with metal and canvas critters. The nearby town of Andrews also has a public campground, of sorts. It's on State Highway 115 (West Broadway), a half mile west of U.S. 385, in a parking lot behind the Chamber of Commerce building. There are 10 full hookup sites there, and you can stay for free on a 3-day limit. (You probably *could* pitch a free-standing tent on this midtown macadam, but wouldn't *that* be a bit tacky?) Restrooms? Well, the Chamber office is open weekdays from 8-5. (Hours and availability subject to change.)

LAKE COLORADO CITY
Lake Colorado City State Recreation Area

Location: West Texas northeast of Big Spring.

Access: From Interstate 20 Exit 210, (7 miles west of Colorado City, 3 miles east of Westbrook), turn southeast onto Farm Road 2836 and travel 5.5 miles; turn north (left) into the recreation area and continue for 0.6 mile to the hookup loops, or 1.2 mile to the standard areas, both on the east (right) side of the park road; **Alternate Access:** From Texas State Highway 163 at a point 7 miles southwest of Colorado City, drive west on Farm Road 2836 for 0.7 mile to the recreation area and proceed as above.

Facilities: 132 campsites, including 79 with partial hookups; sites are medium-sized, with nominal to fair separation; most parking pads are hard-surfaced, medium to long straight-ins, and some will require a touch of additional leveling; large, grassy tent areas; ramadas (sun shelters) for many sites; barbecue grills and/or fire rings; b-y-o firewood; water at faucets throughout; restrooms with showers; holding tank disposal station; paved driveways; adequate supplies and services are available in Colorado City.

Activities & Attractions: Fishing for bass and catfish; fishing piers; boating; boat launch; swimming beach; playground.

Natural Features: Located just above the southwest shore of Lake Colorado City on the West Texas Plains; campground vegetation consists mostly of short grass specked with small hardwoods; elevation 2100'.

Season, Fees & Phone: Open all year; 14 day limit; please see Appendix for reservation information and standard Texas state park fees; park office (915) 728-3931.

Camp Notes: First, the not-so-good news: chances are your campsite will have a great view of the local power plant and its assorted wires and appliances. Now, the good news: the heated cooling water from the juice maker warms the lake, providing a longer-than-usual feeding and growing (and swimming and boating) season for the lake's wildlife (be they finned, feathered, furred or swimsuited).

TEXAS
Southwest
Please refer to the Texas map in the Appendix

HUECO TANKS
Hueco Tanks State Historical Park

Location: Southwest Texas east of El Paso.

Access: From U.S. Highways 62 & 180 at a point 25 miles east of downtown El Paso, 36 miles west of beautiful downtown Cornudas), turn north onto Farm Road 2775 (paved) and travel 5.5 miles; continue ahead, then east, on Park Road 68 for 2 miles to the park entrance station; proceed ahead for 0.05 mile, then turn left for a final half-mile to the campground.

Facilities: 20 campsites, most with partial hookups; sites are medium-sized, level, with fair to good separation; parking pads are paved, medium+ straight-ins; adequate space for large tents on a sandy surface; some sites have framed tent pads; many sites have small ramadas (sun shelters); fire rings and barbecue grills; b-y-o firewood; water at faucets throughout; restrooms with showers; holding tank disposal station; resident ranger-manager; paved driveways; nearest reliable sources of supplies and services (complete) are in El Paso.

Activities & Attractions: Hiking, nature and archaeological trails; pictographs and a few petroglyphs; rock climbing (check park regs); playground; amphitheater.

Natural Features: Located on a desert plain against a backdrop of barren rock hills (locally termed North, East and West Mountain) in the Hueco Mountains area; campground vegetation consists of a few medium to large trees and an assortment of desert brush; elevation 4000'.

Season, Fees & Phone: Open all year; please see Appendix for reservation information and standard Texas state park fees; 14 day limit; park office (915) 857-1135.

Camp Notes: Most campsites have some sort of shade, be it natural or from the small, flat-topped ramadas. (You may still want to bring some of your own rolled or folded shade in case you get one of the sunnier spots.) For untold centuries, desert inhabitants and travelers have gathered rain water from the "tanks", natural, water-collecting basins (*huecos*) in the massive rock formations within the park. Under some circumstances, certain desert desert-dwellers gather *in* and *around* the tanks. Under the right conditions, several varieties of tiny shrimp reproduce and mature in great numbers in the seasonally deep rock-bottom ponds. As the water level is reduced through evaporation, winged and four-legged predators feast on the tasty tidbits.

Texas 12

PINE SPRINGS
Guadalupe Mountains National Park

Location: Southwest Texas east of El Paso.

Access: From U.S. Highways 62 & 180 at a point 0.1 mile west of the settlement of Pine Springs, 9 miles east of the junction of U.S 62 & 180 and Texas State Highway 54, 109 miles east of El Paso, turn northwest onto a paved access road and proceed 0.7 mile to the campground.

Facilities: 43 campsites in 2 loops; about half of the sites are walk-in units, remainder are standard sites, or parking-lot style primarily for rv's; designated handicapped-access unit in the rv lot; walk-in sites are medium-sized, with good to very good separation; standard and rv sites are small to very small, with little separation; parking surfaces for standard/rv units are short to short+, level and paved; walk-ins have framed tent/table pads, generally suitable for large tents; no fire facilities; water at several faucets; restrooms; ranger station nearby; gas and camper supplies are available in Pine Springs.

Activities & Attractions: Visitor center; several hiking trails.

Natural Features: Located on a gentle slope in the Guadalupe Mountains; campground vegetation consists of small pines, junipers, yucca, cactus and other small desert plants; excellent, near and distant mountain/desert views from in and around the campground; elevation 5600'.

Season, Fees & Phone: Open all year; $6.00; 14 day limit; Guadalupe Mountains National Park Headquarters, Pine Springs, (915) 828-3251.

Camp Notes: In keeping with the wilderness park theme of Guadalupe Mountains, the campground appears to have been designed with backpackers and car campers in mind. Most walk-in and standard sites have at least some shade, although you may have to sit down to find it, and rotate your position with the sun to keep it. But this *is* a desert park. In truth, irrespective of the naturally limited shade, many of the walk-ins are very agreeable campsites. The park's other camp, 20-site Dog Canyon, (see description below) can be reached via many, many miles of driving from here.

Texas 13

DOG CANYON
Guadalupe Mountains National Park

Location: Southwest Texas on the Texas-New Mexico border southwest of Carlsbad.

Access: From the junction of U.S. Highway 285 & New Mexico State Highway 137 (at milepost 45 +.6 on U.S. 285, 12 miles northwest of Carlsbad, 24 miles south of Artesia) head southwest on Highway 137 (Queens Highway) for 53 miles to the end of the pavement at the New Mexico-Texas border; continue into the Lone Star State on gravel for another 0.2 mile to the end of the road and the campground. **Alternate Access:** From U.S. Highways 62/180 (locally called the "National Parks Highway") at milepost 25 +.5 (10 miles southeast of Carlsbad, 10 miles north of Whites City), turn west onto Dark Canyon Road/Eddy County Road 408 (paved, but bumpy) and travel 23 miles to a "T" junction; turn south (left) onto New Mexico State Highway 137 and travel 34.5 miles south and southwest to the state border and continue as above.

(Special Note: The first Access is best if you're *southbound* from Roswell and don't need to get gas and grub in Carlsbad; the Alternate Access, which isn't depicted on most highway maps, is the most direct route if you're *northbound* from Carlsbad Caverns National Park and points south; however, if you're northbound and are planning to grab some supplies in Carlsbad, you'll need to double-back south for 10 miles from the city to the Dark Canyon Road turnoff.)

Facilities: 12-17 campsites (depending upon flash flood conditions), including 10-15 walk-in sites, in 2 areas; (a small group camp is also available); sites are generally small to small+, with nominal to fair separation; parking surfaces are gravel, short straight-ins for walk-in sites, medium-length pull-offs for 'trailer' units; adequate space for large tents on framed-and-gravelled tent pads; barbecue grills; charcoal fires only; charcoal is usually for sale, b-y-o is recommended; water at central faucets; restrooms; gas and camper supplies, 15 miles north; nearest year 'round source of supplies and services (complete) is Carlsbad, 65 miles northeast.

Activities & Attractions: Hiking trails; horse corral; small day use area.

Natural Features: Located along a streambed in Dog Canyon on the north-east slope of the Guadalupe Mountains; campground vegetation consists of light to light-medium hardwoods, junipers and a few pines, plus tall grass and desert plants; most sites have at least minimal shade/shelter; closely bordered by dry, rocky hills and mountains; elevation 5900'.

Season, Fees & Phone: Open all year; no fee (subject to change); 14 day limit; Guadalupe Mountains National Park Headquarters, Pine Springs Texas, (915) 828-3251.

Camp Notes: Dog Canyon Campground is only a few yards south of the Texas-New Mexico International Border, and virtually all road access is through New Mexico. Your tent may be sitting in Texas, but if you run a long guy line north from the canvas, the bitter end will be wrapped around a tent peg planted in New Mexico soil. In keeping with the wilderness theme of the park, this place is really designed for tent campers, and as a base camp for hikers and backpackers. In a few respects you might be a bit disappointed with this campground; if so, it would probably be with the simple facilities, not with the desert-mountain scenery.

Texas 14

WILLOW DRAW
Monahans Sandhills State Park

Location: West Texas southwest of Odessa.

Access: From Interstate 20 Exit 86 for the state park (6 miles northeast of the city of Monahans, 31 miles southwest of Odessa), turn north onto Park Road 41 and proceed 0.1 mile to the park entrance; continue ahead for 0.4 mile, then bear left (just before the concession stand) into the campground.

Facilities: 24 campsites, including 19 with partial hookups, in 2 loops; sites are small to medium-sized, with minimal separation; parking pads are paved, short to medium-length straight-ins or pull-offs; some pads may require a little additional leveling; enough space for small to medium-sized tents in most sites; barbecue grills or fireplaces; b-y-o firewood; ramadas (sun shelters) for many sites; water at faucets throughout; restrooms with showers; holding tank disposal station; paved driveways; adequate supplies and services are available in Monahans.

Activities & Attractions: Visitor center with botanical, historical, geological and archaeological exhibits; interpretive trail; sand surfing; (no vehicles permitted on the dunes); scheduled evening programs on summer weekends.

Natural Features: Located amid 20- to 70-feet sand dunes surrounded by brush-dotted plains; elevation 2600'.

Season, Fees & Phone: Open all year; please see Appendix for reservation information and standard Texas state park fees; 14 day limit; park office (915) 943-2092.

Camp Notes: Actually, the park's 3000 acres of sand comprise just a fraction of an immense dune field which stretches west and north from near here into New Mexico. Most of the sandhills you'll pass on the Interstate are so-called "stabilized dunes". But the park's dunes are "active", and thus build and diminish, advance and retreat continually. Interesting, freewayside stop.

Texas 15

BALMORHEA
Balmorhea State Recreation Area

Location: Southwest Texas west of Fort Stockton.

Access: From U.S. Highway 290 & Texas State Highway 17 at a point 4 miles southwest of the town of Balmorhea, on the east edge of Toyahvale, turn south into the park entrance; proceed 0.1 mile beyond the entrance, then turn east (left) and continue for 0.2 mile to the campground. (Note: From Interstate 10, take Exit 192, Exit 206 or Exit 209, depending upon your direction of approach, then follow the connecting highways to Balmorhea.)

Facilities: 34 campsites, majority with partial hookups; sites are medium-sized, level, with minimal to fair separation; parking pads are paved, medium-length straight-ins, or long pull-throughs; ample space for large tents on a grass and sand surface; large ramadas (sun/wind shelters) for most sites; fire rings and barbecue grills; b-y-o firewood; water at faucets; restrooms with showers; holding tank disposal station; paved driveways; gas and groceries are available in Balmorhea.

Activities & Attractions: Swimming in a very large, spring-fed swimming pool (open summer only, extra charge); playground.

Natural Features: Located on a semi-arid plain in Madera Valley near the foothills of the Davis Mountains; campground vegetation consists of mown lawns dotted with a few small hardwoods, and surrounded by desert brush; a canal flows along the south side of the campground; acres and acres of tree-dotted lawns are within the park; elevation 3200'.

Season, Fees & Phone: Open all year; 14 day limit; reservations recommended in summer; please see Appendix for additional reservation information and standard Texas state park fees; park office (915) 375-2370.

Camp Notes: The ramadas here are unique: they resemble miniature, white-washed, red-tile-roofed adobe houses--only with just two sides instead of being fully enclosed. Really distinctive. The established phrase "Oasis of West Texas" accurately describes this place. Generous San Solomon Springs supply about 24 million gallons of 76° water *per day* to what is claimed to be the world's largest spring-fed swimming pool. The name for the community of Balmorhea was coined from the portions of the names of three pioneering individuals who were prominent in the founding of the town in the late 1800's.

Texas 16

DAVIS MOUNTAINS
Davis Mountains State Park

Location: Southwest Texas southwest of Fort Stockton.

Access: From Texas State Highway 118 at a point 2.7 miles northwest of the junction of Texas State Highways 118 & 17 just north of Fort Davis, 48 miles southwest of Kent, turn south into the park entrance and proceed 0.4 mile to the hookup areas, on the left; or continue for another 0.2 mile to the standard areas, also on the left.

Facilities: 90 campsites, including 20 with partial hookups and 27 with full hookups, in 4 sections; standard and partial hookup sites are small+ to medium+ in size, level, with fair to good separation; full hookup units are medium+, some are sloped, with fair separation; parking pads are short to medium-length, gravel straight-ins or long, paved pull-throughs; small ramadas (sun shelters) for some lightly shaded sites; fire rings and/or barbecue grills in most sites; b-y-o firewood is recommended; water at faucets throughout; restrooms with showers; holding tank disposal station; paved driveways; gas and groceries+ are available in Fort Davis.

Activities & Attractions: Trails; interpretive center; scenic drive; amphitheater; Fort Davis National Historic Site and the McDonald Observatory are both nearby.

Natural Features: Located on a flat and on a slope along Keesey Creek in the Davis Mountains; most sites receive light to medium shade/shelter from a mixture of hardwoods, including large oaks; flanked by dry, tree-dotted hills; elevation 4900'.

Season, Fees & Phone: Open all year; 14 day limit; reservations recommended in summer; please see Appendix for additional reservation information and standard Texas state park fees; park office (915) 426-3337.

Camp Notes: Surprisingly, this campground strongly resembles certain camps in, well, uh, Southern California. (Or do the places in Southern Cal resemble this excellent Texas location? Ed.) Golden hills and spreading oaks make good camps, be they in the Lone Star State or elsewhere. Side trips to Fort Davis National historic site and the observatory will really complete the trip to this beautiful region. The University of Texas' McDonald Observatory is perched atop Mount Locke at 6800', just a couple of miles northwest of the state park off Highway 118. The mountain panoramas from the observatory's observation would in themselves be worth the short trip from your campsite. But the observatory also provides an information center, tours, solar viewing sessions. In addition, it hosts "star parties" three times a week. Visitors have the opportunity to view planets, galaxies, nebula and other celestial items through 14-inch and 24-inch telescopes. After a star party in the crisp, cool, clear Davis Mountains air, you'll get back to camp and crawl into your sleeping bag or bunk with a new perspective on the mysteries of the night sky.

Texas 17

COTTONWOOD
Big Bend National Park

Location: Southwest Texas south of Alpine.

Access: From Big Bend National Park Headquarters at Panther Junction (69 miles south of Marathon), travel west on the main park road for 13 miles to Santa Elena Junction; turn south onto a paved road

(Ross Maxwell Scenic Drive) and proceed southwest for 23.2 miles (0.6 mile past Castalon); turn south (left) onto gravel for a final 0.15 mile to the campground. **Alternate Access:** From the park's west boundary near Study Butte (81 miles south of Alpine), travel east on the main park road for 9 miles to Santa Elena Junction, then continue as above.

Facilities: 32 campsites; sites are small+, level, with minimal to nominal separation; parking pads are gravel, short straight-ins or medium to long any-ways; large tent areas on a grass or sandy gravel surface; barbecue grills; charcoal fires only; water at several faucets; vault facilities; gravel driveways; gas and camper supplies at Castalon, Panther Junction, Study Butte and Marathon; adequate supplies and services are available in Alpine.

Activities & Attractions: Castalon historic site; river access; amphitheater; overlook point of superscenic Santa Elena Canyon, 8 miles northwest.

Natural Features: Located on a large flat along the Rio Grande; most sites are situated on a grassy section, sheltered by rows of towering cottonwoods; several sites are on a sandy section, very lightly shaded by mesquite; high, rocky bluffs, buttes and mountains border the river; elevation 2200'.

Season, Fees & Phone: Open all year; $4.00; 14 day limit; Big Bend National Park Headquarters, Panther Junction, (915) 477-2251.

Camp Notes: This section of the park equals some of the scenery that places like Canyonlands, Monument Valley, Grand Canyon and Death Valley can stack up against it. Great country!

Texas 18

THE BASIN
Big Bend National Park

Location: Southwest Texas south of Alpine.

Access: From Big Bend National Park Headquarters at Panther Junction (69 miles south of Marathon), travel west on the main park road for 3 miles to Chisos Basin Junction; turn south onto a paved road and proceed south for 6 miles (to the bottom of a steeeep grade); turn right onto the campground access road and continue (down a steeeeeper grade) for a final half-mile to the campground. **Alternate Access:** From the park's west boundary near Study Butte (81 miles south of Alpine), travel east on the main park road for 19 miles to Chisos Basin Junction, then continue as above.

Facilities: 62 campsites; sites are small to medium-sized, with nominal to fair separation; parking pads are paved/packed gravel, short straight-ins or medium-length pull-offs or pull-throughs, which will probably require additional leveling; medium to large, generally sloped, tent areas on a gravel/earth surface; ramadas (sun shelters) for table/grill areas in some sites; barbecue grills; charcoal fires only; water at several faucets; restrooms; holding tank disposal station; paved/packed gravel driveways; camper supplies at a nearby store, also in Panther Junction, Study Butte and Marathon; adequate supplies in Alpine.

Activities & Attractions: Hiking trails.

Natural Features: Located on a tiered slope in a high basin ringed by the craggy peaks of the Chisos Mountains; sites receive light to medium shelter/shade from pines, junipers, etc.; elevation 5400'.

Season, Fees & Phone: Open all year; $6.00; 14 day limit; Big Bend National Park Headquarters, Panther Junction, (915) 477-2251.

Camp Notes: How about this place! Just when you believe you have this Big Bend Country all figured out as being strictly desert, along comes high and cool and evergreen-scented Chisos Basin. At the risk of stretching the point a bit, the setting resembles a certain remote spot in the North Cascades (minus a few inches of rain and snow).

Texas 19

RIO GRANDE VILLAGE
Big Bend National Park

Location: Southwest Texas south of Alpine.

Access: From Big Bend National Park Headquarters at Panther Junction (69 miles south of Marathon), travel southeast on a paved park road for 20 miles to a "T" intersection; turn left and continue for 0.3 mile; turn right, into the campground. **Alternate Access:** From the park's west boundary near Study Butte (81 miles south of Alpine), travel east on the main park road for 22 miles to Panther Junction, then continue as above.

Facilities: 100 campsites; sites are medium-sized, level, with nominal separation; parking pads are paved/packed gravel, short to long, straight-ins or pull-throughs; ample, grassy space for large tents; a few sites have ramadas (sun shelters); barbecue grills; charcoal fires only; water at several faucets; restrooms; holding tank disposal station; paved driveways; camper supplies at a nearby store, also in Panther Junction, Study Butte and Marathon; adequate supplies and services are available in Alpine.

Activities & Attractions: Self-guiding nature trail; amphitheater; small visitor center (open October to May); river access.

Natural Features: Located on a large flat near the Rio Grande; campground vegetation consists of short grass, well-bedecked with a variety of hardwoods; surrounded by mesquite and other desert brush; flanked by high and dry desert mountains, including the very imposing Sierra del Carmen, to the east, in Mexico; elevation 1850'.

Season, Fees & Phone: Open all year; $6.00; 14 day limit; Big Bend National Park Headquarters, Panther Junction, (915) 477-2251.

Camp Notes: Several of the more private campsites are in their own little coves of greenery in a small side loop at the far end of the campground from the entrance. Depending upon the season and the whims of *El Rio*, you might have either a short stroll or a long hike to the water's edge. Camp visitors at Rio Grande Village typically include vultures and roadrunners.

Texas 20

DRY CREEK
O.C. Fisher Lake/Corps of Engineers Park

Location: West Texas on the west edge of San Angelo.

Access: From U.S. Highway 87 at a point 10 miles northwest of San Angelo and 6 miles southeast of Carlsbad, turn south onto Farm Road 2288 and proceed 0.9 mile; turn southeast (left) onto Old Highway 87 and continue for 0.8 mile; turn southwest (right) onto the campground access road for 0.2 mile to the campground entrance. **Alternate Access:** From U.S. Highway 67 at the southwest corner of San Angelo, take Farm Road 2288 northwest for 11 miles to this campground.

Facilities: 24 campsites, including 9 with partial hookups; sites are medium-sized, with fair to good separation; parking pads are gravel/grass, medium straight-ins or long pull-throughs; a little additional leveling may be required in about half of the sites; medium to large tent areas; ramadas (sun shelters) for some sites; barbecue grills; b-y-o firewood is recommended; water at sites and at central faucets; restrooms with showers; holding tank disposal station; paved main roadways, gravel sub-drives; complete supplies and services are available in San Angelo.

Activities & Attractions: Fishing; boating; boat launch; orv area.

Natural Features: Located on a sloping flat near the bank of the North Concho River at the northwest tip of O.C Fisher Lake; most sites receive ample shade/shelter from large hardwoods; areas of tall grass (certain sections are mown) surround the campground; elevation 1900'.

Season, Fees & Phone: Available all year, with reduced services in winter; $9.00 for a standard site, $11.00 for a partial hookup site; 14 day limit; O.C. Fisher Lake CoE Project Office (915) 949-4757.

Camp Notes: Southeast of here are the Grandview and Highland Range CoE areas, which provide water, vaults and free camping.

Texas 21

RED ARROYO
O.C. Fisher Lake/Corps of Engineers Park

Location: West Texas on the west edge of San Angelo.

Access: From U.S. Highway 67 in the southwest corner of San Angelo (4 miles from midtown), turn west onto Ranch Road 853/Arden Road and proceed 2 miles; turn north onto Farm Road 2288 for 0.75 mile, then bear slightly right onto the South Shore access road; continue ahead for a few yards to a fork; take the right fork northeasterly for 0.5 mile to a second fork; take the left fork this time for a final 0.35 mile to the campground entrance. **Alternate Access:** From U.S. Highway 87 northwest of San Angelo, pick up Farm Road 2288 and follow it 10 miles southeast to the campground.

Facilities: Approximately 45 campsites, including 10 with electrical hookups; sites are medium+ to large, with nominal to very good spacing; parking pads are mostly gravel, medium-length straight-ins or long pull-throughs; some pads may require a bit of additional leveling; ample space for large tents; small ramadas (sun shelters) for some sites; fireplaces; b-y-o firewood; water at a few sites and at central faucets; restrooms with showers; disposal station; paved main roadways, gravel sub-drives; complete supplies and services are available in San Angelo.

Activities & Attractions: Fishing; boating; boat launch; nature trail; hike/bike path; orv area.

Natural Features: Located on the slightly sloping south shore of O.C. Fisher Lake; vegetation consists of acres of grass dotted with a few small hardwoods; surrounded by very gently rolling plains, with a few hills in the distant north; elevation 1900'.

Season, Fees & Phone: Available all year, with limited services in winter; $7.00 to $9.00 for a standard site, $11.00 for a hookup site; 14 day limit; O.C. Fisher Lake CoE Project Office (915)949-4757.

Camp Notes: For a little more natural shade, you might prefer the standard sites near the turnaround loop on the east side of the camping area.

Texas 22

SEMINOLE CANYON
Seminole Canyon State Historical Park

Location: South-west Texas northwest of Del Rio.

Access: From U.S. Highway 90 at a point 9 miles west of Comstock, 19 miles southeast of Langtry, 2 miles southeast of the Pecos River bridge, turn south onto the park road and proceed 0.6 mile to the park headquarters; bear west (right) and continue on a winding road for a 0.9 mile to the campground.

Facilities: 31 campsites, most with partial hookups; sites are medium-sized, with fair to good separation; parking pads are paved, medium to long straight-ins; some pads will require a little additional leveling; large, framed, sand-based tent pads; small ramadas (sun shelters) for all sites; fire rings and barbecue grills; b-y-o firewood; water at faucets throughout; restrooms with showers; holding tank disposal station; paved driveways; gas and groceries are available in Langtry and Comstock.

Activities & Attractions: Visitor center; hiking trail; guided walks to view Indian pictographs; Judge Roy Bean Visitor Center in Langtry; boating and fishing on Amistad Reservoir.

Natural Features: Located on a desert plain near the rim of Seminole Canyon; campground vegetation consists of brush, cactus and other small desert plants; Seminole Canyon is back-filled with the waters of the Rio Grande as a result of the damming of the river and consequent creation of Amistad Reservoir; elevation 1200'.

Season, Fees & Phone: Open all year; 14 day limit; please see Appendix for reservation information and standard Texas state park fees; park office (915) 292-4464.

Camp Notes: The 360° desert view extends out about 150 miles from the campsites (or so it seems). Although at one time a group of displaced Seminole Indians roamed though this region, historians believe the canyon was named for the Seminole-Negro army scouts stationed in nearby Fort Clark during the 1870's. If you're looking for something to occupy a couple of hours while you're in this neighborhood, you might make a trip over to Langtry. The Judge Roy Bean Visitor Center there has impeccably maintained buildings (including a re-creation of Bean's saloon and billiard hall), plus fascinating and beautiful desert gardens. Bean, of course, was the justice known far and wide as the "Law West of the Pecos".

Texas 23

GOVERNORS LANDING
Amistad Recreation Area/NPS

Location: South-west Texas northwest of Del Rio.

Access: From U.S. Highway 90 at a point 1 mile south of the bridge which spans Amistad Reservoir, 22 miles southeast of Comstock, 12 miles northwest of Del Rio, turn west onto Spur 349 for 0.15 mile; turn north (right) onto the paved Governor's Landing access road and proceed 1.1 mile (parallel to the main highway), then turn east (right), and pass under the bridge into the campground (you'll now be on the east side of the highway).

Facilities: 18 campsites; sites are small to medium+ in size, with nil to fairly good separation; parking pads are gravel, mostly medium to long pull-offs or pull-throughs, and some will require additional leveling; small to medium-sized tent areas; most sites have ramadas (sun shelters); barbecue grills; b-y-o firewood; no drinking water; (water is available at the nearby marina, and at park hq, 9 miles southeast); vault facilities; gravel driveways; complete supplies and services are available in Del Rio.

Activities & Attractions: Fishing for bass, crappie, catfish, sunfish; boating, sailing; designated swimming beach; marina.

Natural Features: Located on a short bluff above the south shore of Amistad Reservoir on the Rio Grande; vegetation on the surrounding desert plain consists primarily of desert scrub; elevation 1200'.

Season, Fees & Phone: Open all year; no fee (subject to change); 15-day limit; Amistad Recreation Area, National Park Service, Del Rio, (512) 775-7491.

Camp Notes: There are several other smaller, somewhat more primitive camp spots in this sizeable recreation area run by the National Park Service. The Spur 406 area is on the north shore of the reservoir; San Pedro and Old 277 North & South areas are more or less at the east end. Facilities at those sites include a few ramadas, fireplaces, sani-cans, but no drinking water. All of the foregoing can be reached via paved roads. Governors Landing isn't exactly the type of place you'd send postcards from.

TEXAS
North
Please refer to the Texas map in the Appendix

Texas 24

COPPER BREAKS
Copper Breaks State Park

Location: North-West Texas north of Abilene.

Access: From Texas State Highway 6 at a point 9 miles north of Crowell and 12 miles south of Quanah, turn west onto Park Road 53 and proceed 0.7 mile to the park entrance station; continue ahead for 0.6 mile to the *Kiowa* camp area, or for an additional 0.5 mile to the Comanche camp.

Facilities: *Kiowa*: 11 standard campsites; *Comanche*: 25 campsites with partial hookups and ramadas (sun shelters); (in addition, 6 equestrian sites with paved parking are available in a separate loop); *both areas*: sites are small+ to medium-sized, level, with nominal to fair separation; parking pads are hard-surfaced, medium-length straight-ins; large, grassy areas for tents; barbecue grills and fire rings; b-y-o firewood; water at faucets throughout; restrooms with showers; holding tank disposal station; paved driveways; gas & groceries in Crowell; adequate supplies and services are available in Quanah.

Activities & Attractions: Visitor center; nature trail; hiking and equestrian trails; fishing (said to be very good for catfish, bass and perch); limited boating (5 mph); boat launch.

Natural Features: Located amid multi-colored, juniper-dotted breaks and mesas; Comanche sites receive minimal natural shelter/shade; Kiowa sites are provided with light-medium shelter/shade courtesy of small to large hardwoods and junipers; 60-acre Lake Copper Breaks is the park's main water feature; elevation 1500'.

Season, Fees & Phone: Open all year; 14 day limit; please see Appendix for reservation information and standard Texas state park fees; park office (817) 839-4331.

Camp Notes: Comanche's hookup sites have the most distinctive ramadas you'll find just about anywhere. They resemble tall, three-dimensional spear points. There's excellent tent/pickup/van camping here as well, be it in the Comanche or Kiowa camps. The visitor center's impressive displays surpass those found in many national parks. Worth a stop.

Texas 25

LAKE ARROWHEAD
Lake Arrowhead State Recreation Area

Location: North Texas southeast of Wichita Falls.

Access: From U.S. Highway 281 at a point 8 miles south of Wichita Falls, 11 miles north of Scotland, turn east onto Farm Road 1954; travel east/southeast for 7.5 miles to the park entrance; advance ahead for 0.35 mile, then turn north (left) into the main camp area; or continue past the main camp for another 0.35 mile to the lakeshore area. (Note: access is also possible from U.S. 82/287 in Jolly, via FM 2393.)

Facilities: 67 sites, including 48 with partial hookups; sites are medium+, level, with fair to fairly good separation; parking pads are paved, medium to medium+ straight-ins; large, grassy areas for tents; fire rings and/or barbecue grills; b-y-o firewood; water at faucets throughout; restrooms with showers;

holding tank disposal station; paved driveways; complete supplies and services are available in Wichita Falls.

Activities & Attractions: Fishing; lighted fishing pier; boating; boat launch; swimming beach.

Natural Features: Located along and near the north shore of Lake Arrowhead, a reservoir on the Little Wichita River; sites are very lightly to lightly shaded/sheltered by large mesquite; bordered by tall grass and small brush; surrounded by gently rolling plains; elevation 900'.

Season, Fees & Phone: Open all year; 14 day limit; please see Appendix for reservation information and standard Texas state park fees; park office (817) 528-2211.

Camp Notes: The arrangement of the sites here is novel--and quite effective. Those in the main camp are in *cul de sacs*, each containing a cluster of a half-dozen sites, off of the loop driveway. Plenty of vegetation has been left standing between each *cul de sac*, so there's adequate visual and spatial separation. The small cricket pump for the campground's oil well will lull you to sleep with its *ta-pocketa-ta-pocketa-ta-pocketa-ta-pocketa-ta-pocketa* rhythm.

Texas 26

LAKE EDDELMAN
Graham City Park

Location: North Texas south of Wichita Falls.

Access: From U.S. Highway 380 at a point 2 miles north of Graham, turn west into the campground.

Facilities: 12 campsites with partial hookups for self-contained vehicles; sites are small and closely spaced, level, with nil separation; parking surfaces are grass, medium-length, straight-ins; large tent areas; water at sites; no sanitary facilities (subject to change); gravel driveway; adequate+ supplies and services are available in Graham.

Activities & Attractions: Fishing; limited boating; small boat launch.

Natural Features: Located on the east shore of Lake Eddleman, across the lake from a power plant; sites are very lightly shaded; bordered by low hills; elevation 1000'.

Season, Fees & Phone: Available all year; no fee (subject to change); 5 day limit; Graham City-Young County Parks Department (817) 549-3324.

Camp Notes: There isn't much visible from the camp at Lake E. except the very prominent power pumper. (But, as one camper put it, "The electricity has to come from *somewhere*".) The lake is named for a former mayor of the city of Graham who was instrumental in securing support for construction of the lake.

Texas 27

KINDLEY
Young County Park

Location: North Texas south of Wichita Falls.

Access: From U.S. Highway 380 at a point 7 miles northwest of Graham, turn south (at the east end of the bridge) into the campground.

Facilities: Approximately 6 actual campsites, but room for 15-50 campers (depending upon how friendly they are) in a more or less open camping arrangement; parking areas are grass/earth any-which-way-you-can; large tent areas; water at a central faucet; restrooms; gravel/earth driveways; adequate+ supplies and services are available in Graham.

Activities & Attractions: Fishing; limited boating; small boat launch (shallow water).

Natural Features: Located on the northeast shore of Lake Graham; sites are lightly shaded by large hardwoods; bordered by low hills; elevation 1000'.

Season, Fees & Phone: Available all year; no fee (subject to change); 5 day limit; Graham City-Young County Parks Department (817) 549-3324.

Camp Notes: Here's a very simple stop which, taking into account the current rental rate, might be worth considering as an enroute, or perhaps even weekend, stop. Like Lake Eddelman (described above), it's only a few yards from a high-traffic highway. But Kindley gets a thumbs-up for surroundings.

FORT RICHARDSON
Fort Richardson State Historical Park

Location: North Texas southeast of Wichita Falls.

Access: From U.S. Highway 281 at a point 0.9 mile south of courthouse square in Jacksboro, turn southwest into the park entrance to the park headquarters; continue on the main park road west, then north, then around to the south for 1 mile to the campground.

Facilities: 23 campsites, some with partial hookups, in 2 sections; sites are small+ to medium-sized, essentially level, with nominal to fairly good separation; parking pads are hard-surfaced, medium to long, primarily straight-ins, plus several pull-throughs; large tent pads for most sites; fire rings; b-y-o firewood; water at faucets throughout; restrooms with showers; holding tank disposal station; paved driveways; adequate supplies and services are available in Jacksboro.

Activities & Attractions: Restored buildings of Fort Richardson, a frontier outpost of the late 1860's and 1870's; interpretive center; hiking and nature trails; playground.

Natural Features: Located on the edge of a plain along a line of large trees, or slightly below the plain in a wooded area along Lost Creek; elevation 1100'.

Season, Fees & Phone: Open all year; 14 day limit; please see Appendix for reservation information and standard Texas state park fees; park office (817) 567-3506.

Camp Notes: Fort Richardson and its counterpart, Fort Griffin, 60 miles southwest of here, (see separate information) were frontier posts during the era of the Indian Wars. Both forts eventually became state historical parks with interesting exhibits and good campgrounds. But note the dramatically different destinies of the shanty towns which sprang up in association with the two military installations: Jacksboro went on to become a prosperous, modern community which fathered the national 4-H Clubs; the town of Fort Griffin, conversely, now has only a few residents and virtually no commerce.

FORT GRIFFIN
Fort Griffin State Historical Park

Location: West Texas northeast of Abilene.

Access: From U.S. Highway 283 in what's left of the settlement of Fort Griffin (15 miles north of Albany, 18 miles south of Throckmorton), turn southeast into the park entrance; continue slightly southeast, then curve northeast (left) for 0.4 mile to the campground.

Facilities: 20 campsites, including 15 with partial hookups, in 2 loops; sites are generally spacious, level, with nominal to fair separation; parking pads are gravel, mostly medium+ to long straight-ins, plus a couple of pull-throughs; ample space for large tents on a grassy surface; barbecue grills and fire rings; b-y-o firewood; water at faucets throughout; restrooms with showers; holding tank disposal station; paved main driveway, gravel sub-drives; gas and groceries+ in Throckmorton; limited+ supplies and services are available in Albany.

Natural Features: Located on a grassy flat along the bank of the Clear Fork of the Brazos River; sites receive very light to light shade from scattered small to large mesquite; surrounded by plains and low hills; elevation 1400'.

Activities & Attractions: Remains of Fort Griffin; the official State of Texas Longhorn Herd resides here; visitor center; nature trail; amphitheater; river and pond fishing for bass, catfish, and crappie; fishing tournaments.

Season, Fees & Phone: Open all year; 14 day limit; please see Appendix for reservation information and standard Texas state park fees; park office (915) 762-3592.

Camp Notes: According to historical literature, Fort Griffin was more of a frontier eyesore than an Old West showplace. (Or put another way, life in and around this outpost resembled an earthy, Clint Eastwood "spaghetti western" rather than an heroic, John Wayne classic.) Fort Griffin is still depicted as a town on highway maps, but there's very little around here that hints of civilization.

ABILENE
Abilene State Recreation Area

Location: West Texas south of Abilene.

Access: From U.S. Highway 277 at its junction with Farm Road 89 (22 miles southwest of Abilene), proceed east on Farm Road 89 for 7.5 miles; turn south (right) into the park entrance; continue ahead for 0.8 mile to the main camp loops. **Alternate Access:** From U.S. Highway 83 or U.S. 84, east of the park, the simplest route is via Farm Road 613 from Tuscola to Buffalo Gap, then southwest on Farm Road 89 to the park; or just follow the signs along the back roads (preferably not at night, though).

Facilities: 95 campsites (includes a 48-site group trailer camp), most with partial hookups; (in addition, 8 units with screened shelters are also available); sites in the main camp loops are medium-sized, level, with very good separation; parking pads are paved/packed gravel, medium-length straight-ins or pull-offs; large tent pads for some sites; fire rings; b-y-o firewood; water at sites; restrooms with showers; holding tank disposal stations; paved driveways; camper supplies in Buffalo Gap; complete supplies and services are available in Abilene

Activities & Attractions: Swimming pool; hiking trail; fishing and boating at Lake Abilene, just west of this park.

Natural Features: Located on bottomland along Elm Creek among the low hills of the Callahan Divide, which partitions the headwaters of the Brazos and Colorado Rivers; a very dense woodland with huge hardwoods and some evergreens covers the campsites; elevation 1900'.

Season, Fees & Phone: Open all year; 14 day limit; please see Appendix for reservation information and standard Texas state park fees; park office (915) 572-3204.

Camp Notes: The above *Facilities* section primarily describes the 2 loops with individual, hookup campsites (#'s 49 to 83) which are the most commonly used. Sites 1-48, which are designated as group trailer units, are in one of the most peculiar arrangements you may ever see in a campground. The park's large pecan groves provide plenty of pleasant, very welcome, shade in this semi-arid region. Nearby Buffalo Gap was named for the only cleft in the Callahan Divide. The pass was used as a natural throughway by thousands of migrating bison in early times.

SPANISH OAKS
Possum Kingdom State Recreation Area

Location: North-central Texas west of Fort Worth.

Access: From U.S. Highway 180 in the community of Caddo, head north on Park Road 33 for 16.5 miles to the park entrance station/headquarters; continue ahead for 0.3 mile to a fork; take the left fork for 0.5 mile to Spanish Oaks Campground.

Facilities: 58 campsites, about half with partial hookups; sites are small+ to medium-sized, level, with nominal to good separation; parking pads are hard-surfaced, short to long, mostly straight-ins; plenty of space for large tents; ramadas (sun shelters) for some sites; barbecue grills and fire rings; b-y-o firewood; water at faucets throughout; restrooms with showers; holding tank disposal station; paved driveways; camper supplies in the park; limited supplies and services are available in Caddo.

Activities & Attractions: Swimming beach; boating; boat launch; fishing; lighted fishing pier; playground.

Natural Features: Located on a grassy flat along the south shore of Possum Kingdom Lake, a reservoir on the Brazos River; sites receive very light shade from large hardwoods and junipers; the lake is in a canyon surrounded by the juniper-blanketed Palo Pinto Mountains; elevation 1000'.

Season, Fees & Phone: Open all year; 14 day limit; please see Appendix for reservation information and standard Texas state park fees; park office (817) 549-1803.

Camp Notes: Possum Kingdom could win the award for "Cutest Park Name in the West", or something like that. Excellent scenery, both near and far.

LAKEVIEW & SHADY GROVE
Possum Kingdom State Recreation Area

Location: North-central Texas west of Fort Worth.

Access: From U.S. Highway 180 in the community of Caddo, head north on Park Road 33 for 16.5 miles to the park entrance station/headquarters; continue ahead for 0.3 mile to a fork; take the right fork for 0.5 mile to the Lakeview and Shady Grove Campgrounds.

Facilities: 60 campsites, half with partial hookups; sites are small+ to medium-sized, with fair to very good separation; parking pads are hard-surfaced, short to long, mostly straight-ins; many pads may require additional leveling; ample space for large tents; some sites have framed and gravelled tent pads; ramadas (sun shelters) for some sites; barbecue grills and fire rings; b-y-o firewood; water at faucets throughout; restrooms with showers; holding tank disposal station; paved driveways; camper supplies in the park; limited supplies and services are available in Caddo.

Activities & Attractions: Swimming beach; boating; boat launch; fishing; lighted fishing pier; playgrounds.

Natural Features: Located on a slope above the shore of Possum Kingdom Lake, a reservoir on the Brazos River; sites receive light to medium shelter/shade from large hardwoods and junipers; the lake is in a sizeable canyon surrounded by the forested Palo Pinto Mountains; elevation 1000'.

Season, Fees & Phone: Open all year; 14 day limit; please see Appendix for reservation information and standard Texas state park fees; park office (817) 549-1803.

Camp Notes: Many dandy campsites here. It's a tough choice between the elevated sites with commanding views in Lakeview and Shady Grove, or the lakeside units in the park's Spanish Oaks campground.

LAKE MINERAL WELLS
Lake Mineral Wells State Park

Location: North Texas west of Fort Worth.

Access: From U.S. Highway 180 at a point 4 miles east of midtown Mineral Wells, 15 miles west of Weatherford, turn north onto Park Road 71 and proceed north for a quarter-mile to the park entrance station; continue north and east for another 0.3 mile to a fork; swing sharply around to the left and proceed northwest across the dam for 0.4 mile; the road curves around the southwest corner of the lake then heads northeast for a final 0.4 mile to 1 mile to the 3 main camp areas, on the right.

Facilities: 88 campsites, including 77 with partial hookups; (15 units with screened shelters, an equestrian camp with 20 sites, and primitive camp areas are also available); sites are small+, most are tolerably level, with fair to good separation; parking pads are paved, short to medium-length straight-ins; mostly medium-sized tent areas; fire rings; b-y-o firewood; water at faucets throughout; restrooms with showers; holding tank disposal station; paved driveways; gas and groceries in Cool, 2 miles east; adequate+ supplies and services are available in Mineral Wells.

Activities & Attractions: Hiking and horse trails; swimming beach; fishing; fishing pier; boating; boat launch and dock.

Natural Features: Located along the west shore of 650-acre Lake Mineral Wells; sites receive light to medium shade/shelter from medium-sized hardwoods and brush; surrounded by hilly, woody-brushy terrain; elevation 1000'.

Season, Fees & Phone: Open all year; 14 day limit; please see Appendix for reservation information and standard Texas state park fees; park office (817) 328-1171.

Camp Notes: "Mineral Wells", like "Furnace Creek" or "Rock Springs", is one of those authentic Old West names, so its not surprising to find a horse camp and miles of trails here.

HOLIDAY
Benbrook Lake/Corps of Engineers Park

Location: North-Central Texas south of Fort Worth.

Access: From U.S. Highway 377 at a point 6 miles southwest of Interstate 20 exit 429 for Benbrook, 0.25 mile northeast of the bridge which crosses Clear Fork of the Trinity River, 9 miles northeast of Cresson, turn east onto South Lakeview Drive and proceed 1.8 miles to the park entrance station; turn south (right) to the main camp loops, or continue ahead and north, to a stretched-out string of several scattered shoreside standard sites.

Facilities: 92 campsites, including 62 with partial hookups; sites are medium to medium+ in size, with fairly good overall separation; parking pads are paved, medium to long straight-ins; many pads will require a little additional leveling; medium to large tent areas, some are a bit sloped; ramadas (sun shelters) for nearly all sites; barbecue grills plus some fireplaces; some firewood is available for gathering in the area; water at hookup sites and at several additional faucets; restrooms with showers; holding tank disposal station; paved driveways; gas and groceries on the main highway; complete supplies and services are available in Benbrook.

Activities & Attractions: Boating; boat launches; fishing; trail; photography blinds.

Natural Features: Located above the west shore of Benbrook Lake; sites receive light to medium shade/shelter from large hardwoods; encircled by plains; elevation 700'.

Season, Fees & Phone: Open all year; $7.00-$9.00 for a standard site, $11.00 for a partial hookup site; 14 day limit; Benbrook Lake CoE Project Office (817) 292-2400.

Camp Notes: If you just want an 'ordinary' lake view, the main campground has many good-sized, semi-private campsites to choose from. But for a deluxe nighttime view of the Fort Worth skyline rising in the distance, you might want to check out the small group of sites on a knoll along the shore north of the main camp.

Texas 35

DINOSAUR VALLEY
Dinosaur Valley State Park

Location: North-Central Texas southwest of Fort Worth.

Access: From U.S. Highway 67 at the southwest corner of Glen Rose, turn west onto Farm Road 205/Park Road 59 and proceed 2.8 miles to a fork; continue northwest (bear right) on Park Road 59 for an additional 0.6 mile to the park entrance station/headquarters; proceed slightly ahead, then take the next three right-hand turns in succession for a final 0.4 mile to the campground.

Facilities: 46 campsites, including 40 with partial hookups; (backpacking sites in 7 areas with no facilities are also available); sites are small+ to medium-sized, level, with nominal to good separation; parking pads are hard-surfaced, medium-length straight-ins; adequate space for medium to large tents; fireplaces, plus some barbecue grills; b-y-o firewood; water at faucets throughout; restrooms with showers; holding tank disposal station; paved driveways; adequate supplies and services are available in Glen Rose.

Activities & Attractions: Dinosaur tracks and other outdoor exhibits; 5-mile Cedar Break Trail System of nature and hiking trails; visitor center.

Natural Features: Located on a wooded flat in a valley along the bank of the Paluxy River; sites receive light to medium shade from large junipers/cedars; and hardwoods; bordered by rocky hills; elevation 700'.

Season, Fees & Phone: Open all year; 14-day limit; reservations recommended Spring through fall; please see Appendix for reservation information and standard Texas state park fees; park office (817) 897-4588.

Camp Notes: *It's half-past eleven on a still and steamy, moonless night in early August. You're sitting by a flickering campfire, gazing up to a zillion stars, and pondering the great creatures of aeons past. Suddenly, there's a loud splash by the river, and then a lumbering crashing through the trees, and then.....*

Texas 36

CLEBURNE
Cleburne State Recreation Area

Location: North-Central Texas southwest of Fort Worth.

Access: From U.S. Highway 67 at a point 6 miles southwest of the city of Cleburne, 17 miles northeast of Glen Rose, turn southeast onto Park Road 21 and travel 6 miles to the park entrance station/headquarters; continue westerly on the park road for 0.8 mile to 1.5 miles to the 5 camp areas, situated around the west end of the lake.

Facilities: 58 campsites, including 31 with partial hookups, and 27 with full hookups, in 5 areas; (6 units with screened shelters are also available); sites are medium-sized, with nominal to fairly good separation; parking pads are paved, short to medium-length straight-ins; majority of pads will probably require a little additional leveling; adequate, slightly sloped spaces for medium to large tents; fire rings; b-y-o firewood; water at faucets throughout; restrooms with showers; holding tank disposal station; paved driveways; complete supplies and services are available in Cleburne.

Activities & Attractions: Fishing for bass and catfish in summer, stocked rainbow trout in January; limited boating; swimming area; fossilized creek bed; playground.

Natural Features: Located around the west shore of 116-acre, spring-fed Cedar Lake; campsites are moderately sheltered/shaded by large junipers/cedars and hardwoods; surrounded by wooded slopes; elevation 800'.

Season, Fees & Phone: Open all year; 14 day limit; please see Appendix for reservation information and standard Texas state park fees; park office (817) 645-4215.

Camp Notes: Since Cleburne is so reachably close to the Dallas-Fort Worth megalopolis, "you don't stand a prayer of a chance" of getting a campsite here on a summer weekend without a 90-day rez. A lot of campers must feel it's worth the wait.

Texas 37

JUNIPER POINT
Lake Texoma/Corps of Engineers Park

Location: North Texas northwest of Denison.

Access: From U.S. Highway 377 at a point 14 miles north of its junction with U.S. 82 at Whitesboro, at the south end of the bridge which spans Lake Texoma, turn east into the East unit, or west into the West unit.

Facilities: 70 campsites, including 13 with electrical hookups and 31 with partial hookups, in 2 areas; sites are small to medium-sized, with nominal to fair separation; parking pads are paved or gravel, short to long straight-ins; most pads will require at least a touch of additional leveling; medium to large, generally a little sloped, areas for tents; barbecue grills and/or fire rings; a limited amount of firewood is available for gathering in the area; water at partial hookup sites and at several faucets; restrooms with showers, plus auxiliary vaults; holding tank disposal station; paved driveways; gas and groceries are available within 1 mile south of the campground.

Activities & Attractions: Boating; boat launches; fishing; Cross Timbers Hiking Trail (a trail map/brochure is available, check with the campground attendant).

Natural Features: Located on a major point of land on the south shore of Lake Texoma; most sites in the East unit are near the base of a lakeside slope; sites in the West unit are on the top and sides of hilly terrain; campsites are lightly to moderately shaded by large junipers (or call 'em cedars, or whatever) and hardwoods; elevation 600'.

Season, Fees & Phone: April to November; $8.00 for a standard site, $11.00 for an electrical hookup site, $12.00 for a partial hookup site; 14 day limit; Lake Texoma CoE Project Office, Denison, (214) 465-4990.

Camp Notes: Campsites in the East unit are a little more deluxe than those on the West side. Camping on the West side, however, is more informal, with sites that are considerably more scattered over the slopes. The campground is said to be popular with Scout groups throughout the region because the Cross Timbers Trail, a 14-mile route along the south side of the lake, is a Scout-accredited route.

Texas 38

PRESTON BEND
Lake Texoma/Corps of Engineers Park

Location: North Texas northwest of Denison.

Access: From U.S. Highways 69 & 75 in Denison, travel west on Farm Road 120 for 8 miles to Pottsboro, then continue north on FM 120 for 9.5 miles; turn east (right) onto the park access road and proceed 0.7 mile to the park entrance and the campground. **Alternate Access:** From U.S. Highway 82 at a point 3 miles west of U.S. Highways 69 & 75 in Sherman and 15 miles east of Whitesboro, turn north onto Farm Road 1417 and proceed 6.5 miles to FM 120; turn west (left) onto FM 120 for 2 miles to Pottsboro and continue on as above.

Facilities: 44 campsites, some with electrical hookups; sites are small+ to medium-sized, with fair separation; parking pads are gravel, medium-length straight-ins; additional leveling will be required in many sites; adequate space for medium to large tents; barbecue grills; some firewood is available for gathering in the surrounding area; water at several faucets; restrooms with showers, plus auxiliary vaults; holding tank disposal station; paved main driveways; gas and groceries are available at a number of spots within 5 miles south of the park turnoff.

Activities & Attractions: Boating; boat launch; fishing (especially good for stripers, also largemouth bass, crappie, assorted catfish); designated swimming beach.

Natural Features: Located on sloping/hilly terrain on a peninsula extending from the south shore of 89,000-acre Lake Texoma; sites are mostly on slopes overlooking a small bay; sites receive moderate shade/shelter from large hardwoods and a few evergreens; elevation 600'.

Season, Fees & Phone: May to October; $8.00 for a standard site, $11.00 for an electrical hookup site; 14 day limit; Lake Texoma CoE Project Office, Denison, (214) 465-4990.

Camp Notes: This area's history dates back as far as the early days of the Texas Republic when a trading post, and later a fort, were established at Preston Bend on the Red River.

Texas 39

EISENHOWER
Eisenhower State Recreation Area

Location: North Texas north of Denison.

Access: From Texas State Highway 75A at the south end of Denison Dam on Lake Texoma, 4 miles north of Denison, head west on Farm Road 1310 for 1.9 miles to the park entrance station; just beyond entrance, turn north (right) into the *Armadillo Hill* area; or continue ahead (northwesterly) for 1 to 2 miles to the *Bois d'Arc*, *Fossil Ridge* or *Elm Point* areas.

Facilities: *Armadillo Hill*: 12 standard campsites and 45 campsites with partial hookups; *Bois d'Arc*: 50 campsites with full hookups; *Fossil Ridge*: 22 standard campsites; *Elm Point*: 23 standard campsites; (35 units with screened shelters and a 37-site group trailer area are also available); sites are small+ to medium-sized, with fair to good separation; parking pads are hard-surfaced, short to medium-length straight-ins or pull-offs in standard and partial hookup sites; pads are paved, long pull-throughs in full hookup sites; additional leveling will be needed in some sites; medium to large tent areas; some sites have framed tent pads; barbecue grills, plus some fire rings; b-y-o firewood; water at faucets throughout; restrooms with showers; holding tank disposal station; paved driveways; complete supplies and services are available in Denison.

Activities & Attractions: Boating; boat launch; very good fishing for native white bass, also striped bass, black bass, crappie and cats; fishing piers; designated swimming beach; playgrounds; hiking trails.

Natural Features: Located on hilly terrain atop several small points/ridges high above the shore at the southeast corner of Lake Texoma; sites receive light to moderate shade/shelter from medium to large hardwoods and a few junipers/cedars; elevation 700'.

Season, Fees & Phone: Open all year; 14-day limit; please see Appendix for reservation information and standard Texas state park fees; park office (214) 465-1956.

Camp Notes: Although the park is indeed above the southeast shore of the lake, only a few sites have lake or distant views. But the dense vegetation which obstructs the view also helps to provide additional privacy for many sites. If you're from outside the region, the origin of the name of the *Bois d'Arc* camp area may throw you for a loop. It's the name of a tree commonly found in the Southwest Plains. Regionally pronounced like "*boh*-dark", it produces a curious fruit that resembles a hard green apple covered with deep dimples. (Many campers call them "horse apples".) It's probably a "no-brainer" to realize that the park was named for General and U.S. President Dwight D. Eisenhower. But why this park? The famous statesman was born in nearby Denison.

Texas 40

DAMSITE
Lake Texoma/Corps of Engineers Park

Location: North Texas northwest of Denison.

Access: From Texas State Highway 75A at a point just south of Denison Dam, 6 miles south of Colbert, OK, and 3 miles north of Denison, turn east onto a road signed for the Lake Texoma Project

Office/Headquarters; proceed 0.3 mile to a fork; bear right and continue for 0.4 mile to the campground. (Bearing left will take you across the river to the Oklahoma side of Damsite--see below.)

Facilities: 32 campsites, including 20 with electrical hookups, in 2 loops; sites are small to medium-sized, with minimal to nominal separation; parking pads are gravel, short to medium-length straight-ins; a few pads may require some additional leveling; adequate, grassy space for medium to large tents; ramadas (sun shelters) for a few sites; fire rings; b-y-o firewood is recommended; water at several faucets; restroom with showers; auxiliary vault facilities; holding tank disposal station; paved driveways, gravel sub-drives; complete supplies and services are available in Denison.

Activities & Attractions: Fishing; day use area with shelter.

Natural Features: Located on a grassy shelf above the south bank of the Red River just below Denison Dam; some sites are on an open grassy flat and others are in a stand of hardwoods; elevation 500'.

Season, Fees & Phone: April to October; $8.00 for a standard site, $11.00 for an electrical hookup site; 14 day limit; Lake Texoma CoE Project Office, Denison, (214) 465-4990.

Camp Notes: Reportedly the fishing on the river here is excellent, especially when the power plant is generating electricity. (Maybe the fish feel the megawatt *tingle* and wonder what's going on and come up for a look-see.) The Oklahoma side of Damsite is visible across the river from this campground. In Oklahoma there are about a dozen sites on a tree-dotted slope with vault facilities, gravel driveways and pads, central water and a nominal fee. But the Texas camp is a damsite better than the one on the Oklahoma side.

Texas 41

COFFEE MILL LAKE
Caddo National Grassland

Location: North Texas northwest of Paris.

Access: From U.S. Highway 82 in Honey Grove, travel north on Farm Road 100 for 10.8 miles; turn west (left) onto Farm Road 409 and proceed 4.3 miles; turn south (left) onto a gravel access road and continue for 0.1 mile to the campground.

Facilities: 14 campsites; sites are small+, with fair separation; parking surfaces are gravel, tolerably level, as-long-as-you-require, pull-offs; adequate, slightly sloped space for large tents on an earthen surface; fireplaces; firewood is available for gathering in the area; water at several faucets; vault facilities; gravel driveways; limited supplies and services are available in Honey Grove.

Activities & Attractions: Boating; small boat launch; fishing.

Natural Features: Located on slightly sloping terrain on the north shore of 700-acre Coffee Mill Lake; campsites are lightly to moderately shaded by large hardwoods and some pines on a surface of sparse grass; bordered by very dense forest; elevation 600'.

Season, Fees & Phone: Open all year; no fee (subject to change); 14 day limit; Caddo National Grassland Headquarters, Decatur, (817) 627-5475.

Camp Notes: The campsites here really are closer to being park n' walk or park-along sites, since the tables and grills are several yards from the loop driveway/parking area. Compared to its companion camp on Lake Davy Crockett (see separate description), Coffee Mill is probably the nicer of the two, if only by the slim margin of having a little more elbow room. But Lake Davy Crockett itself is perhaps a little nicer-looking than the lake here. Call it a draw. The Coffee Mill Recreation Area is also listed as 'East Coffee Mill Recreation Area' on some maps in current distribution. There may be (or may have been) a 'West Coffee Mill' somewhere, but there's no evidence of it being a developed area.

Texas 42

LAKE DAVY CROCKETT
Caddo National Grassland

Location: North Texas northwest of Paris.

Access: From U.S. Highway 82 in Honey Grove, travel north on Farm Road 100 for 10.8 miles; turn west (left) onto Farm Road 409 and proceed 1.4 miles; turn southeast (left) onto a paved driveway and continue for 0.1 mile to the campground.

Facilities: 6 campsites; (several additional camp/picnic sites are located at the northeast corner of the lake, along FM 409); sites are small+, with fair separation; parking pads are gravel, medium to long pull-offs; slight additional leveling probably will be needed; enough space for medium to large tents on an earthen surface; fireplaces; firewood is available for gathering in the area; water at central faucets; vault facilities; gravel driveway; limited supplies and services are available in Honey Grove.

Activities & Attractions: Boating; small boat launch; fishing.

Natural Features: Located on a tiny, forested point on the west shore of 400-acre Lake Davy Crockett; sites are moderately shaded/sheltered by large hardwoods and some pines and cedars; elevation 600'.

Season, Fees & Phone: Open all year; no fee (subject to change); 14 day limit; Caddo National Grassland Headquarters, Decatur, (817) 627-5475.

Camp Notes: This is one of the smallest and most primitive of any of the campgrounds operated by the feds in Texas. (In fact, using a camera with only a moderately wide-angle lens, you can stand at the entrance and take in the entire place on one frame of film.) But size isn't always everything, and the views of this attractive, forest-rimmed lake are quite good from just about any spot in the campground. When you come right down to it, this nice-sized, woodsy lake may be just the right type of place to name after the legendary Tennesseean-turned-Texan who was "raised in the woods 'till he knew every tree". Ol' Davy, the story goes, camped not far from here when he first came to Texas.

Texas 43

LAKE BONHAM
City of Bonham Water Authority Recreation Area

Location: North Texas southeast of Denison.

Access: From Texas State Highway 78 at a point 3 miles north of Bonham, turn north onto Farm Road 898 and travel 1.3 miles; turn east onto Recreation Road 3 and proceed 2 miles east, then north for 0.2 mile to the park entrance, and the campground on the left.

Facilities: 87 campsites with partial hookups; sites are small, with nominal to fair separation; parking pads are gravel, short+ to long straight-ins; many pads will require a little additional leveling; generally small areas for tents; no fire facilities; (b-y-o long extension cord for electrical hookups); water at faucets throughout; restrooms with showers; holding tank disposal stations; paved main driveway, gravel sub-drives; adequate+ supplies and services are available in Bonham.

Activities & Attractions: Swimming beach; playground; golf course (par 3, 9 holes); boating; boat launch (extra fee); waterskiing; fishing (good for largemouth bass, crappie, catfish).

Natural Features: Located near the shore of a bay at the southeast corner of Lake Bonham, a 1300-acre reservoir on Bois d'Arc Creek (a tributary of the Red River); most sites are well-sheltered/shaded by large cedars/junipers and some hardwoods on a surface of sparse grass; elevation 600'.

Season, Fees & Phone: Open all year; $6.00 for a standard (i.e., no hookup) site, $9.00 for a partial hookup site; 14 day limit; lake manager's office (214) 583-8001.

Camp Notes: Of the pair of parks with campgrounds in the Bonham area (also see info for Bonham SRA), this would probably be the better choice of the two if you're oriented toward water recreation. However, the lake and its shoreline are attractive enough for 'just' camping and sitting and enjoying the view.

Texas 44

HACKBERRY HOLLOW
Bonham State Recreation Area

Location: North Texas southeast of Denison.

Access: From Texas State Highway 78 at a point 1.5 miles south of Bonham, 9 miles north of Bailey, turn southeast onto Farm Road 271 and proceed 2 miles; turn east (left) onto Park Road 24 for 0.1 mile; turn north (left) and continue around the lake for 0.6 mile to the park headquarters and the campground, just beyond the headquarters complex.

Facilities: 21 campsites, including 11 with partial hookups, in 2 loops; sites are small, with nominal separation; parking pads are gravel, short straight-ins; additional leveling may be required in some sites; generally small areas for tents, may be slightly sloped; tent pads for some sites; barbecue grills or fire rings; b-y-o firewood; water at faucets throughout; restrooms with showers; holding tank disposal station; paved main roadway, gravel driveways; adequate+ supplies and services are available in Bonham.

Activities & Attractions: Swimming beach; fishing; lighted fishing pier; limited boating; boat launch and dock; playground.

Natural Features: Located on a slope on the northeast shore of 65-acre Bonham State Park Lake; most sites receive medium shade/shelter from large hardwoods and some junipers/cedars; the lake is ringed by dense vegetation; elevation 600'.

Season, Fees & Phone: Open all year; reservations recommended well in advance for weekends, April to November; please see Appendix for additional reservation information and standard Texas state park fees; park office (214) 583-5022.

Camp Notes: Hackberry Hollow and its sites are a bit on the small side (by Texas standards). But the park scenery and local historical points, including the Sam Rayburn Library and home, make this a good short-term/weekend base camp.

Texas 45

PILOT KNOLL
Lewisville Lake/Corps of Engineers Park

Location: North Texas north of Dallas.

Access: From Interstate 35E on the north edge of Lewisville, take Exit 454A for Farm Road 407/Justin; head west on Farm Road 407 for 4 miles; turn north (right) onto Chinn Chapel Road and travel 2.7 miles to a "T" intersection; turn easterly onto a paved road and proceed 0.6 mile to the park entrance station; continue ahead for a few yards, then left for 0.3 mile to the campground. **Alternate Access:** From Interstate 35W at the exit for Farm Road 407/Justin/Lewisville, travel east on Farm Road 407 for 10 miles to Chinn Chapel Road and continue as above.

Facilities: 56 campsites with partial hookups; sites are good-sized, with nominal to fair separation; parking pads are gravel, long to very long straight-ins or pull-throughs; additional leveling will be needed in many sites; small to medium-sized, sloped tent spaces on grass (or the parking pad); fire rings; some firewood is available for gathering in the area; water at faucets throughout; vault facilities; showers; holding tank disposal station; paved driveway; limited supplies and services are available along FM 407.

Activities & Attractions: Boating; boat launch; fishing for bass, crappie, catfish.

Natural Features: Located on a small point of land at the west tip of a major arm (Hickory Creek inlet) at the southwest side of Lewisville Lake; campground vegetation consists of large hardwoods which provide light-medium to medium shelter/shade; open lake views or cove views from all sites; bordered by dense woodland; elevation 500'.

Season, Fees & Phone: Open all year; $11.00; 14 day limit; Lewisville Lake CoE Project Office (214) 434-1666.

Camp Notes: Except on the three big summer holiday weekends, this backroad campground never is filled to capacity. Its location, roughly midway between the twin forks of Interstate 35, makes it an easy destination from either "Cowtown" or "Big D".

Texas 46

OAKLAND
Lewisville Lake/Corps of Engineers Park

Location: North Texas north of Dallas.

Access: From Interstate 35E, Exit 457 for Lake Dallas/Hickory Creek (the first exit north of the long bridge which spans the Hickory Creek arm of the lake, 7 miles north of Lewisville, 11 miles southeast of Denton), from the east side of the freeway, turn east onto Carlisle Drive and proceed 0.4 mile; turn southeast (right) onto Main Street and travel 2 miles (past Westlake Park); turn west (right) onto the campground access road for a last half-mile to the campground entrance station and the campground.

Facilities: 84 campsites, most with partial hookups, in 4 main sections; sites are medium-sized, with nominal to fair separation; parking pads are mostly hard-surfaced, medium to long straight-ins; a little additional leveling may be needed in some sites; adequate space for large tents; ramadas (sun shelters) for many sites; assorted fire facilities; some firewood is available for gathering in the vicinity, b-y-o to be sure; water at faucets throughout; restrooms; showers; holding tank disposal stations; paved driveways; limited supplies and services are available in Lake Dallas.

Activities & Attractions: Boating; boat launches; fishing; playground; swimming beach and changehouse in Westlake Park.

Natural Features: Located on a half-dozen small points (or 'pointlettes') on a peninsula on the south-west shore of 23,000-acre Lewisville Lake, an impoundment on Elm Fork of the Trinity River; sites receive very light to light-medium shade from large hardwoods; elevation 500'.

Season, Fees & Phone: Open all year; $9.00 for a standard site, $11.00 for a partial hookup site; 14 day limit; Lewisville Lake CoE Project Office (214) 434-1666.

Camp Notes: Oakland has a totally different character from its fellow campground at Lewisville Lake City Park, in clear view just across the lake. Since only 10 or 15 minutes' drive separates the two, it might pay to check both.

Texas 47

LAKE LEWISVILLE
Lake Lewisville State Park

Location: North Texas north of Dallas.

Access: From Texas State Highway 121 at a point 6.7 miles northeast of Interstate 35E Exit 450 in Lewisville and 20 miles southwest of McKinney, travel north on Farm Road 423 for 5.2 miles; turn west (left) onto Hackberry Road and proceed west, then zigzag a few times, for a total of 3.2 miles from FM 423 to the park entrance station; continue ahead, then west (right) for 0.4 mile to the campground; **Alternate Access:** From U.S. Highway 380 at a point 14 miles east of Denton, go south on FM 423 for 5.6 miles to Hackberry Road, then west to the park.

Facilities: 50 campsites with partial hookups; (38 units with screened shelters are also available); sites are medium+ in size, with fair separation; parking pads are paved, medium-length straight-ins; minor additional leveling may be needed in some sites; large, framed tent pads; ramadas (sun shelters) for most sites; barbecue grills and fire rings; b-y-o firewood; water at sites; restrooms with showers; holding tank disposal station; paved driveway; nearly complete supplies and services are available in The Colony, 4 miles south on FM 423.

Activities & Attractions: Boating; boat launch; fishing; ball field.

Natural Features: Located near the 'base' (vs the 'tip') of a peninsula extending from the middle-east shore of Lewisville Lake; sites receive very light to medium shade/shelter from hardwoods on large areas of mown grass; bordered by plains and agricultural land; elevation 500'.

Season, Fees & Phone: Open all year; 14 day limit; reservations recommended well in advance for weekends; please see Appendix for additional reservation information and standard Texas state park fees; park office (214) 292-1442.

Camp Notes: This is a bit of alright. Heck, you can camp out in this nicely groomed park in ranch country, and yet drive only a half-hour or so to go mall-hopping in Big D. Note that there are slight differences among the various agencies that operate campgrounds on the lake as to whether the body of water should be called "Lake Lewisville" or "Lewisville Lake". No biggie.

Texas 48

LEWISVILLE LAKE
Lewisville City Park

Location: North Texas north of Dallas.

Access: From Interstate 35E on the north edge of Lewisville, take Exit 454A for Farm Road 407/Justin; from the east side of the freeway, proceed east on Lake Park Road for 1.2 miles (past the golf course); turn north (left) onto Kingfisher Drive for 0.1 mile to the campground entrance station and the campground.

Facilities: 107 campsites, including 95 with partial hookups; sites are small, with minimal to nominal separation; parking pads are gravel, mostly medium to medium+ straight-ins; most pads will require a little additional leveling; adequate space on tent pads for medium to large tents; (tents permitted only in tent sites and in 4 designated hookup sites); barbecue grills, plus a few fire rings; b-y-o firewood; water at faucets throughout; restrooms with showers; holding tank disposal station; mostly paved driveways; security fence; gas and groceries nearby; complete supplies and services are available in Lewisville.

Activities & Attractions: 18-hole municipal golf course; swimming beach; athletic fields; sailing/windsurfing; boating; boat launch; fishing; fishing barge; playground.

Natural Features: Located on gently sloping terrain near the south shore of Lewisville Lake; campground vegetation consists of mown lawns, and rows of large hardwoods and pines which provide light to medium shade/shelter for most sites; elevation 500'.

Season, Fees & Phone: Open all year; $6.00 for a standard/tent site, $8.00-$10.00 for a partial hookup site; weekly rates available; 14 day limit; park office (214) 221-5754.

Camp Notes: The sites may be a little on the small side and closely spaced, but there's still more room here than in, for instance, the average national park campground. The camp's landscaping matches that of the golf course.

Texas 49

TWIN COVES
Grapevine Lake/Corps of Engineers Park

Location: North Texas northwest of Dallas.

Access: From Farm Road 1171 at a point 5.5 miles west of Interstate 35E Exit 452 for Lewisville/Main Street, 10.3 miles east of the Interstate 35W exit for Farm Road 1175 north of Roanoke, turn south onto Old Settlers Road and proceed 0.9 mile; turn west (right) onto Simmons Road and wind southwesterly for 0.8 mile; turn west (right) onto Wichita Trail for 1.1 miles, then turn south (left) for a final mile to the campground entrance station and thence the campground.

Facilities: 45 campsites, most with partial hookups; sites are medium-sized, with nominal to fairly good separation; parking pads are paved, medium to long straight-ins; most pads will require a little additional leveling; adequate, though typically sloped, space for medium to large tents; ramadas (sun shelters) for all sites; barbecue grills and fire rings; b-y-o firewood is recommended; water at faucets throughout; restrooms with showers, plus auxiliary vaults; holding tank disposal station; paved driveways; gas and groceries+ 3 miles east on FM 1171; complete supplies and services are available in Lewisville.

Activities & Attractions: Boating; boat launch; marina; fishing; pier; swimming; nature trail; amphitheater; playground.

Natural Features: Located on a small point on the north shore of 7300-acre Grapevine Lake; large hardwoods provide light to medium shade; elevation 500'.

Season, Fees & Phone: Open all year; $9.00 for a standard site, $11.00 for a partial hookup site; 14 day limit; Grapevine Lake CoE Project Office (817) 481-4541.

Camp Notes: This is one of those rare land harbors where you can bunk for a spell in secluded comfort if you're trying to avoid process servers, telephone solicitors or a cranky spouse, and still be within the D-FW metro area. No one would even *think* of looking for you here, let alone be able to *find* the place. And for a welcome break from camp meals and monotony, you can even get pizza and videos a couple of miles east.

Texas 50

SILVER LAKE
Grapevine Lake/Corps of Engineers Park

Location: North Texas northwest of Dallas.

Access: From Texas State Highway 26 at the far northeast corner of Grapevine, 1.25 miles southwest of the Grapevine Lake Project Office/Headquarters, turn north onto North Dooley Street and proceed 1 mile; turn west (left) to the campground entrance station. **Alternate Access:** From Interstate 35E, take Exit 450 for Lewisville, head southwest on State Highway 121 for 5 miles, then travel along Highway 26 for 3 miles; *or*: from the western terminus of Interstate 635, take Highway 121 north to the Bethel Road exit, go west on Bethel Road to Highway 26, then southwest on Highway 26 for 2 miles; just keep in mind that the park is near the southeast end of the lake, not far from the project office.)

Facilities: 62 campsites, including 26 with partial hookups, in 2 complex loops; sites are small to medium-sized, with nominal separation; parking pads are paved or gravel, short+ to long, straight-ins or pull-offs; most pads will require a little additional leveling; slightly sloped space for medium to large tents on a grassy surface; ramadas (sun shelters) for most sites; barbecue grills; b-y-o firewood is suggested; water at faucets throughout; restrooms with showers; holding tank disposal station; paved driveways; complete supplies and services are available in Grapevine.

Activities & Attractions: Boating; boat launch; marina; fishing; playground.

Natural Features: Located on a pair of small, gently sloping points flanking a cove on the south shore of 7300-acre Grapevine Lake; sites receive very light to light-medium shade from large hardwoods; elevation 500'.

Season, Fees & Phone: Open all year; $9.00 for a standard site, $11.00 for a partial hookup site; 14 day limit; Grapevine Lake CoE Project Office (817) 481-4541.

Camp Notes: If you like sailing, or just enjoy watching a promenade of vividly colored hulls and sails gliding across deep blue water, this is the spot for you.

COLLIN
Lavon Lake/Corps of Engineers Park

Location: North Texas northeast of Dallas.

Access: From Texas State Highway 78 on the north edge of Wylie, head north on Farm Road 2514 for 2.7 miles; at a long, north-to-west curve, continue north for a few yards, then turn east (right) onto the park access road and proceed 0.9 mile; turn north (left) to the campground entrance station, then ahead for 0.2 mile to the campsites.

Facilities: 44 campsites, including 32 with partial hookups; sites are small to medium-sized, with nominal to fair separation; parking pads are gravel, medium-length, straight-ins for hookup units, pull-offs for standard sites; additional leveling will be needed in many sites; medium to large areas for tents, most are sloped; ramadas (sun shelters) for most sites; barbecue grills; b-y-o firewood; water at faucets throughout; restrooms with showers; holding tank disposal station; paved driveways; limited+ supplies and services are available in Wylie.

Activities & Attractions: Swimming beach in the nearby day use area; boating; boat launch; fishing.

Natural Features: Located on a very small point just above the southwest shore of 21,000-acre Lavon Lake; sites receive minimal to light shade/shelter from small to large hardwoods; elevation 500'.

Season, Fees & Phone: March to October; $7.00 for a standard site, $11.00 for a partial hookup site; 14 day limit; Lavon Lake CoE Project Office (214) 442-5711.

Camp Notes: This campground is in a high-class neighborhood: *Dallas'* famed Southfork Ranch is just a few miles west of here. Just follow FM 2514 and you'll find it. If you'd prefer a camp spot which provides more anonymity, check out Clear Lake Park or Ticky Creek Park, on the lake's north shore. Both have free camp/picnic sites, drinking water, grills and boat ramps. Clear Lake has restrooms, Ticky Creek has vaults. Clear Lake is at the end of a major peninsula, Ticky Creek is at the tip of a small point.

EAST FORK
Lavon Lake/Corps of Engineers Park

Location: North Texas northeast of Dallas.

Access: From Texas State Highway 78 on the north edge of Wylie, proceed north on Farm Road 2514 for 0.7 mile; turn east (right) onto a paved lake access road and proceed 1.5 miles; turn northeast (left) for 0.2 mile to the campground entrance station and the campground. (Note: southwestbound travelers approaching from Lavon on Highway 78 may find it a bit quicker to turn north off the highway at a point 1 mile northeast of Wylie; head north to the lake headquarters/project office, then turn west onto the main the east-west lake access road to East Fork Park, for a total of 2.4 miles from Highway 78.)

Facilities: 50 campsites with partial hookups; sites are good-sized, level, with nominal to fair separation; parking pads are paved, medium to medium+ straight-ins; plenty of space for tents on a grassy surface; ramadas (sun shelters) for all sites; barbecue grills; b-y-o firewood; water at sites; restrooms with showers; disposal station; paved driveway; limited+ supplies and services are available in Wylie.

Activities & Attractions: Boating; boat launch; fishing; swimming beach, next door at Avalon Park.

Natural Features: Located on top of a bluff above the south shore of Lavon Lake; campground vegetation consists of a large area of mown grass dotted with hardwoods; elevation 500'.

Season, Fees & Phone: Open all year; $11.00 14 day limit; Lavon Lake CoE Project Office (214) 442-5711.

Camp Notes: There's a feeling of roominess that comes from having a couple of acres of grassy infield within the camp loop drive. Many sites enjoy a good lake view, too. (Of course, a big reason for the sense of space and the good lake views is the sparse population of large trees--but you can't always have everything.) Subjectively, this still is the best campground on the lake.

LAVONIA
Lavon Lake/Corps of Engineers Park

Location: North Texas northeast of Dallas.

Access: From Texas State Highway 78 at a point 1 mile northeast of Lavon (at the junction of Highway 78 with Farm Road 6) and 2 miles south of Copeville, turn west onto Collin County Road 486 (RD 486, paved) and proceed 1 mile to a 3-way intersection just after the road swings south; turn west (right) for 0.15 mile to the campground entrance station and the campground. (Note: Travelers approaching from the southwest may find it quicker to pick up RD 486, which is a loop road, near the southwest corner of Lavonia, then zigzag north for 1.5 miles to the campground.)

Facilities: 53 campsites, including 38 with partial hookups, in 3 loops; sites are medium-sized, with nominal to fairly good separation; parking pads are paved for hookup sites, gravel for standard sites, medium to medium+ straight-ins; pads will require a little to a lot of additional leveling; large, grassy areas for tents, though generally sloped; ramadas (sun shelters) for most sites; barbecue grills; b-y-o firewood; water at faucets throughout; restrooms with showers; holding tank disposal station; paved driveways; limited supplies and services are available in Lavon.

Activities & Attractions: Boating; boat launch; fishing (crappie, catfish); amphitheater; day use area.

Natural Features: Located on a grassy, rolling slope above the south shore of Lavon Lake, a flood-control reservoir which impounds the East Fork of the Trinity River and its tributaries; sites receive very little to very light shade from scattered hardwoods; elevation 500'.

Season, Fees & Phone: Open all year; $7.00 for a standard site, $11.00 for an electrical hookup site; 14 day limit; Lavon Lake CoE Project Office (214) 442-5711.

Camp Notes: Lavon Lake's camps tend to fill up on most nice weekends from early April to well into October, so it might be good to plan your arrival for as early as is feasible.

Texas 54

LITTLE RIDGE
Lavon Lake/Corps of Engineers Park

Location: North Texas northeast of Dallas.

Access: From Texas State Highway 78 on the southwest edge of Copeville (just opposite the turnoff for Business Route 78), turn west onto Collin County Road 489 (paved) and proceed 1.7 miles; turn southwest (left) onto a gravel road for 0.3 mile to the hookup loop; or continue ahead to the standard camp/picnic sites.

Facilities: 74 campsites, including 31 with partial hookups; sites are small+ to medium-sized, with nominal to fair separation; parking pads are paved, medium-length straight-ins for hookups; mostly gravel, straight-ins or pull-throughs for standard units; slight additional leveling may be required; ample space for tents; ramadas (sun shelters) for most sites; barbecue grills; b-y-o firewood; restrooms with showers in the hookup loop; restrooms, plus auxiliary vaults, in the standard district; paved driveways; limited supplies and services are available in Copeville.

Activities & Attractions: Boating; boat launch; fishing.

Natural Features: Located at the tips of a pair of small points on the southeast shore of Lavon Lake; campground vegetation consists of open, grassy sections dotted with hardwoods; elevation 500'.

Season, Fees & Phone: Standard sites are available all year, with limited services October to March; hookup sites are open March to October; no fee for a standard camp/picnic site; $11.00 for a hookup site; 14 day limit; Lavon Lake CoE Project Office (214) 442-5711.

Camp Notes: Well, it's like this: Little Ridge is a good, breezy, somewhat out-of-the-way location with a couple of drawbacks worth contemplating. A minor minus point is the proximity of some residences behind the campground. OK, we all probably can live with that--this isn't a wilderness camp. But the big bummer is the power plant which looms over the campground. The thing to do is to just ignore the steam and sizzle from the juice maker.

Texas 55

WAXAHACHIE CREEK
Bardwell Lake/Corps of Engineers Park

Location: North-Central Texas south of Dallas.

Access: From Texas State Highway 34 at a point 1.1 miles northeast of Bardwell, 0.7 mile southwest of the Bardwell Lake Causeway, 6 miles southwest of Ennis, turn northwest onto a paved county road and proceed 1.7 miles to the park entrance; continue ahead for a few yards, then turn left or right to the campsites. (Note: From Interstate 45, take Exit 251 at Ennis for this and the other Bardwell Lake campgrounds.)

Facilities: 47 campsites, majority with partial hookups; sites are small to small+, with minimal to fair separation; parking pads are gravel, medium-length straight-ins; most pads will require a little additional leveling; enough space for medium to large tents; ramadas (sun shelters) for most sites; barbecue grills; b-y-o firewood is recommended; water at hookup sites and at central faucets; vault facilities; showers; paved main driveways, gravel sub-drives; gas and groceries in Bardwell; adequate+ supplies and services are available in Ennis.

Activities & Attractions: Boating; boat launches; fishing; nature trail.

Natural Features: Located on a slope above the northwest shore of Bardwell Lake, an impoundment on Waxahachie Creek; most sites are well sheltered/shaded by large hardwoods; the lake is encircled by near-level prairie, woods and cropland; elevation 400'.

Season, Fees & Phone: March to November; $9.00 for a standard site, $11.00 for a partial hookup site; 14 day limit; Bardwell Lake CoE Project Office (214) 875-5711.

Camp Notes: Waxahachie Creek's campsites are the best-shaded of all those on the lake. Sites on the southeast side of the park are spaced a little better than others. The day-trippers weren't forgotten here. Some of the best sites have been tagged as day use units. Waxahachie is a derivation of an Indian word meaning "Buffalo Cow".

Texas 56

Mott
Bardwell Lake/Corps of Engineers Park

Location: North-Central Texas south of Dallas.

Access: From Texas State Highway 34 at a point 0.6 mile northeast of Bardwell, 1.2 miles southwest of the Bardwell Lake Causeway, 8 miles southwest of Ennis, turn south/southeast onto Farm Road 985 and proceed 1.7 miles; turn northeast (left) to the park entrance station; continue ahead for 0.35 mile, then turn left to the majority of sites, or right to a few scattered sites.

Facilities: 50 campsites, about half with partial hookups; sites are small+, with nominal to fair separation; parking pads are paved or gravel, medium to long straight-ins, plus a few very long, paved pull-throughs; most pads will probably require a little additional leveling; large, generally sloped, grassy tent areas; ramadas (sun shelters) for many sites; barbecue grills; b-y-o firewood; water at hookup sites and at central faucets; vault facilities; holding tank disposal station; paved driveways; gas and groceries in Bardwell; adequate+ supplies and services are available in Ennis.

Activities & Attractions: Boating; boat launch; fishing.

Natural Features: Located on a grassy slope above the southwest shore of Bardwell Lake; sites receive minimal to medium shade/shelter from large, spreading hardwoods; bordered by prairie, woodland and cultivated land; elevation 400'.

Season, Fees & Phone: Open all year; $7.00 for a standard site, $9.00 for a partial hookup site; 14 day limit; Bardwell Lake CoE Project Office (214) 875-5711.

Camp Notes: Scenario: You're camped-out here in the very merry month of May, but camp life becomes too sedate. Solution: For a generous splash of local color and mirth, you can motor up to Ennis for the National Polka Festival. Sounds like it might be a lot of fun.

Texas 57

High View
Bardwell Lake/Corps of Engineers Park

Location: North-Central Texas south of Dallas.

Access: From Texas State Highway 34 at a point 1.5 miles northeast of Bardwell, 0.3 mile southwest of the Bardwell Lake Causeway, 7 miles southwest of Ennis, turn southeast onto a paved county road and proceed 0.4 mile; turn east (left) to the park entrance station; campsites are just beyond and to the left of the gate, and also at the end of the point.

Facilities: 49 campsites, most with partial hookups; sites are small+, with nominal separation; parking pads are hard-surfaced, medium to long straight-ins; a little additional leveling may be required; ample, grassy spaces for tents, though they may be sloped; ramadas (sun shelters) for many sites; barbecue grills; b-y-o firewood; vault facilities; holding tank disposal station; paved driveways; gas and groceries in Bardwell; adequate+ supplies and services are available in Ennis.

Activities & Attractions: Boating; boat launch; fishing.

Natural Features: Located along the top and side of a long point on the west shore of Bardwell Lake; sites are unshaded to very lightly shaded by large hardwoods and two cedars; good lake views from all sites; elevation 400'.

Season, Fees & Phone: Open all year; $7.00 for a standard site, $9.00 for a partial hookup site; 14 day limit; Bardwell Lake CoE Project Office (214) 875-5711.

Camp Notes: Directly across the lake from High View is Love Park (also called Lower Love Park). To get there, turn south off Highway 34 onto Lakeview Road at a point 2 miles northeast of the causeway which crosses the lake, then zigzag south and southwest for 2.6 miles. Love has about a dozen sites along or just above the lakeshore on a grassy, tree-dotted slope, ramadas, bbq grills, water, vault facilities and a boat ramp. The campground appears to be particularly popular with tent and small vehicle campers. Love is free.

Texas 58

PURTIS CREEK
Purtis Creek State Recreation Area

Location: East-central Texas southeast of Dallas.

Access: From U.S. Highway 175 at the south edge of Eustace (7 miles south of Mabank, 12 miles north of Athens), head north on Farm Road 316 for 3.5 miles; turn north (left, since the road is east-west at this point) and proceed 0.15 mile to the entrance station; just past the entrance, turn west (left), go across the dam, then north for a total of 1 mile to the campground. (Access is also available from Texas State Highway 198 in Phalba, then south on Farm Road 316 for 7 miles.)

Facilities: 59 campsites with partial hookups; sites are small+ to medium-sized, reasonably level, with fair to good separation; parking pads are paved, medium-length straight-ins; enough space for medium to large tents; fire rings; b-y-o firewood; water at faucets throughout; restrooms with showers; disposal station; paved driveways; gas and groceries in Eustace.

Activities & Attractions: Fishing lighted fishing piers; idle-speed boating; boat launch and dock; hiking trail.

Natural Features: Located on the south-west shore of 350-acre Purtis Creek Lake; sites are well-shaded/sheltered by large hardwoods; surrounding countryside is very gently rolling prairie and woodland; elevation 500'.

Season, Fees & Phone: Open all year; 14 day limit; reservations recommended for weekends, Spring through Fall; please see Appendix for additional reservation information and standard Texas state park fees; park office (214) 425-2332.

Camp Notes: Not many sites have a lake view. But most campers come here for the fishing, so they get plenty of lake views in other ways. The lake was designed from the ground up (oops! pun time), with fishing as its number one priority, so there are acres of fish attractors left standing in the water. Many shoreline spots are said to be ideal for fishing, so you may not need a boat to enjoy some angling action

===

TEXAS
Central
Please refer to the Texas map in the Appendix

Texas 59

FRIENDSHIP
Hords Creek Lake/Corps of Engineers Park

Location: West Texas south of Abilene.

Access: From Texas State Highway 153 at a point 7 miles west of Coleman, 6 miles east of Glen Cove, turn south onto a paved access road and proceed 0.3 mile to a point just beyond the project office; turn southwest (right) for 0.2 mile, then right again to the campground. **Alternate Access:** From U.S. Highway 67 in Valera, travel north on Farm Road 503 for 7 miles, then turn west (left) onto Texas 153 for 1.4 miles to the access road, and continue as above.)

Facilities: 23 campsites; (a group camp area is also available); sites are medium+ in size, with fairly good separation; parking pads are paved, medium to long straight-ins, and most will require a little additional leveling; adequate, though slightly sloped, space for large tents; ramadas (sun shelters) for most sites; fireplaces; b-y-o firewood is recommended; water at central faucets; vault facilities; holding tank disposal station; paved driveways; gas and camper supplies in Glen Cove; adequate supplies and services are available in Coleman.

Activities & Attractions: Swimming beach; fishing; boating; boat launch.

Natural Features: Located on an easy slope on the northeast corner of Hords Creek Lake; nearly all sites have at least light shade/shelter provided primarily by large oak trees; plenty of mown grass throughout the park; surrounded by gently rolling plains; elevation 1900'.

Season, Fees & Phone: Available all year, with reduced services October to April; no fee (subject to change); 14 day limit; Hords Creek Lake CoE Project Office (915) 625-2322.

Camp Notes: Some sites are more or less lakeside, and most have at least some sort of lake (and dam) view. The campsites are situated in pairs or small clusters and are spread out over quite an area.

Texas 60

LAKESIDE
Hords Creek Lake/Corps of Engineers Park

Location: West-Central Texas south of Abilene.

Access: From Texas State Highway 153 at a point 8 miles west of Coleman, 5 miles east of Glen Cove, turn south onto a paved access road and proceed south/southeast for 0.8 mile to the campground. **Alternate Access:** From U.S. Highway 67 in Valera, travel north on Farm Road 503 for 7 miles, then turn west (left) onto Texas 153 for 2.5 miles to the access road, and continue as above.)

Facilities: 38 campsites with partial hookups; sites are medium+ to large, with nominal to fair separation; parking pads are paved, medium to long straight-ins, or long pull-throughs; most pads will require a little additional leveling; adequate, though slightly sloped, space for large tents; ramadas (sun shelters) for most sites; fireplaces; b-y-o firewood is recommended; water at sites; restrooms with showers, plus auxiliary vault facilities; holding tank disposal station; paved driveways; gas and camper supplies on the highway; adequate supplies and services are available in Coleman.

Activities & Attractions: Swimming beach; fishing; boating; boat launch.

Natural Features: Located on a slight slope on a point of land on the north shore of Hords Creek Lake; sites receive light to medium shade/shelter from large oak trees on a surface of mown grass; surrounded by gently rolling plains; elevation 1900'.

Season, Fees & Phone: Available all year, with reduced services and fees October to April; $11.00; 14 day limit; Hords Creek Lake CoE Project Office (915) 625-2322.

Camp Notes: All of the sites were built with ramadas; but, because the campground's trees are now fully developed, the shelters really aren't needed for shade (but handy to shed the rain that falls in barrels a couple of times a year).

Texas 61

FLAT ROCK
Hords Creek Lake/Corps of Engineers Park

Location: West-Central Texas south of Abilene.

Access: From Texas State Highway 153 at a point 7 miles west of Coleman, 6 miles east of Glen Cove, turn south onto a paved access road and proceed south past the project office, across the dam, then west for a total of 2.3 miles to the campground. **Alternate Access:** From U.S. Highway 67 in Valera, travel north on Farm Road 503 for 7 miles, then turn west (left) onto Texas 153 for 1.4 miles to the access road, and continue as above.

Facilities: 68 campsites with partial hookups, in 4 areas; sites are medium to medium+ in size, with fairly good separation; parking pads are paved, medium to long straight-ins or pull-throughs, and most will require a little additional leveling; adequate, though slightly sloped, space for large tents; ramadas (sun shelters) for most sites; fireplaces; b-y-o firewood is recommended; water at sites; restrooms with showers; holding tank disposal station; paved driveways; gas and camper supplies on the highway; adequate supplies and services are available in Coleman.

Activities & Attractions: Swimming beach; fishing (fairly good for black bass, crappie, catfish); boating; boat launch.

Natural Features: Located on easy slopes on several small points of land on the south shore of Hords Creek Lake; sites have light to medium shade/shelter provided primarily by large oak trees, plus plenty of mown grass; surrounded by gently rolling plains; elevation 1900'.

Season, Fees & Phone: May to September; $9.00 for a site in Area 2 (tents, pop-ups, etc., no trailers), $11.00 for other sites; 14 day limit; Hords Creek Lake CoE Project Office (915) 625-2322.

Camp Notes: Flat Rock is the most popular camping area on the lake. One explanation is that shoreline and boat fishing offshore of the several points of land within and near the campground is said to be somewhat better than on the easier-to-reach north side of the lake. Or is it merely a "grass is greener" situation on the south shore?

LAKE BROWNWOOD
Lake Brownwood State Recreation Area

Location: West-Central Texas southeast of Abilene.

Access: From Texas State Highway 279 at a point 15 miles northwest of Brownwood, 18 miles south of Cross Plains, head east on Park Road 15 for 6 miles to the park entrance station; turn north (left) to the *Council Bluff* area; or continue for 0.4 mile, then swing north (left) and go 0.3 mile to the *Willow Point* area; or continue ahead on the main park road for a few yards past the Willow Point turnoff to a fork; take the right fork south for 0.3 mile to the *Comanche Trails* area. **Alternate Access:** From U.S. Highway 183 midway between Rising Star and Early, take FM 2273 west for 7.7 miles, then FM 2559 south for 5 miles to Park Road 15, then east on PR 15 for 2.3 miles to the park entrance station and continue as above.

Facilities: *Council Bluff*: 20 campsites with full hookups; *Willow Point*: 12 standard campsites and 32 campsites with partial hookups; *Comanche Trails*: 20 campsites with partial hookups; (10 units with screened shelters are also available in Comanche Trails); sites are small to medium-sized, level to slightly sloped, with nominal to good separation; parking pads are paved, mostly medium-length straight-ins; large tent areas; barbecue grills and/or fire rings; b-y-o firewood; water at faucets throughout; restrooms with showers; holding tank disposal station; gas and groceries are available in and near the park; complete supplies and services are available in Brownwood.

Activities & Attractions: Swimming beaches; hiking and nature trails; boat launches and docks; fishing; fishing pier.

Natural Features: Located on the west shore of Lake Brownwood, an impoundment on Pecan Bayou; majority of campsites have at least a glimpse of the lake; sites are lightly shaded by hardwoods; elevation 1400'.

Season, Fees & Phone: Open all year; 14 day limit; reservations recommended for summer; please see Appendix for additional reservation information and standard Texas state park fees; park office (915) 784-5223.

Camp Notes: There are a dozen dandy standard/tent sites along the shore at the end of Willow Point. The most private sites are in the Comanche Trails area. The latter has a nice beach adjacent to it. Lake Brownwood has more than 70 miles of shoreline.

PROMONTORY
Proctor Lake/Corps of Engineers Park

Location: North-Central Texas northwest of Waco.

Access: From Texas State Highway 16 at a point 6 miles south of De Leon, 10 miles north of Comanche, turn east/southeast onto Farm Road 2318 and proceed 5 miles to the campground entrance; continue ahead for 0.2 mile, then turn left or right to the camp areas.

Facilities: 55 campsites, including 26 sites designated as 13 double units, most with partial hookups; sites are small+ to medium-sized, with nominal to good separation; parking pads are paved or gravel, short to medium-length, primarily straight-ins; some pads may require a little additional leveling; ample space for large tents in most sites; ramadas (sun shelters) for most sites; fireplaces or fire rings; b-y-o firewood is recommended; water at sites and at central faucets; restrooms with showers; holding tank disposal station; adequate to adequate+ supplies and services are available in De Leon and Comanche.

Activities & Attractions: Boating; boat launch; fishing; fishing pier.

Natural Features: Located on a hilly peninsula on the west shore of Proctor Lake, a flood-control impoundment on the Leon River; sites receive light to medium shade from large hardwoods; lake views from nearly all sites; the lake has a low, wooded shoreline, but low hills can be seen in the distant east and north; elevation 1200'.

Season, Fees & Phone: Open all year; $9.00 for a standard site, $11.00 for an electrical hookup site; 14 day limit; Proctor Lake CoE Project Office (817) 879-2424.

Camp Notes: The amount of territory allotted to camping on this lake is quite large. Many sites are situated in small clusters on a number of hilltop points, and thus aren't crowded. The district which contains most of the hookups and all of the double units, on the other hand, is somewhat congested.

Texas 64

COPPERAS CREEK
Proctor Lake/Corps of Engineers Park

Location: North-Central Texas northwest of Waco.

Access: From U.S. Highways 67/377 at a point 6 miles northeast of Comanche, 6 miles southeast of Proctor, turn north onto Farm Road 2861 and proceed north for 1.8 miles, then west for 0.4 mile; turn northwest (right) to the campground entrance station; bear northeast (right) for 0.4 mile or turn west-northwest (left) for 0.5 mile to the camping areas. **Alternate Access:** From Texas State Highway 16 at a point 11 miles south of De Leon, 5 miles north of Comanche, turn east onto Farm Road 2861 and proceed 4 miles to the campground turnoff.

Facilities: 60 campsites, including 49 with partial hookups; sites are small+ to medium-sized, with minimal to fair separation; parking pads are gravel, short to medium-length, primarily straight-ins; most pads will require a little additional leveling; generally sloped space for medium to large tents; ramadas (sun shelters) for many sites; fireplaces; b-y-o firewood is recommended; water at sites and at central faucets; restrooms with showers; holding tank disposal station; paved main driveways, mostly gravel sub-drives; adequate+ supplies and services are available in Comanche.

Activities & Attractions: Boating; boat launches; fishing (crappie, largemouth bass, stripers, etc.); fishing pier; amphitheater.

Natural Features: Located on a pair of small points flanking a bay on the south shore of Proctor Lake, a flood-control impoundment on the Leon River; sites receive light to medium shade from large hardwoods; elevation 1200'.

Season, Fees & Phone: Open all year; $9.00 for a standard site, $11.00 for an electrical hookup site; 14 day limit; Proctor Lake CoE Project Office (817) 879-2424.

Camp Notes: The campsites here may not be the Corps' best, but at least they aren't in a run-down neighborhood: the local country club is just a few, brush-busting yards across the ravine west of the west area.

Texas 65

SOWELL CREEK
Proctor Lake/Corps of Engineers Park

Location: North-Central Texas northwest of Waco.

Access: From U.S. Highways 67/377 at the southwest edge of the community of Proctor, 12 miles northeast of Comanche, turn west onto Farm Road 1476 and proceed 1.1 miles; turn south (left) onto Recreation Road 6 (paved) for 0.3 mile, then west (right) to the campground entrance station; sites are straight ahead or to the right of the entrance.

Facilities: 69 campsites with partial hookups; sites are small+ to medium-sized, reasonably level, with nominal to fair separation; parking pads are mostly gravel/partially paved, medium-length straight-ins; ample space for large tents; majority of sites have ramadas (sun shelters); fireplaces or fire rings; b-y-o firewood is recommended; water at sites; restrooms with showers; holding tank disposal station; paved main driveways, gravel sub-drives; gas and groceries+ in Proctor; adequate+ supplies and services are available in Comanche.

Activities & Attractions: Boating; boat launches; fishing (crappie, largemouth bass, stripers, hybrids, catfish); fishing pier.

Natural Features: Located along the gently sloping shore of a large bay on the east side of Proctor Lake; sites are very lightly to lightly shaded by large hardwoods on a grassy surface; this geographical area is regionally called "Pecan Valley"; elevation 1200'.

Season, Fees & Phone: Open all year; $9.00 for a standard site, $11.00 for an electrical hookup site; 14 day limit; Proctor Lake CoE Project Office (817) 879-2424.

Camp Notes: Proctor Lake is a favorite haunt of bass clubs and crappie clubs. Tournaments are held quite often. The lake's free campground, High Point, is a mile northwest of here, via FM 1476, then southwest 0.7 mile. It lacks most of the comforts of Sowell Creek, but does have nearly two-dozen sites with very light shade, drinking water, vaults, a disposal station, a boat ramp and some good views.

Texas 66

MERIDIAN
Meridian State Recreation Area

Location: Central Texas Northwest of Waco.

Access: From Texas State Highway 22 at a point 3.5 miles southwest of Meridian, 12 miles northeast of Cranfills Gap, turn west onto Park Road 7, then bear southwest for 0.2 mile to the park entrance/headquarters; the main campground is located just across the park road from the entrance; semi-primitive sites are located in a half-dozen clusters along the park roads.

Facilities: 15 campsites in the main campground, including 7 with partial hookups and 8 with full hookups; (a couple-dozen small, semi-primitive sites with short pads, tables and fireplaces, plus 17 units with screened shelters, are also available); sites are small to medium-sized, acceptably level, with nominal to fairly good separation; parking pads are paved, short to medium-length straight-ins or medium+ pull-throughs; small to medium-sized tent areas; fire rings; b-y-o firewood; water at sites; restrooms with showers; paved driveway; limited+ supplies and services are available in Meridian.

Activities & Attractions: Extensive network of nature and hiking trails, including a trail around the lakeshore; designated swimming area; limited boating; boat launch; fishing.

Natural Features: Located on a hilltop among densely wooded hills; sites receive light to light-medium shelter/shade primarily from large junipers/cedars; 70-acre Lake Meridian serves as the geographical and recreational hub of the park; elevation 1000'.

Season, Fees & Phone: Open all year; 14 day limit; reservations recommended for summer weekends; please see Appendix for additional reservation information and standard Texas state park fees; park office (817) 435-2536.

Camp Notes: Meridian was designed chiefly for, and is visited by, people who enjoy hiking, wildlife watching, toe dipping, pebble plopping and other very elementary pursuits.

Texas 67

CEDRON CREEK
Whitney Lake/Corps of Engineers Park

Location: Central Texas northwest of Waco.

Access: From Texas State Highway 22 at a point 4 miles west of Laguna Park and 14 miles southeast of Meridian, travel northwest on Farm Road 56 for 8.5 miles; turn northeast (right) onto Farm Road 1713 and proceed 4 miles; turn southeast (right) to the park entrance station and the campground. (Note: For campers approaching from Dallas-Fort Worth on Interstate 35, it might be quicker to take Texas 22 to the city of Whitney, then Farm Road 933 northwest out of Whitney for 3.5 miles to Farm Road 1713; go south on FM 1713 and across the bridge that spans the midpoint of the lake to the south shore for a final 6 miles to the campground turnoff.)

Facilities: 57 campsites with partial hookups; sites are medium to large, with fair separation; parking pads are paved, medium to very long straight-ins or pull-throughs; most pads will require a little additional leveling; medium to large, generally sloped, tent areas; ramadas (sun shelters) for all sites; barbecue grills and fireplaces; b-y-o firewood is suggested; water at sites; restrooms with showers; holding tank disposal station; paved driveways; gas and groceries are available on FM 1713 and in Laguna Park.

Activities & Attractions: Swimming beach; boating; boat launch; fishing (good for stripers, also largemouths, cats, bream).

Natural Features: Located on the south-west shore of Whitney Lake; sites receive very light to medium shade principally from large hardwoods; elevation 600'.

Season, Fees & Phone: Open all year; $11.00; 14 day limit; Whitney Lake CoE Project Office (817) 622-3332.

Camp Notes: Cedron Creek is the only full-service campground on this side of the lake. Two other areas along the shore, northwest of here, are Steeles Creek and Plowman Creek. Each of these "no charge" parks has room for roughly 20 camping parties, tables and grills, drinking water, vaults, and a boat ramp.

MᴄCᴏᴡɴ Vᴀʟʟᴇʏ
Whitney Lake/Corps of Engineers Park

Location: Central Texas northwest of Waco.

Access: From Texas State Highway 22 in the city of Whitney, take Farm Road 933 through town and northwest for 3.5 miles; turn southwest (left) onto Farm Road 1713 and proceed 4 miles to a "Y" intersection; continue south on Spur 1713 (instead of following FM 1713 to the west) for 0.5 mile to the park boundary; turn east (left) for 0.1 mile to the campground entrance station and the campground.
Alternate Access: From State Highway 174 near Blum, travel southeast on Farm Road 933 (through Blum) for 14 miles to FM 1713, and continue as above.

Facilities: 55 campsites, most with partial hookups; sites are medium to large, with nominal to fairly good separation; parking pads are mostly paved, medium to long straight-ins or long to very long pull-throughs; ample space for large tents; ramadas (sun shelters) for all sites; fire rings; some firewood may be available for gathering in the vicinity, b-y-o is suggested; water at faucets throughout; restrooms with showers; holding tank disposal station; paved main driveways, gravel sub-drives; gas and groceries on FM 1713; limited+ supplies and services are available in Whitney.

Activities & Attractions: Swimming beach; boating; boat launch (on the opposite side of the bay); fishing; playground.

Natural Features: Located on slightly sloping and rolling terrain along and near the north-east shore of Whitney Lake; some sites look out onto the open lake, others overlook a bay; shoreside sites are minimally to lightly sheltered, others are well-sheltered; elevation 600'.

Season, Fees & Phone: Open all year; $9.00 for a standard site, $11.00 for a partial hookup site; 14 day limit; Whitney Lake CoE Project Office (817) 622-3332.

Camp Notes: This locale is along the narrowest segment of the main part of the lake. The scenic/photo possibilities seem just a bit better here, due to the visual enhancement which stems from being a little closer to the opposite shore.

Lᴀᴋᴇ Wʜɪᴛɴᴇʏ
Lake Whitney State Recreation Area

Location: Central Texas northwest of Waco.

Access: From Texas State Highway 22 at the southeast corner of the city of Whitney, turn west onto Farm Road 933 (Colorado Street) and proceed 0.7 mile; turn southwest onto Farm Road 1244 and follow it for 2.4 miles to the park entrance station; continue for 0.2 mile to a 3-way intersection; proceed ahead for 0.2 mile to the full hookup sites, or turn left for a mile to most standard sites.

Facilities: 137 campsites, including 7 with partial hookups and 35 with full hookups; (26 units with screened shelters are also available); overall, sites are medium-sized, at least tolerably level, with fair to fairly good separation; full hookup units have long, paved parking pads; most remaining sites have short to medium-length, gravel straight-ins; lots of space for tents; ramadas (sun shelters) for most standard sites; assorted fire appliances; b-y-o firewood; water at faucets throughout; restrooms with showers; holding tank disposal station; paved main driveways, some gravel sub-drives; limited+ supplies and services are available in Whitney.

Activities & Attractions: Swimming beach; boating; boat launch; fishing (good lake for stripers); trail bike area.

Natural Features: Located on a large point of land on the north-east shore of Whitney Lake; full hookup sites are in a hardwood grove a short distance from the lake; most other sites are on small points along a light-to-moderately shaded blufftop overlooking the lake; elevation 600'.

Season, Fees & Phone: Open all year; 14-day limit; please see Appendix for reservation information and standard Texas state park fees; park office (817) 694-3793.

Camp Notes: The campsites possess two distinctively different personalities: open and rugged and windblown along the bluff; or sheltered, refined and park-like in the grove.

LOFERS BEND EAST
Whitney Lake/Corps of Engineers Park

Location: Central Texas northwest of Waco.

Access: From Texas State Highway 22 at a point 3.4 miles north of Laguna Park, 1 mile north of Whitney Dam, 5 miles south of Whitney, turn northwest onto the park access road and proceed 0.4 mile to the park entrance station; turn north (right) for 0.5 mile to the campground entrance station; campsites are situated in 4 clusters off of the main campground driveway.

Facilities: 56 campsites, most with partial hookups; sites are medium to large, with fair to good separation; parking pads are paved or gravel, mostly medium to long straight-ins; a little additional leveling may be required in some sites; adequate, generally level, space for large tents; ramadas (sun shelters) for many sites; fireplaces, plus some barbecue grills; a limited amount of firewood is available for gathering in the general area, b-y-o to be sure; water at sites; restrooms with showers; holding tank disposal station; paved driveways; gas and groceries in Laguna Park; limited+ supplies and services are available in Whitney.

Activities & Attractions: Boating; boat launches; fishing; playground; designated swimming beach at Lofers Bend West (see separate information).

Natural Features: Located on the east shore of Whitney Lake; campground vegetation consists of stands of hardwoods and evergreens, plus scattered hardwoods on large sections of mown grass; sites receive light to light-medium shelter/shade; the lake is rimmed by low, light-colored cliffs topped by dense vegetation; elevation 600'.

Season, Fees & Phone: Open all year; $9.00 for a standard site, $11.00 for a partial hookup site; 14 day limit; Whitney Lake CoE Project Office (817) 622-3332.

Camp Notes: This is a good-looking lake--and you can see a lot of it from many of the campsites here. Those that don't have great lake views have a little more seclusion instead.

LOFERS BEND WEST
Whitney Lake/Corps of Engineers Park

Location: Central Texas northwest of Waco.

Access: From Texas State Highway 22 at a point 3.4 miles north of Laguna Park, 1 mile north of Whitney Dam, 5 miles south of Whitney, turn northwest onto the park access road and proceed 0.4 mile to the park entrance station; turn south (left) for 0.3 mile to the campground entrance station; turn west (right) just past the entrance and continue for 0.3 mile to the campsites, situated in a half-dozen sections off of the main campground driveway.

Facilities: 68 campsites, majority with partial hookups; (a group camp area is also available); sites are medium to large, with fair to very good separation; parking pads are gravel, mostly medium to long straight-ins, plus a few pull-throughs; a little additional leveling may be required in some sites; adequate space for large tents, those close to the shore may be a little sloped; ramadas (sun shelters) for many sites; assorted fire facilities; a limited amount of firewood may be available for gathering in the vicinity, b-y-o is recommended; water at sites; restrooms; vault facilities; showers; holding tank disposal station; paved main driveways, gravel sub-drives; gas and groceries in Laguna Park; limited+ supplies and services are available in Whitney.

Activities & Attractions: Boating; boat launch; fishing; swimming beach; playground; day use area.

Natural Features: Located on a point on the east shore of Whitney Lake; sites receive very light to moderate shelter/shade from large hardwoods; the lake is encircled by low cliffs and bluffs topped by dense vegetation; elevation 600'.

Season, Fees & Phone: April to November; $9.00 for a standard site, $11.00 for a partial hookup site; 14 day limit; Whitney Lake CoE Project Office (817) 622-3332.

Camp Notes: Across the southeast tip of the lake from Lofers Bend West are two small CoE parks with about 10 free-use picnic/camp sites each. Walling Bend and Soldiers Bluff have tables, grills, central water and vaults.

WOLF CREEK II
Navarro Mills Lake/Corps of Engineers Park

Location: North-Central Texas northeast of Waco.

Access: From Texas State Highway 31 at a point 4 miles northeast of Dawson, 17 miles southwest of Corsicana, turn northwest onto Farm Road 667 and travel 5 miles; turn southwest (left) onto Farm Road 744 and proceed 2.4 miles to Farm Road 1578; turn southwest (left) onto Farm Road 1578 for 2 miles to a fork; turn right to the west section or left to the east section. **Alternate Accesses:** From State Highway 22 in the city of Frost, travel southeast on Farm Road 667 for 8 miles to its junction with Farm Road 744, then southwest on FM 744 for 1.5 miles to FM 1578 and continue as above; or from State Highway 171 in Malone, head northeast on Farm Road 744 for 12 miles to Farm Road 1578 and continue as above.

Facilities: 45 campsites; sites vary from small to large, about half are slightly sloped, with nominal to good separation; parking surfaces are gravel/grass, medium-length straight-ins or pull-offs; plenty of tent space; ramadas (sun shelters) for some sites; barbecue grills or fireplaces; b-y-o firewood is suggested; water at several faucets; vault facilities; paved main driveways, gravel sub-drives; gas and camper supplies on FM 744; gas and groceries+ are available in Dawson.

Activities & Attractions: Boating; boat launch; fishing; swimming beach.

Natural Features: Located on gently sloping terrain above the north shore of Navarro Mills Lake; several sites are lakeside, on a small point; sites receive minimal to light shade from large hardwoods; bordered by prairie, woodland and cropland; elevation 400'.

Season, Fees & Phone: April to November; no fee (subject to change); 14 day limit; Navarro Mills Lake CoE Project Office (817) 578-1431.

Camp Notes: Here's a bargain basement camp that's worth considering. Wolf Creek II may not have showers and hookups like its big brother, Wolf Creek I (see info), but the views are just as good and there's lots of elbow room.

WOLF CREEK I
Navarro Mills Lake/Corps of Engineers Park

Location: North-Central Texas northeast of Waco.

Access: From Texas State Highway 31 at a point 4 miles northeast of Dawson, 17 miles southwest of Corsicana, turn northwest onto Farm Road 667 and proceed 3.2 miles; turn southwest (left) onto Farm Road 639 and continue for 1.5 miles, then turn sharply south (left) to the park entrance station; sites are located in several sections from 0.2 mile to 1.5 miles south/southeast of the entrance. **Alternate Access:** From Texas State Highway 22 in the city of Frost, proceed southeast on Farm Road 667 for 10 miles to Farm Road 639 and continue as above.

Facilities: 52 campsites, half with partial hookups; sites are small+ to medium-sized, with nominal to fairly good separation; parking pads are mostly gravel, short to very long straight-ins, plus a few paved pull-throughs; a little additional leveling may be needed; adequate space for large tents, may be sloped; ramadas (sun shelters) for some sites; assorted campfire appliances; b-y-o firewood is suggested; water at sites and at central faucets; restrooms with showers; holding tank disposal station; paved main driveways, paved or gravel sub-drives; gas and groceries+ are available in Dawson.

Activities & Attractions: Boat launch; fishing; playground.

Natural Features: Located on moderately sloping terrain near the north shore of Navarro Mills Lake; sites receive very light to medium shelter/shade from large hardwoods, plus some pines and junipers/cedars; encircled by prairie, woodland and cropland; elevation 400'.

Season, Fees & Phone: Available all year, with limited services November to April; $9.00 for a standard site, $11.00 for a partial hookup site; 14 day limit; Navarro Mills Lake CoE Project Office (817) 578-1431.

Camp Notes: Most of the campsites have excellent views of the lake and its pastoral shoreline. A lot of campers like this place because the sites are situated in clusters which are quite distant from one another.

OAK
Navarro Mills Lake/Corps of Engineers Park

Location: North-Central Texas northeast of Waco.

Access: From Texas State Highway 31 at a point 4 miles northeast of Dawson, 17 miles southwest of Corsicana, turn northwest onto Farm Road 667 and proceed 1.4 miles (0.25 mile past the project office); turn west (left) onto the park access road and proceed 0.2 mile to the park entrance station; continue ahead for 0.3 mile, then turn left or right to the campsites.

Facilities: 47 campsites, including 25 with partial hookups, in 2 loops connected by a string; sites are small+ to medium-sized, with nominal to fair separation; parking pads are paved or gravel, medium to long straight-ins; many pads will require a little additional leveling; slightly sloped spaces for medium to large tents; ramadas (sun shelters) for most sites; barbecue grills; a small amount of firewood is available for gathering in the vicinity, b-y-o to be sure; water at hookup sites and at central faucets; restrooms with showers; holding tank disposal station; paved driveways; gas and groceries+ are available in Dawson.

Activities & Attractions: Boating; boat launch and dock; fishing; fishing pier; swimming beach; Alliance Creek Nature Trail; playground.

Natural Features: Located on moderately rolling and sloping terrain near the northeast shore of Navarro Mills Lake; sites receive minimal to medium+ shelter/shade from large hardwoods; elevation 400'.

Season, Fees & Phone: Open all year; $9.00 for a standard site, $11.00 for a partial hookup site; 14 day limit; Navarro Mills Lake CoE Project Office (817) 578-1431.

Camp Notes: Of the four campgrounds on Navarro Mills Lake, Oak seems to offer the greatest variety of campsite surroundings. If you'd like to learn more about the local environment in which you're camping, an excellent booklet for the Alliance Creek Nature Trail is available from the project office.

LIBERTY HILL
Navarro Mills Lake/Corps of Engineers Park

Location: North-Central Texas northeast of Waco.

Access: From Texas State Highway 31 on the northeast corner of the community of Dawson, turn northwest onto Farm Road 709 and proceed northwest, northeast, then northwest again, for 3.8 miles to the park entrance station; continue ahead for 0.2 mile, then turn left or right to the camp areas.

Facilities: 102 campsites, including 82 with partial hookups, in 4 major sections; sites vary considerably, but the majority are medium to medium+, with nominal to good separation; parking pads are paved, short to medium+ straight-ins; most pads will require a touch of additional leveling; ample space for large tents; ramadas (sun shelters) for all sites; barbecue grills, fireplaces or fire rings; b-y-o firewood is recommended; water at hookup sites and at central faucets; restrooms with showers; holding tank disposal station; paved driveways; gas and groceries+ are available in Dawson.

Activities & Attractions: Boating; boat launches and docks; marina; fishing; fishing pier; swimming beach; playground.

Natural Features: Located along the edge of a short bluff just above the south-east shore of Navarro Mills Lake; campground vegetation consists of large tracts of grass, well-dotted with large hardwoods, plus a few pines and cedars/junipers; shade varies from very light to light-medium; the lake is encircled by prairie, cropland and woodland; elevation 400'.

Season, Fees & Phone: Open all year; $9.00 for a standard site, $11.00 for a partial hookup site; 14 day limit; Navarro Mills Lake CoE Project Office (817) 578-1431.

Camp Notes: Although many of the campsites are somewhat closely spaced, lots of shoulder room has been left around many others. Spacing is best on the east side of the campground. Liberty Hill is the nicest and most popular camp on the lake.

FAIRFIELD LAKE
Fairfield Lake State Recreation Area

Location: East-Central Texas southeast of Dallas.

Access: From U.S. Highway 84 at the southeast side of the city of Fairfield (1.5 miles east of the Interstate 45 exits for Fairfield), travel north/northeast on Farm Road 488 for 1.8 miles, then continue northeast on Farm Road 2570 for another 1.3 miles; turn east (right) onto Farm Road 3285/Park Road 64 for 3 miles to the park entrance; continue around the south end of the lake, then up the east shore for 3 miles to 4 miles to the 3 camp areas.

Facilities: 135 campsites, including 90 with partial hookups; sites are small+ to medium-sized, with nominal to good separation; parking pads are hard-surfaced, medium-length straight-ins or long pull-throughs which may require a little additional leveling; adequate space for medium to large tents; assorted fire facilities; b-y-o firewood; water at faucets throughout; restrooms with showers; holding tank disposal station; paved driveways; adequate supplies and services are available in Fairfield.

Activities & Attractions: Fishing; lighted fishing pier; boating; boat launch and docks; swimming area; hiking trails; playground; amphitheater.

Natural Features: Located on slightly rolling terrain on nearly 1500 acres along the south-east shore of Fairfield Lake, an impoundment on Big Brown Creek; sites are well sheltered by large hardwoods and a few cedars; lake views through the trees from some sites; bordered by the woodland and grassland of the Post Oak Savannah; elevation 500'.

Season, Fees & Phone: Open all year; 14-day limit; please see Appendix for reservation information and standard Texas state park fees; park office (214) 389-4514.

Camp Notes: There is also a backpacking/primitive camping area on the lake's south-west shore. The camp can only be reached via a 4.5 mile trail from a parking area at the park entrance station/headquarters.

Texas 77

FORT PARKER
Fort Parker State Recreation Area

Location: North-Central Texas east of Waco.

Access: From Texas State Highway 14 at a point 6.5 miles south of Mexia, 6 miles north of Groesbeck, turn west onto Park Road 28 for 0.2 mile to the park entrance station; continue ahead (northwest, then north) for 0.8 mile, then around to the south (left) for 0.2 mile; swing north (right, just past the shelters) into the campground.

Facilities: 25 campsites with partial hookups; (in addition, 10 units with screened shelters are also available); sites are medium-sized, with nominal to fair separation; most parking pads are gravel, medium to long straight-ins; most pads will require a little additional leveling; adequate space for large tents; fire rings; b-y-o firewood; water at faucets throughout; restrooms with showers; holding tank disposal station; limited+ supplies and services are available in Groesbeck; adequate supplies and services can be found in Mexia.

Activities & Attractions: Fishing (crappies, cats, largemouths and sunnies); fishing pier; swimming; boat launch; Old Fort Parker and Confederate Reunion Grounds State Historical Parks, just south and north, respectively, of this park.

Natural Features: Located on the gently sloping east shore of Lake Fort Parker, a reservoir on the Navasota River; sites are very well-sheltered/shaded by large hardwoods; lake views from most sites; the area is in the boundary between the Post Oak Savannah to the East and the Blackland Prairie region to the West; elevation 500'.

Season, Fees & Phone: Open all year; 14-day limit; please see Appendix for reservation information and standard Texas state park fees; park office (817) 562-5751.

Camp Notes: The campsites and roadways are sheltered by tunnels of trees--a really neat effect. The large water birds often use the row of reeds along the campground's share of the shore as a feeding and resting spot. Highway signs in the nearby towns display the spirit and good-natured sense of humor found in so many communities throughout Texas. Groesbeck's steadfast enthusiasm for its high school football team, "Home of the Fightin' Goats"; and Mexia's self-proclaimed "A Great Place ... However You Pronounce It" suggest that there are a lot of nice, real people around here.

Texas 78

AIRPORT
Waco Lake/Corps of Engineers Park

Location: Central Texas west of Waco.

Access: From Interstate 35 Exit 339 on the north edge of Waco, take Farm Road 3051 west, then southwest, for 6 miles to the northeast corner of the airport; continue ahead onto Airport Road for 0.4 mile; turn west/southwest (right) onto Airport Drive and continue for 0.8 mile, then bear left onto Skeet Eason Drive (be careful not to take the terminal turnoff); follow Skeet Eason Drive around for 1.7 miles; turn southwest (left, by the radar site) to the park entrance and the campground. (Note: Unless you hanker for a grand tour of Waco and the surrounding countryside, it's best to stick to the above *relatively* straightforward access, vs some of the more exotic, published routes.)

Facilities: 88 campsites, including 20 with partial hookups; sites are small+ to medium+, with nominal to fairly good separation; parking surfaces are gravel or earth, short to medium in standard sites, long in hookup units; some additional leveling probably will be needed; medium to large tent areas; ramadas (sun shelters) for some sites; barbecue grills or fireplaces in some sites; b-y-o firewood is suggested; water at hookup sites and at central faucets; vault facilities (basically); showers; holding tank disposal station; paved or gravel driveways; gas and groceries are available within a mile.

Activities & Attractions: Beach; boat launch; fishing; picnicking.

Natural Features: Located on a short bluff along a point on the north shore of Waco Lake; sites receive light to medium shade/shelter from large junipers/cedars and hardwoods; lake views from many sites; elevation 500'.

Season, Fees & Phone: Open all year, with reduced services October to April; $7.00 for a standard site, $11.00 for a partial hookup site; 14 day limit; Waco Lake CoE Project Office (817) 756-5359.

Camp Notes: For being so close to the city (and consequently seeing heavy use on occasion), this place isn't too bad. If you're an airplane watcher, you've got it made.

Texas 79

SPEEGLEVILLE I
Waco Lake/Corps of Engineers Park

Location: Central Texas west of Waco.

Access: From Texas State Highway 6 at a point 8 miles west/northwest of Interstate 35 Exit 330 at the south edge of Waco, 2 miles northwest of the causeway which crosses Waco Lake, 3 miles southeast of the junction of State Highway 36 and Farm Road 185, take the exit for "Speegleville Road" to the northeast side of the divided highway; proceed east/northeast (past the Speegleville Fire Station on your left) for 1.2 miles to a 4-way intersection with Spur 412; continue ahead (across Spur 412, no turn), northeast, then curve north-northwest, for another 1.5 miles; turn northeast (right) to the park entrance station and the campground.

Facilities: 93 campsites with partial hookups in 9 areas; site size varies from small to large, most are at least reasonably level, with nominal to fairly good separation; parking pads are paved, medium to long straight-ins or pull-throughs; adequate space for medium to large tents; ramadas (sun shelters) for most sites; barbecue grills; b-y-o firewood is suggested; water at sites; restrooms with showers; holding tank disposal stations; paved driveways; gas and groceries are available at the junction of Texas Highway 6 & Farm Road 185.

Activities & Attractions: Boating; boat launch; fishing for crappie, white bass, catfish, plus "Florida" largemouths, wipers and stripers; nature trail; amphitheater; evening programs in summer; clubhouse.

Natural Features: Located along the north-west shore of Waco Lake; sites receive ample shade from large junipers/cedars and hardwoods on mown grass; the area is bordered by near-level agricultural land; elevation 500'.

Season, Fees & Phone: Open all year; $11.00; 14 day limit; Waco Lake CoE Project Office (817) 756-5359.

Camp Notes: Speegleville I gets a pair of "thumbs-up" as the best camp on Waco Lake. Dozens of first-rate, lakeside campsites here.

Texas 80

SPEEGLEVILLE III
Waco Lake/Corps of Engineers Park

Location: Central Texas west of Waco.

Access: From Texas State Highway 6 near the north-west end of the causeway which crosses Waco Lake (7 miles west-northwest of Interstate 35 Exit 330 at the south edge of Waco, 5 miles southeast of the junction of Highway 36 and Farm Road 185), turn northeast onto the park access road and proceed 0.1

mile to the park entrance station; turn right to a small group of hookup sites, or continue ahead for 0.4 mile, then right for 0.3 mile to the main hookup area. (Special Note for southeastbound traffic on Highway 6: after exiting from the divided highway, you'll need to find the underpass which will take you to the north side of the 4-lane road and onto the park access road.)

Facilities: 14 sites with partial hookups; (10 standard camp/picnic sites are also available); sites are medium-sized, with fair separation; parking pads are paved, medium to long straight-ins, most of which will probably require some additional leveling; adequate space for large tents; ramadas (sun shelters) for all sites; barbecue grills; b-y-o firewood; vault facilities; showers; holding tank disposal station; paved driveways; gas and groceries within 3 miles north or south.

Activities & Attractions: Boating; fishing; model airplane field.

Natural Features: Located near the west shore of Waco Lake; most sites are well-shaded/sheltered by large hardwoods; bordered by agricultural land; elevation 500'.

Season, Fees & Phone: Open all year; $9.00 for a standard site, $11.00 for a partial hookup site; 14 day limit; Waco Lake CoE Project Office (817) 756-5359.

Camp Notes: OK, this is Speegleville III; and Speegleville I is detailed elsewhere. What happened to Speegleville II? It's mostly just a lake access area. One more nearby CoE area is Midway Park, at the southeast end of the lake causeway, with a couple dozen free picnic/camp sites, tables, fireplaces, water and vaults.

Texas 81

FORT FISHER
City of Waco Park

Location: Central Texas in Waco.

Access: From Interstate 35 exit 335B for University Parks Drive and Farm Road 434, proceed to the east side of the freeway, turn north for a few yards, then east into the park; the main campground is on the east side of the park, behind the office/info center. **Additional Access:** the full hookup sites are located in the North Park area, on the west side of the freeway via an underpass by the river, (but you'll need to check in at the office prior to settling-in anyway).

Facilities: 110 campsites, including 90 with partial hookups and 10 with full hookups; (15 units with screened shelters are also available); sites are small, level, with minimal to nominal separation; parking pads/areas are paved or grass, medium-length straight-ins (pull-throughs for full hookups); large, grassy tent areas; no fire facilities; water at faucets; restrooms with showers; holding tank disposal station; paved driveways; complete supplies and services are available nearby.

Activities & Attractions: Texas Ranger Hall of Fame; museum; replicas of frontier buildings; information center.

Natural Features: Located on a grassy flat on the south bank of the Brazos River; a baker's dozen of sites are on a short step or rise, a few yards directly across from a marble orchard; most sites are very lightly to moderately shaded by large hardwoods on mown lawns; elevation 400'.

Season, Fees & Phone: Open all year; $10.00 for a tent, $11.00 for a partial hookup site, $12.00 for a full hookup site, $12.00 for a shelter; reservations accepted, contact the park office (see Notes); park office (800) 922-6386 or (817) 753-4931.

Camp Notes: This is one of the nicest big city park camps you'll find anywhere. Although the freeway is close at hand, its proximity really isn't an issue with campers who stay here. There's *usually* room for drop-ins during most of the year. Major exceptions: Baylor University Homecoming and home game weekends, plus the end of November and early December during the Masonic Lodge get-together. If you're interested in Western history, this stop is especially worthwhile.

Texas 82

MOTHER NEFF
Mother Neff State Park

Location: Central Texas northwest of Temple.

Access: From Texas State Highway 236 at a point 5 miles north of The Grove, 1.7 miles south of the junction of Highway 236 and Farm Road 107 west of Moody, turn west into the park and proceed 0.1 mile; bear right around the traffic circle, then turn north (right) and continue for 0.1 mile to the campground. (Note: From Interstate 35, northbound, take Exit 299 in Temple, then travel northwest on

State Highway 36 to the park; from Interstate 35, southbound, take Exit 315 in Eddy, then go west on Farm Road 107.)

Facilities: 21 campsites, including 6 with partial hookups; sites are small+ to medium-sized, basically level, with fair separation; parking pads are gravel, medium to long straight-ins; large areas for tents; barbecue grills and fire rings; b-y-o firewood; water at hookup sites and at central faucets; restrooms with showers; holding tank disposal station; paved driveways; gas and groceries are available in The Grove.

Activities & Attractions: Hiking trail; playground; limited fishing; historic sites.

Natural Features: Located on a large, slightly rolling flat along the north bank of the Leon River; large hardwoods provide moderately dense shade/shelter for all sites; surrounding countryside is comprised of woodland, prairie and farmland; elevation 700'.

Season, Fees & Phone: Open all year; 14 day limit; please see Appendix for reservation information and standard Texas state park fees; park office (817) 853-2389.

Camp Notes: For anyone who is enthusiastic about Texas' many outstanding state parks, a trip here could be likened to undertaking a pilgrimage to Mecca. This is the Lone Star State's first state park, established on land donated by Isabella Eleanor Neff in 1916. (Mrs. Neff was a teacher and was older than most other frontier settlers. Consequently, she acquired the appellation "Mother Neff".) Mother Neff State Park has a surprisingly similar counterpart in the Pacific Northwest. In Oregon's great Willamette Valley is Sarah Helmick State Park. Both parks are approximately equal in size and have nearly identical geography (large hardwoods, lots of grass, on a riverbank, bordered by farmland). Furthermore, both Mother Neff and Sarah Helmick hold the distinction of being the first state parks established by the citizens of their respective states.

Texas 83

CEDAR RIDGE
Belton Lake/Corps of Engineers Park

Location: Central Texas west of Temple.

Access: From Texas State Highway 36 at a point 2 miles northwest of its junction with State Highway 317 northwest of Temple, 3 miles southeast of the Belton Lake (Leon River) causeway, 9 miles southeast of The Grove, turn south/southwest (left) onto Cedar Ridge Park Road and proceed 1.25 miles; turn southeast (left) to the entrance station for the main campground (hookup) area. (Special Access Note: From Interstate 35, Exit 299 or Exit 301 in Temple, take State Highway 36 north for 7 miles to the Cedar Ridge turnoff.)

Facilities: 40 campsites with partial hookups; sites are generally good-sized, with nominal to fairly good separation; parking pads are gravel, medium to medium+ straight-ins; a few pads may require a bit of additional leveling; adequate space for large tents; ramadas (sun shelters) for most sites; barbecue grills; a limited amount of firewood may be available for gathering in the area, b-y-o suggested; water at sites; vault facilities; showers; holding tank disposal station; paved driveways; several gas and groceries stops are within 4 miles.

Activities & Attractions: Boating; boat launch; fishing for largemouth bass, catfish, panfish, and some walleye.

Natural Features: Located on a short bluff above a long arm (Cedar Creek inlet) on the east side of Belton Lake; sites are lightly to moderately sheltered/shaded by large hardwoods and junipers/cedars; elevation 600'.

Season, Fees & Phone: Open all year; $11.00; 14 day limit; Belton Lake CoE Project Office (817) 939-1829.

Camp Notes: In addition to the pay campground, two dozen free campsites are available in the vicinity. Just continue past the fee campground to the simple sites, which are scattered along the next mile of access road. Make-do camping is also available at Leona, White Flint, and Owl Creek Parks, off Texas 36, northwest of here. These parks offer tables, fireplaces, vaults, boat ramps and seclusion.

Texas 84

TEMPLE'S LAKE
Belton Lake/Corps of Engineers Park

Location: Central Texas west of Temple.

Access: From Texas State Highway 317 at a point 3 miles south of its junction with State Highway 36 west of Temple and 6 miles north of Belton, turn west onto Farm Road 2305 and proceed 3.3 miles to the park entrance station; turn right or left to the campsites. (Special Access Note: From Interstate 35, northbound, take Exit 293 in Belton, then travel Highway 317 northwest to FM 2305, then west to the park; from Interstate 35, southbound, take Exit 301 in Temple, then Farm Road 2305 west to Highway 317, jog south for 50 yards, then continue west on FM 2305 to the campground.)

Facilities: 58 campsites; sites are generally small, with nominal separation; parking pads are gravel, short to medium-length pull-offs or straight-ins; a touch of additional leveling may be needed in some sites; adequate space for large tents, may be slightly sloped; all sites have ramadas (sun shelters); barbecue grills, plus some fire rings; b-y-o firewood is recommended; water at a number of faucets; restrooms with showers; holding tank disposal station; paved main driveways, gravel sub-drives; gas and groceries are available at several points within 4 miles.

Activities & Attractions: Swimming beach; changehouse; boating; boat launches; fishing.

Natural Features: Located near the tip of a major point of land on the southeast shore of Belton Lake, an impoundment on the Leon River; some sites are shoreside, but most are part-way up a hillside, on a somewhat level section; sites are minimally to lightly shaded by large hardwoods on a surface of natural grass; elevation 600'.

Season, Fees & Phone: Available all year, with limited services October to April; $8.00; 14 day limit; Belton Lake CoE Project Office (817) 939-1829.

Camp Notes: Some of the widest views on the lake are from this park. Even though at times it's busy with day traffic, this camp would be good choice if you need a tent site.

Texas 85

LIVE OAK RIDGE
Belton Lake/Corps of Engineers Park

Location: Central Texas west of Temple.

Access: From Texas State Highway 317 at a point 3 miles south of its junction with State Highway 36 west of Temple and 6 miles north of Belton, turn west onto Farm Road 2305 and proceed 1.7 miles; turn south (left) onto Farm Road 2271 and continue for 0.9 mile; turn west (right) for 0.15 mile to the park entrance station and the campground. (Special Access Note: From Interstate 35, northbound, take Exit 293 in Belton, then Highway 317 northwest to FM 2305, then FM 2305 west to FM 2271; from Interstate 35, southbound, take Exit 301 in Temple, then Farm Road 2305 west to Highway 317, jog south for 50 yards, then continue west on FM 2305 to FM 2271 and continue as above.)

Facilities: 48 campsites with partial hookups; sites are small+ to medium-sized, with nominal to fair separation; parking pads are gravel, medium to long straight-ins; many pads will require at least a bit of additional leveling; slightly sloped spaces for large tents; ramadas (sun shelters) for most sites; barbecue grills and fireplaces; some firewood may be available for gathering in the area, b-y-o suggested; water at sites; restrooms with showers; holding tank disposal station; paved driveways; several gas and groceries stops are within 3 miles.

Activities & Attractions: Boating; boat launch; pier; fishing for bass, catfish, panfish, and some walleye; amphitheater.

Natural Features: Located on a gentle slope on a short bluff above a small bay on the southeast shore of Belton Lake, a flood-control impoundment on the Leon River; sites are lightly to moderately shaded, principally by medium to large oaks (of course); elevation 600'.

Season, Fees & Phone: Open all year; $11.00; 14 day limit; Belton Lake CoE Project Office (817) 939-1829.

Camp Notes: Good views from a number of sites along the edge of the bluff, but sites farther from the lake are a bit larger, with longer pads and a little more shade.

Texas 86

WESTCLIFF
Belton Lake/Corps of Engineers Park

Location: Central Texas west of Temple.

Access: From Texas State Highway 317 at a point 6 miles south of its junction with State Highway 36 west of Temple and 3 miles north of Belton, turn northwest onto Farm Road 439 and travel northwest (past the Belton Lake Project Office), then west, for 4.5 miles; turn northwest (right) onto Sparta Road and proceed 0.65 mile; bear northeast (right) onto Westcliff Road for a final 0.7 mile to the entrance station and the campground. (Special Access Note: From Interstate 35, northbound, take Exit 293 in

Belton, then proceed northwest on Highway 317 to FM 439; from I-35, southbound, take Exit 301 in Temple, then Farm Road 2305 west to Highway 317, then south to pick up FM 439 and continue as above.)

Facilities: 25 campsites, including 20 with partial hookups; sites are small to small+, acceptably level, with nominal to fair separation; parking pads are paved, medium to long pull-throughs or pull-offs; medium to large areas for tents; small ramadas (sun shelters) for most sites; barbecue grills and/or fire rings; a limited amount of firewood may be available for gathering in the area; water at faucets throughout; restrooms with showers; mostly paved driveways; gas and camper supplies are available on FM 439.

Activities & Attractions: Swimming beach; boating; boat launch; fishing for largemouth bass, catfish, panfish, walleye.

Natural Features: Located around a cove on the south shore of Belton Lake, against a backdrop of a high, wooded bluff; standard sites are lightly sheltered/shaded by large hardwoods and junipers/cedars, hookup sites are essentially unsheltered; elevation 600'.

Season, Fees & Phone: Open all year; $9.00 for a standard site, $11.00 for a partial hookup site; 14 day limit; Belton Lake CoE Project Office (817) 939-1829.

Camp Notes: Many campers choose this as the nicest park on the lake. The hookup units are right along the open shore, so bring a bailing bucket for soggy times when the north wind picks up.

Texas 87

DANA PEAK
Stillhouse Hollow Lake/Corps of Engineers Park

Location: Central Texas southwest of Temple.

Access: From U.S. Highway 190 at the exit for Simmons Road and Farm Road 2410 (5 miles west of I-35 exit 293 in Belton, 6 miles east of Harker Heights), proceed to the south side of the divided highway; head west/southwest on Farm Road 2410 for 5.3 miles; turn south (left) onto Comanche Gap Road and continue south, then southeast, for 3 miles; turn south (right) to the campground entrance station and the campground. **Alternate Access:** From U.S. Highway 190 at the west edge of Harker Heights, turn southeast onto Farm Road 2410 and proceed 2.6 miles to Comanche Gap Road and continue as above.

Facilities: 45 campsites with partial hookups; sites are small+ to medium-sized, slightly sloped, with nominal separation; most parking pads are paved, medium to long straight-ins; ample, grassy space for large tents; ramadas (sun shelters) for all sites; barbecue grills, plus a few fire rings; b-y-o firewood; restrooms with showers; holding tank disposal station; paved driveways; nearly complete supplies and services are available in Harker Heights.

Activities & Attractions: Boating; boat launch; swimming beach; fairly good fishing for crappie, white bass, hybrids, largemouth bass, catfish and some walleye; fishing pier.

Natural Features: Located at the 'base' of a long point on the north-west shore of Stillhouse Hollow Lake; large hardwoods provide light-medium shade for most sites; the lake is bordered by wooded hills; elevation 600'.

Season, Fees & Phone: Open all year; $11.00; 14 day limit; phone c/o Belton Lake CoE Project Office (817) 939-1829.

Camp Notes: This is probably the most versatile of the campgrounds on the lake: good campsites, lake views from throughout, a good source of supplies nearby. A boat isn't absolutely needed to have some luck fishing here. Besides using the pier, some anglers find that it's productive to use flotation gear (like so-called "belly boats") to wade out to the offshore drop-offs.

Texas 88

STILLHOUSE
Stillhouse Hollow Lake/Corps of Engineers Park

Location: Central Texas southwest of Temple.

Access: From U.S. Highway 190 at the exit for Simmons Road and Farm Road 2410 (5 miles west of Interstate 35 exit 293 in Belton, 6 miles east of Harker Heights), proceed to the south side of the divided highway; begin heading west on Farm Road 2410, then almost immediately curve south onto Simmons Road and continue southeasterly for 2 miles to the camping area.

Facilities: 13 campsites; most sites are park n' walks, small and closely spaced; adequate, slightly sloped parking for smaller vehicle or combinations in a paved parking lot; ample space for tents on a grassy surface; ramadas (sun shelters) for some sites; barbecue grills; b-y-o firewood; water at central faucets; restrooms with showers; paved driveways; nearly complete supplies and services are available in Harker Heights.

Activities & Attractions: Boat launch; boating; marina; fishing.

Natural Features: Located on a grassy, gentle slope just above the shore at the northeast corner of Stillhouse Hollow Lake; large hardwoods provide light-medium shelter/shade for most sites; the lake is bordered by wooded hills; elevation 600'.

Season, Fees & Phone: Available all year; no fee (subject to change); 14 day limit; phone c/o Belton Belton Lake CoE Project Office (817) 939-1829.

Camp Notes: In reality, this does look more like a picnic area than a campground. The traffic flow is uncontrolled (i.e., no security gate as at the lake's other camping areas). Nonetheless, it's OK to camp here, and maybe it is worth a try. Small tent campers on a budget often use it because the tent-pitching possibilities are quite good and the scenic views out across the lake are fine too. Plus, the place has showers (albeit very basic, one-button jobs). The price is right, as well.

UNION GROVE
Stillhouse Hollow Lake/Corps of Engineers Park

Location: Central Texas southwest of Temple.

Access: From Interstate 35 Exit 286 for Farm Road 1670 on the north edge of Salado, travel northwest on Farm Road 1670 for 1 mile; pick up Farm Road 2484 and continue northwest, then west, for another 5.5 miles; turn northwest (right) on the park access road and proceed northwest, then east, for 0.9 mile; turn north (left) to the campground entrance station; just beyond the entrance, bear right to the hookup area or left to the standard area.

Facilities: 35 campsites, including 14 with partial hookups; sites are small+, with nominal to fair separation; parking pads are gravel, medium to long straight-ins, some are extra wide; a little additional leveling will be required in most sites; generally slightly sloped spaces for medium to large tents; barbecue grills and fire rings; b-y-o firewood is suggested; water at sites and at central faucets; restrooms (showers are planned); holding tank disposal station; paved main driveway, gravel sub-drives; limited supplies and services are available at the freeway interchanges and in Salado.

Activities & Attractions: Boating; boat launch; fishing; fishing pier.

Natural Features: Located on a point on the south-west shore of Stillhouse Hollow Lake, an impoundment on the Lampasas River; sites receive light to light medium shelter/shade from large hardwoods and junipers/cedars; the lake is bordered by low, wooded hills; elevation 600'.

Season, Fees & Phone: Open all year; $9.00; 14 day limit; phone c/o Belton Lake CoE Project Office (817) 939-1829.

Camp Notes: Almost all sites at Union Grove are just a few feet from the water's edge. This relatively small lake is somewhat more formidable than it seems at first glance. Its deep blue waters are well in excess of a hundred feet deep in the segment above the original stream bed.

JIM HOGG
Georgetown Lake/Corps of Engineers Park

Location: Central Texas north of Austin.

Access: From Interstate 35 Exit 262 for Lake Georgetown/Andice (the northernmost of the exits for Georgetown), travel northwest on Ranch Road 2338 for 5.7 miles; turn southwest onto the park access road and proceed southwest, then southeast, for 1.5 miles to the park entrance station; continue ahead for another 0.3 mile, then turn east (left) to the campground entrance station and the campground.

Facilities: 148 campsites with partial hookups in 2 loops; sites are medium to medium+, with fair to good separation; parking pads are paved, medium+ to long straight-ins; a number of pads will require a little additional leveling; large, grassy areas for tents, may be a little sloped; ramadas (sun shelters) for all sites; barbecue grills; b-y-o firewood is suggested; water at sites; restrooms with showers; holding tank disposal station; paved driveways; virtually complete supplies and services are available in Georgetown.

Activities & Attractions: Boating; boat launch; generally good fishing for black bass, white bass, crappie, and catfish.

Natural Features: Located on a slope on top of a point above the north shore of Georgetown Lake on the northeast corner of the Texas Hill Country; sites close to the lake are lightly shaded, those farther back are substantially more sheltered/shaded by junipers/cedars and hardwoods; bordered by forested hills; elevation 800'.

Season, Fees & Phone: Open all year; $11.00; 14 day limit; Georgetown Lake CoE Project Office (512) 863-3016.

Camp Notes: This is the newer of the lake's two campgrounds, (also see Cedar Breaks). Consequently, the sites and the parking pads here were made somewhat larger and longer in order to accommodate contemporary tents and rv's. (Actually, considering the terrain, those at Cedar Breaks probably couldn't have been made much larger and longer anyway.) Both are good camps. Governor Jim Hogg, for whom the park is named, was the first native Texan to be elected governor, and one of the most prominent politicians in the late 1800's. Known as the "People's Governor", Hogg was a newspaperman and lawyer who developed a reputation as a champion of legal, political and social reforms for the public good.

Texas 91

CEDAR BREAKS
Georgetown Lake/Corps of Engineers Park

Location: Central Texas north of Austin.

Access: From Interstate 35 Exit 262 for Lake Georgetown/Andice (the northernmost of the exits for Georgetown), travel northwest on Ranch Road 2338 for 3.3 miles; turn south onto the dam/Cedar Breaks access road and proceed past the project office, southwest across the dam, then swing northwest to the park entrance station for a total of 2 miles; continue ahead for an additional 0.2 mile, then turn west (left) to the campground entrance station and the campground.

Facilities: 63 campsites with partial hookups; sites are small+ to medium-sized, with fair to good separation; parking pads are paved, medium-length straight-ins; most pads will require at least a bit (and some will need quite a bit) of additional leveling; small to medium-sized, mostly sloped, areas for tents; ramadas for all sites; barbecue grills; b-y-o firewood is recommended; water at sites; restrooms with showers; holding tank disposal station; paved driveways; virtually complete supplies and services are available in Georgetown.

Activities & Attractions: Boating; boat launch; generally good fishing for black bass, white bass, crappie, catfish; (quite a few bass tournaments are held here annually); hiking trail.

Natural Features: Located on a moderately steep slope above the south shore of Georgetown Lake on the northeast corner of the Texas Hill Country; large junipers/cedars and oaks provide adequate shelter/shade for most sites; bordered by forested hills; elevation 800'.

Season, Fees & Phone: Open all year; $11.00; 14 day limit; Georgetown Lake CoE Project Office (512) 863-3016.

Camp Notes: This is a really spiffy campground. In fact, Cedar Breaks might be the best-looking Corps campground west of I-35. The 'Cedar Breaks' are cedar-(juniper, whatever) covered, multi-hued cliffs in the area. Georgetown Lake's camps are favorite stops of snowbirds during their fall and spring migratory flights to and from The Valley.

Texas 92

BLACK ROCK
Lower Colorado River Authority Park

Location: Central Texas northwest of Austin.

Access: From Texas State Highway 29 at its junction with State Highway 261 (17 miles east of Llano, 13 miles west of Burnet), proceed northwest on Highway 261 for 2.7 miles; turn east (right) into the campground. (Note: If approaching from Llano, you can save a couple of miles by taking Farm Road 1431 from Highway 29 north to Highway 261, then left for a few yards to the campground.)

Facilities: 22 campsites; sites are medium to large, with nominal to fair separation; parking pads are sandy gravel, mostly medium to long straight-ins; a little additional leveling will probably be required in most sites; ample space for large tents; barbecue grills; b-y-o firewood; water at central faucets; restrooms; holding tank disposal station; paved driveway; nearest reliable sources of supplies and services (adequate) are in Llano and Burnet.

Activities & Attractions: Boating; boat launch; fishing.

Natural Features: Located on a moderate slope above the southwest shore of Lake Buchanan, a major impoundment on the Colorado River, in the Texas Hill Country; sites are lightly shaded by large hardwoods on a surface of sparse grass; hundreds of yards of beaches, adjacent; surrounded by wooded hills; elevation 1000'.

Season, Fees & Phone: Open all year; $4.00 for a site, plus $3.00 daily park entrance fee; 10 day limit semiannually; Lower Colorado River Authority Office, Austin, (512) 473-4083.

Camp Notes: For a hookup site, or a standard site with a little more greenery, you might try the city-county park complex in Llano. From State Highways 16/71 at courthouse square in midtown Llano, drive west on Ranch Road 152 for 2 miles, then north (right) into the park. There are some nice tent sites on a tree-dotted, grassy slope above the Llano River; hookup sites are on an unshaded flat just above the slope. A swimming pool and a golf course, plus limited boating and fishing, provide added interest.

INKS LAKE
Inks Lake State Park

Location: Central Texas northwest of Austin.

Access: From Texas State Highway 29 at a point 9 miles west of Burnet, 2 miles east of Buchanan Dam, 21 miles east of Llano, turn south onto Park Road 4 and proceed 3.4 miles; turn west (right) into the park entrance; turn right to a hookup and standard area, or left to a standard area. **Alternate Access:** From U.S. Highway 281, at a point 5 miles south of Burnet, 9 miles north of Marble Falls, follow Park Road 4 west and north (past Longhorn Cavern State Park) for 12 miles to the Inks Lake State Park entrance.

Facilities: 197 campsites, including 54 with partial hookups; (22 units with screened shelters are also available); sites are small to small+, slightly sloped, with nominal to fairly good separation; parking pads are hard-surfaced, short to medium-length straight-ins; ample space for large tents; barbecue grills, plus fireplaces or fire rings; b-y-o firewood; water at faucets throughout; restrooms with showers; holding tank disposal station; paved driveways; camper supplies in the park; adequate+ supplies in Burnet and Marble Falls.

Activities & Attractions: Swimming beach; 7.5 miles of hiking trails (map available at hq); boating; boat launch; fishing.

Natural Features: Located on slightly sloping and rolling terrain on the east shore of Inks Lake, a small (relatively speaking) impoundment on the Colorado River; large hardwoods and junipers provide light to medium shade/shelter; ringed by the forested hills of the Texas Hill Country; elevation 900'.

Season, Fees & Phone: Open all year; reservations recommended March to December, especially weekends; please see Appendix for additional reservation information and standard Texas state park fees; park office (512) 793-2223.

Camp Notes: What makes this park so much of a favorite of family campers? It's probably because Inks Lake is "right in the middle" of the area's attractions--Longhorn Cavern, river cruises, historical sites and several big lakes.

PACE BEND
Travis County Park

Location: Central Texas northwest of Austin.

Access: From Texas State Highway 71 at a point 16 miles southeast of its junction with U.S. 281 south of Marble Falls, 11 miles northwest of Bee Cave, turn northeast onto Ranch Road 2322 and proceed 5 miles; bear right to the recreation area entrance station; continue ahead for 0.7 mile to a "T", then turn right to the campsites, spread out along the next several miles of park road; the hookup loop is situated 2 miles from the "T".

Facilities: Approximately 400 campsites, including 20 with partial hookups; hookup sites are small+ to medium-sized, reasonably level, with nominal separation; standard sites vary from small to large, level to lumpy, close to distant; parking pads in hookup sites are paved, medium-length straight-ins; other sites have dirt parking; adequate space for medium to large tents; barbecue grills; b-y-o firewood; water at hookup sites and at central faucets; restrooms with showers in hookup loop, vault facilities in other areas; holding tank disposal station; mostly gravel/dirt driveways, paved in hookup loop; several gas and grocery stops are within 4 miles.

Activities & Attractions: Designated swimming areas; hiking trail; boating; boat launch; playground.

Natural Features: Located on a peninsula above the south-east shore of Lake Travis, a sinuous, 65-mile-long, 2-mile-wide impoundment on the Colorado River; sites receive light to medium shade; bordered by the green slopes of the Texas Hill Country; elevation 700'.

Season, Fees & Phone: Open all year; $4.00 for a standard site, $11.00 for a partial hookup site, plus $3.00 daily park entrance fee; limit of 7 days within a 30 day period; Travis County Parks Department, Austin, (512) 320-5780; seasonal park phone (512) 264-1482.

Camp Notes: According to knowledgeable local campers, "unless you like lots of music" with your outdoor experience, "camp here on weekdays, not on the weekends". Lake Travis' shape resembles a happy dragon in a Chinese New Year parade.

Texas 95

MANSFIELD
Travis County Recreation Area

Location: Central Texas northwest of Austin.

Access: From U.S. Highway 183 on the northwest corner of Austin, 1 mile south of Cedar Park, travel southwest, then west, on Ranch Road 620 for 5 miles to the west end of Mansfield Dam; turn north (right) to the park entrance station and then go 0.1 mile to the campsites. **Alternate Access:** From Texas State Highway 71 in the community of Bee Cave (8 miles northwest of Oak Hill, 27 miles southeast of the junction of Highway 71 and U.S. 281, turn northeast onto Ranch Road 620 and proceed north and east for 9 miles to the west end of Mansfield Dam; turn north (left) into the park.

Facilities: Approximately 20 campsites; sites are small+ to medium-sized, generally a bit sloped, with nominal separation; parking surfaces are sandy gravel, any-way-you-can-maneuver-'em; medium to large areas for tents; barbecue grills; b-y-o firewood; water at a central faucet; restrooms; holding tank disposal station; gravel driveways; complete supplies and services are available within 5 miles.

Activities & Attractions: Boating; boat launch; fishing.

Natural Features: Located on a hilltop and on a slope above Lake Travis, a major impoundment on the Colorado River, in the Texas Hill Country; sites receive light to medium shade from large hardwoods and a few junipers; flanked by wooded hills and ridges; elevation 700'.

Season, Fees & Phone: Open all year; $4.00 for a site, plus $3.00 daily park entrance fee; limit 7 days within a 30-day period; Travis County Parks Department, Austin, (512) 320-5780; seasonal park phone (512) 266-2600.

Camp Notes: This roughcut area has been included because: (a) It's economical; (b) It's close to a great city; (c) It's the largest of the local/county campgrounds in the metro area; and (d) It would be a handy place to hang out whenever you come to the capitol to powwow with the minions of government.

Texas 96

MCKINNEY FALLS
McKinney Falls State Park

Location: Central Texas in southeast Austin.

Access: From Interstate 35 at exit 228 for William Cannon Drive, take William Cannon Drive east, southeast, then south for 2.5 miles; turn easterly (left) onto Colton-Bluff Springs Road and proceed 1 mile; turn north, continuing on Colton-Bluff Springs Road, then pick up Scenic Loop (after Colton-Bluff Springs turns east), for a final 1.7 miles to the park road; turn northwest (left) for 0.4 mile to the park entrance; continue ahead for 0.3 mile, then left into the campground. **Alternate Access:** From U.S. Highway 183 at a point 4 miles south of its junction with State Highway 71, turn west onto Scenic Loop and follow it for 2 miles to the park turnoff and continue as above.

Facilities: 84 campsites, including 70 with partial hookups; sites are medium to medium+, most are a little sloped, with fair to very good separation; parking pads are paved, medium-length straight-ins or long pull-throughs; space for large tents (many sites have tent pads); barbecue grills and fire rings; b-y-o firewood; water at faucets throughout; restrooms with showers; holding tank disposal station; paved driveways; complete supplies and services are within 5 miles.

Activities & Attractions: McKinney Falls; visitor center; Onion Creek Hike and Bike Trail; historical sites; playground.

Natural Features: Located on hilly terrain above Onion Creek on the east edge of the Texas Hill Country where the Hills meet the Plains; sites are moderately sheltered/shaded by large hardwoods and a few junipers/cedars; elevation 500'.

Season, Fees & Phone: Open all year; 14 day limit; reservations suggested for spring and fall; please see Appendix for additional reservation information and standard Texas state park fees; park office (512) 243-1643.

Camp Notes: It's worth camping here just to enjoy this wooded island of tranquility within the city. Many campers, however, use this as an economical and yet comfortable base of ops for exploring the town, or when visiting family. Onion Creek winds through the park for nearly two miles and provides tranquil pools, sections of fast water, and two waterfalls that drop over the rims of barren rock shelves.

Texas 97

ENCHANTED ROCK
Enchanted Rock State Natural Area

Location: Central Texas west of Austin.

Access: From U.S. Highway 290 just west of midtown Fredericksburg, head north on Ranch Road 965 for 17 miles; turn west (left) into the park entrance; continue around the entrance station and across the bridge to the campground. **Alternate Access:** From Texas State Highway 16 at a point 16 miles south of Llano, 19 miles north of Fredericksburg, travel southwest on Ranch Road 965 for 8.5 miles, then turn west to the park entrance and continue as above. (Important Note: rv's, buses, trailers, or anything longer than 20 feet aren't allowed to cross the bridge.)

Facilities: 46 standard or park n' walk campsites; (in addition, 60 backpacking spots--about 20 in each of 3 areas--are available within 1.5 to 3 miles of the park entrance); sites are large, with good to excellent separation; large to very generous tent spaces; ramadas (sun/partial wind shelters); barbecue grills and fire rings; firewood is usually for sale, or b-y-o; water at several faucets; restrooms with showers; nearest supplies and services are in Llano (adequate) and Fredericksburg (virtually complete).

Activities & Attractions: Hiking trails; climbing.

Natural Features: Located in the Texas Hill Country on a flat above Sandy Creek or around the base and side of an enormous, dome-shaped, smooth-surfaced, rocky hill; sites near the stream are well-shaded/sheltered by large hardwoods; hillside sites generally are lightly sheltered; elevation 1400'.

Season, Fees & Phone: Open all year; 14 day limit; reservations recommended 60-90 days in advance for spring and fall; please see Appendix for additional reservation information and standard Texas state park fees; park office (915) 247-3903.

Camp Notes: If you're not a tent camper, it would be worth it to become one for awhile in order to enjoy spending some time on an extraordinary geological-botanical island. This is one of the finest tent camps you'll find anywhere. Enchanted Rock itself is made of billion-year-old pink granite, and is one of the oldest exposed chunks of stone in North America. Like similar formations, (especially Independence Rock in Independence Rock State Historic Site in Wyoming) what you see rising 400' above the landscape is only the "tip of the iceberg", so to speak. The "iceberg", however, is an ancient, cooled mass of molten material. A trail to the summit of Enchanted Rock provides relatively easy access to some good Hill Country vistas.

Texas 98

LADY BIRD JOHNSON
Fredericksburg Municipal Park

Location: Central Texas west of Austin.

Access: From Texas State Highway 16 at a point 3 miles southwest of Fredericksburg, 21 miles northeast of Kerrville, turn west onto the park road and proceed 0.5 mile to the park headquarters and the campground.

Facilities: 113 campsites, most with full hookups; sites are small and closely spaced; parking pads are gravel/hard-surfaced, short+ to medium-length straight-ins which may require a little additional leveling; enough space for large tents; no fire facilities; (bbq grills are available in the day use area): water at faucets throughout; restrooms with showers; paved driveways; virtually complete supplies and services are available in Fredericksburg.

Activities & Attractions: Golf course; swimming pool; tennis and volleyball courts; athletic fields; playgrounds; fishing.

Natural Features: Located on a gentle slope covered by rows of large hardwoods on sparse grass, in the Texas Hill Country; most sites are quite favorably shaded/sheltered; views of distant hills to the south from some sites; elevation 1700'.

Season, Fees & Phone: Open all year; $6.00 for tent camping, $10.00 for a partial hookup site, $11.00 for a full hookup site, $3.00 for an extra vehicle; winter rates available; 14 day limit April to October; reservations ($2.00 extra), recommended well in advance, contact the park office (512) 997-4202.

Camp Notes: Don't count on being able to just "drop in" for a site in this popular park. They're booked as much as a year in advance for some weekends, holidays and Fredericksburg's Oktoberfest. Add to that the occasional rv club bookings for 50 to 100 sites at a time. And then, too, there are the Snowbirds, and..... It's easily worth parting with some pocket change for a phone call to assure yourself of having a site. Even though the campground itself provides somewhat close quarters, there's plenty of room in the adjacent, spacious, well-maintained park grounds.

Texas 99

PEDERNALES FALLS
Pedernales Falls State Park

Location: Central Texas west of Austin.

Access: From U.S. Highway 290 at its junction with Farm Road 3232 (9 miles east of the junction of U.S. 290 and U.S 281 north of Blanco, 34 miles west of Austin), travel north on Farm Road 3232 for 6.5 miles to a "T" intersection at the park boundary; jog east (right) then north (left) and proceed 2.5 miles to the park entrance/headquarters; continue ahead for 0.8 mile, then turn southeast (right) for 0.3 mile to the campground. **Alternate Access:** From U.S. 281/290 at a point just southeast of Johnson City, travel east on Farm Road 2766 for 8 miles to the park boundary and continue as above.

Facilities: 69 campsites with partial hookups (a primitive, 21-site backpacking area and a group camp are also available); sites are small+ to medium-sized, with fair to quite good separation; parking pads are hard-surfaced, medium-length straight-ins; about half of the pads may require a little additional leveling; most sites have large tent pads; barbecue grills; b-y-o firewood; water at sites; restrooms with showers; holding tank disposal station; paved driveways; limited supplies and services are available in Johnson City.

Activities & Attractions: Swimming area; (because of safety considerations, water activities are restricted in the falls area and for three miles below the falls, so check the 'regs' before dipping your tootsies into the Pedernales); tubing; hiking trails; nature trail; falls overlook; amphitheater; fishing; day use area; Lyndon B. Johnson National Historic Park is near Johnson City.

Natural Features: Located on gently to moderately sloping terrain above the Pedernales River in the Texas Hill Country; sites receive very light to light-medium shade/shelter from large hardwoods and junipers/cedars; elevation 950'.

Season, Fees & Phone: Open all year; 14 day limit; reservations recommended for weekends March through November; please see Appendix for additional reservation information and standard Texas state park fees; park office (512) 868-7304.

Camp Notes: Just enough vegetation was cleared to place the parking pad, table and tent area in these sites, thus providing a snug but private arrangement. 'Falls' is in the name of the park, but don't come here expecting a Texas Niagara. The maximum drop in one spot is about 25 feet. The park has six miles of river frontage within its boundaries, so wading, swimming and tubing in the stream's shallow, quiet sections are the biggest reasons campers and day-trippers wait in line to enjoy this park. Foot trails lead down to the river from the campground and the day use areas.

Texas 100

BLANCO
Blanco State Recreation Area

Location: Central Texas north of San Antonio.

Access: From U.S. Highway 281 on the south edge of the city of Blanco, 0.1 mile north of the Blanco River bridge, turn south/southwest onto Park Road 23 for a few yards to the park entrance station; just beyond the entrance, turn southwest (right) for 0.1 mile, then southeast (right) across the river for 0.1 mile and up the riverbank to the campground.

Facilities: 31 campsites, including 21 with partial hookups and 10 with full hookups; in addition, 7 units with screened shelters are also available; sites are small+, level, with nominal separation; parking pads are hard surfaced/packed gravel, medium to long straight-ins; adequate space for large tents; small ramadas (sun shelters) for partial hookup sites; barbecue grills and fire rings; b-y-o firewood; water at faucets throughout; restrooms with showers; holding tank disposal station; paved driveways; limited supplies and services are available in Blanco.

Activities & Attractions: Limited boating, canoeing; fishing; group pavilion; playground.

Natural Features: Located on a shelf above the south bank of the Blanco River in the Texas Hill Country; sites receive minimal to medium natural shade/shelter predominantly from large hardwoods on a surface of mown grass; small dams have been constructed on the river which have created a pair of long, thin, lakes; bordered by wooded slopes; elevation 1400'.

Season, Fees & Phone: Open all year; 14 day limit; reservations recommended for summer; please see Appendix for additional reservation information and standard Texas state park fees; park office (512) 833-4333.

Camp Notes: This park may be small (only 100 acres), but nearly all of it is waterfront property. You could probably spend hours poking along on the banks of this waterway.

Texas 101

GUADALUPE RIVER
Guadalupe River State Park

Location: Central Texas north of San Antonio.

Access: From Texas State Highway 46 at a point 7.4 miles east of the junction of Texas 46 and U.S. Highway 281, 13 miles east of Boerne, turn north onto Park Road 31 and proceed north/northeast 3 miles to the park entrance station; continue ahead for 1.5 miles to the *Cedar Sage* area, or 1.7 miles to the *Turkey Sink* area, or 1.9 miles to the *Wagon Ford* area.

Facilities: *Cedar Sage*: 37 standard campsites; *Turkey Sink* 48 campsites with partial hookups; *Wagon Ford*: 20 walk-in campsites; *all areas*: sites are small+ to medium-sized, basically level, with nominal to very good separation; parking pads are hard-surfaced, short to medium-length straight-ins; large tent pads; fire rings and/or barbecue grills; b-y-o firewood; water at faucets throughout; restrooms with showers; holding tank disposal station; paved driveways; gas and groceries in the hamlet of Bergheim, 3 miles west on Highway 46.

Activities & Attractions: River access (in the day use area); canoeing, rafting; playgrounds; fishing.

Natural Features: Located on wooded flats some distance above the Guadalupe River (but no river views) in the Texas Hill Country; most sites receive light to medium shade/shelter from large hardwoods and junipers/cedars; elevation 1000'.

Season, Fees & Phone: Open February to December (closed during January for a public deer hunt); 14 day limit; reservations recommended for summer; please see Appendix for additional reservation information and standard Texas state park fees; park office (512) 438-2656.

Camp Notes: The Guadalupe, accompanied by its great cypress trees, is, of course, the park's most notable feature. What predominates throughout the park, however, is not so much the river but the beautiful Hill Country woodlands which envelope it. What may impress you most about camping here is the atmosphere of serenity and seclusion the park offers. Behind the typical tranquility in the shadows of recent natural history, however, is an event that for a time changed the river which placidly makes its way through the Hill Country. In August 1978, torrential rains deluged the Hill Country with as much as 30 inches of water. The ensuing floodwaters crested 63 feet above the Guadalupe's standard banks. Monstrous rafts of timber and trash plunged headlong through the streambed, uprooting robust cypress trees and ripping the tops off others. In the wake of the flood, debris was left tangled and trapped in the tallest treetops. Now, years later, after an extensive natural and human cleanup, the landscape has substantially recovered from the cataclysm. Guadalupe River is once again the kind of park you'd definitely want to come back to.

Texas 102

HILL COUNTRY
Kerrville State Recreation Area

Location: Central Texas south of Kerrville.

Access: From Texas State Highway 173 at a point just south of the Kerrville city limits and 9 miles north of Camp Verde, turn west into the campground.

Facilities: 83 campsites, including 15 with partial hookups and 20 with full hookups, in 4 loops; (8 units with screened shelters are also available); sites are small to medium-sized, with nominal to fairly good separation; parking pads are packed gravel, short to medium-length straight-ins in the standard sites, or hard-surfaced, long pull-throughs in the hookup loops; some sites may require a little additional leveling; large tent areas; ramadas (sun shelters) for some standard sites; various fire facilities; b-y-o firewood;

water at faucets throughout; restrooms with showers; holding tank disposal station; paved driveways; complete supplies and services are available in Kerrville.

Activities & Attractions: Fishing; lighted fishing pier; boating; boat launch; hiking trails; playground; amphitheater; recreation hall; (the foregoing items are nearby in the park's Riverside area).

Natural Features: Located on a hillside a short distance above the Guadalupe River in the Texas Hill Country; sites receive light to light-medium shelter from large hardwoods and junipers; elevation 1600'.

Season, Fees & Phone: Open all year; 14 day limit; please see Appendix for reservation information and standard Texas state park fees; park office (512) 257-5392.

Camp Notes: Although it lacks the waterfront setting preferred by many campers, the atmosphere up here is more open and breezy than in the park's Riverside unit, described below.

Texas 103

RIVERSIDE
Kerrville State Recreation Area

Location: Central Texas south of Kerrville.

Access: From Texas State Highway 173 at a point just south of the Kerrville city limits and 9 miles north of Camp Verde, turn east onto a park access road and proceed 0.2 down to the camping areas.

Facilities: 40 campsites, including 24 with partial hookups, in 3 areas; (8 units with screened shelters are also available); sites are small+ to medium-sized, basically level, with nominal to fair separation; parking pads are packed gravel, medium-length straight-ins in the standard sites, or hard-surfaced, long pull-throughs in the hookup sites; assorted fire appliances; b-y-o firewood; water at faucets throughout; restrooms with showers; holding tank disposal station; paved driveways; complete supplies and services are available in Kerrville.

Activities & Attractions: Fishing for crappie, catfish and bass; lighted fishing pier; boating; boat launch; hiking trail along the riverbank; playground; amphitheater.

Natural Features: Located along the Guadalupe River in the Texas Hill Country; sites receive light to medium shelter mostly from large hardwoods; the impounded river is known as Flat Rock Lake in this segment; elevation 1600'.

Season, Fees & Phone: Open all year; 14 day limit; please see Appendix for reservation information and standard Texas state park fees; park office (512) 257-5392.

Camp Notes: For a change of pace: If you're a tent camper whose patience and canvas are both wearing thin, try camping in the simple screened shelters in the string of "Cliff Dwellings" along the edge of the river. The Guadalupe has been slightly impounded in several spots near here to form what amounts to a chain of long, slender lakes with a slow current. The river and its banks are nicely maintained through town and in the recreation area.

Texas 104

LOST MAPLES
Lost Maples State Natural Area

Location: Central Texas southwest of Kerrville.

Access: From the junction of Texas State Highway 39 & Ranch Road 187 southwest of Kerrville, travel south on Ranch Road 187 for 15 miles (to a point 4 miles north of Vanderpool); turn west/northwest onto a paved access road and proceed 0.15 mile to the park entrance station/headquarters; continue ahead for 0.3 mile, then turn north (right) into the campground. **Alternate Access:** From the junction of U.S. Highway 83 & Ranch Road 337 in Leakey, head east on RR 337 for 17 miles to the hamlet of Vanderpool; turn north (left) onto Ranch Road 187 and proceed for miles; turn west (left) onto the park access road and continue as above.

Facilities: 30 campsites, most with partial hookups; (40 walk-in primitive sites are also available); sites are small and closely spaced; parking pads are paved/packed gravel, short to medium-length straight-ins which may require a touch of additional leveling; medium to large, grassy tent areas; ramadas (sun/partial wind shelters) for some sites; barbecue grills and fire rings; b-y-o firewood; water at sites; restrooms with showers; paved driveway; gas and camper supplies near Vanderpool; nearest sources of limited supplies and services are Utopia (14 miles south) or Leakey (21 miles west).

Activities & Attractions: Hiking trails; nature trail; nature study.

Natural Features: Located on a shelf near the base of a hill in a narrow canyon along the Sabinal River in the Texas Hill Country; campground vegetation consists of short grass dotted with a few small hardwoods; bordered by high, well-wooded hills; elevation 1600'.

Season, Fees & Phone: Open all year; 14 day limit; please see Appendix for reservation information and standard Texas state park fees; park office (512) 966-3413.

Camp Notes: Although summer is a fine time to visit Lost Maples, it's mid-autumn (October-November) when the park really shows its true colors (no pun intended). It's a visual feast throughout the several weeks of intense coloration. (Suggestion: call ahead to make sure there'll be room for you during this often-busy period.) Another state natural area in this region, Hill Country State Natural Area southwest of Bandera and a few miles due east of the tiny town of Tapley, offers limited camping opportunities. It's accessible from Farm Road 1077, which isn't depicted on many maps. FM 1077 links Texas State Highway 173 with FM 462; it runs parallel to FM 470. Hill Country SNA has a few primitive sites in a roadside camp, and hike-in camping within a pair of designated backcountry areas, one to three miles from the trailhead near the park headquarters. Unlike most state park areas throughout the West, there are no ready-made campsites. You pick the spot, and then make sure all traces of your stay are obliterated when you leave. Drinking water and vaults are available at the trailhead. Campfires aren't permitted, so pack a reliable camp stove. A call to the park headquarters (512-796-4413) should provide you with any additional information which you may require to start you on a rustic and rewarding experience.

Texas 105

GARNER: CENTRAL
Garner State Park

Location: South-Central Texas west of San Antonio.

Access: From U.S. Highway 83 at a point 7 miles north of Concan, 9 miles south of Leakey, turn east/southeast onto Park Road 29 and proceed 0.3 mile to the park entrance station; the *Shady Meadows* and *River Crossing* areas, plus "Late Arrivals" are near the entrance.

Facilities: *Shady Meadows* 29 campsites with partial hookups; *River Crossing*, 18 campsites with partial hookups, some with screened shelters; (in addition, 40 angled camp slots are available in a paved parking lot with restrooms and showers in the "Late Arrivals" zone); *both areas*: sites are small+ to medium-sized, generally level, with nominal to fair separation; parking pads are paved or packed gravel, mostly medium-length straight-ins; adequate space for medium to large tents; barbecue grills and fire rings; b-y-o firewood; water at faucets throughout; restrooms with showers; holding tank disposal station nearby; paved driveways; gas and groceries are available along the highway.

Activities & Attractions: Swimming; trails; mini-golf; playground.

Natural Features: Located in the Texas Hill Country in a valley along or near the bank of the Frio River (River Crossing), or on a flat at the base of a hill several hundred yards from the river (Shady Meadows); lots of grass, and light-medium to medium shade from large hardwoods and some junipers; high, wooded hills surround the park; elevation 1300'.

Season, Fees & Phone: Open all year; 14 day limit; reservations recommended for summer weekends; please see Appendix for additional reservation information and standard Texas state park fees; park office (512) 232-6132.

Camp Notes: This is one of Texas' most scenic parks. True, the loops closest to the river's edge are busy (even jammed) much of the summer. Still lots of good camping, though.

Texas 106

GARNER: NORTH
Garner State Park

Location: South-Central Texas west of San Antonio.

Access: From U.S. Highway 83 at a point 7 miles north of Concan, 9 miles south of Leakey, turn east/southeast onto Park Road 29 and proceed 0.3 mile to the park entrance station; turn left (northeast) and proceed 0.8 mile to the *Rio Frio*, *Live Oak* and *Persimmon Hill* areas.

Facilities: *Live Oak*: 65 campsites with partial hookups in a single large loop; *Persimmon Hill*: 35 standard campsites in a single large loop; *Rio Frio*: 114 standard campsites in 2 large concentric loops; *all areas*: sites are small to medium-sized, fairly level, with minimal (in Rio Frio) to fair separation; parking pads are paved or packed gravel, short+ to medium-length straight-ins; adequate space for medium to large tents on a grass or earth surface; barbecue grills and fire rings; b-y-o firewood; water at faucets throughout; restrooms with showers; holding tank disposal station near the park entrance; paved driveways; gas and groceries are available along the highway.

Activities & Attractions: Swimming; trails; mini-golf; playground.

Natural Features: Located in the Texas Hill Country in a valley along or very near the bank of the Frio River; sites receive very light to medium shade, mostly from large hardwoods; wooded hills surround the park; elevation 1300'.

Season, Fees & Phone: Open all year; 14 day limit; reservations recommended for summer weekends; please see Appendix for additional reservation information and standard Texas state park fees; park office (512) 232-6132.

Camp Notes: For breathing room, try the back side of Rio Frio or Live Oak.

Texas 107

GARNER: SOUTH
Garner State Park

Location: South-Central Texas west of San Antonio.

Access: From U.S. Highway 83 at a point 7 miles north of Concan, 9 miles south of Leakey, turn east/southeast onto Park Road 29 and proceed 0.3 mile to the park entrance station; continue ahead (southeast) for 0.6 mile, over the hill and down to the *Oakmont* and *Pecan Grove* areas.

Facilities: *Oakmont*: 50 campsites with partial hookups in a complex loop; *Pecan Grove*: 104 standard campsites, including some with screened shelters in a complex loop; *both areas*: sites are small to small+, reasonably level, with minimal to nominal separation; parking pads are paved or packed gravel, short to medium-length straight-ins; adequate space for medium to large tents; barbecue grills and fire rings; b-y-o firewood; water at faucets throughout; restrooms with showers; holding tank disposal station near the park entrance; paved driveways; gas and groceries are available along the highway.

Activities & Attractions: Swimming; trails; mini-golf; playground.

Natural Features: Located in the Texas Hill Country in a valley along the bank of the Frio River; lots of grass, and very light to medium shade from large hardwoods; high, wooded hills surround the park; elevation 1300'.

Season, Fees & Phone: Open all year; 14 day limit; reservations recommended for summer weekends; please see Appendix for additional reservation information and standard Texas state park fees; park office (512) 232-6132.

Camp Notes: Best sites in the park? Oakmont and Pecan Grove, both by the man-made swimmin' hole, are the most popular.

Texas 108

POTTERS CREEK
Canyon Lake/Corps of Engineers Park

Location: Central Texas north of San Antonio.

Access: From Farm Road 306 at a point 11 miles northwest of Sattler, 0.1 mile east of the junction of Farm Roads 306 and 484, 9 miles east of U.S. Highway 281 at Spring Branch, turn south/southwest onto a paved access road and proceed 2.5 miles to the entrance station and the campground; campsites are located both east and west of the entrance.

Facilities: Approximately 70 campsites, including 18 with partial hookups, in 2 sections; sites are medium-sized, with fair to fairly good separation; parking spaces are gravel or grass, medium-length straight-ins, some of which may require additional leveling; ample space for large tents; barbecue grills or fireplaces; b-y-o firewood is recommended; water at some sites and at central faucets; vault facilities; holding tank disposal station; paved or gravel driveways; gas and groceries and other services are available at several points along Farm Road 306.

Activities & Attractions: Fishing; boating; boat launch.

Natural Features: Located on a gentle to moderate slope on the north shore of Canyon Lake in the Texas Hill Country; sites receive very light to medium shade/shelter from large hardwoods; the lake is encircled by high, tree-covered hills; elevation 900'.

Season, Fees & Phone: Available all year, with reduced services October to April; $7.00 for a standard site. $9.00 for a partial hookup site; 14 day limit; Canyon Lake CoE Project Office (512) 964-3341.

Camp Notes: Overall, this is one of the more open (less tree-sheltered) campgrounds on Canyon Lake. (The sites farther from the shore generally offer a little more shelter.) The plus side is that there isn't a lot of greenery to restrict your view of the lake and its residentialized shoreline.

Texas 109

CANYON
Canyon Lake/Corps of Engineers Park

Location: Central Texas north of San Antonio.

Access: From Farm Road 306 at a point 7.5 miles north of Sattler, 3.5 miles southeast of the junction of Farm Roads 306 and 484, 12 miles east of U.S. Highway 281 at Spring Branch, turn southwest onto a paved access road and proceed 1.7 miles to the entrance station and the campground.

Facilities: 210 campsites in 6 areas; sites vary from small to medium in size, with nominal to very good separation; parking pads are gravel, mostly short to medium-length pull-offs/straight-ins; additional leveling will be required in many sites; medium to large tent spaces, though they may be sloped; ramadas (sun shelters) for many sites; barbecue grills or fireplaces; b-y-o firewood is suggested; water at several faucets; vault facilities; holding tank disposal station; paved driveways; gas and groceries and other services are available at several points along Farm Road 306.

Activities & Attractions: Fishing; boating; boat launch; marina; swimming beach.

Natural Features: Located on a hilly peninsula on the northeast side of Canyon Lake, a flood-control impoundment on the Guadalupe River; vegetation consists of large sections of grass interspersed with stands of hardwoods and junipers; natural shelter/shade varies from none to light-medium; surrounded by the high, tree-covered hills of the Texas Hill Country; el. 900'.

Season, Fees & Phone: Available all year, with reduced services October to April; $7.00; 14 day limit; Canyon Lake CoE Project Office (512) 964-3341.

Camp Notes: There are some good lakefront sites here. But probably the best are in area 5, way up on top of a hill near the end of the peninsula. There are some commanding views of the lake (and of much of the Hill Country) from that vantage point.

Texas 110

JACOBS CREEK
Canyon Lake/Corps of Engineers Park

Location: Central Texas north of San Antonio.

Access: From Farm Road 306 at a point 7.5 miles north of Sattler, 3.5 miles southeast of the junction of Farm Roads 306 and 484, 12 miles east of U.S. Highway 281 at Spring Branch, turn southwest onto a paved access road; Area 1 is near the turnoff; Areas 2 and 3 are 0.8 mile ahead.

Facilities: Approximately 40 campsites; sites are small+ to medium-sized, with nominal to fairly good separation; parking surfaces are gravel/earth, short pull-offs; additional leveling will probably be needed in some sites; space for small to medium-sized tents; ramadas (sun shelters) for some sites; fireplaces; b-y-o firewood is recommended; water at several faucets; restrooms and vault facilities; paved driveways; gas and groceries and other services are available at several points along Farm Road 306.

Activities & Attractions: Fishing; boating; boat launch; sailboat/windsurfer launch area.

Natural Features: Located on a hilly point on the northeast side of Canyon Lake, a flood-control reservoir on the Guadalupe River, in the Texas Hill Country; sites receive light to medium shelter/shade from hardwoods and junipers; surrounded by tree-covered hills; elevation 900'.

Season, Fees & Phone: Available all year, with reduced services October to April; no fee (subject to change); 14 day limit; Canyon Lake CoE Project Office (512) 964-3341.

Camp Notes: Unfortunately, what are probably the best sites in the place are designated as picnic sites. (Score one for the day-trippers.) Nonetheless, there are some good lakeview sites along the edge of a hill, as well as a few tucked away back in the trees in Area 2. A mile-and-a-half southeast of Jacobs Creek is North Park. It's meant more for day use, but there are some nice, private camp/picnic sites which are available without charge. (The turnoff to North Park is about 50 yards south of the turnoff to Jacobs Creek.)

COMAL
Canyon Lake/Corps of Engineers Park

Location: Central Texas north of San Antonio.

Access: From Texas State Highway 46 at its junction with Farm Road 3159 (4.5 miles east of the junction of Texas 46 with U.S. Highway 281, 23 miles northwest of New Braunfels), proceed northeast on Farm Road 3159 for 6 miles to Startzville (a small community 6 miles west of Sattler); turn northwest (left) onto Farm Road 2673 and proceed 0.5 mile to the northwest corner of Startzville; turn north/northeast (right) onto Canyon Park Drive and proceed 2.3 miles; (note that Canyon Park Drive winds through a residential neighborhood north for 1.3 miles, then east for several blocks, then curves north again); turn east (right) and go a final 0.5 mile to the campground.

Facilities: Approximately 50 campsites; sites are medium to medium+, with fair to good separation; most parking surfaces are gravel/earth, straight-ins/pull-offs, and about half may require additional leveling; adequate space for large tents; ramadas (sun shelters) for some sites; fireplaces or barbecue grills; water at central faucets; vault facilities; holding tank disposal station; paved driveways; limited supplies and services are available in Startzville.

Activities & Attractions: Swimming beach; fishing; boat launch.

Natural Features: Located on a point on the south-west shore of Canyon Lake in the Texas Hill Country; some sites are along the unsheltered lakeshore, others are several yards above the water's edge, well-sheltered by large hardwoods; elevation 900'.

Season, Fees & Phone: Available all year, with reduced services and fees October to April; $7.00; 14 day limit; Canyon Lake CoE Project Office (512) 964-3341.

Camp Notes: Comal might rate at or near the top of the list of Canyon Lake's camps. (The resident roadrunner thinks very highly of the place.) However, on Saturdays and Sundays you'll usually find more tranquility elsewhere. Incidentally, Startzville isn't shown on most maps, but it is certainly more than just a wide spot on the road.)

CRANES MILL
Canyon Lake/Corps of Engineers Park

Location: Central Texas north of San Antonio.

Access: From Texas State Highway 46 at its junction with Farm Road 3159 (4.5 miles east of the junction of Texas 46 with U.S. Highway 281, 23 miles northwest of New Braunfels), proceed northeast on Farm Road 3159 for 6 miles to Startzville (a small community 6 miles west of Sattler); turn northwest (left) onto Farm Road 2673 and travel 4.3 miles to the campground. (Note: if you're approaching from New Braunfels, it might be a bit quicker to take Farm Road 2722 from Texas 46 to Startzville.)

Facilities: Approximately 60 campsites; sites are medium to medium+, generally level or nearly so, with nominal to fairly good separation; parking surfaces are gravel/earth/grass, pull-offs or straight-ins; ample space for large tents; ramadas (sun shelters) for some sites; fireplaces; b-y-o firewood is suggested; water at several faucets; vault facilities; holding tank disposal station; paved main driveway, gravel/earth sub-drives; limited supplies and services are available in Startzville.

Activities & Attractions: Fishing; boating; boat launch; marina.

Natural Features: Located along the top and sides of a point at the west end of Canyon Lake in the Texas Hill Country; sites are lightly shaded/sheltered by large hardwoods; lake views from most sites; the lake is encircled by tree-covered hills; elevation 900'.

Season, Fees & Phone: Available all year, with reduced services October to April; $7.00; 14 day limit; Canyon Lake CoE Project Office (512) 964-3341.

Camp Notes: The trees in this camp appear to have been affected more than those in the lake's other recreation areas by flooding. (There are plans to perform some re-planting.) Crane's Mill and the other Canyon Lake campgrounds aren't in the same league as most other CoE lake parks; the facilities are, shall we say, somewhat more "basic" than those you'll find in the spiffier Corps camps.

FRIENDSHIP
Granger Lake/Corps of Engineers Park

Location: Central Texas northeast of Austin.

Access: From Texas State Highway 95 in midtown Granger, head easterly on Farm Road 971 for 6.6 miles; turn south (right) onto the park access road and continue for 0.7 mile; turn west (right) to the campground entrance station and the campground. **Alternate Access:** From State Highway 95 at a point 0.8 mile south of its junction with State Highway 29, 6 miles north of the city of Taylor, turn east/northeast onto Farm Road 1331 and travel 6.2 miles; turn north (left) onto the dam access road and drive 3.2 miles to the north end of the dam and Farm Road 971; turn northwest (left) onto Farm Road 971 for 1.3 miles to the park access road and continue as above.

Facilities: 50 campsites with partial hookups; sites are medium-sized, with nominal separation; parking pads are paved, medium-length straight-ins; a little additional leveling will be required in many sites; ample space for tents on a grassy slope; large ramadas (sun shelters) for all sites; barbecue grills and fire rings; b-y-o firewood; water at faucets throughout; restrooms with showers; holding tank disposal station; paved driveways; gas and groceries are available in Granger.

Activities & Attractions: Nice, sand and grass swimming beach; boating; boat launch; fishing.

Natural Features: Located on a moderate slope above the northeast corner of Granger Lake; campground vegetation consists of expanses of mown grass dotted with small, planted hardwoods; the camp area is bordered by larger hardwoods, near-level prairie and cultivated land; elevation 500'.

Season, Fees & Phone: April to October; $11.00; 14 day limit; Granger Lake CoE Project Office (512) 859-2668.

Camp Notes: If you're strapped for a campsite on a summer holiday weekend because of a last-minute "go" decision, odds are that you'll find one here, or at one of Granger Lake's other top notch campgrounds. Wide-open views.

WILLIS CREEK
Granger Lake/Corps of Engineers Park

Location: Central Texas northeast of Austin.

Access: From Texas State Highway 95 at a point 2.4 miles north of its junction with State Highway 29, 8 miles north of Taylor, 2.7 miles south of Granger, turn northeast onto Williamson County Road 346 (paved) and proceed 3.8 miles to the park entrance; the campground is on the north (left) just past the gate. (Note: watch for the sharp, right-then-left jog in the county road at the "T" intersection, 2.2 miles from the highway.)

Facilities: 12 campsites; sites are medium-sized, level, with nominal separation; parking pads are paved, medium-length straight-ins; excellent, grassy tent areas; ramadas (sun shelters) for all sites; barbecue grills and fire rings; b-y-o firewood; water at a central faucet; vault facilities; paved driveways; gas and groceries in Granger; nearly complete supplies and services are available in Taylor.

Activities & Attractions: Fishing (said to be good in this area); boating; boat launch; pier; day use area.

Natural Features: Located on a flat along the shore of Willis Creek inlet, one of two major arms of Granger Lake, on the lake's northwest corner; campground vegetation consists of mown grass flecked with a few trees; the lake is encircled by near-level agricultural land and prairie; elevation 500'.

Season, Fees & Phone: Open all year; no fee (subject to change); 14 day limit; Granger Lake CoE Project Office (512) 859-2668.

Camp Notes: Remember the story of the City Mouse and the Country Mouse? Well, if the lake's other campground's are the city critters, this one is the country cousin. The other camps, which are very nice indeed, may have more in the way of creature comforts; but this small spot has an uncluttered, unsophisticated, clean-cut, country character which you might enjoy. Considering the current cost of camping at Willis Creek, it's a great buy.

WILSON H. FOX
Granger Lake/Corps of Engineers Park

Location: Central Texas northeast of Austin.

Access: From Texas State Highway 95 at a point 0.8 mile south of its junction with State Highway 29, 6 miles north of the city of Taylor, turn east/northeast onto Farm Road 1331 and proceed 6 miles; turn north (left) onto the dam access road for 0.25 mile, then turn west (left) onto the park access road and continue for 0.6 mile to the park entrance station; just past the entrance, hang two sharp right turns into the campground.

Facilities: 58 campsites with partial hookups; sites are medium-sized, level, with nominal separation; parking pads are paved, medium-length straight-ins; plenty of space for tents on a grassy surface; large ramadas (sun shelters) for all sites; barbecue grills and fire rings; b-y-o firewood; water at faucets throughout; restrooms with showers; holding tank disposal station; paved driveways; gas and groceries on Highway 95; nearly complete supplies and services are available in Taylor.

Activities & Attractions: Swimming beach; boating; boat launch; fishing; fishing pier.

Natural Features: Located on a blufftop at the southeast corner of Granger Lake, a flood control impoundment on the San Gabriel River; campground vegetation consists of expanses of mown grass dotted with small, planted hardwoods; the camp area is ringed by larger hardwoods; bordered by near-level prairie and cropland; elevation 500'.

Season, Fees & Phone: Open all year; $11.00; 14 day limit; Granger Lake CoE Project Office (512) 859-2668.

Camp Notes: This super campground is open all year (usually) and is never full. OK, so the scenic views may not be as majestic as those in the (more crowded) camps in the Hill Country, a few miles west. But the facilities and immediate surroundings here take second place to few other CoE camps in these parts.

TAYLOR
Granger Lake/Corps of Engineers Park

Location: Central Texas northeast of Austin.

Access: From Texas State Highway 95 at a point 0.8 mile south of its junction with State Highway 29, 6 miles north of the city of Taylor, turn east/northeast onto Farm Road 1331 and proceed 4.8 miles; turn northwest (left) for 0.1 mile to the park entrance station; 0.1 mile beyond the entrance turn southwest (left) for 0.3 mile to the campground.

Facilities: 48 campsites with partial hookups in 2 loops; sites are medium-sized, with nominal separation; parking pads are paved, medium-length straight-ins; most pads will probably require a little additional leveling; ample space for large tents, may be sloped; good-sized ramadas (sun shelters) for all sites; barbecue grills and fire rings; b-y-o firewood; water at faucets throughout; restrooms with showers; holding tank disposal station; paved driveways; gas and groceries on Highway 95; nearly complete supplies and services are available in Taylor.

Activities & Attractions: Boating; boat launch; fishing; hiking trail; trailside museum; day use area.

Natural Features: Located on a blufftop and on a slope near the south-west end of Granger Lake; the bluff overlooks the San Gabriel River inlet, one of two major arms of the lake; campground vegetation consists of mown grass dotted with hardwoods; surrounded by near-level farmland and prairie; elevation 500'.

Season, Fees & Phone: April to October; $11.00; 14 day limit; Granger Lake CoE Project Office (512) 859-2668.

Camp Notes: Like the other full-service campgrounds on Granger Lake, the location of this one was designed right from the start with campers in mind, and perhaps even a little more than the others. Although there's a common entrance point, the camp loops are several hundred yards removed from day-tripper traffic.

LAKE BASTROP: NORTH SHORE
Lower Colorado River Authority Park

Location: Central Texas southeast of Austin.

Access: From Texas State Highway 95 at a point 4 miles north of Bastrop, 13 miles south of Elgin, turn east onto Farm Road 1441 and proceed 2.6 miles; turn south onto a paved road and continue for 0.3 miles to the recreation area entrance and the campground. **Alternate Access:** From State Highway 21 at a point 6 miles northeast of Bastrop, turn west onto Farm Road 1441 and proceed 4 miles to the recreation area turnoff and continue as above.

Facilities: 66 campsites, about two-thirds with partial hookups; sites are small, with nominal separation; parking surfaces are grass, medium to long straight-ins which may require a little additional leveling; adequate space for large tents; barbecue grills; b-y-o firewood is suggested; water at faucets throughout; restrooms with showers; disposal station; paved driveways; adequate+ supplies and services in Bastrop.

Activities & Attractions: Fishing (bass, crappie, catfish, perch); boating; boat launch.

Natural Features: Located on a gentle slope on the north shore of 900-acre Lake Bastrop; large hardwoods and a few pines, on a surface of sparse grass, provide medium shade for most sites; el. 400'.

Season, Fees & Phone: May to September; $7.00 for a standard/tent site, $10.00 for a partial hookup site, plus $5.00 park entrance fee; park office (512) 321-3307.

Camp Notes: North Shore and its counterpart at the opposite end of the lake (see South Shore) are primarily fishing camps. Fishing is cyclical here, being particularly dependant upon weed conditions. Generally speaking, though, crappie fishing is excellent in spring; and the perch, reportedly, can be harvested in quantity on just about anything--bare hooks, small hunks of plastic tubing, swatches of shop rags, fallen leaves from trees.....

LAKE BASTROP: SOUTH SHORE
Lower Colorado River Authority Park

Location: Central Texas southeast of Austin.

Access: From Texas State Highway 21 at a point 2 miles northeast of Bastrop, 11 miles southwest of the junction of Highway 21 with U.S. 290 near Paige, turn north/northwest onto Bastrop County Road 352 (paved) and proceed 1.7 miles to the park office and the campground. (This segment of Texas 21 is a 4-lane-divided road; a crossover is provided for northeastbound traffic.)

Facilities: 82 campsites, including 49 with partial hookups; (for hookups, b-y-o long extension cord); sites are small to small+, with nominal separation; parking and tent surfaces are grass/earth, pitch-'em-'n-park-'em however you can; barbecue grills; b-y-o firewood is suggested; water at faucets throughout; restrooms with showers; holding tank disposal station; paved main driveway; adequate+ supplies and services are available in Bastrop.

Activities & Attractions: Fishing; fishing pier; boating; boat launch; (extra space for boat trailers in adjacent parking lots); hiking trail; designated swimming area.

Natural Features: Located on the slightly sloping south shore of 900-acre Lake Bastrop; sites are generally well shaded/sheltered by large hardwoods and junipers/cedars; bordered by dense woodland; about two-thirds of the sites have lake views; elevation 400'.

Season, Fees & Phone: Open all year; $7.00 for a standard/tent site, $10.00 for a partial hookup site, plus $5.00 park entrance fee; park office (512) 321-3307.

Camp Notes: This is a surprisingly popular spot, particularly with tent campers. Even though the campsites are rather closely spaced, no one seems to mind it. The lake's waters provide the coolant for the local electrical generating plant, so fishing is best in winter and early spring. It's entirely possible to fish from the pier here, but any really serious angling requires a boat.

BASTROP
Bastrop State Park

Location: Central Texas southeast of Austin.

Access: From Texas State Highway 21 at its intersection with Loop 150 (1 mile east of Bastrop), turn east onto Park Road 1A and proceed 0.4 mile to the entrance station; continue ahead for 0.25 mile to a "Y" intersection; jog left for 0.05 mile, then right for 0.2 mile (through the parking lot and past the pool) to the standard and full hookup area; or turn right at the "Y" and proceed 1 mile to the partial hookup and walk-in area.

Facilities: 72 campsites, including 7 walk-ins, 29 with partial hookups and 25 with full hookups, in 3 principal areas; (primitive, trailside camping is also available); sites are small+ to medium-sized, passably level, with nominal separation; parking pads are paved, short to medium-length straight-ins or long pull-throughs; ample space for large tents; barbecue grills; b-y-o firewood; water at faucets throughout; restrooms with showers; holding tank disposal station; paved driveways; adequate+ supplies and services are available in Bastrop.

Activities & Attractions: Lost Pines Hiking Trail (8.5-mile loop); swimming pools (1 regular pool, 2 duckie pools); 9-hole goof course; limited fishing on 10 Acre Lake.

Natural Features: Located on gently rolling, pine-needle-cushioned terrain in the hilly Lost Pines area; sites are moderately sheltered/shaded by lofty loblolly pines, plus large hardwoods and junipers/cedars; elevation 400'.

Season, Fees & Phone: Open all year; 14 day limit; reservations recommended March to December; please see Appendix for additional reservation information and standard Texas state park fees; park office (512) 321-2101.

Camp Notes: Actually, the main attractions here are the Lost Pines themselves. The errant conifers, which are normally associated with the great stands of timber in East Texas a hundred or more miles from here, 'lost their way' and found themselves in needle-needy Central Texas.

Texas 120

BUESCHER
Buescher State Park

Location: Central Texas southeast of Austin.

Access: From Texas State Highway 71 north of Smithville, (12 miles southeast of Bastrop, 21 miles northwest of LaGrange), turn east/northeast onto Farm Road 153 and proceed 0.5 mile; turn north (left) to the park entrance station; just past the entrance, bear right onto Park Road 1E and continue for 0.8 mile to the trailer (partial hookups) area; or bear left onto Park Road 1C for 0.5 mile to the multi-use (partial hookup) loop; or bear either left or right and continue for 1 mile to the standard/tent area at the opposite end of the park.

Facilities: 65 campsites, including 40 with partial hookups; (4 units with screened shelters are also available); sites are small+, more or less level, with nominal to fairly good separation; parking pads are mostly hard-surfaced, short to medium-length straight-ins; medium to large tent spots; (tent pads in standard area); barbecue grills and fire rings; b-y-o firewood; water at hookup sites and at central faucets; restrooms with showers; disposal station; paved driveways; adequate supplies and services in Smithville.

Activities & Attractions: Hiking Trail (7.7-mile loop); fishing (crappie, catfish, bass, stocked rainbows); limited boating.

Natural Features: Located on a large, tree-dotted flat (standard/tent area) or on slightly rolling, well-wooded terrain (other areas), around 25-acre Park Lake in the Lost Pines; sites receive medium to moderately dense shelter from a blend of hardwoods, pines and junipers/cedars; bordered by hilly, dense woodland; elevation 300'.

Season, Fees & Phone: Open all year; 14 day limit; reservations recommended April to October; please see Appendix for additional reservation information and standard Texas state park fees; park office (512) 237-2241.

Camp Notes: First choice would probably be the "multi-use" sites. For a lake view, try the tent area.

Texas 121

LOCKHART
Lockhart State Recreation Area

Location: South-Central Texas northeast of San Antonio.

Access: From U.S. Highway 183 just south of midtown Lockhart, turn southwest onto Farm Road 20 and proceed 2 miles; turn south (left) for 0.15 mile to the park entrance; continue ahead, then right and across the bridge for 0.3 mile, then a final left, into the campground.

Facilities: 20 campsites, including 10 with partial hookups and 10 with full hookups, in 2 sections; (a primitive camping area is also available); sites are small to small+, with minimal to nominal separation; parking pads are hard-surfaced, medium pull-offs or straight-ins in the partial hookups, medium to long straight-ins in the full hookups; a little additional leveling may be required in some sites; space for medium to large tents; ramadas (sun shelters) for full hookup sites; barbecue grills and fire rings; b-y-o firewood; water at sites; restrooms with showers; paved driveways; virtually complete supplies and services are available in Lockhart.

Activities & Attractions: Golf course (9 holes, 3000 yards, par 35); swimming pools (a big pool and a duckie pool); basketball court; playground; recreational hall; stream fishing for panfish, cats and a few bass.

Natural Features: Located on a grassy, gentle slope (full hookups) and a small, streamside flat (partials) along Plum Creek; full hookups lack natural shade, partial hookups are moderately shaded by hardwoods; elevation 500'.

Season, Fees & Phone: Open all year; 14 day limit; reservations recommended for summer; please see Appendix for additional reservation information and standard Texas state park fees; park office (512) 398-3479.

Camp Notes: This park and its links were built by the CCC (which may have turfed more golf courses than most of us realize). No fishing allowed along the fairways, though.

PALMETTO
Palmetto State Park

Location: South-Central Texas east of San Antonio.

Access: From U.S. Highway 183 at a point 2.5 miles southeast of Interstate 10 exit 632 for Luling/Lockhart, 12 miles northwest of Gonzales, turn southwest onto Park Road 11 and proceed 2 miles to the park headquarters; continue ahead for a quarter-mile, then southeast (left) to the standard sites; or continue ahead, across the bridge, then east (left) for 1.3 miles to the hookup loop.

Facilities: 37 campsites, including 19 with partial hookups; sites are small+ to medium+, reasonably level, with nominal to fairly good separation; parking pads are packed gravel, short straight-ins in the standard sites or hard-surfaced, medium-length straight-ins in the hookup sites; large tent spots; barbecue grills and/or fire rings; b-y-o firewood; water at faucets throughout; restrooms with showers; holding tank disposal station; paved driveways; gas and camper supplies are available in the hamlet of Ottine, just outside the park.

Activities & Attractions: Palmetto and River Nature Trails; swimming and floating on the lake; limited fishing.

Natural Features: Located on a bench on bottomland a few feet above the San Marcos River; a slender, shallow (6-foot average depth) backwater pond (Oxbow Lake) parallels the river; sites are quite well-sheltered/shaded by large hardwoods; encircled by dense forest; elevation 350'.

Season, Fees & Phone: Open all year; 14-day limit; please see Appendix for reservation information and standard Texas state park fees; park office (512) 672-3266.

Camp Notes: The park's soft, melodic name is derived from the attractive, multi-frond dwarf palmetto plant (also called the "blue palm" and, would you believe, the "swamp palm"). Palmetto is quite common here and it adds a touch of the tropics to the bottomland. A really excellent booklet for the self-guiding nature trails is available at the trailheads. The booklet is highly useful to casual nature observers and experienced botanists alike.

NAILS CREEK
Lake Somerville State Recreation Area

Location: East-Central Texas southeast of Bryan.

Access: From U.S. Highway 290 at a point 6 miles east of Giddings, head northeast on Farm Road 180 for 13 miles to the park entrance station; continue ahead, then right, for 0.2 mile to the campground.
Alternate Access: From Texas State Highway 21 at a point 9 miles northwest of Lincoln, 14 miles southwest of Caldwell, turn southeast onto Farm Road 141 and travel 8 miles (passing through Dime Box) to the junction of Farm Roads 141 and 1697; continue southeast of Farm Road 1697 for another 7 miles to its junction with Farm Road 180; turn northeast (left) onto FM 180 for a final 3.4 miles to the park.

Alternate-Alternate Access: From U.S. 290 in the burg of Burton, pick your way through town on Farm Road 390 for 1 mile to the northeast corner of Burton; turn northwest (left) onto Farm Road 1697 and continue for 10 miles to its junction with Farm Road 180; turn northeast (right) onto FM 180 for a final 3.4 miles to the park entrance.

Facilities: 40 campsites with partial hookups, in 2 loops; (an equestrian camp with 10 standard sites is also available); sites are medium to medium+ in size, level, with fair to very good separation; parking pads are hard-surfaced, medium-length straight-ins; plenty of room for tents; barbecue grills and fire rings; b-y-o firewood; water at faucets throughout; restrooms with showers; paved driveways; gas and camper supplies are available near the park.

Activities & Attractions: Boating; boat launch; fishing; swimming beach; hiking and horse trails; interpretive center.

Natural Features: Located on a point on the west shore of Somerville Lake; campsites are moderately sheltered/shaded by large hardwoods and junipers/cedars; bordered by dense woodland; elevation 300'.

Season, Fees & Phone: Open all year; 14 day limit; please see Appendix for reservation information and standard Texas state park fees; Nails Creek unit office (409) 289-2392.

Camp Notes: This is a dandy little out-of-the-way place. Most of the campsites are tucked into their own little tree-lined nooks, thus delivering a good measure of seclusion. There's a fine day use area at the tip of the point which provides room to stretch and to look out across the lake. The origin of the name for the nearby village of Dime Box? It acquired its unique name from an old local custom. Farmers and other residents in outlying areas often were unable to make the trip into town to buy small quantities of necessities. So they'd leave a note in a small box next to their mailbox asking the postman to bring a few items from town on his next trip. Accompanying the note inside the box was a silver dime, left as compensation for the postman's special services.

Texas 124

BIRCH CREEK
Lake Somerville State Recreation Area

Location: East-Central Texas southwest of Bryan.

Access: From Texas State Highway 36 in Lyons (4 miles northwest of Somerville, 13 miles southeast of Caldwell), turn west/southwest onto Farm Road 60 and drive 7 miles; turn south (left) onto Park Road 57 and proceed south/southeast for 4 miles to the park entrance; just beyond the entrance, turn southwest (right) to the *Old Hickory* section, or northeast (left) for 0.6 mile to the *Post Oak* area, or 1.4 miles to the *Youpon* area. **Alternate Access:** From State Highway 21 at a point 7 miles southwest of Caldwell, 16 miles northeast of Lincoln, travel southeast on Farm Road 60 for 10.5 miles to Park Road 57.

Facilities: *Old Hickory*, *Post Oak*, *Youpon*: a total of 103 campsites with partial hookups; (20 standard sites in an equestrian camp and 30 sites in a group trailer area are also available); sites are small+ to medium-sized, most are acceptably level, with fair to very good separation; parking pads are paved/packed gravel, medium-length straight-ins; medium to large tent areas; barbecue grills, plus fire rings or fireplaces; b-y-o firewood; water at sites; restrooms with showers; disposal station; paved driveways; gas and camper supplies are available on Park Road 57.

Activities & Attractions: 21-mile hiking/horse trail to the Nails Creek Unit of the park on the lake's west shore; hiking and nature trails; boating; boat launch; limited fishing.

Natural Features: Located near the north shore of Somerville Lake; majority of sites receive light to medium shade and good wind shelter from hardwoods and a few small cedars; bordered by dense woodland; elevation 300'.

Season, Fees & Phone: Open all year; 14 day limit; reservations recommended for weekends, April to October; please see Appendix for additional reservation information and standard Texas state park fees; Birch Creek unit office (409) 535-7763.

Camp Notes: Agreeably small, private campsites in Post Oak and Old Hickory; Youpon's are a bit larger and more airy. If you're into birding, be sure to ask for the *Birds of Lake Somerville SRA Field Checklist* pamphlet at the office. It includes over 260 species actually observed within or near the park. The 21-mile foot trail to the Nails Creek Unit of the sra is the longest trail in the Texas state park system.

Texas 125

BIG CREEK
Somerville Lake/Corps of Engineers Park

Location: East-Central Texas southwest of Bryan.

Access: From Texas State Highway 36 in the small community of Lyons (4 miles northwest of Somerville, 13 miles southeast of Caldwell), turn west/southwest onto Farm Road 60 and proceed 4 miles; turn south onto Recreation Road 4 and follow it south/southeast for 3.5 miles (to a point just beyond a sharpish left curve in the road); turn south (right) for 0.1 mile to the campground entrance station; just beyond the entrance, bear right to most standard sites, or left to the hookup units.

Facilities: 52 campsites, including 21 with partial hookups, in 2 loops; sites are small to small+, most are sloped, with nominal separation; parking pads are gravel, medium-length straight-ins; large, grassy areas for tents; barbecue grills; a limited amount of firewood is available for gathering in the vicinity; water at faucets throughout; restrooms with showers; holding tank disposal station; paved driveways; gas and groceries on R4 and in Lyons; limited supplies and services are available in Somerville.

Activities & Attractions: Fishing (some stripers and white bass near the dam in spring, or trotlining for catfish any time); boating; boat launch.

Natural Features: Located on a pair of small points at the tip of a large point on the north shore of Somerville Lake, a flood control impoundment on Yegua Creek; a small cove separates the two "pointlettes"; campground vegetation consists of light to medium-dense large hardwoods on a grassy surface; bordered by dense vegetation; elevation 300'.

Season, Fees & Phone: Open all year; $9.00 for a standard site, $11.00 for a partial hookup site; 14 day limit; Somerville Lake CoE Project Office (409) 596-1622.

Camp Notes: All sites have faucets, but be prepared to travel a couple-hundred yards from the standard/tent loop to the campground's other facilities.

Texas 126

OVERLOOK
Somerville Lake/Corps of Engineers Park

Location: East-Central Texas southwest of Bryan.

Access: From Texas State Highway 36 at a point 4 miles south of Somerville, turn west onto Farm Road 1948 and proceed 0.15 mile; turn north (the first right turn after the railroad tracks) onto the Overlook Park/Somerville Dam access road and proceed 0.6 mile; turn northwest (left, then a quick jog to the right) down onto the campground access road and parallel the main road for 0.4 mile to the campground entrance station and the campground.

Facilities: 50 campsites, including 25 with partial hookups; sites are small to medium-sized, reasonably level, with minimal to fair separation; parking pads are gravel, medium-length straight-ins; large, grassy tent areas; ramadas (sun shelters) for a few sites; barbecue grills, plus some fireplaces; b-y-o firewood; water at hookup sites and at central faucets; restrooms with showers; disposal station; paved main driveway, gravel sub-drives; limited supplies and services are available in Somerville.

Activities & Attractions: Boating; fishing; playground.

Natural Features: Located on the gently sloping southeast shore of Somerville Lake; sites are very lightly to lightly shaded by large hardwoods; elevation 300'.

Season, Fees & Phone: Open all year; $9.00 for a standard site, $11.00 for a partial hookup site; 14 day limit; Somerville Lake CoE Project Office (409) 596-1622.

Camp Notes: A couple of good-sized islands just offshore add an element of interest to the view from Overlook. At the risk of doing some hair-splitting, it might be noted that "Overlook", as applied to the campground, is a bit of a misnomer, since most sites are close to lake level and strictly speaking don't "look over" a great deal of lake scenery. "Overlook" might pertain to the picnic spot on the knoll at the end of the park's point. (Or maybe it's because everyone driving along the dam road on the embankment above the campground has a clear visual shot of the whole place.) At the north end of the dam is Welch City Park (see info below). It has restrooms, showers and room for 100 (or maybe 200) campers.

Texas 127

WELCH
Somerville City Park

Location: East-Central Texas southwest of Bryan.

Access: From Texas State Highway 36 on the north edge of Somerville, turn west onto Thornberry Drive; proceed west for 1.5 miles to the project headquarters, then southwest for 0.2 mile to the top of the dam, and finally swing around to the northwest for a final 0.2 mile to the park entrance and the campground.

Facilities: Approximately 100 campsites in more or less of a park-'em-'n-pitch-'em-however-you-like-'em, open camping arrangement; parking and tent areas are grass/earth, and are either tolerably level or sloped; some tables and barbecue grills; b-y-o firewood; water at central faucets; restrooms with showers; gravel/dirt driveways; limited supplies and services are available in Somerville.

Activities & Attractions: Boating; boat launch; fishing (mostly in spring, by the dam.)

Natural Features: Located along the shore and on a hilly point on the east side of Somerville Lake, just north of the dam on Yegua Creek; sites are minimally to lightly shaded by hardwoods, mostly along the water's edge and on the point; large, open grassy areas; elevation 300'.

Season, Fees & Phone: Open all year, with reduced services in winter; $7.00; 14 day limit; City of Somerville Public Works Department (409) 596-2286.

Camp Notes: Call this one an "Action Extra". What you need to do in this camping area is to stake out a fair-sized piece of property, preferably around one of the few tables and grills. Then enjoy the scenery and your camping *compadres*. There are some shaded, edgewater spots below the dam embankment; but a hilltop site out on the point might be even better. When the lake level is at a typical late summer low, it is said to be possible to take a leisurely stroll out to the island just offshore of the park, (as long as you wear a lifejacket and don't mind getting your toes wet). Judging by the reports of how popular Welch is on summer weekends, what it lacks in facilities it makes up for in good times.

Texas 128

YEGUA CREEK
Somerville Lake/Corps of Engineers Park

Location: East-Central Texas southwest of Bryan.

Access: From Texas State Highway 36 at a point 4 miles south of Somerville, turn west onto Farm Road 1948 and proceed 2.7 miles; turn northwest (right) onto the Yegua Creek access road and proceed 0.9 mile to the campground entrance station; bear right just after the entrance to the campground. (Note: If you're approaching from the west on U.S. Highway 290, several miles can be saved by taking Farm Road 1948, from a point 2 miles east of Burton, then north and east for a total of 14 miles to the Yegua Creek access road.)

Facilities: 95 campsites, including 45 with partial hookups; sites are small+ to medium-sized, with nominal to fair separation; most parking pads are gravel, medium to long straight-ins; many pads will require a little additional leveling; ample space for large tents, may be sloped; ramadas (sun shelters) for some sites; barbecue grills; b-y-o firewood is suggested; water at faucets throughout; restrooms with showers; holding tank disposal station; paved driveways; gas and groceries on Farm Road 1948.

Activities & Attractions: Boating; boat launches and docks; fishing; fishing pier; nature trail; amphitheater; off road vehicle (orv) area.

Natural Features: Located on the south-east shore of Somerville Lake, on a point flanked by a long, slender bay on one side and the open lake on the other; campground vegetation consists of very light to medium-dense hardwoods and expansive tracts of grass and wildflowers; elevation 300'.

Season, Fees & Phone: Open all year; $9.00 for a standard site, $11.00 for a partial hookup site; 14 day limit; Somerville Lake CoE Project Office (409) 596-1622.

Camp Notes: There are some really nifty tent campsites at and near the very end of the point. Good views (just ignore the dam). (Incidentally, the name of the place is pronounced like "*Yay*-wah"--an Indian word for "mare".)

Texas 129

ROCKY CREEK
Somerville Lake/Corps of Engineers Park

Location: East-Central Texas southwest of Bryan.

Access: From Texas State Highway 36 at a point 4 miles south of Somerville, turn west onto Farm Road 1948 and proceed 5 miles; turn northeast (right) onto the Rocky Creek access road and proceed 1.1 miles to the campground entrance station; turn right into a hookup loop, or continue ahead for 0.4 mile to the remaining loops. **Alternate Access:** From U.S. Highway 290 at a point 2 miles east of Burton, 11 miles west of Brenham, turn northwest onto Farm Road 1948 and follow it northwest, north, northeast, then east for a total of 10 miles to the Rocky Creek Access Road and continue as above.

Facilities: 153 campsites, including 35 with partial hookups, in a half-dozen loops and sub-loops; sites are small+ to medium-sized, with minimal to fair separation; most parking pads are gravel, medium to long straight-ins; most pads will require at least a little additional leveling; large, generally sloped, grassy tent areas; ramadas (sun shelters) for a few sites; barbecue grills; b-y-o firewood is suggested; water at sites and at central faucets; restrooms with showers; holding tank disposal station; paved driveways; gas and camper supplies on Farm Road 1948.

Activities & Attractions: Boating; boat launch and dock; fishing; playground; amphitheater.

Natural Features: Located on a narrow peninsula which extends from the south shore of Somerville Lake; large hardwoods provide light to medium shade for most sites; several acres of grassy slopes; long stretches of open, grassy shoreline/beach; elevation 300'.

Season, Fees & Phone: Open all year; $9.00 for a standard site, $11.00 for a partial hookup site; 14 day limit; Somerville Lake CoE Project Office (409) 596-1622.

Camp Notes: Rocky Creek is a favorite spot of many campers because ..... well, as one camper put it, "because the lake is almost all around it, and it's just a good place to camp".

TEXAS

South

Please refer to the Texas map in the Appendix

Texas 130

CASTROVILLE
Castroville Regional Park

Location: South Texas west of San Antonio.

Access: From U.S. Highway 90 at the west edge of Castroville, turn south onto South Athens Street and go 0.3 mile, then turn west (right) onto Lisbon Street for 0.2 mile; the street swings south, then almost immediately turn west again into the park entrance; the camping area is south of the swimming pool.

Facilities: Approximately 40 campsites, most with full hookups; sites are very small (hookups) to medium-sized (tents), level, and closely spaced; parking surfaces are gravel/grass, medium-length, parallel pull-throughs; large tent areas adjacent to hook-ups; no fire facilities; (barbecue grills in day use area); not all sites have tables; rustic restrooms; open-air showers; gravel driveways; adequate supplies and services are available in Castroville.

Activities & Attractions: Swimming pool; limited fishing; playground; large day use area.

Natural Features: Located on a grassy flat along the Medina River; hardwoods provide very light to medium shade/shelter for most sites; mown grass; elevation 800'.

Season, Fees & Phone: Open all year; $6.00 for a standard (tent) site, $9.00 for a hookup site; reservations accepted, contact the park office (512) 538-2224.

Camp Notes: To be very above-board about it: This park and its facilities aren't exactly in the multi-star category. (Like most small-town parks, the principal motivation behind operating a campground is probably to bring a little extra commerce into the area--and there's certainly nothing unprincipled about that.) Although capital improvements may be slow in arriving, the park does, nonetheless, provide a fairly economical and convenient-to-town stop for U.S. 90 travelers. Chances are, another reason why campers stop and spend some time is because there are a lot of nice people around here.

Texas 131

CALLIHAM
Choke Canyon State Park

Location: South Texas between San Antonio and Corpus Christi.

Access: From Texas State Highway 72 in the community of Calliham (11 miles west of Three Rivers, 12 miles east of Tilden), turn northeast onto Park Road 8 and proceed 1.1 miles to the park entrance; continue ahead for 1.2 miles to a "T" intersection; turn southeast (right) for 0.1 mile, then turn south (right) and go another 0.6 mile to the walk-in tent area; or continue on the main road as it curves around to the north for a final mile to the hookup area.

Facilities: 58 campsites, including 39 partial hookup units and 19 walk-in sites; in addition, 20 units with screened shelters are also available; hookup sites are generally medium to large, level, with nominal to very good separation; parking pads are hard-surfaced, medium-length straight-ins; most sites have large, framed tent pads and ramadas (sun/partial-wind shelters); fire rings and barbecue grills; b-y-o firewood;

water at faucets throughout; restrooms with showers; holding tank disposal station; paved driveways; gas and camper supplies in Calliham; limited supplies and services are available in Three Rivers.

Activities & Attractions: Tennis courts; swimming pool; swimming beach; athletic field; basketball courts; playground; fishing; fishing jetties; boat launch; trails.

Natural Features: Located on a peninsula on the south shore of Choke Canyon Reservoir; sites receive very light to medium shade/shelter from large hardwoods; surrounded by brushy plains; elevation 200'.

Season, Fees & Phone: Open all year; 14 day limit; please see Appendix for reservation information and standard Texas state park fees; Calliham unit office (512) 786-3868.

Camp Notes: A distinctive feature here are two 'lakes within a lake', so to speak. The peninsula contains a 5-acre lake, and a 90-acre lake which was created by damming a bay.

Texas 132

SOUTH SHORE
Choke Canyon State Park

Location: South Texas between San Antonio and Corpus Christi.

Access: From Texas State Highway 72 at a point 4 miles west of Three Rivers, 7 miles east of Calliham, 19 miles east of Tilden), turn northwest onto the park access road for 0.2 mile to the park entrance; continue ahead for 0.1 mile, then right for 1.5 miles to the riverside area (hookups and walk-ins); or proceed ahead for 0.8 mile to the lakeside unit (walk-ins only).

Facilities: 55 campsites, including 20 with partial hookups, in 2 major areas; hookup sites are small+ to medium-sized, with nominal separation; parking pads for hookup sites are hard-surfaced, level, medium-length straight-ins; adequate space for large tents; ramadas (sun/partial-wind shelters) for walk-in sites; fire rings and barbecue grills; b-y-o firewood; water at many sites and at central faucets; restrooms with showers; holding tank disposal station; paved driveways; limited supplies and services are available in Three Rivers.

Activities & Attractions: Fishing; boating; multi-lane boat launches on the lake; launch on the river for small boats and canoes; playgrounds.

Natural Features: Located on grassy flats above the outlet channel (riverside) and on a grassy, easy slope above the south shore (lakeside) of Choke Canyon Reservoir, an impoundment on the Frio River; sites receive very light to light-medium shade from hardwoods; elevation 200'.

Season, Fees & Phone: Open all year; 14 day limit; please see Appendix for reservation information and standard Texas state park fees; South Shore unit office (512) 786-3538.

Camp Notes: This area holds the distinction of being the westernmost habitat of alligators in the United States. (Hmmmmm. Whatever happened to that armadillo that just waddled by the tent.....? Ed.)

Texas 133

LAKE CORPUS CHRISTI
Lake Corpus Christi State Recreation Area

Location: South Texas northwest of Corpus Christi.

Access: From Texas State Highway 359 at a point 6 miles southwest of Interstate 37 exit 36 for Mathis, 2 miles northeast of Sandia, turn west/northwest onto Park Road 25 and proceed 1.9 miles to the park entrance station; standard area 1 and the hookup loops are straight ahead, standard area 2 is to the right.

Facilities: 108 campsites, including 23 with partial hookups and 25 with full hookups, in 4 areas; (25 units with screened shelters are also available; sites are generally medium to large, with fair to fairly good separation; standard sites have mostly short+ to medium-length, basically paved, straight-ins; hookup sites have long, paved pull-throughs; most pads will require at least a little additional leveling; large tent areas, though most are a bit sloped; large ramadas (sun shelters) for many standard sites; barbecue grills or fire rings; water at faucets; restrooms with showers; holding tank disposal station; paved driveways; adequate supplies and services are available in Mathis, 5 miles north.

Activities & Attractions: Fishing for catfish, perch, bass, crappie; fishing piers; boating; boat launch; swimming; nature trail.

Natural Features: Located around the rim of a bay on the gently sloping southeast shore of Lake Corpus Christi in a valley on the edge of the South Texas Brush Country; shade from large hardwoods varies from minimal to medium; plenty of mown grassy areas; elevation 150'.

Season, Fees & Phone: Open all year; 14 day limit; please see Appendix for reservation information and standard Texas state park fees; park office (512) 547-2635.

Camp Notes: If you prefer a campsite with a bit more privacy, try standard area 1. Standard area 2's sites, though, are a tad roomier. And if you need water and juice, either of the two hookup districts should look good.

Texas 134

GOLIAD
Goliad State Historical Park

Location: South Texas southeast of Victoria.

Access: From U.S. Highways 183 & 29A at a point 0.8 mile south of Goliad, turn west onto Park Road 6 and proceed 0.1 mile to the park entrance/headquarters; just beyond the entrance, turn south (left) to the hookup/shelter loop; or continue south, then east, passing under the highway, for 0.5 mile to the primitive walk-in sites.

Facilities: 20 campsites with full hookups; (10 primitive campsites and 5 screened shelters are also available); hookup sites are medium-sized, with fairly good separation; parking pads are hard-surfaced, long pull-throughs which may require a touch of additional leveling; large, grassy tent areas; barbecue grills and fire rings; water at sites and at central faucets; restrooms with showers; paved driveways; adequate supplies and services are available in Goliad.

Activities & Attractions: Reconstruction of Mission Espiritu Santo; interpretive exhibits; nature trail; swimming pool; limited fishing and boating; playground; birthplace of General Ignacio Zaragoza, just south of the main park.

Natural Features: Located on a gently sloping flat on the inside of a bend of the San Antonio River; most sites are well shaded by large hardwoods; surrounded by dense woodland; no river views from hookup sites; (primitive sites are along the riverbank); elevation 200'.

Season, Fees & Phone: Open all year; 14 day limit; please see Appendix for reservation information and standard Texas state park fees; park office (512) 645-3405.

Camp Notes: The historic mission, whose renewal was begun a half century ago by local citizens, is quite an impressive structure. But who was General Ignacio Zaragoza, you ask? He was the Texas-born Mexican army leader who defeated the French in 1862, thus ensuring Mexico's independence. The date, May 5, 1862, is celebrated as the famous Mexican national holiday, *Cinco de Mayo*.

Texas 135

COLETO CREEK
Guadalupe-Blanco River Authority Regional Park

Location: South Texas southeast of Victoria.

Access: From U.S. Highway 59 at a point 12 miles southeast of Victoria, 4 miles northeast of Fannin, 13 miles northeast of Goliad, turn north onto Coleto Park Road (paved) and proceed 0.4 mile, then turn northeast (right) for 0.15 mile to the park entrance/headquarters; continue ahead for 0.25 mile, then turn left onto a gravel driveway for a final 0.3 mile to the campground.

Facilities: 33 campsites with partial hookups; sites are medium-sized, with fair separation; parking pads are gravel, generally level, medium+ straight-ins; large, grassy tent areas; barbecue grills; b-y-o firewood; water at faucets throughout; restrooms with showers; holding tank disposal station; gravel driveways; gas and groceries are available on the main highway; adequate supplies and services are available in Goliad.

Activities & Attractions: Fishing for black bass, assorted catfish, hybrid stripers, crappie; lighted fishing pier; boating; boat launch; designated swimming beach; day use area.

Natural Features: Located on a grassy slope on a small point of land on the south shore of 3100-acre Coleto Creek Reservoir; sites receive very light to medium shade/shelter from large hardwoods; elevation 150'.

Season, Fees & Phone: Open all year; $11.00 per vehicle for tent campers, $14.00 per vehicle for rv's, trailers, pickup campers, pop-ups, $6.00 for an extra vehicle; 14 day limit; reservations suggested for spring through fall weekends; contact the park office (512) 575-6366.

Camp Notes: Virtually all sites have a lake view, and some are right along the shore (handy for campside mooring, as many camping boaters have found). The lake's grassy, tree-dotted, low shoreline provides a quite pleasant plains environment.

LAKE TEXANA
Lake Texana State Park

Location: South Texas northeast of Victoria.

Access: From Texas State Highway 111 at a point 6.5 miles southeast of Edna, 0.5 mile west of the causeway which crosses Lake Texana, turn north into the park entrance; continue ahead for 0.5 mile to a "T" intersection; turn northwest (left) and continue north then northeast for 0.4 mile to 0.8 mile to the camp loops.

Facilities: 141 campsites, including 86 with partial hookups, in 2 loops; sites are medium-sized, level, with fair to good separation; parking pads are hard-surfaced, short+ to medium-length straight-ins, and many are double-wide; adequate space for medium to large tents; barbecue grills and fire rings; b-y-o firewood; water at faucets throughout; restrooms with showers; holding tank disposal station; paved driveways; adequate supplies and services are available in Edna.

Activities & Attractions: Fishing; lighted fishing piers; boating; boat launches; swimming areas; playgrounds.

Natural Features: Located on peninsulas adjacent to a major arm of Lake Texana along the lake's middle-west shore; the lake is a reservoir on the Navidad River; sites are light to moderately shaded/sheltered by large hardwoods; alligators; bordered by the woodlands and grasslands of the Gulf Coastal Plain; elevation 100'.

Season, Fees & Phone: Open all year; 14 day limit; reservations suggested for summer, and maybe Thanksgiving weekend; please see Appendix for additional reservation information and standard Texas state park fees; park office (512) 582-5718.

Camp Notes: Attractive park: lots of grass, lots of trees, lots of shoreline, lots of water. The lake is named for the ghost town of Texana, a mid-1800's port city located on the Navidad River. Texana prospered for nearly a half-century but is now long-forgotten.

BRACKENRIDGE PLANTATION
Lavaca-Navidad River Authority Park

Location: South Texas northeast of Victoria.

Access: From Texas State Highway 111 at a point 6.7 miles southeast of Edna, (0.2 mile east of Lake Texana State Park, 0.3 mile west of the causeway which crosses Lake Texana, turn south onto a paved access road and proceed 1.1 miles; turn east (left) into the campground.

Facilities: 100 campsites with full or partial hookups; sites are medium-sized, with nominal to fairly good separation; parking pads are hard-surfaced, medium to long straight-ins, some of which may require a little additional leveling; large tent areas; barbecue grills and fire rings; b-y-o firewood; water at sites; restrooms with showers; holding tank disposal stations; paved driveways; gas and camper supplies at the marina; adequate supplies and services are available in Edna.

Activities & Attractions: Fishing; boating; boat launch; nature trail; volleyball court; athletic field; playground.

Natural Features: Located along the west shore of Lake Texana, a reservoir on the Navidad River, on the site of the former Brackenridge Plantation; sites are lightly to moderately well shaded/sheltered by large hardwoods; alligators; bordered by grassy fields; elevation 100'.

Season, Fees & Phone: Open all year; $10.00 for a partial hookup site, $12.00 for a full hookup site; additional charges for extra tents and vehicles; weekly, monthly, and winter rates available; reservations accepted, contact the park office (512) 782-5249.

Camp Notes: The story of Brackenridge Plantation and its founding family reads like the script from a TV mini-series--and it's a case of History being more interesting than Hollywood. (If you're interested in Texas history, you should be able to obtain a copy of the handout that's distributed by the local historical commission from someone in the campground or at the marina.) Even Abraham Lincoln plays a cameo role in this 19th century drama.

PORT LAVACA PIER
City of Port Lavaca Park

Location: South Texas southeast of Victoria.

Access: From Texas State Highway 35 on the east edge of Port Lavaca, 0.3 mile southwest of the Lavaca Bay causeway, turn southeast onto a short street for 0.15 mile to a "T" intersection, then northeast (left) for 0.2 mile to the camping area. (Note: Texas 35 is a 4-lane divided highway, but a crossover is provided at this point for southwestbound traffic; the easiest way to spot the turnoff point is to look for a large community center with a squarish, white, green-topped lighthouse on the corner of the property).

Facilities: 51 campsites with partial hookups; sites are very small to small, essentially level, with zero separation; parking surfaces are gravel or grass, short to medium+ straight-ins; space for medium to large tents; small ramadas (sun/partial wind shelters) for 19 sites; no campsite fire facilities (bbq barrels in the day use area); water at sites and at central faucets; restrooms with showers; holding tank disposal station; paved driveway; nearly complete supplies and services are available in Port Lavaca.

Activities & Attractions: Fishing; Port Lavaca State Fishing Pier (more than a half-mile-long) extends into Lavaca Bay; boat launch; well-sheltered boat moorage; swimming pool; small playground.

Natural Features: Located on the shore of Lavaca Bay; a few short palms dot the grassy sections; sea level.

Season, Fees & Phone: Open all year; $8.00 for a regular hookup site, $9.00 for a hookup site with a ramada; park office (512) 552-4402.

Camp Notes: Since it's so close to a normally very busy highway, this isn't what you'd call an ideal Gulf Coast resort campground (with all due respects to the palm trees and the sea breeze). Still, it's certainly accessible to a sizable city's services--and there may be some goings-on at the community center next door which may be of interest.

GOOSE ISLAND
Goose Island State Recreation Area

Location: South Texas northeast of Corpus Christi.

Access: From Texas State Highway 35 at a point 0.5 mile north of the Copano bay Bridge, 7 miles north of Rockport-Fulton, 24 miles south of Tivoli, turn east onto Park Road 13 and proceed 1.6 miles, then turn south (right) for 0.3 mile to the park entrance/headquarters; continue straight ahead for 0.3 mile to the *Island* area, or turn west-northwest (right) to the *Wooded* area.

Facilities: *Island* area: 45 campsites with partial hookups; sites are small, level, closely spaced; parking pads are gravel, short straight-ins or pull-offs; medium to large tent areas, ramadas (sun/wind shelters); barbecue grills; *Wooded* area: 82 campsites, including 57 with partial hookups; sites are medium to large, level, with fair to excellent separation; parking pads are paved, medium to long straight-ins; adequate space for a large tent; barbecue grills and fire rings; ***both areas***: b-y-o firewood; water at faucets throughout; restrooms with showers; holding tank disposal station; paved driveways; nearly complete supplies and services are available in the Rockport-Fulton area.

Activities & Attractions: Fishing (including a 1600' pier); boat launch; trails; recreation hall; 'The Big Tree', a spreading coastal live oak more than 1000 years old, is 2 miles northeast.

Natural Features: Located on a beach on Goose Island (Island area) and in a stand of oaks (Wooded area) on the Gulf Coast; no natural shade to speak of on the island, ample shade/shelter in the woods; sea level.

Season, Fees & Phone: Open all year; 14 day limit; please see Appendix for reservation information and standard Texas state park fees; park office (512) 729-2858.

Camp Notes: The Wooded area (which includes some excellent standard/tent sites) is nice; the Island area is nice. It would be difficult to think of many seaside campgrounds in the West which offer a more interesting selection of, well, *nice* campsites. Definitely recommended.

PORT ARANSAS
Nueces County Park

Location: South Texas northeast of Corpus Christi.

Access: From midtown Port Aransas at the intersection of Alister Street and Beach Street, proceed east/northeast on Beach for 0.8 mile to the park; turn north and continue for 0.2 mile to the park office and the campground. **Alternate Access**: The above access is best if approaching on Park Road 53 from Corpus Christi; but from the Port A Ferry Terminal on the northwest corner of town, easiest way to the park is to head east/northeast on Cotter Street, cross Alister Street, and continue as Cotter makes a couple of jogs through a residential area; after passing the U of T Marine Science Institute, turn south to the campground, for a total of 1.6 miles from the ferry.

Facilities: 75 campsites with partial hookups in the primary camp area; (additional, primitive sites are available on the beach); sites are small, level, and closely spaced; parking pads are paved/gravel, short to medium-length straight-ins; large, grassy tent areas; tiny ramadas (sun shelters) for all sites; no fire facilities; (b-y-o grill and charcoal); water at faucets throughout; restrooms and showers; holding tank disposal station; paved driveways; adequate supplies and services are available in Port A.

Activities & Attractions: Surf fishing; fishing from a 1200-foot-long pier; swimming.

Natural Features: Located at the northern tip of Mustang Island, a few yards from the Gulf of Mexico; vegetation consists of sparse grass between and around campsites in the primary camp area; sea level.

Season, Fees & Phone: Open all year; $5.00 for a primitive site, $10.00 for a partial hookup site; 14 day limit; park office (512) 749-6117.

Camp Notes: A study in contrasts: the park's relatively rustic real estate, overshadowed and out-architectured by the high-rise condos next door.

MUSTANG ISLAND
Mustang Island State Park

Location: South Texas east of Corpus Christi.

Access: From Texas State Highway 358 (Padre Island Drive) at the southeast end of the John F. Kennedy Causeway (the highly arched viaduct which spans Laguna Madre and links Corpus Christi and Padre Island), proceed southeast on Park Road 22 for 1.3 miles to a large "Y" intersection; turn north (left) onto Park Road 53 and proceed 5 miles; turn east (right) into the park entrance; continue ahead for 0.15 mile, then north into the main campground; or continue ahead for another 0.3 mile to the beach area.

Facilities: *Main area*: 48 campsites with partial hookups in 2 parallel rows along both sides of a wide, paved driveway; sites are small, level, with minimal separation; parking surfaces are basically paved, short, wide straight-ins; adequate space for large tents (free-standing); ramadas (sun shelters) for all sites; barbecue grills; b-y-o firewood/charcoal; water at faucets throughout; restrooms with showers; holding tank disposal station; paved driveway; *Beach area*: dozens of good-sized, primitive sites, some with ramadas, are available along more than a mile of Gulfside beach; plenty of space for tents and vehicles; b-y-o charcoal and grill; central water, freshwater rinse showers and vault facilities are available on the beach; gas and groceries are available near the "Y" mentioned in the Access section above.

Activities & Attractions: Swimming; surfing; surf fishing.

Natural Features: Located on Mustang Island about 300 yards west of the Gulf of Mexico; the windswept, treeless area's vegetation consists primarily of tall grass, shrubs and other smaller plants; a total of about 5.5 miles of beach are within the park; sea level.

Season, Fees & Phone: Open all year; reservations accepted for hookup sites; please see Appendix for additional reservation information and standard Texas state park fees; park office (512) 749-5246.

Camp Notes: The hookup area is OK, but it looks like it would be a lot more fun to camp on the beach!

PADRE BALLI
Nueces County Park

Location: South Texas southeast of Corpus Christi.

Access: From Texas State Highway 358/Padre Island Drive at the southeast end of the John F. Kennedy Causeway (the highly arched viaduct which spans Laguna Madre and links Corpus Christi and Padre Island), proceed southeast on Park Road 22 for 1.3 miles to a large "Y" intersection; bear south (right) and continue on Park Road 22 for 1.6 miles; turn east (left) into the park's main entrance and proceed 0.4 mile (around the traffic circle) almost to the surf; turn south (right) for another 0.1 mile to the park office and the campground.

Facilities: 66 campsites with partial hookups in a large, paved parking lot (more or less), plus room for a couple-dozen campers in a large, paved standard (non-hookup) parking lot; additionally, an unlimited number of primitive sites are available on the beach; sites are small and closely spaced; parking areas are basically level, medium to long pull-offs, pull-throughs or straight-ins; enough space for medium to large tents; small ramadas (sun shelters) for hookup sites; no fire facilities; restrooms with showers for hookup campers; outside, freshwater rinse showers for standard and primitive campers; laundry; holding tank disposal station; gas and groceries near the "Y".

Activities & Attractions: Beachcombing, surf-slogging; lighted, 1200-foot-long fishing pier; surf fishing.

Natural Features: Located on the Gulf side of Padre Island, a hundred yards west of the beach (hookup and non-hookup sites) or on the beach (primitive sites); patches of grass provide the only natural shade; sea level.

Season, Fees & Phone: Open all year; $5.00 for a standard or primitive site, $10.00 for a partial hookup site; 3-day limit; park office (512) 949-8121.

Camp Notes: It is said that the Bob Hall Fishing Pier here is one of the most popular fishing spots in Texas.

Texas 143

MALAQUITE BEACH
Padre Island National Seashore

Location: South Texas southeast of Corpus Christi.

Access: From Texas State Highway 358 (Padre Island Drive) at the southeast end of the John F. Kennedy Causeway (the highly arched viaduct which spans Laguna Madre and links Corpus Christi and Padre Island), proceed southeast on Park Road 22 for 1.3 miles to a large "Y" intersection; bear south (right) and continue on Park Road 22 for 10 miles to the park boundary; continue on the paved park road for another 4.5 miles; turn east (left) onto a paved access road for 0.1 mile, then hang a final left into the campground.

Facilities: 50 campsites in somewhat of a paved parking lot arrangement; sites are small+, level and closely spaced; parking spaces are small+ to medium-sized, straight-ins or pull-offs; adequate space for a medium-sized, free-standing tent on the pavement (if your vehicle isn't too large), or for a large tent on the beach; no fire facilities; (b-y-o grill and charcoal); water at central faucets; restrooms; outside showers (no soap allowed); holding tank disposal station; gas and groceries near the "Y".

Activities & Attractions: Beachcombing; visitor center; nature trail; surf fishing; 4wd travel and primitive camping on the beach along the length of the island, south of this area.

Natural Features: Located on Malaquite beach on Padre Island along the Gulf of Mexico; a dune, covered with tall grass and flowering plants, rises behind (west) of the campground; Gulf views from all campsites; sea level.

Season, Fees & Phone: Open all year; $5.00; 14 day limit; Padre Island National Seashore Headquarters (512) 937-2621.

Camp Notes: The segment of Padre Island which is within the boundaries of the national seashore is, in its essence, a low, slender, 70-mile-long, treeless, grassy dune with a fabulous beach. The strictly objective description (above) aside, this is a tent/pickup/van/small trailer beach camper's delight.

Texas 144

SEA WIND
Kaufer-Hubert Memorial/Kleberg County Park

Location: South Texas south of Kingsville.

Access: From U.S. Highway 77 at a point 3.5 miles north of Riviera, 5.5 miles south of Ricardo, turn east onto Farm Road 628 and travel 10 miles, (the road curves south/southeast at about 8.5 miles) to the park entrance; turn east (left) into the park, continue ahead for 0.4 mile, then turn right, into the campground.

Facilities: 134 campsites with full hookups in 2 sections; sites are small, level, with nil separation; parking pads are basically paved, long straight-ins; adequate space for medium to large tents on a grass/gravel surface; no fire facilities; (bbq grills in day use area); water at faucets throughout; restrooms with showers; laundry; holding tank disposal station; paved driveways; gas and groceries in Riviera.

Activities & Attractions: Saltwater fishing (reportedly excellent for trout); lighted fishing pier; boating; boat launch; athletic fields; walking/jogging trail with fitness course; playground; 2-story, covered observation deck; recreation hall; bird walk.

Natural Features: Located near the shore of Cayo Del Grullo, a major arm of Baffin Bay on the Gulf Coast; vegetation consists of patches of grass between sites, and medium-sized hardwoods which provide limited shade for some sites; one group of sites partly encircles a small, round, treatment pond ("Kaufer Lake"); sea level.

Season, Fees & Phone: Open all year; $9.00 for tents/no hookups, $12.00 for full hookups; long-term rates available; reservations recommended November to April; park office (512-297-5738).

Camp Notes: The catch-phrase for this spot might be "You name it, they've got it". The long term rates are reasonable (attn: Snowbirds), and you can even get a telephone hooked-up to your rv (or to your tent, for that matter). (No cable TV at last report, so b-y-o satellite dish or dx antenna.)

Texas 145

ADOLPH THOMAE, JR.
Cameron County Park

Location: South Texas northeast of Harlingen.

Access: From the junction of U.S. Highways 77 & 83 in Harlingen, travel east on Tyler Avenue through Harlingen, then north on Farm Road 106, for a total of 11 miles, to Rio Hondo; continue on Farm Road 106 to a point 3 miles east of Rio Hondo; turn north (left) onto Farm Road 2925 and proceed north, then east for 12 miles to Arroyo City; continue for a final 3 miles to the east end of town to the park entrance and campground. (Note: there are at least six ways to get here from various points in the area, but the above access should serve the majority of travelers.)

Facilities: 35 campsites, including many with full-hookups; sites are small, level, with fair to fairly good separation; parking pads are sandy gravel, medium-length straight-ins; small to medium-sized, grass/gravel tent areas; no fire facilities; (b-y-o grill, charcoal only); water at several faucets; restrooms with showers; paved driveways; gas and groceries in Arroyo City; limited supplies and services are available in Rio Hondo.

Activities & Attractions: Saltwater fishing; lighted fishing pier; boating; boat launch; nature trail.

Natural Features: Located on the Coastal Plain along the south bank of Arroyo Colorado waterway; campground vegetation consists of tall grass, brush and medium-height trees; sites receive limited to medium shade; bordered by the Laguna Atascosa National Wildlife Refuge; sea level.

Season, Fees & Phone: Open all year $10.00 for a standard site, $12.00 for a full hookup site; reservations accepted, contact the park office (512) 761-5493.

Camp Notes: If you or your campmates enjoy saltwater fishing, boating, or wildlife watching, this park would be a good choice. There are miles of well-sheltered waters around here.

Texas 146

ISLA BLANCA
Cameron County Park

Location: South Texas northeast of Brownsville.

Access: From Texas State Highway 100 at the east end of Port Isabel, travel across the Queen Isabella Causeway, which spans Laguna Madre (the waterway between South Padre Island and the mainland), to the Island; at the traffic triangle 0.1 mile from the east end of the causeway, turn southeast (right) onto Padre Boulevard and continue for 1.6 mile to the park entrance station and the campground.

Facilities: Approximately 400 campsites, most with partial or full hookups; sites are small, level and closely spaced; parking surfaces are partially paved, medium to long pull-throughs; enough space for a small to medium-sized tent (permitted in designated sites only); no fire facilities; water at faucets throughout; restrooms with showers; holding tank disposal station; paved driveways; gas, groceries and other services on the Island, within 1 mile; adequate+ supplies and services are available in Port Isabel.

Activities & Attractions: Long, sandy beaches; paved bike trail; extensive (and busy) day use facilities; well-sheltered harbor and marina; popular children's swimming area within walking distance at Dolphin Cove.

Natural Features: Located at the southern tip of South Padre Island, a few yards from the Gulf of Mexico; campground vegetation consists of sparse grass dotted with a few palms; (b-y-o shade); sea level.

Season, Fees & Phone: Open all year; $10.00 for a standard (tent) site, $11.00 for a partial hookup site, $12.00 for a full hookup site; long term rates available; 6 month limit; reservations accepted, only in person or by mail (P.O. Box 2106, South Padre Island, TX, 78597), recommended December to April; park office (512) 761-5493.

Camp Notes: In Tropical Texas, the Gulf Coast is often referred-to as the "Third Coast". Count on daytime temps in the balmy 70's throughout most of the winter. By a margin of a fraction of a degree of latitude, this is the southernmost public campground in the West.

Texas 147

FALCON
Falcon State Recreation Area

Location: South Texas south of Laredo.

Access: From U.S. Highway 83 at a point 3 miles south of Falcon, 14 miles north of Roma, turn west onto Farm Road 2098 and proceed 2.7 miles; turn northwest (right) onto Park Road 46 for 0.9 mile, then west (left) for 0.7 mile to the park entrance station/headquarters; proceed ahead for 0.6 mile, then right, to the camping areas.

Facilities: 31 campsites with partial hookups 31 sites with full hookups, plus 55 picnic/camp sites; (24 units with screened shelters are also available); sites are small+, mostly level, with nominal to fair separation; parking pads are gravel, medium+ pull-throughs; adequate space for medium to large tents; small ramadas (sun shelters) in all sites; barbecue grills or fire rings; b-y-o firewood; water at faucets throughout; restrooms with showers; holding tank disposal stations; paved driveways; gas and groceries in Falcon Heights, 5 miles south on U.S. 83.

Activities & Attractions: Fishing; boating; boat launch and dock; playground.

Natural Features: Located on a bluff above the lower east shore of Falcon Reservoir in the Rio Grande Valley; most sites have minimal or very limited natural shade, but are bordered by trees and bushes; surrounding terrain consists of low, brush-covered hills; elevation 250'.

Season, Fees & Phone: Open all year; 14 day limit; please see Appendix for reservation information and standard Texas state park fees; park office (512) 848-5327.

Camp Notes: Unless you really need a sewer hookup, you might consider getting a partial hookup campsite (i.e., those numbered in the 100's). The partials tend to be somewhat more private because of the greater vegetation between sites.

Texas 148

BENTSEN-RIO GRANDE VALLEY
Bentsen-Rio Grande Valley State Park

Location: South Texas west of McAllen.

Access: From U.S. Highway 83 at the west edge of the city of Mission, travel west on Loop 374 for 1.6 miles; turn south (left) onto Route 2062 and proceed 2.7 miles to the park entrance; continue ahead for 0.5 mile to the camping areas. (Note: If you're southbound on U.S. 83 in Tierra Blanca, 7 miles west of Mission, just angle southeast off U.S. 83 onto Loop 374, then travel 4 miles to pick up Route 2062.)

Facilities: 142 campsites, including 77 with full hookups; sites are small to medium-sized, level, with generally fair separation; parking pads are packed gravel, long pull-throughs in the hookup loop, and short, gravelly straight-ins in the standard section; tent areas are small in the hookup section, large in the standard area; barbecue grills and fire rings; b-y-o firewood; water at faucets throughout; restrooms with showers; mostly paved driveways; gas and groceries nearby; nearly complete supplies and services are available in Mission.

Activities & Attractions: Rio Grande and Singing Chaparral self-guiding trails (guide booklets available); boating; fishing.

Natural Features: Located on a wooded flat a few hundred yards northeast of the Rio Grande; most sites are moderately shaded by large hardwoods; the twin 'question marks' of Ox-Bow Lake lie adjacent to the park; elevation 150'.

Season, Fees & Phone: Open all year; 14 day limit; please see Appendix for reservation information and standard Texas state park fees; park office (512) 585-1107.

Camp Notes: Ox-Bow Lake is an interesting phenomenon: formerly part of a channel on the Rio Grande, only the lake's two, unconnected ends (shaped like question marks or fishhooks) remained after the river changed course. The northwest curl of what could be called 'the lake with two ends and no middle' is pump-fed from the river to maintain the water level. (The southeast end is now actually only a marsh.) Brer' Rabbit would love the thickets in this park!

TEXAS
East
Please refer to the Texas map in the Appendix

Texas 149

PAT MAYSE: WEST
Pat Mayse Lake/Corps of Engineers Park

Location: North-East Texas north of Paris.

Access: From U.S. Highway 271 in Arthur City, (15 miles north of Paris and just south of the Texas-Oklahoma border at the Red River), turn west onto Farm Road 197 and travel 7 miles, to a point 2.8 miles west of the settlement of Chicota; turn south (left) onto a paved access road and proceed south for 0.5 mile, then east (left) for 0.5 mile to the park entrance station; continue ahead, then south (right) for 0.7 mile to a fork; take the left fork to the A Loop or the right fork to the B and C Loops.

Facilities: 86 campsites, including 75 with electrical hookups, in 3 loops; sites are small to medium-sized, with nominal to fairly good separation; parking pads are paved, medium to long, mostly straight-ins; additional leveling will be needed in at least half the sites; mostly medium-sized, tolerably level, areas for tents; barbecue grills; fire rings; some firewood is available for gathering in the area; water at several faucets; restrooms with showers, plus vault facilities; holding tank disposal station; paved driveways; gas and groceries are available in Chicota.

Activities & Attractions: Boating; boat launch; swimming beach; fishing (said to be good for stripers, also sand bass, crappie, catfish); amphitheater.

Natural Features: Located on three small points on a major point of land on the mid-north shore of Pat Mayse Lake; campsites are moderately shaded/sheltered by large hardwoods; elevation 500'.

Season, Fees & Phone: Open all year, with limited services November to March; $8.00 for a standard site, $11.00 for an electrical hookup site; 14 day limit; Pat Mayse Lake CoE Project Office (214) 732-3020.

Camp Notes: Because the campsites vary considerably in size, levelness, and view, it would pay to take the time to look around, given the opportunity. The A Loop has the restrooms, but the B Loop has several very nice sites.

Texas 150

PAT MAYSE: EAST
Pat Mayse Lake/Corps of Engineers Park

Location: North-East Texas north of Paris.

Access: From U.S. Highway 271 in Arthur City, (15 miles north of Paris and just south of the Texas-Oklahoma border at the Red River), turn west onto Farm Road 197 and travel 5 miles, to a point 1 mile west of the settlement of Chicota; turn south (left) onto a paved access road and proceed 1.4 miles to a fork; take the left fork to the A Loop or the right fork to the B Loop, each an additional 0.4 mile south.

Facilities: 30 campsites in 2 loops; sites are small+ to medium-sized, with reasonably good separation; parking pads are gravel, medium to long straight-ins; most pads will require additional leveling; large, typically a little sloped, tent areas; barbecue grills and fire rings; some firewood is available for gathering in the area; water at central faucets; vault facilities; holding tank disposal station; paved main driveways, gravel sub-drives; gas and groceries are available in Chicota.

Activities & Attractions: Boating; boat launch; swimming beach; fishing.

Natural Features: Located on hilly terrain on a pair of points just above the north shore of 6000-acre Pat Mayse Lake, an impoundment on Sanders Creek, a tributary of the Red River; sites are moderately sheltered/shaded by large hardwoods on a surface of sparse grass; bordered by dense forest; elevation 500'.

Season, Fees & Phone: Open all year; $6.00; 14 day limit; Pat Mayse Lake CoE Project Office (214) 732-3020.

Camp Notes: Unlike many other Corps camps, those on this lake don't appear to have undergone extensive landscaping jobs--not much in the way of immense parcels of seeded and mown lawns, or regimented rows of obviously planted trees. Although the lake itself was man-made, the natural, well-forested surrounding country seems to have been more or less left to its own devices. What there is now is a pleasant, naturally realistic area.

Texas 151

SANDERS COVE
Pat Mayse Lake/Corps of Engineers Park

Location: North-East Texas north of Paris.

Access: From U.S. Highway 271 at a point 2 miles north of Powderly, 13 miles north of Paris, 2 miles south of Arthur City, turn west onto Farm Road 906 and drive 1.7 miles; turn southwest (left) onto the park access road and proceed 0.8 mile to the park entrance station; turn right to the C Loop, or continue ahead for 0.4 mile, then turn right or left to the A or B Loops.

Facilities: 79 campsites, including 47 with electrical hookups, in 3 loops; sites are medium to medium+, with fair to fairly good separation; parking pads are gravel, medium to long straight-ins; most pads will require additional leveling; adequate space for large tents, may be a little sloped; barbecue grills and fire rings; some firewood is available for gathering in the surrounding area; water at central faucets; vault facilities; holding tank disposal station; paved main driveways, gravel sub-drives; gas and groceries are available in Chicota, 4 miles northwest.

Activities & Attractions: Boating; boat launches and docks; fishing; swimming beach; nature trail.

Natural Features: Located on rolling and sloping terrain on a trio of small points at the east end of Pat Mayse Lake; sites receive medium to moderately dense shade/shelter from tall pines and hardwoods; the lake is surrounded by dense forest; elevation 500'.

Season, Fees & Phone: Open all year; $6.00 for a standard site, $10.00 for an electrical hookup site; 14 day limit; Pat Mayse Lake CoE Project Office (214) 732-3020.

Camp Notes: Also accessible from U.S. 271 is Lamar Point, the only camp on the lake's south shore. From 7 miles north of Paris, take Farm Road 1499 west for 6 miles, then Farm Road 1500 north for 5 miles. Lamar Point is a free area with a couple-dozen sites, drinking water, vaults, a dump station, a swimming area, and a boat ramp. It's a basic, practical, isolated camp that's well-worth the price.

Texas 152

CLEAR SPRINGS
Wright Patman Lake/Corps of Engineers Park

Location: North-East Texas southwest of Texarkana.

Access: From U.S. Highway 59 at a point 9 miles southwest of Texarkana, turn northwest onto Farm Road 2148 and proceed 1 mile (just to the north end of the dam); turn west (left) onto a paved access road and continue for 1.3 miles; turn south (left) for 0.3 mile, then hang a quick right to the campground entrance and the campsites. **Alternate Access:** From U.S. Highway 67 at a point 8 miles west of Texarkana, 5 miles east of Redwater, turn south onto Farm Road 2148 and proceed 3.9 miles to the access road and continue as above.

Facilities: 105 campsites, including 92 with partial hookups, in 5 sections; sites are small+ to medium-sized, about half are slightly sloped, with fair separation; parking pads are paved or gravel, medium to long straight-ins; ample space for large tents; assorted fire facilities; some firewood is available for gathering in the surrounding area; water at sites and at central faucets; restrooms with showers; holding tank disposal station; mostly paved driveways; gas and groceries are available along the main highways.

Activities & Attractions: Swimming beach; boating; boat launch; fishing; playground.

Natural Features: Located at the north tip of Wright Patman Lake, a 20,000-acre impoundment on the Sulphur River; campground vegetation consists of mostly light to medium-dense, tall pines on a floor of pine needles and sparse grass; elevation 250'.

Season, Fees & Phone: Open all year; $7.00 for a standard site, $11.00 for a partial hookup site; 14 day limit; Wright Patman Lake CoE Project Office (214) 838-8781.

Camp Notes: Not-so-old timers may remember that this reservoir's original handle was Lake Texarkana. In 1973 the President (whoever he was) signed a House of Representatives bill which renamed it in recognition of the prominent Texas congressman from the state's First Congressional District.

Texas 153

ROCKY POINT
Wright Patman Lake/Corps of Engineers Park

Location: North-East Texas southwest of Texarkana.

Access: From U.S. Highway 59 at a point 12 miles southwest of Texarkana and 10 miles north of Queen City, turn northwest (the first turn south of the Sulphur River Bridge) onto a paved access road and proceed 0.3 mile to a "T" intersection; turn west (left) and continue for 0.4 mile to a 4-way intersection; turn southwest (left again) for a final mile to the park entrance station and the campground.

Facilities: 126 campsites with partial hookups; sites are small+ to medium-sized, with fair separation; parking pads are hard-surfaced, medium+ to long straight-ins, plus a few pull-throughs; a little additional leveling may be needed in some sites; large, slightly sloped tent areas; assorted fire facilities; some firewood may be available for gathering in the area; water at sites; restrooms with showers; disposal station; paved driveways; gas and groceries are available at several stops along the highway within 3 miles.

Activities & Attractions: Swimming beach; boating; boat launch; fishing (said to be very good for crappie and catfish in season); Cat Squirrel Nature Trail; playground.

Natural Features: Located on a large, gently rolling slope on the southeast shore of Wright Patman Lake; campground vegetation consists of mostly light to medium-dense, tall hardwoods and pines on sparse grass; bordered by moderately dense woods; elevation 250'.

Season, Fees & Phone: Open all year; $11.00; 14 day limit; Wright Patman Lake CoE Project Office (214) 838-8781.

Camp Notes: It seems that this is the most popular campground on the lake, probably due in part to its location on the main segment of the lake and its easy accessibility from a four-lane highway. (Well, *easy* if you discount the somewhat convoluted route you must follow once you leave the main road.) They hang out the "CAMPGROUND FULL" shingle on most weekends, May to mid-September.

Texas 154

ATLANTA
Atlanta State Recreation Area

Location: North-East Texas southwest of Texarkana.

Access: From U.S. Highway 59 near the north edge of Queen City, turn northwest onto Farm Road 96 and travel 7.2 miles; turn north (right) onto Farm Road 1154 for 1.7 miles, then northwest (left) on Park Road 42 for 0.25 mile to the park entrance; continue ahead for 0.1 mile to a "Y" intersection; bear west (slightly left) for 0.4 mile to the *Knights Bluff* loop (standard & full hookups); or turn east (right) for 1 mile to the *Wilkins Creek* loop (partial hookups) and *White Oak Ridge* area (partial hookups). **Alternate Access:** From Texas State Highway 77 at a point 6 miles northwest of Atlanta, head north on Farm Road 96 for 4.6 miles, then pick up FM 1154 and continue as above.

Facilities: 59 campsites, including 43 with partial hookups and 8 with full hookups; sites are small+ to medium-sized, just a bit off-level, with fair to good separation; parking pads are hard-surfaced, short straight-ins or long pull-throughs; adequate space for large tents; barbecue grills and fire rings; b-y-o firewood; water at faucets throughout; restrooms with showers; disposal station; paved driveways; limited+ supplies and services are available in Queen City.

Activities & Attractions: Swimming beach; nature trail; 3.5-mile hiking trail; boating; boat launch; fishing; amphitheater; playground; mini bike area.

Natural Features: Located near the south shore of Wright Patman Lake; sites receive medium shade/shelter from tall pines and large hardwoods; elevation 250'.

Season, Fees & Phone: Open all year; 14 day limit; reservations recommended for summer weekends; please see Appendix for additional reservation information and standard Texas state park fees; park office (214) 796-6476.

Camp Notes: The favorite loop is Knights Bluff, which is actually below the bluff, and is the closest area to the lake shore. But you really couldn't go wrong anywhere here.

Texas 155

LAKE BOB SANDLIN
Lake Bob Sandlin State Recreation Area

Location: North-East Texas northwest of Longview.

Access: From U.S. Highway 271 on the west edge of Mount Pleasant, travel southwest on Farm Road 127 for 10.4 miles; turn south (left) onto Farm Road 21 and proceed 1 mile; turn east (left) for 0.3 mile to the park entrance; continue ahead for 0.1 mile, then turn northeast (left) for 0.7 mile to the campground. (Important Note: This is one of at least 8 principal accesses to this park; please check the state highway map for other routes; just bear in mind that the park is off of FM 21, south of the junction of FM's 21 & 127 and north of the causeway which crosses the lake.)

Facilities: 75 campsites with partial hookups; (primitive camp areas and 20 units with screened shelters are also available); sites are small+ to medium-sized, very slightly sloped, with nominal to fairly good separation; parking pads are paved, medium-length straight-ins; medium-sized tent areas; small ramadas (sun shelters) for some (less-shaded) sites; barbecue grills or fire rings; b-y-o firewood; water at sites; restrooms with showers; disposal station; paved driveways; gas and groceries on FM 21.

Activities & Attractions: Swimming; boating; boat launch and dock; fishing; fishing pier; hiking trail.

Natural Features: Located a few yards from the northwest shore of Lake Bob Sandlin, a 9500-acre reservoir on Big Cypress Creek; sites are shaded/sheltered by tall pines and short pines, big hardwoods and little hardwoods, plus a generous amount of low-level vegetation; low terrain around the lake; elevation 400'.

Season, Fees & Phone: Open all year; please see Appendix for reservation information and standard Texas state park fees; 14 day limit; park office (214) 572-5531.

Camp Notes: The dense vegetation frustrates the lake view from most of the campsites. That's probably OK, since this isn't much of a *view* lake, but rather more of a *do* lake.

Texas 156

DAINGERFIELD
Daingerfield State Park

Location: North-East Texas north of Longview.

Access: From Texas State Highways 11 & 49 at a point 2.7 miles east of Daingerfield and 2.5 miles west of Hughes Springs, turn south onto Park Road 17 and proceed 0.5 mile southwest to the park entrance station; proceed ahead for 0.2 mile, then south (left) to the *Big Pine* and *Dogwood* areas; or continue west, then north, for an additional 0.4 mile to the *Mountain View* area.

Facilities: *Big Pine*: 10 campsites with full hookups; *Dogwood*: 18 campsites with partial hookups; *Mountain View*: 12 standard campsites; *all areas*: sites are small+ to medium+, acceptably level, with fair to very good separation; parking pads are paved, medium to long straight-ins in Dogwood and Mountain View, long pull-throughs in Big Pine; adequate spaces for large tents, many on framed tent pads; barbecue grills; b-y-o firewood; water at sites; restrooms with showers; paved driveways; adequate supplies and services are available in Daingerfield.

Activities & Attractions: Swimming beach; 2.5-mile hiking trail; limited boating (5 mph); boat launch; fishing; fishing pier.

Natural Features: Located near the east and north shores of 80-acre Daingerfield Lake; sites receive medium to moderately dense shelter/shade from large and small hardwoods, lofty pines, and large ferns; elevation 400'.

Season, Fees & Phone: Open all year; 14 day limit; reservations suggested for weekends; please see Appendix for additional reservation information and standard Texas state park fees; park office (214) 645-2921.

Camp Notes: Some of the campsites appear to have been painstakingly hewn from dense forest, leaving just enough room in their small, woody nooks for the essentials. The result is a group of cozy camps with an excellent privacy factor. This is such a neat park, in a way it's too bad that there isn't room for more than 40 campers here. But then again, maybe that's the whole point.

ALLEY CREEK
Lake O' The Pines/Corps of Engineers Park

Location: North-East Texas north of Longview.

Access: From Texas State Highway 49 at a point 3 miles northwest of Jefferson, travel west on Farm Road 729 for 14 miles to the park access road (0.5 mile west of the Alley Creek bridge); turn south onto the access road and proceed southeast for 0.4 mile, then turn southwest (right) to the campground entrance station; continue ahead for 0.4 mile, then turn right to the hookup area, or left into the standard area. **Alternate Access:** From Texas State Highway 155 at its junction with Farm Road 729, head southeast on FM 729 for 6.5 miles to the park turnoff, and continue as above.

Facilities: Approximately 45 campsites, including 30 with partial hookups; sites are small+ to medium-sized, reasonably level, with fair separation; parking pads are mostly paved, medium to medium+ straight-ins; adequate space for large tents; barbecue grills; some firewood is available for gathering in the general area; water at hookup sites and at central faucets; restrooms with showers; holding tank disposal station; paved driveways; gas and groceries are available at several points along FM 729.

Activities & Attractions: Swimming beach; boating; boat launch; fishing; day use area.

Natural Features: Located on a bluff at the end of a major point of land near the north-east shore of Lake O' The Pines, a 19,000-acre reservoir on Cypress Creek; sites receive medium shade/shelter from tall pines and hardwoods; lake views through the trees; the lake is surrounded by low, forested hills; elevation 250'.

Season, Fees & Phone: March to October; $7.00 for a standard site, $11.00 for a partial hookup site; 14 day limit; Lake O' The Pines CoE Project Office (214) 665-2336.

Camp Notes: If you're inclined to favor smaller (and correspondingly less-busy) campgrounds, this would be your best choice for Lake O' The Pines. Nice camp.

JOHNSON CREEK
Lake O' The Pines/Corps of Engineers Park

Location: North-East Texas north of Longview.

Access: From Texas State Highway 49 at a point 3 miles northwest of Jefferson, travel west on Farm Road 729 for 11 miles to the park access road (0.05 mile west of the Johnson Creek bridge); turn south onto the access road for 0.5 mile, then turn southwest (right) to the campground entrance station; campsites are located in 6 areas along a 1-mile loop drive. **Alternate Access:** From Texas State Highway 155 at its junction with Farm Road 729, proceed southeast on FM 729 for 9 miles to the park turnoff, and continue as above.

Facilities: 85 campsites, including 63 with partial hookups; sites are small+ to medium-sized, with minimal to fair separation; parking pads are paved, medium to medium+ straight-ins; additional leveling will probably be required in most sites; adequate space for large tents, generally sloped; assorted fire appliances; b-y-o firewood is suggested; water at hookup sites and at central faucets; restrooms with showers; disposal station; paved driveways; gas and groceries are available at several points along FM 729.

Activities & Attractions: Swimming beaches; boating; boat launches; fishing; extensive day use facilities adjacent.

Natural Features: Located at the end of a major point of land, on sloping terrain above the north-east shore of Lake O' The Pines, a reservoir on Cypress Creek; sites receive light-medium shade/shelter from a good mixture of tall pines and hardwoods; the lake is surrounded by low, forested hills; elevation 250'.

Season, Fees & Phone: Open all year; $7.00 for a standard site, $11.00 for a partial hookup site; 14 day limit; Lake O' The Pines CoE Project Office (214) 665-2336.

Camp Notes: Like most full-service Corps camps in this region, the campground has a controlled-access system in order to keep day-tripper traffic to a minimum. But it also has its own separate swim beach and boat launch. Handy.

BUCKHORN CREEK
Lake O' The Pines/Corps of Engineers Park

Location: North-East Texas north of Longview.

Access: From Texas State Highway 49 at a point 3 miles northwest of Jefferson, head west on Farm Road 729 for 8 miles; turn southwest onto Farm Road 726 and proceed 2.4 miles; turn north (right) for 0.15 mile to the campground entrance station and the campsites. **Alternate Access:** From U.S. Highway 259 at a point 3 miles north of Diana, travel east on Farm Road 726 for 17 miles (to 0.4 mile northeast of the north-east end of the dam) to the park access road and continue as above.

Facilities: 99 campsites, including 61 with partial hookups; sites are small to medium-sized, with minimal to fair separation; parking pads are mostly paved (gravel for standard sites), medium to medium+ straight-ins; additional leveling will be required in the majority of sites; adequate, though generally sloped, space for large tents; barbecue grills or fire rings; b-y-o firewood is suggested; water at hookup sites and at central faucets; restrooms with showers; holding tank disposal station; paved driveways; gas and camper supplies 6 miles west on FM 726, gas and groceries are available on FM 729.

Activities & Attractions: Boating; boat launch; fishing (bass, catfish, crappie).

Natural Features: Located on sloping, rolling terrain around a small bay at the southeast end of Lake O' The Pines, a reservoir on Cypress Creek; sites receive light to medium shade/shelter from tall pines and hardwoods; the lake is bordered by low, forested hills; elevation 250'.

Season, Fees & Phone: March to October; $7.00 for a standard site, $11.00 for a partial hookup site; 14 day limit; Lake O' The Pines CoE Project Office (214) 665-2336.

Camp Notes: If the north-south-east-west access instructions above seem a trifle foggy, it's because the long, slender lake lies in a northwest-southeast line. Unlike the typical reservoir, the dam is at an angle across the line of the lake.

BRUSHY CREEK
Lake O' The Pines/Corps of Engineers Park

Location: North-East Texas north of Longview.

Access: From Texas State Highway 49 at a point 3 miles northwest of Jefferson, proceed west on Farm Road 729 for 8 miles; turn southwest (left) onto Farm Road 726 and drive 5.1 miles (to just past the south-west end of the dam); turn north (right) for 0.1 mile to the campground entrance station; just beyond the entrance, turn northwest (left) and continue for 0.9 mile to the campground. **Alternate Access:** From U.S. Highway 259 at a point 3 miles north of Diana, travel east on Farm Road 726 for 14 miles to the park access road and continue as above.

Facilities: 104 campsites, including 71 with partial hookups, in a complex of loops and sub-loops; sites are small+, with minimal to fair separation; parking pads are mostly paved, (gravel parking for standard sites), medium to medium+ straight-ins; additional leveling will be required in most sites; large tent areas, some are sloped; barbecue grills or fire rings; b-y-o firewood is suggested; water at hookup sites and at central faucets; restrooms with showers; holding tank disposal station; paved driveways; gas and camper supplies are available 3.5 miles west on FM 726.

Activities & Attractions: Swimming beach; boat launch; fishing.

Natural Features: Located on a slope at the southeast end of Lake O' The Pines, a flood control and water supply reservoir on Cypress Creek; sites are moderately shaded by tall pines and hardwoods; elevation 250'.

Season, Fees & Phone: Open all year; $7.00 for a standard site, $11.00 for a partial hookup site; 14 day limit; Lake O' The Pines CoE Project Office (214) 665-2336.

Camp Notes: If you arrive after dark on the gatekeeper's night off (but before the bewitching hour when the gate is locked), it'll be no easy task to grope your way around the campground. Just don't overshoot the loops and end up in the drink. With luck, one of the nice, lakeside sites will be available. Things will look much better in the morning.

CADDO LAKE
Caddo Lake State Park

Location: East border of Texas northeast of Longview.

Access: From Texas State Highway 43 at a point 1 mile north of Karnack, 14 miles northeast of Marshall, and 1 mile south of the Cypress Bayou bridge, take Farm Road 2198 east for 1 mile; turn north onto Park Road 2 to the park entrance station/headquarters; continue ahead for another mile to the camping areas.

Facilities: 48 campsites, including 20 with partial hookups and 8 with full hookups, in 3 strings; (8 units with screened shelters are also available); sites are small to medium-sized, level, with good to very good separation; parking pads are paved, medium-length straight-ins for standard and partial hook-ups, or long pull-throughs for full hookup units; adequate space for large tents on tent pads; barbecue grills and fire rings; b-y-o firewood; water at faucets throughout; restrooms with showers; holding tank disposal station; paved driveways; gas and groceries are available near the park and in Karnack.

Activities & Attractions: Visitor center with displays related to history and natural history of the area; 0.75-mile Caddo Forest Nature Trail; 3-mile hiking trail; fishing; fishing pier (on Sawmill Pond); boating; boat launch; playground.

Natural Features: Located near the south bank of Big Cypress Bayou, the headwater of Caddo Lake, and adjacent to a mill pond off of the bayou; vegetation consists of tall pines and hardwoods which provide ample shade/shelter for most sites; bordered by very dense forest and cypress swamps; total lake area is 32,700 acres; elevation 200'.

Season, Fees & Phone: Open all year; reservations recommended for weekends year 'round; please see Appendix for additional reservation information and standard Texas state park fees; park office (214) 679-3351.

Camp Notes: Caddo Lake is steeped in Indian mythology, and backwoods tales and good ol' campfire yarns. According Caddo Indian legend, the lake was created when an earthquake created a rift that quickly filled with water. In scientific actuality, the lake was formed by the Great Raft, a series of natural log jams that blocked the Red River and backed up the water into its tributaries. The lake is a maze of bayous, channels and cypress swamps. The park deserves at least one trip to see it. Definitely a unique spot.

TYLER: NORTH
Tyler State Park

Location: East Texas north of Tyler.

Access: From Interstate 20 Exit 562 for Tyler, Hawkins, and Tyler State Park, head north on Farm Road 14 for 2 miles; turn west (left) onto Park Road 16 and proceed 0.2 mile to the park entrance station/headquarters; continue ahead for 0.5 mile to a fork; bear right for 0.05 mile to 2 miles to (in listed order) the *Cedar Point*, *Lakeview*, and *Big Pine* areas.

Facilities: *Cedar Point*: 20 campsites with partial hookups; *Lakeview*: 18 campsites with partial hookups; *Big Pine*: 39 campsites with full hookups; sites are small+, with nominal to fair separation; parking pads are hard-surfaced, medium to long pull-throughs or straight-ins for partial hookups, long pull-throughs for full hookups; most pads will require additional leveling; available tent space is small and sloped; assorted fire facilities; b-y-o firewood; water at sites; restrooms with showers; holding tank disposal station; paved driveways; complete supplies and services are available in Tyler.

Activities & Attractions: Swimming beach; hiking trails; nature trail; fishing (stocked bass and catfish, bream); fishing pier; limited boating (5 mph); amphitheater.

Natural Features: Located on hilly terrain above the north shore of a 64-acre lake in the East Texas Pineywoods; sites receive light-medium to medium shade/shelter from tall pines and hardwoods; elevation 500'.

Season, Fees & Phone: Open all year; 14 day limit; reservations recommended for weekends; please see Appendix for additional reservation information and standard Texas state park fees; park office (214) 597-5338.

Camp Notes: Fishing in the spring fed lake is said to be excellent. The lake is regularly stocked with channel catfish and black bass; it also produces good catches of sunfish. The lake's 400-foot swimming beach is along the north shore. It's within walking distance of many of the campsites in the Lakeview and Cedar Point loops.

Texas 163

TYLER: SOUTH
Tyler State Park

Location: East Texas north of Tyler.

Access: From Interstate 20 Exit 562 for Tyler, Hawkins, and Tyler State Park, head north on Farm Road 14 for 2 miles; turn west (left) onto Park Road 16 and proceed 0.2 mile to the park entrance station/headquarters; continue ahead for 0.5 mile to a fork; bear left for 0.5 mile to 1 mile to (in listed order) the *Sumac Bend*, *Hickory Hollow*, *Red Oak*, and *Dogwood Ridge* areas.

Facilities: *Sumac Bend*: 8 standard sites; *Hickory Hollow*: 10 standard campsites; *Red Oak*: 14 standard campsites: *Dogwood Ridge*: 9 standard campsites; (35 units with screened shelters, a large group standard camp, and a large group trailer camp with partial hookups are also available nearby); sites are small to medium-sized, with nominal to fairly good separation; parking pads are hard-surfaced, short to medium-length straight-ins; most pads will require additional leveling; tent spaces vary, but are generally sloped; Red Oak has large tent pads; assorted fire facilities; b-y-o firewood; water at faucets throughout; restrooms with showers nearby; paved driveways; complete supplies and services are available in Tyler.

Activities & Attractions: Swimming beach; hiking trails; nature trail; fishing (stocked bass and catfish, bream); fishing pier; limited boating (5 mph); amphitheater.

Natural Features: Located on hilly terrain above the south shore of a small lake; sites receive light-medium to medium+ shade/shelter from tall pines and hardwoods; elevation 500'.

Season, Fees & Phone: Open all year; reservations recommended for weekends; please see Appendix for additional reservation information and standard Texas state park fees; park office (214) 597-5338.

Camp Notes: Beautiful, woodsy park. Most sites don't have lake views but it's "right down there". If you're camping in a tent, perhaps the best overall sites are in the Red Oak loop. Red Oak not only has large tent pads, but the sites are good-sized as well. However, be prepared to do some sloped slumbering if you select an earthen tent spot in any of the four tent loops.

Texas 164

MARTIN CREEK LAKE
Martin Creek Lake State Recreation Area

Location: East Texas southeast of Longview.

Access: From Texas State Highway 43 at a point 4 miles southwest of Tatum and 15 miles northeast of Henderson, turn southeast onto Farm Road 1716 and proceed 0.9 mile; turn south/southeast (right) onto Rusk County Road 2181D for 0.15 mile to the park entrance station; continue ahead for another 0.2 mile, then bear west (right) for a last 0.2 mile to the campground.

Facilities: 60 campsites with partial hookups; (2 primitive camping areas and 21 units with screened shelters are also available); sites are small+ to medium-sized, with fair to good separation; parking pads are paved, mostly medium-length straight-ins; a bit of additional leveling may be needed in some sites; adequate space for medium to large tents; some framed tent pads; ramadas (sun shelters) for a few sites; fire rings; b-y-o firewood; water at sites; restrooms with showers; holding tank disposal station; paved driveways; limited supplies and services are available in Tatum.

Activities & Attractions: Swimming beach; playground; boating; boat launches; extensive day use facilities; fishing for largemouth bass, crappie, channel cat and sunfish; (the water used as a coolant for the local coal-fired power plant warms the lake in winter, and is said to help produce very good fishing as a result).

Natural Features: Located near the north shore of 5000-acre Martin Creek Lake; most sites are very well-shaded/sheltered by tall pines and hardwoods; encircled by dense forest; elevation 350'.

Season, Fees & Phone: Open all year; 14 day limit; please see Appendix for reservation information and standard Texas state park fees; park office (214) 836-4336.

Camp Notes: One of the primitive camping areas is on a good-sized, well-wooded island which is reachable via a long, pedestrian boardwalk and a trail, or in a boat. The camp is on a pair of coves at the opposite (east) side of the island from the picnic spots, so there's still enough of the ol' spirit of adventure associated with island camping. Nifty idea.

RUSK
Rusk-Palestine State Park

Location: East Texas northwest of Nacogdoches.

Access: From U.S. Highway 84 at a point 3.3 miles west of its junction with U.S. 69 in Rusk, 28 miles east of Palestine, turn south onto Park Road 76 and proceed south, then southeast for 0.4 mile to the park entrance station/headquarters; continue ahead for 0.15 mile to the A (full hookup) loop; or for an additional 0.1 mile (across the choo-choo track) to the B (partial hookup) area.

Facilities: 94 campsites, including 62 with partial hookups and 32 with full hookups, in areas; sites are generally small+ to medium-sized, with nominal to fair separation; parking pads are hard-surfaced, short to medium-length straight-ins in the B area, or long pull-throughs in the A loop; a smidgen of additional leveling may be required in some sites; medium to large tent spaces; barbecue grills and fire rings; b-y-o firewood; water at sites; restrooms with showers; holding tank disposal station; paved driveways; adequate supplies and services are available in Rusk.

Activities & Attractions: Texas State Railroad terminal; 4-hour round-trip from here to Palestine, seasonally (extra charge); tennis courts; limited fishing; fishing pier.

Natural Features: Located on slightly hilly/bumpy terrain; sites receive light-medium to medium shade from tall pines and hardwoods; a small lake/pond (stocked with white bass, catfish, perch) lies a short distance south of the campground; elevation 500'.

Season, Fees & Phone: Open all year; 14 day limit; reservations recommended for weekends, March to November; please see Appendix for additional reservation information and standard Texas state park fees; park office (214) 683-5126.

Camp Notes: A trip on the gleaming yellow Texas State Railroad is a high point of a trip to this region. The railroad tracks pass right by the campground (so does the highway, for that matter). The train crew gives you plenty of "toots" to signal an arrival or departure. What the heck--that's the fun of it all. No night trains, anyway.

MISSION TEJAS
Mission Tejas State Historical Park

Location: East Texas west of Nacogdoches.

Access: From Texas State Highway 21 at the south end of the hamlet of Weches, 21 miles northeast of Crockett, turn northwest to the park entrance/headquarters; continue ahead for 0.5 mile to the campground.

Facilities: 15 campsites, including 7 with partial hookups and 5 with full hookups; sites are small to medium-sized, with nominal separation; parking pads are gravel, medium-length straight-ins; additional leveling will be needed in most sites; enough space for small to medium-sized tents, though a little sloped; barbecue grills and fire rings; b-y-o firewood; water at all sites; restrooms with showers; holding tank disposal station; paved driveways; gas and groceries are available in Weches.

Activities & Attractions: Mission San Francisco de los Tejas, first Spanish mission in Texas (established in 1690), rebuilt by the Civilian Conservation Corps (in 1935); original settler's log home; hiking trail; nature trail (a nice guide booklet is available); playground.

Natural Features: Located on sloping terrain along a stream bed; sites receive medium shade/shelter from towering pines and hardwoods; surrounded by rather dense forest; a small pond is several yards east of the campground; elevation 350'.

Season, Fees & Phone: Open all year; 14 day limit; please see Appendix for reservation information and standard Texas state park fees; park office (409) 687-2394.

Camp Notes: How many parks can you name which have an old mission in the center of the camp loop? Well, this one does. Actually, the present mission building was constructed of logs and shingles the way the CCC *thought* it should look. But let's not be finicky. The reconstruction serves well as a reminder of a singularly significant event in Texas history.

RATCLIFF LAKE
Davy Crockett National Forest

Location: East Texas southwest of Nacogdoches.

Access: From Texas State Highway 7 at a point 1 mile southwest of Ratcliff, 2.5 miles northeast of Kennard, 20 miles northeast of Crockett, turn north onto the recreation area access road (paved) and proceed 1 mile (around to the north side of the lake) to the main complex of camp loops; or follow the main driveway for another 0.5 mile to the small loop on the east shore.

Facilities: 68 campsites, including about 21 with electrical hookups; sites are small+ to medium-sized, reasonably level, with good to very good separation; parking pads are paved, short to medium-length straight-ins; large, framed tent pads; fire rings; firewood is available for gathering; water at several faucets; restrooms and natural temperature showers; holding tank disposal station; paved driveways; gas and groceries are available in Kennard and Ratcliff.

Activities & Attractions: Hiking trails; fishing; limited boating (hand-powered or electric motors); amphitheater.

Natural Features: Located on the north and east shores of several-acre Ratcliff Lake; sites are quite well shaded/sheltered by tall hardwoods and some pines; some lake views; surrounded by dense forest; elevation 350'.

Season, Fees & Phone: Open all year; $6.00 for a standard site, $9.00 for an electrical hookup site; 14 day limit; Neches Ranger District, Crockett, (409) 544-2046.

Camp Notes: This is the second time around, so to speak, for this national forest. As was the case with the other national forests in Texas, these lands, which, of course, were all originally in the public domain, were obtained by private timber interests in the 1800's. Because of subsequent owners' inability to protect them from theft and fire, (and to pay the taxes on them during the Great Depression), the lands were re-acquired, consolidated into a single national forest, and named for the folk hero, former congressman and defender of the Alamo.

RAGTOWN
Sabine National Forest

Location: East Texas east of Nacogdoches.

Access: From Texas State Highway 87 at a point 6.5 miles southeast of Shelbyville, 23 miles northwest of Milam, turn east onto Farm Road 139 and travel 6.7 miles to its junction with Farm Road 3184; continue east on Farm Road 3184 for 3.7 miles; at the end of Farm Road 3184, pick up Forest Road 132 (paved) for a final 1.5 miles to the campground entrance; continue for an additional 0.4 mile to the campsites.

Facilities: 25 campsites; sites are small+ to medium-sized, with good separation; parking pads are paved, short to long straight-ins, many are extra wide; many pads will require a touch of additional leveling; large, framed tent pads in most sites; barbecue grills and/or fireplaces; firewood is available for gathering; water at central faucets; restrooms with natural-temperature showers; auxiliary vault facilities; holding tank disposal station; paved driveways; gas and groceries in Shelbyville; nearest source of adequate supplies and services is Center.

Natural Features: Located on a short bluff above the west shore of Toledo Bend Reservoir, an impoundment on the Sabine River; most sites are very well shaded/sheltered by tall hardwoods and pines, some decorated with hanging moss; glimpses of the lake; slightly hilly terrain in the surrounding area; elevation 250'.

Activities & Attractions: Mother Nature's Pathway nature trail; boating; boat launch; fishing.

Season, Fees & Phone: March to October; $5.00; 14 day limit; Tenaha Ranger District, San Augustine, (409) 275-2632.

Camp Notes: A number of the campsites, even though they're "singles", have two tables and two tent pads. (They might come in handy if you have a big family--or if you want to ask the rest of the campers in the neighborhood over for a catfish dinner or to spend the night.) This really is a fine forest camp.

RED HILLS LAKE
Sabine National Forest

Location: East Texas east of Nacogdoches.

Access: From Texas State Highway 87 at a point 3.7 miles north of Milam, 23 miles southeast of Shelbyville, turn east onto a paved access road and proceed 0.4 mile to the campground; turn left or right to the campsites.

Facilities: 27 campsites, including a half-dozen with electrical hookups, in 3 loops; sites are small to medium-sized, with fair to good separation; parking pads are paved or gravel, short to medium-length straight-ins or pull-offs; most pads will require additional leveling; medium to large tent areas; some framed tent pads; barbecue grills and/or fireplaces; some firewood is available for gathering in the area; water at several faucets; restrooms with natural-temperature showers; paved driveways; limited+ supplies and services are available in Hemphill.

Activities & Attractions: Swimming beach (extra fee); pier; Tower Trail; limited boating (person propulsion); boat launch; some fishing (mostly for kids).

Natural Features: Located around the shore and on a hillside above the shore of several-acre Red Hills Lake; sites receive moderately dense shade/shelter from tall pines and hardwoods; closely encircled by low, heavily forested hills; elevation 300'.

Season, Fees & Phone: March to October; $6.00 for a standard site, $9.00 for an electrical hookup site; 14 day limit; Yellowpine Ranger District, Hemphill, (409) 787-3870.

Camp Notes: This is one of two national forest campgrounds which are easy-in-easy-out stops along Texas 87. The other camp, Willow Oak on Toledo Bend Reservoir, can be reached from a point 15 miles south of Hemphill, then 0.6 mile east. Willow Oak has about a dozen park n' walk camp/picnic sites, water and vaults, right by the boat ramp. It's all your's for just a few greenbacks per night.

INDIAN MOUNDS
Sabine National Forest

Location: East Texas southeast of Nacogdoches.

Access: From Texas State Highway 87 near the north side of the city of Hemphill, turn east onto Farm Road 83 and travel 7 miles; turn south onto Farm Road 3382 and proceed 3.8 miles; at the end of Farm Road 3382, turn southeast (left) and continue on pavement for 0.6 mile to a "Y" intersection; turn right for a final 0.6 mile to the campsites. (Special Note: the above access includes no gravel travel; it would be all too easy to continue straight ahead on the gravel road at the end of FM 3382, only to suddenly find yourself on a narrow path deep in the woods, with no turnaround space; a pair of *Double Eagle* editors now know this.)

Facilities: Approximately 30 campsites; sites are large, with good separation; parking pads are hard-surfaced, short+ to long straight-ins; additional leveling will be needed in some sites; adequate space for large tents on cleared earth or framed tent pads; fire rings; firewood is available for gathering in the area; water at several faucets; vault facilities; paved driveway; limited+ supplies and services are available in Hemphill.

Activities & Attractions: Boating; boat launch; fishing.

Natural Features: Located on a short bluff above the west shore of Toledo Bend Reservoir, an impoundment on the Sabine River; vegetation consists of tall hardwoods, super-sized pines and a considerable quantity of lower vegetation which provide moderately dense shade/shelter for all sites; bordered by quite steep terrain; elevation 250'.

Season, Fees & Phone: March to October; $4.00; 14 day limit; Yellowpine Ranger District, Hemphill, (409) 787-3870.

Camp Notes: Much of the original campground has been abandoned and left to the primeval forest from whence it was hewn. There must be a message in this.

MILL CREEK
Sam Rayburn Reservoir/Corps of Engineers Park

Location: East Texas southeast of Nacogdoches.

Access: From U.S. Highway 96 in the small community of Brookeland (7 miles south of Pineland, 14 miles north of Jasper), turn west onto Loop 149 and proceed 0.9 mile; continue west on Spur 165 for 0.6 mile to the campground entrance station; campsites are directly ahead or 0.2 mile to the right of the entrance.

Facilities: 110 campsites, including 53 with electrical hookups and 57 with partial hookups; sites are medium-sized, roughly half are level, with fair to good separation; parking pads are paved, medium to long, mostly straight-ins; large, grassy areas for tents; ramadas (sun shelters) for many sites; barbecue grills; some firewood may be available for gathering in the surrounding area, b-y-o is suggested; water at some sites and at several faucets; restrooms with showers; holding tank disposal station; paved driveways; gas and groceries on Highway 96; limited supplies and services are available in Pineland.

Activities & Attractions: Swimming beach; boating; boat launch; fishing; day use facilities.

Natural Features: Located on a large, slightly rolling, grassy flat on a small point at the east end of 115,000-acre Sam Rayburn Reservoir; sites receive light to medium shade/shelter from tall pines and hardwoods; bordered by dense woodland; elevation 200'.

Season, Fees & Phone: Open all year; $11.00; 14 day limit; Sam Rayburn Reservoir CoE Project Office (409) 384-5716.

Camp Notes: The small, main point of land on which the campground is situated is partly split by a narrow cove, providing even more water frontage. Most of the campsites thus have lake views, and quite a few border the cove. Suggestion: check out the loop to the right of the entrance first. Mill Creek is, deservedly, a very popular place.

SAN AUGUSTINE
Sam Rayburn Reservoir/Corps of Engineers Park

Location: East Texas southeast of Nacogdoches.

Access: From U.S. Highway 96 in Pineland, head west on Farm Road 83 for 5.3 miles; turn south onto Farm Road 1751 and proceed 4 miles to the campground entrance station; turn right into the first loop, or continue ahead for 0.45 mile to the main camp area. **Alternate Access:** From Texas State Highway 147 in Broaddus, travel east on Farm Road 83 for 13 miles to Farm Road 1751, and continue as above.

Facilities: 100 campsites with partial hookups; sites are small+, with nominal to fair separation; parking pads are paved/packed gravel, short to long straight-ins; many pads will require additional leveling; large tent areas, generally a bit sloped; ramadas (sun shelters) for most sites; barbecue grills; some firewood is available for gathering in the area; water at sites; restrooms with showers; holding tank disposal station; paved driveways; limited supplies and services are available in Pineland.

Activities & Attractions: Boating; boat launch; fishing.

Natural Features: Located on a point on a major arm (Ayisn Bayou) on the north-east shore of Sam Rayburn Reservoir; sites receive medium shade/shelter from tall pines and hardwoods; bordered by dense forest; elevation 200'.

Season, Fees & Phone: Open all year; $11.00; 14 day limit; Sam Rayburn Reservoir CoE Project Office (409) 384-5716.

Camp Notes: After trying to find your way through the camp's maze of loop driveways, you may suddenly acquire an unexplained craving for a piece of cheese, and an aversion for cats. The nearby town of Pineland is notable for at least two reasons: according to the local highway signs, its official population is 1111; it is also the location of Farm to Market Road 1, (or Farm Road 1 or just plain FM 1).

POWELL
Sam Rayburn Reservoir/Corps of Engineers Park

Location: East Texas southeast of Nacogdoches.

Access: From U.S. Highway 96 in Pineland, travel west on Farm Road 83 for 9.5 miles; turn south onto Farm Road 705 and proceed 11 miles; turn east (left) onto the park access road and proceed 0.25 mile to the park entrance station and the campsites. **Alternate Access:** From Texas State Highway 147 in Broaddus, travel east on Farm Road 83 for 8.5 miles to Farm Road 705, and continue as above.

Facilities: 84 campsites; sites are good-sized, with fair to good separation; parking pads are gravel, medium-length straight-ins; large, grass-and-pine-needle-covered tent areas; ramadas (sun shelters) for a few sites; barbecue grills and fire rings; some firewood is available for gathering in the area; water at central faucets; restrooms with showers; auxiliary vault facilities; holding tank disposal station; paved driveways; gas and groceries at the junction of FM's 83 & 705; limited supplies and services are available in Pineland.

Activities & Attractions: Swimming beach; boating; boat launch; marina; fishing (generally good for black bass, "Florida" bass, stripers, white bass and crappie, catfish, bream).

Natural Features: Located on gently rolling terrain at the southeast tip of a peninsula extending from the north shore of 115,000-acre Sam Rayburn Reservoir; sites receive medium to moderately dense shade/shelter from tall pines and hardwoods; elevation 200'.

Season, Fees & Phone: Open all year; $9.00; 14 day limit; Sam Rayburn Reservoir CoE Project Office (409) 384-5716.

Camp Notes: Except possibly during Memorial Day weekend, you can count on getting a site here when all of the other full-service campgrounds around the lake are "full-up". Subjectively, this one is several notches down on the tally board of the fee camps around the lake. Not that there's anything really wrong with it. The others are just better.

Texas 174

RAYBURN
Sam Rayburn Reservoir/Corps of Engineers Park

Location: East Texas southeast of Nacogdoches.

Access: From U.S. Highway 96 in Pineland, travel west on Farm Road 83 for 9.5 miles; turn south onto Farm Road 705 and proceed 11.1 miles; turn west (left) onto Farm Road 3127 for 1 mile, then south on Spur 3127 for 0.7 mile; turn east (left) for a final 0.6 mile to the park entrance; campsites are scattered along and near the shore throughout the park. **Alternate Access:** From Texas State Highway 147 in Broaddus, travel east on Farm Road 83 for 8.5 miles to Farm Road 705, and continue as above.

Facilities: 77 campsites; sites are small+, with fair separation; parking surfaces are grass/earth, tolerably level, medium-length straight-ins/pull-offs; ample space for large tents; ramadas (sun shelters) for a few sites; assorted fire facilities; some firewood is available for gathering in the area; water at several faucets; vault facilities; holding tank disposal station; paved driveways; gas and groceries at the junction of FM's 83 & 705; limited supplies and services are available in Pineland.

Activities & Attractions: Boating; boat launch; fishing.

Natural Features: Located on a grassy slope at the southernmost tip of a peninsula extending from the north shore of Sam Rayburn Reservoir, a 115,000-acre impoundment on the Neches River; sites receive medium to moderately dense shade/shelter from lofty pines and hardwoods; bordered by dense forest; elevation 200'.

Season, Fees & Phone: Open all year; no fee (subject to change); 14 day limit; Sam Rayburn Reservoir CoE Project Office (409) 384-5716.

Camp Notes: It's curious that this large, but simple, park--named for the distinguished Texan who served as Speaker of the U.S. House of Representatives longer than any other man in history--should have remained in this relatively uncomplicated state of development. Maybe, though, "Mr. Sam" would have preferred it this way.

Texas 175

JOHNSON HILL
Sam Rayburn Reservoir/Corps of Engineers Park

Location: East Texas southeast of Nacogdoches.

Access: From Texas State Highway 147 at a point 3.5 miles south of Broaddus, 1 mile north of the causeway which spans the middle of Sam Rayburn Reservoir, 9 miles north of Zavalla, turn west onto Farm Road 2851 and proceed 0.9 mile to the campground; continue ahead or turn to the left to the campsites.

Facilities: Approximately 30 campsites; sites are medium to large, with fair to good separation; parking pads are gravel, medium to long straight-ins; ample space for large tents; ramadas (sun shelters) for a few sites; some fire rings, plus a few barbecue grills; firewood is available for gathering in the area; water at central faucets; vault facilities; paved driveways; gas and groceries in Broaddus.

Activities & Attractions: Designated swimming beach; boating; boat launch; day use facilities.

Natural Features: Located on the north shore of Sam Rayburn Reservoir; sites are moderately shaded by tall pines and hardwoods; bordered by dense forest; elevation 200'.

Season, Fees & Phone: March to November; no fee (subject to change); 14 day limit; Sam Rayburn Reservoir CoE Project Office (409) 384-5716.

Camp Notes: The best sites here--those closest to the lake--have been tagged for day use. Most of the campsites, however, are situated away from the lake, back in the woods. Still not too bad for a freebie, though. There's another campground on this side of the lake not far from here that might be worth a try: Harvey Creek, an Angelina National Forest recreation area. To get there, from Texas Highway 147 in Broaddus, take Farm Road 83 southeast for 3.1 miles, then Farm Road 2390 south for 5.5 miles. Harvey Creek has about three dozen sites, drinking water, vaults, day use facilities and a boat ramp. It's right along the middle-north shore of the main body of the lake.

Texas 176

CASSELLS-BOYKIN
Cassells-Boykin State Park

Location: East Texas southeast of Nacogdoches.

Access: From Texas State Highway 147 at a point 0.6 mile south of the causeway which spans the middle of Sam Rayburn Reservoir, 8 miles south of Broaddus, 6 miles north of Zavalla, turn northwest onto Farm Road 3123 and proceed 0.8 mile to the park entrance; turn right or left to the camp areas.

Facilities: 30 campsites in 2 loops; sites are medium-sized, with fair separation; parking pads are gravel, long straight-ins; adequate space for large tents; fire rings for a few sites; b-y-o firewood; water at central faucets; vault facilities; holding tank disposal station; paved driveways; gas and groceries within 1 mile; limited supplies and services are available in Zavalla.

Activities & Attractions: Boating; boat launch; fishing.

Natural Features: Located on a short bluff and along the shoreline on a small point on the south shore of Sam Rayburn Reservoir; most sites receive light-medium to medium shaded/shelter from pines and hardwoods; bordered by dense forest; elevation 200'.

Season, Fees & Phone: Open all year; 14 day limit; please see Appendix for standard Texas state park fees; park office (409) 384-5231.

Camp Notes: Really, just about the only reason for camping here would be to have a lake view campsite conveniently close to a fourth-priority highway. The state park's facilities are nearly dead-ringers for those at Johnson Hill, the corresponding CoE camp just off this highway on the north side of the lake. Most of the sites at Johnson Hill lack waterfront scenery--but the Corps camp is a freebie. Otherwise, for not much more *dinero*, there are several other, far superior, places around Rayburn Reservoir at which you can park it and pitch it. (Possibly Cassells-Boykin will have been improved by the time you arrive in the neighborhood.)

Texas 177

CANEY CREEK
Angelina National Forest

Location: East Texas southeast of Nacogdoches.

Access: From Texas State Highway 63 at a point 4.3 miles east of Zavalla, 28 miles northwest of Jasper, turn northeast onto Farm Road 2743 and proceed 5.3 miles; turn north (left) onto Forest Road 336 (paved) and continue for 1.3 miles to the campground.

Facilities: 128 campsites in 5 loops; sites are medium-sized, basically level, with nominal to good overall separation; parking pads are mostly hard-surfaced, medium to long straight-ins; large, framed tent pads; fireplaces; firewood is available for gathering in the area; water at central faucets; restrooms with natural temperature showers; holding tank disposal station; paved driveways; limited supplies and services are available in Zavalla.

Activities & Attractions: Swimming beach (extra charge); short nature trail; boating; boat launch; fishing; amphitheater.

Natural Features: Located on a point on the south shore of Sam Rayburn Reservoir; sites are very well shaded/sheltered by large hardwoods and pines; bordered by dense forest; el. 200'.

Season, Fees & Phone: Open all year; $6.00; 14 day limit; Angelina Ranger District, Lufkin, (409) 634-7709.

Camp Notes: Seasoned, national forest campers may occasionally refer to a particular campground as being a "classic, little forest camp". Well, this one could be termed a "classic, big forest camp". There may very well be in excess of six score of sites in the five loops, but you'll not see much of your loopmates, let alone the rest of the campground. The loop driveways closely parallel the shoreline, which consists of a half-dozen small coves. Although most sites are actually quite close to the water, only some have lake views, and even then it's typically a glimpse through the trees. On the whole, it's a choice spot.

Texas 178

SANDY CREEK
Angelina National Forest

Location: East Texas southeast of Nacogdoches.

Access: From Texas State Highway 63 at a point 15 miles southeast of Zavalla, 17 miles northwest of Jasper, turn north onto Forest Road 333 and proceed 2.6 miles to the campground.

Facilities: 27 campsites, including several park n' walk units, in 3 loops; sites are small+ to medium-sized, with fair to fairly good separation; parking pads are paved/gravel, short to medium-length straight-ins; most pads will require additional leveling; enough space for small to medium-sized tents in most sites; large, framed tent pads for some units; fireplaces; firewood is available for gathering in the area; water at several faucets; vault facilities; natural temperature showers; paved driveways; limited supplies in Zavalla, adequate+ supplies and services in Jasper.

Activities & Attractions: Swimming beach (extra charge); boating; boat launch; fishing.

Natural Features: Located on the top and sides of a short ridge on a small point on the south shore of 115,000-acre Sam Rayburn Reservoir; sites are well shaded/sheltered by large hardwoods and pines; bordered by dense forest; elevation 200'.

Season, Fees & Phone: Open all year; $5.00; 14 day limit; Angelina Ranger District, Lufkin, (409) 634-7709.

Camp Notes: Most visitors to this region are oriented toward camping on Sam Rayburn Reservoir, be it at a 'basic' camp like this one, or at one of the full-featured CoE facilities. However, for a less-grand, but not less-pleasant, experience, you might want to try Boykin Springs, an Angelina National Forest camp that's off the well-worn path. It can be reached from Highway 63, 4 miles northwest of the Sandy Creek turnoff and 10.7 miles southeast of Zavalla, then via Forest Road 313 south for 3 miles. Boykin Springs has a couple-dozen sites, water, restrooms, hiking trail and a 10-acre lake.

Texas 179

TWIN DIKES
Sam Rayburn Reservoir/Corps of Engineers Park

Location: East Texas southeast of Nacogdoches.

Access: From U.S. Highway 96 at a point 9 miles north of Jasper and 11 miles south of Pineland, turn west onto Recreation Road 255 (R 255, paved) and proceed 4.8 miles; turn north (right) to the campground entrance station; campsites are situated left and right of the entrance. **Alternate Access:** From Texas State Highway 63 at a point 15 miles northwest of Jasper and 17 miles southeast of Zavalla, head northeast on Recreation Road 255 for 8 miles (to a point 0.8 mile east of the dam) to the campground turnoff and continue as above.

Facilities: 38 campsites; sites are medium-sized, with nominal to fair separation; parking surfaces are gravel/earth, pull-offs or straight-ins, generally of ample size; additional leveling (or maneuvering) will be needed in most sites; medium to large areas for tents, mostly sloped; ramadas (sun shelters) for a few sites; barbecue grills, plus some fire rings; some firewood is available for gathering in the area; water at several faucets; restrooms with showers; holding tank disposal station; paved main driveways, gravel sub-drives; gas and groceries within 3 miles.

Activities & Attractions: Boating; boat launch; fishing (one of the best for bass); visitor center, 3 miles west, at the dam.

Natural Features: Located on a bluff above the south shore of Sam Rayburn Reservoir; sites receive medium shade from tall hardwoods and some pines; bordered by moderately dense forest; elevation 200'.

Season, Fees & Phone: Open all year; $9.00; 14 day limit; Sam Rayburn Reservoir CoE Project Office (409) 384-5716.

Camp Notes: Call this one a "practical" or "usable" campground. OK, so it may not have the first-cabin facilities or manicured landscaping of some of the more "polished" campgrounds in the state. But many campsites have lake views, quite a few are lakeside, and a number of them are good-sized and well-spaced. Worth looking at.

Texas 180

MAGNOLIA RIDGE
B.A. Steinhagen Lake/Corps of Engineers Park

Location: East Texas north of Beaumont.

Access: From U.S. Highway 190 at a point 13 miles northeast of Woodville, 1.2 miles west of the causeway which spans Steinhagen Lake, 15 miles southwest of Jasper, turn northwest onto Farm Road 96 and proceed 0.9 mile; turn northeast (right) onto the park access road for another mile to the campground entrance station; continue ahead for 0.35 mile, then turn right, into the campground.

Facilities: 36 campsites, including 27 with partial hookups, in 2 main sections; sites are medium-sized, reasonably level, with nominal to fair separation; parking pads are gravel, medium to long straight-ins; adequate space for medium to large tents; ramadas (sun shelters) for many sites; barbecue grills or fire rings; firewood is available for gathering in the area; water at sites and at central faucets; vault facilities; holding tank disposal station; paved driveways; gas and groceries along the main highway, on both east and west shores of the lake.

Activities & Attractions: Fishing; boating; boat launches.

Natural Features: Located on the northwest shore of B.A. Steinhagen Lake, a reservoir which impounds the Neches River at its confluence with the Angelina River; a very dense forest of hardwoods and pines surrounds the campground; not much of a view of the open lake because of the shoreline "logjam"; alligators ("all sizes of 'em"); elevation 100'.

Season, Fees & Phone: Open all year; $7.00 for a standard site, $9.00 for a partial hookup site; 14 day limit; B.A. Steinhagen Lake CoE Project Office (409) 429-3491.

Camp Notes: You might expect Tarzan, Jane and Cheetah to swing in for dinner. It just *looks* like that kind of place--hanging moss, swinging vines, mysterious swamps, jungle critters, and all that. An interesting, even intriguing, locale. (And if you need to get out of your camper or tent during the night, take a bright light and watch where you step.....)

Texas 181

WALNUT RIDGE
Martin Dies, Jr. State Park

Location: East Texas north of Beaumont.

Access: From U.S. Highway 190 at a point 11 miles southwest of Jasper, 0.1 mile east of the causeway which spans Steinhagen Lake, 17 miles northeast of Woodville, turn north onto Park Road 48 and proceed 0.3 mile to the unit entrance station; continue north for 0.9 mile, then curve south/southwest for a final mile to the campground entrance. (Note: the camp driveway is a one-way half-loop; entry is at the southwest corner of the campground.)

Facilities: 82 campsites, including 58 with partial hookups; (25 units with screened shelters are also available); sites are medium-sized, essentially level, with fair to fairly good separation; parking pads are hard-surfaced, medium-length straight-ins; medium to large areas for tents; assorted fire facilities; b-y-o firewood; water at faucets throughout; restrooms with showers; holding tank disposal station; paved driveways; gas and groceries along the main highway, on both east and west shores of the lake.

Activities & Attractions: Hiking and nature trails; fishing; fishing pier; boating; boat launches; swimming beach (at the Hen House Ridge Unit, south of the main highway).

Natural Features: Located on a large flat on the east shore of 17,000-acre B.A. Steinhagen Lake; sites are sheltered primarily by moderately dense, tall hardwoods; the campground is on a virtual island, surrounded by either the open lake or the brackish backwater; bordered by very dense forest; alligators; elevation 100'.

Season, Fees & Phone: Open all year; 14 day limit; reservations recommended for weekends; please see Appendix for additional reservation information and standard Texas state park fees; park office (409) 384-5231.

Camp Notes: This place will provide you with some idea of what camping in Texas' famous Big Thicket, which lies south and west of here, might be like.

Texas 182

HEN HOUSE RIDGE
Martin Dies, Jr. State Park

Location: East Texas north of Beaumont.

Access: From U.S. Highway 190 at a point 11 miles southwest of Jasper, 0.35 mile east of the causeway which spans Steinhagen Lake, 17 miles northeast of Woodville, turn south onto Park Road 48 and proceed 0.6 mile to the park entrance station/headquarters and the campground.

Facilities: 100 campsites, including 42 with partial hookups and 14 with full hookups; (21 units with screened shelters are also available); sites are medium to medium+ in size, level, with fairly good to very good separation; parking pads are hard-surfaced, medium to long, pull-throughs in the hookup sites, straight-ins in standard sites; generally adequate space for medium to large tents; ramadas (sun shelters) for a few sites; assorted fire facilities; b-y-o firewood; water at faucets throughout; restrooms with showers; disposal station; paved driveways; gas and groceries on the main highway on the east and west shores.

Activities & Attractions: Swimming beach; hiking & nature trails; fishing; fishing pier; boating; boat launch; playground.

Natural Features: Located on the east shore of B.A. Steinhagen Lake; campground vegetation consists of medium-dense, lofty hardwoods and pines, plus some low brush; the campground is bisected by Gum Slough, a narrow backwater of the lake; surrounded by near-level, very heavily wooded terrain; alligators; elevation 100'.

Season, Fees & Phone: Open all year; 14 day limit; reservations recommended for weekends; please see Appendix for additional reservation information and standard Texas state park fees; park office (409) 384-5231.

Camp Notes: It's mostly the standard sites which have good lake views. (Many of the hookup sites have slough views, though.) There are some super standard sites along the beach, at the far south edge of the campground. The state park is named for a Texas state senator from Lufkin.

Texas 183

LAKE LIVINGSTON
Lake Livingston State Recreation Area

Location: East Texas north of Houston.

Access: From U.S. Highway 59 at a point 2.4 miles south of the junction of U.S 59 & U.S. 190 in Livingston, 5 miles north of Goodrich, turn southwest onto Farm Road 1988 and proceed 3.8 miles; turn northwest (right) onto Farm Road 3126 for 0.5 mile, then turn west (left) onto Park Road 65 for 0.2 mile to the park entrance station; continue ahead for another 0.2 mile, then turn south (left) for 0.3 mile, or north (right) for 1 mile, to the camp loops. (Special Access Note: the above access works well if approaching from the north; from the south, on U.S. 59 in Goodrich, head northwest on FM 1988 for 6 miles to pick up FM 3126.)

Facilities: 163 campsites, including 147 with partial hookups, in 4 loops; (10 units with screened shelters are also available); sites are small+ to medium-sized, acceptably level, with good separation; most parking pads are hard-surfaced, medium-length straight-ins; large, framed tent pads; fireplaces; b-y-o firewood; water at sites; restrooms with showers; holding tank disposal stations; paved driveways; adequate supplies and services are available in Livingston.

Activities & Attractions: Fishing; boating; boat launches; 4 miles of hiking and nature trails; swimming pool; activity center; playgrounds; observation tower; amphitheater.

Natural Features: Located on the southeast shore of Lake Livingston, an 85,000-acre reservoir on the Trinity River; sites are well shaded/sheltered by tall pines and hardwoods; bordered by dense woodland; elevation 150'.

Season, Fees & Phone: Open all year; 14 day limit; reservations recommended for most weekends; please see Appendix for additional reservation information and standard Texas state park fees; park office (409) 365-2201.

Camp Notes: Less than a dozen campsites have lake frontage; the remainder are a few minutes' walk or a short drive to the water's edge. Most sites are wooded and quite private.

DOUBLE LAKE
Sam Houston National Forest

Location: East Texas north of Houston.

Access: From Texas State Highway 150 at a point 1.9 mile southwest of midtown Coldspring, (at the southwest city limit), turn south onto Farm Road 2025 and proceed 0.4 mile; turn southeast (left) onto Forest Road 210 (paved) and proceed for another 0.6 mile to the recreation area; bear right for 0.6 mile, or turn left for 0.9 mile, to the campsites. **Alternate Access:** From U.S. Highway 59 at the north edge of Cleveland, take Farm Road 2025 northwest for 16 miles to Forest Road 210 and continue as above.

Facilities: 49 campsites; sites are medium+ in size, with good separation; parking pads are paved, short to medium-length straight-ins; most pads will require some additional leveling; large, framed tent pads; fireplaces; firewood is available for gathering in the area; water at several faucets; restrooms with showers; paved driveways; limited supplies and services are available in Coldspring.

Activities & Attractions: Small, sandy swimming beach (extra charge); fishing (lake is stocked with bass, bream, catfish); limited boating (hand-propelled or small electric motors); access point for the 140-mile-long Lone Star Trail; 5-mile trail to Big Creek Scenic Area; lake shore trail.

Natural Features: Located on the north-east and south-west shores of several-acre Double Lake on the edge of the Big Thicket region; campsites are sheltered/shaded by moderately dense, large hardwoods and some pines; surrounded by very dense forest; elevation 350'.

Season, Fees & Phone: Open all year; $8.00; 14 day limit; San Jacinto Ranger District, Cleveland, (713) 592-6461.

Camp Notes: In early Texas, the Big Thicket was a haven for settlers looking for solitude. During the War Between the States it became a haunt for deserters, draft-dodgers and others trying to avoid the conflict. Nowadays, the remaining natural areas of the Thicket are highly regarded for their scenic, historical and scientific value.

HUNTSVILLE
Huntsville State Park

Location: South-East Texas north of Houston.

Access: From Interstate 45 Exit 109 for Huntsville State Park/Park Road 40 (7 miles south of Huntsville, 6 miles north of New Waverly), proceed west on Park Road 40 for 1.3 miles to the park entrance station; continue ahead for a quarter-mile to a fork (at the interpretive center); bear left to the *Raven Hill* (hookups) and *Coloneh* areas, or bear right to the *Prairie Branch* (hookups) area.

Facilities: 191 campsites, including 64 with partial hookups; (30 units with screened shelters are also available); sites are small+ to medium-sized, with fair separation; parking pads are gravel, mostly medium to long straight-ins (long pull-throughs in Raven Hill); most pads will require at least a little additional leveling; large areas for tents; barbecue grills; b-y-o firewood, (some gatherable wood may be available on adjacent national forest lands); water at faucets throughout; restrooms with showers; holding tank disposal station; paved driveways; complete supplies and services are available in Huntsville.

Activities & Attractions: 8-mile hiking trail around the lake; interpretive center and trail; swimming beach; fishing; fishing piers; limited (size and speed restrictions) boating; boat launch; mini-golf; playground.

Natural Features: Located on a forested slope above 200-acre Lake Raven; sites are shaded/sheltered by moderately dense, tall hardwoods and pines; deer are frequent visitors; surrounded by dense forest; elevation 400'.

Season, Fees & Phone: Open all year; 14-day limit; please see Appendix for reservation information and standard Texas state park fees; park office (409) 295-5644.

Camp Notes: There's quite a bit of history associated with the area. The park was originally constructed of local materials by the CCC back in the 1930's. Sam Houston lived near here, on a plantation he named "Raven Hill" The Cherokee Indians had given Houston the name *Coloneh*, which means "Raven".

STUBBLEFIELD
Sam Houston National Forest

Location: South-East Texas north of Houston.

Access: From Interstate 45, *northbound*, take Exit 102 for New Waverly to the west side of the freeway to Farm Road 1375; travel west on Farm Road 1375 (past the ranger station and across Lake Conroe) for 10.5 miles; turn northwest (right) onto a paved access road and continue for 3 miles (after the first half-mile, the road curves northeasterly); turn south (right) into the campground. **Alternate Access:** From I-45, *southbound*, take Exit 103, then go south for 1.3 miles on a west frontage road to Farm Road 1375 and continue as above.

Facilities: 28 campsites; sites are medium-sized, level, with fair to fairly good separation; parking pads are gravel, short to medium-length straight-ins; ample space for large tents on a grassy surface; fireplaces; firewood is available for gathering; water at several faucets; restrooms with natural-temp showers; paved driveway; limited supplies and services are available in New Waverly.

Activities & Attractions: A segment of the 140-mile-long Lone Star Hiking Trail passes through the campground; off road vehicle (orv) trail.

Natural Features: Located on a forested flat at the northernmost tip of Lake Conroe; tall hardwoods and some tall pines provide medium shade/shelter for most sites; surrounded by dense forest; elevation 400'.

Season, Fees & Phone: Open all year; $5.00; 14 day limit; Raven Ranger District, New Waverly, (409) 344-6205.

Camp Notes: As a guideline, camping is best here in spring and fall, 'cause it's pretty still and steamy here during most of the summer. (The slender portion of Lake Conroe which borders the campground is also still and steamy.) This rec area is sometimes called Stubblefield Lake. Another forest camp in this neck of the woods is Kelly's Pond, with 8 sites, a vault, but no drinking water and no fee. It's accessible by turning south off FM 1375 at the point opposite the turnoff to Stubblefield, then following gravel and dirt roads southeast then southwest for 2 miles.

STEPHEN F. AUSTIN
Stephen F. Austin State Historical Park

Location: South-East Texas west of Houston.

Access: From Interstate 10 Exit 723 for San Felipe (48 miles west of Houston, 3 miles east of Sealy), turn north onto Farm Road 1458 and proceed through San Felipe for 2.1 miles; turn west (left) onto Park Road 38 and proceed west, then northwest for 0.8 mile to the park entrance station; continue ahead for 0.7 mile to the campground.

Facilities: 80 campsites, including 40 with full hookups; in addition, 20 units with screened shelters are also available; sites are medium+, level, with fair to fairly good separation; most parking pads are hard-surfaced, medium-length straight-ins in the standard sites, long pull-throughs in the hookup sites; plenty of tent space on a grassy surface; barbecue grills and fire rings; b-y-o firewood; water at faucets throughout; restrooms with showers; holding tank disposal station; paved driveways; gas and groceries in San Felipe.

Activities & Attractions: Historical points of interest; swimming pool; 18-hole golf course; short hiking trail.

Natural Features: Located on acres and acres of mown lawns, well-sheltered/shaded by large hardwoods; bordered on the north and east by the Brazos River; surrounded by dense woodland; elevation 150'.

Season, Fees & Phone: Open all year; 14 day limit; reservations recommended for spring and fall weekends, particularly for hookup sites; please see Appendix for additional reservation information and standard Texas state park fees; park office (409) 885-3613.

Camp Notes: This entire place is so neatly trimmed, it would be easy to mistake the day use area and campground for the park's golf course. (Hint: The golf course has fewer trees.) The history of the area is as old as Texas itself. Austin ("The Father of Texas") brought the first Texas colonists here under a contract with Mexico.

BRAZOS BEND
Brazos Bend State Park

Location: South-East Texas southwest of Houston.

Access: From U.S. Highway 59 at the exit for Farm Road 762 near Richmond, head south on Farm Road 762 for 17.5 miles; turn east onto Park Road 72 for 0.6 miles to the park entrance station/headquarters; continue east, then north for 3.7 miles to the campground. (Access is also possible from Texas Highway 288, then by traveling west on FM 1462 to the park.)

Facilities: 77 campsites, including 42 with partial hookups, in 2 loops; (14 units with screened shelters and a primitive camping area are also available); sites are small+ to medium-sized, level, with nominal to fairly good separation; parking pads are hard-surfaced, medium to long straight-ins; plenty of space for large tents; barbecue grills and fire rings; b-y-o firewood; water at faucets throughout; restrooms with showers; holding tank disposal station; paved driveways; gas and groceries are available on Farm Road 762.

Activities & Attractions: Interpretive center; hiking trails, nature trails, hike/bike trail; observation deck and tower; playground; fishing; fishing pier.

Natural Features: Located on nicely wooded, mown-grass flats along the Brazos River floodplain on the Gulf Coastal Plain; alligators (one of the best places in the state to view them in the wild); a half-dozen small lakes lie within the park; bordered by dense woodland; total park area is nearly 5000 acres; elevation 100'.

Season, Fees & Phone: Open all year; 14 day limit; reservations recommended far in advance for spring, fall and early winter weekends; please see Appendix for additional reservation information and standard Texas state park fees; park office (409) 553-3243.

Camp Notes: It's easy to see why plans for weekend camping here during much of the year need to be made well in advance. This is one of the most naturally beautiful state parks in Texas. Once you're inside the park amidst all of the almost jungle-like greenery, it's difficult to remember that one of the nation's five largest cities is just 50 miles away. Worth waiting for.

GALVESTON ISLAND
Galveston Island State Park

Location: South-East Texas southwest of Galveston.

Access: From Interstate 45 Exit 1A for 61st Street in Galveston, proceed south on 61st Street (Butterowe St.) for 1.7 miles to Seawall Boulevard/Farm Road 3005; turn southwest (right) onto Seawall and continue for 9.5 miles; turn southeast (left) for 0.15 mile, then southwest (right) for 0.2 mile to the beach area; or turn northwest (right) onto a park road and proceed 1.3 miles to the trailer loop.

Facilities: 170 campsites with partial hookups; (10 units with screened shelters are also available); sites are small+, level and closely spaced; parking pads are hard-surfaced, medium-length straight-ins; ample space for large tents on a surface of mown grass; ramadas (sun/partial wind shelters) for all beach sites; barbecue grills and fire rings; b-y-o firewood; water at faucets throughout; restrooms with showers; holding tank disposal station; paved driveways; gas and groceries are available within 1.5 miles northeast or southwest.

Activities & Attractions: Swimming; interpretive area and trail; (trailer loop is reservable for groups).

Natural Features: Located a few yards from the Gulf (beach area) or on a mown lawn adjacent to a tallgrass plain/marsh (trailer loop) on Galveston Island; no natural shade (b-y-o shade for the trailer loop); sea level.

Season, Fees & Phone: Open all year; 14 day limit; please see Appendix for reservation information and standard Texas state park fees; park office (409) 737-1222.

Camp Notes: Depending upon your architectural preferences, the unique design of the beach camp is either proper, pleasing, stylish, cute, chic, exotic or outlandish. The campsites--set in rows, each site with a slant-roofed, two-sided, port-holed, cast-concrete ramada, with a barbecue out back--might remind you of open-air condos in a beachfront subdivision. The engineering is entirely practical, however. The camp's sturdy structures were designed to withstand the forces of hurricanes that hammer the Gulf Coast from time to time. There's nothing like this campground anywhere else in the West.

SEA RIM
Sea Rim State Park

Location: South-East Texas south of Beaumont.

Access: From Texas State Highway 87 at a point 25 miles southwest of Port Arthur, 10 miles west of the small community of Sabine Pass, 22 miles northeast of High Island, and 52 miles northeast of Galveston, turn south into the park entrance, then jog east and south into the campground.

Facilities: 20 campsites with partial hookups in a parking lot arrangement; (primitive sites with vault facilities are available along several miles of beach, as well as several 'camping platforms', see *Camp Notes* section); sites are very small, level and closely spaced; parking surfaces are paved, short straight-ins; space for free-standing tents on the pavement is inversely proportional to the size of your vehicle; (possible tent-pitching on the beach); barbecue grills; b-y-o firewood; water at faucets throughout; restrooms with showers; holding tank disposal station; gas and groceries are available in Sabine Pass.

Activities & Attractions: Interpretive center; observation deck; 0.7-mile-long boardwalk nature trail through marshlands; fishing and crabbing; beach activities.

Natural Features: Located on the edge of the Coastal Plain, a few yards from the Gulf of Mexico; bounded by an expansive, tallgrass plain/marsh to the north, and a short dune/bluff on the Gulf side; alligators; abundant waterfowl in winter; sea level.

Season, Fees & Phone: Open all year; 14 day limit; reservations recommended for weekends; please see Appendix for additional reservation information and standard Texas state park fees; park office (409) 971-2559.

Camp Notes: Sea Rim is sizable--15,000+ acres--and quite undeveloped, (although perhaps "natural" might be more appropriately descriptive). The highway neatly bisects the park into two distinctive zones: a narrow, five-mile strip of coastal beach on the south, broad tidal marshlands to the north. The park is named for the section of Gulf shoreline where marsh grasses extend into the surf in a zone known as a 'sea rim marsh'. The marshlands include boat/canoe trails for navigating the wetlands. If you have a paddleable or poleable boat, you can also spend the night on one of a half-dozen camping platforms in the marsh. (Most alligators can't climb the ladders leading up to the platforms.) From the main campground, if you have a tall vehicle (or a yurt with a crow's nest), you'll be able to see the sea from your campsite.

Oklahoma

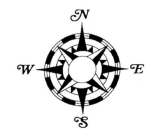

Public Campgrounds

The Oklahoma map is located in the Appendix on page 177.

Oklahoma 1

BLACK MESA
Black Mesa State Park

Location: Oklahoma Panhandle west of Guymon.

Access: From Oklahoma State Highway 325 at a point 20.5 miles northwest of Boise City, 15 miles southeast of Kenton, turn west onto a paved access road (signed for Lake Etling and the state park) and travel 4.5 miles to a "T" intersection; turn north (right, continuing on the paved road) for 1.2 miles, west (left) for 0.5 mile, then north again for a final 0.3 mile to the campground. **Alternate Access:** From U.S. Highways 50/64 at the Oklahoma-New Mexico border, travel northeast to the burg of Felt, OK; head due north on the paved county road out of midtown Felt for 12 miles to Oklahoma State Highway 325; turn west (left) onto Highway 325 and proceed 5.5 miles to the signed state park turnoff and continue as above.

Facilities: 32 campsites, many with partial hookups; sites are small+, with nominal separation; parking pads are gravel, medium-length straight-ins or pull-offs; a number of pads will require some additional leveling; space for medium to large tents in most sites; ramadas (sun shelters) for some sites; barbecue grills; b-y-o firewood; water at sites and at central faucets; restrooms with showers; holding tank disposal station; paved driveway; limited supplies and services are available in Boise City.

Activities & Attractions: Fishing; boating (wakeless, 6 mph); boat launch; nature trail.

Natural Features: Located along or near the south shore of Lake Carl Etling, in a canyon on the High Plains; vegetation consists principally of scattered, large hardwoods and range grass; petrified forest; elevation 4400'.

Season, Fees & Phone: March to November; please see Appendix for standard Oklahoma state park fees; 14 day limit; park office (405) 426-2222.

Camp Notes: Black Mesa is a candidate for being the birthplace of those "edge of the earth" wisecracks. Even though it's at the tip of the Oklahoma outback, you'll still usually have some company from local fishermen.

Oklahoma 2

HARDESTY
Optima Lake/Corps of Engineers Park

Location: Oklahoma Panhandle northeast of Guymon.

Access: From Oklahoma State Highway 3 at a point 2 miles east of Hardesty and 18 miles west of the junction of Oklahoma 3 & U.S. Highway 83 at Bryans Corner, turn north onto a paved lake access road and proceed 1.9 miles; turn northwesterly (left) onto the park access road for 0.4 mile, then go west (left) for a final 0.4 mile to the campground.

Facilities: 65 campsites, including 48 with electrical hookups; sites are medium-sized, with nominal separation; parking pads are hard-surfaced, short to long pull-offs or straight-ins; additional leveling will probably be required in many sites; ample space for tents, though they may be a bit sloped; ramadas (sun/partial wind shelters) for all sites; barbecue grills and fire rings; b-y-o firewood (unquestionably, b-y-o firewood); water at central faucets; restrooms with showers; holding tank disposal station; paved driveways; gas and groceries are available in Hardesty.

Activities & Attractions: Fishing; boating; boat launch; swimming beach.

Natural Features: Located on a gentle slope in a shallow basin above Optima Lake, a reservoir on the North Canadian River (also called the Beaver River), on the High Plains; campground vegetation consists of range grass, dozens of small hardwoods, plus a few small pines and junipers; elevation 2800'.

Season, Fees & Phone: Available all year, with limited services October to April; $8.00 for a standard site, $11.00 for a partial hookup site; 14 day limit; Optima Lake CoE Project Office (405) 888-4226.

Camp Notes: If you appreciate the sense of freedom and space and timelessness of a classic High Plains environment, this might be a good spot for you. Although summer days may be a touch on the warm side, the altitude and the prairie wind should cooperate in cooling the country at night.

Oklahoma 3

PRAIRIE DOG POINT
Optima Lake/Corps of Engineers Park

Location: Oklahoma Panhandle northeast of Guymon.

Access: From Oklahoma State Highway 94 at a point 2 miles north of the junction of Highway 9 & Oklahoma State Highway 3 near Hardesty and 13 miles south of Hooker, turn east onto the paved park access road and proceed 2.2 miles; turn south (right) for 0.2 mile to the campground.

Facilities: 50 campsites, most with electrical hookups; sites are medium-sized, with nominal separation; parking pads are hard-surfaced, short to long pull-offs or straight-ins; additional leveling will probably be required in many sites; ample space for tents, though may be a bit sloped; ramadas (sun/partial wind shelters) for all sites; barbecue grills and fire rings; b-y-o firewood; water at central faucets; restrooms with showers; holding tank disposal station; paved driveways; gas and groceries are available in Hardesty.

Activities & Attractions: Fishing; boating; boat launch.

Natural Features: Located on a gently sloping point above Optima Lake, a reservoir on the North Canadian River (Beaver River), on the High Plains; campground vegetation consists of range grass, numerous small hardwoods, plus a some small pines and junipers; elevation 2800'.

Season, Fees & Phone: (See Camp Notes section); Optima Lake CoE Project Office (405) 888-4226

Camp Notes: (Special editorial note: Prairie Dog currently is a campground without a cause. Water levels at Optima Lake have been quite low in recent years, with a consequential shortage of campers. Prairie Dog has been mothballed until such time as useage-demand warrants its re-opening. The facilities, which are more weathered than they are used, are excellent. We have included information on this major campground just in case nature decides to fill the cup at Optima Lake, and Prairie Dog is revived from its state of suspended animation.)

Oklahoma 4

ANGLER POINT
Optima Lake/Corps of Engineers Park

Location: Oklahoma Panhandle northeast of Guymon.

Access: From Oklahoma State Highway 3 at a point 2 miles east of Hardesty and 18 miles west of the junction of Oklahoma 3 & U.S. Highway 83 at Bryans Corner, turn north onto a paved lake access road and proceed 2.7 miles to the south end of the dam; bear right, drive past the project office, continue down the slope on the east (river) side of the dam, and across the outlet channel to the campground.

Facilities: 21 campsites; sites are medium-sized, level, with fair separation; parking pads are medium to long straight-ins; adequate space for large tents on a grassy surface; ramadas (sun shelters) for a couple of sites; barbecue grills and fire rings; b-y-o firewood; water at central faucets; vault facilities; paved driveway; gas and groceries are available in Hardesty.

Activities & Attractions: Fishing (on the river and on the lake); boating, boat launch on the lake; Trestle Pond Trail.

Natural Features: Located on a large, grassy flat along the north bank of the North Canadian River (Beaver River), below Optima Lake Dam; sites receive minimal to light shade from large hardwoods; bordered by very gently rolling plains; elevation 2700'.

Season, Fees & Phone: Available all year, subject to weather conditions, with reduced services October to April; no fee; 14 day limit; Optima Lake CoE Project Office (405) 888-4226.

Camp Notes: A "point" is usually associated with a promontory on a lake, but in this case it's a vague reference to a spot along the river. Typical of Corps lakes, fishing on the outlet stream can often produce results when all else fails. Fishing has been sporadic on Optima Lake because of generally low water levels, although some good-sized hybrid stripers ("wipers") have been landed, and trotlining for catfish has been productive.

BEAVER
Beaver State Park

Location: Oklahoma Panhandle northeast of Guymon.

Access: From U.S. Highway 270/Oklahoma State Highway 23 at a point 1.7 miles north of Beaver, 1 mile north of the Beaver River Bridge and 6 miles south of Forgan, turn west onto the campground access road and proceed 0.1 mile to the campground. (Note that the campground access road is a quarter mile north of the park's day use area access road.)

Facilities: 12 campsites, including 7 with partial hookups; sites are small, level, and closely spaced; parking pads are gravel, medium-length straight-ins; enough space for medium to large tents; barbecue grills and/or fire rings; b-y-o firewood; water at hookup sites and at central faucets; restrooms with showers; holding tank disposal station; paved driveway; limited supplies and services are available in Beaver.

Activities & Attractions: Dune riding/scrambling; fishing; day use area.

Natural Features: Located on a small, grassy flat along or near the shore of a small lake; large hardwoods provide hookup sites with very light morning shade only, standard sites are somewhat more evenly shaded; fairly good wind shelter from adjacent trees and the terrain; bordered by small hills and sand dunes; surrounded by open plains; elevation 2500'.

Season, Fees & Phone: Open all year; please see Appendix for standard Oklahoma state park fees; 14 day limit; park office (405) 625-3373.

Camp Notes: Unless you're an orv enthusiast, this bantam boondock by the banks of the Beaver *probably* won't be worth going more than a few miles out of the way for (and that is stated guardedly, but candidly). However, the park's pleasant little picnic area is worth a short stay for a snack or a snooze on the way through the Panhandle.

OKLAHOMA

Northwest

Please refer to the Oklahoma map in the Appendix

SUPPLY
Fort Supply Lake/Corps of Engineers Park

Location: Northwest Oklahoma northwest of Woodward.

Access: From U.S. Highways 183/270 and Oklahoma State Highway 3 at the southeast edge of the town of Fort Supply, turn south onto a paved lake access road and proceed 0.7 mile (0.3 mile past the project office) to a "T" intersection; bear slightly right, continue for 0.1 mile, then turn left into the campground.

Facilities: 21 campsites with partial hookups; sites are medium-sized, with nominal separation; parking pads are paved, medium to long straight-ins; a little additional leveling will be needed in some sites; ample space for large tents; some sites have ramadas (sun shelters); barbecue grills and fire rings; a limited amount of firewood is available for gathering in the vicinity; water at sites; restrooms with showers; holding tank disposal station; paved driveway; gas and groceries are available in Fort Supply.

Activities & Attractions: Swimming beach; fishing for bass, catfish, crappie, walleye; boat launch.

Natural Features: Located on the northwest shore of Fort Supply Lake; sites are minimally to lightly shaded by large hardwoods on mown grass; tree-lined shoreline, surrounded by low, grassy hills; elevation 2000'.

Season, Fees & Phone: Available all year, with reduced services November to April; $12.00 for a partial hookup site; 14 day limit; Fort Supply Lake CoE Project Office (405) 766-2701.

Camp Notes: This is a visually pleasing, shoreside camp. Although it's next door to the day use area and swim beach, campground traffic is restricted. The lake's other campground, Cottonwood Point, is a large area located about a mile south of Supply Park. Most sites there have electrical hookups, but only vault facilities are available, and its season is limited. Plans call for adding restrooms and showers to Cottonwood Point.

BOILING SPRINGS
Boiling Springs State Park

Location: Northwest Oklahoma northeast of Woodward.

Access: From Oklahoma State Highway 34 at a point 1.4 miles north of Woodward, turn east onto State Highway 34C and proceed 5 miles to the park office; continue east (bear right at the fork after the office) on the main park road for 0.75 mile; turn north (left) to the camping areas. **Alternate Access:** From Oklahoma State Highway 50 in Mooreland, proceed west on State Highway 50B for 5 miles to the east park boundary; continue for 0.8 mile, then turn north (right) to the camping areas.

Facilities: 50 campsites, including 35 with partial hookups and 10 with full hookups, in 2 areas; (2 large group camps are also available); sites are small to medium-sized, with minimal to nominal separation; most parking pads are gravel/grass, short to long straight-ins, some of which may require a little additional leveling; tent space varies from small to large; barbecue grills; b-y-o firewood is suggested; water at faucets throughout; restrooms with showers; holding tank disposal station; paved driveways; virtually complete supplies and services are available in Woodward.

Activities & Attractions: Boiling Springs; swimming pool (extra charge); hiking trails; playground.

Natural Features: Located on slightly rolling and sloping terrain on the north side of the valley of the North Canadian River; large hardwoods and evergreens provide light to light-medium shade/shelter; elevation 1900'.

Season, Fees & Phone: Open all year; reservations accepted for assigned sites; please see Appendix for reservation information and standard Oklahoma state park fees; park office (405) 256-7664.

Camp Notes: The sites in Area 3 (assigned, i.e., reservable, loop, all partial hookups) are a little larger and better-separated than those in Area 4 (unassigned, assorted sites). Placid, woodsy atmosphere throughout this park. The park is in the last stand of Big Timber in Western Oklahoma. The park is named for cool springs which "boil up" through the white sands of the North Canadian River floodplain at a rate of 200 gallons per minute.

ALABASTER CAVERNS
Alabaster Caverns State Park

Location: Northwest Oklahoma northeast of Woodward.

Access: From Oklahoma State Highway 50 at a point 6 miles south of Freedom, 18 miles north of Mooreland, turn east onto Oklahoma State Highway 50A and proceed 0.6 mile; turn southeast (right, near the park office) into the primary camp area (includes all hookup sites); or continue ahead on the main park road, then down the hill for 0.5 mile to bottom area.

Facilities: 20 campsites, including 10 with partial hookups; sites are small to small+, with nominal to fair separation; parking pads are gravel, medium-length pull-throughs or straight-ins, most of which probably will require some additional leveling; medium to large areas for tents; barbecue grills and fire rings; b-y-o firewood is suggested; water at hookup sites and at central faucets; restrooms with showers; holding tank disposal station; paved main driveways; gas and groceries and a few other services are available in Freedom.

Activities & Attractions: Guided tours through alabaster and selenite crystal caverns; hiking trails (including a trail to a natural rock bridge); swimming pool; (extra charge for tours and pool.)

Natural Features: Located on an upper slope (main camp), or in a small canyon along a small stream (bottom area); sites receive light to medium shade/shelter from large hardwoods and evergreens; surrounded by tree-dotted hills, buttes, canyons and plains; elevation 1800'.

Season, Fees & Phone: Open all year; please see Appendix for standard Oklahoma state park fees; 14 day limit; park office (405) 621-3381.

Camp Notes: Halloween is one of the favorite camping times here. (The park stages an annual ghostly get-together then.) There is a wonderful variety of shape, color and hue in this region.

LITTLE SAHARA
Little Sahara State Recreation Area

Location: Northwest Oklahoma northeast of Woodward.

Access: From U.S. Highway 281 at a point 3.5 miles south of Waynoka, 1 mile north of the Cimarron River bridge, 8 miles north of the junction of U.S. 281 & U.S. 412, turn west into the park entrance; most sites are south (left) of the entrance, a small area is north of the entrance.

Facilities: Approximately 30 campsites, including 21 with partial hookups; sites are small and closely spaced; most parking pads are gravel, medium-length straight-ins which may require a bit of sideways leveling (i.e., backed-in vehicles will have a portside tilt); space for small to medium-sized tents on a gravel surface; fire rings; b-y-o firewood; water at hookup sites and at central faucets; restrooms with showers; paved driveway; limited supplies and services are available in Waynoka.

Activities & Attractions: Dune riding.

Natural Features: Located on a bluff/hilltop above the valley of the Cimarron River; a few tent sites are lightly shaded by large hardwoods, otherwise most sites are unshaded; several acres of dunes lie within the park; elevation 1500'.

Season, Fees & Phone: Open all year; please see Appendix for standard Oklahoma state park fees; 14 day limit; park office (405) 824-1471.

Camp Notes: The hookup sites are right along the fairly busy highway, but several nice little tent sites are several yards farther from the road. Although there are extensive areas of public land in the West on which orvs, dune buggies and scramble bikes are permitted, this is one of perhaps only a dozen or so parks with campgrounds which are specifically designed to accommodate off-highway motor sports.

SANDY BEACH
Great Salt Plains State Park

Location: North-central Oklahoma northwest of Enid.

Access: From Oklahoma State Highway 38 at a point 5 miles south of its junction with State Highway 11, 10 miles north of Jet, turn south into *Sandy Beach 1*; or continue slightly south, then west, to *Sandy Beach 2*. (Note: Sandy Beach 2 can also be accessed from a point 1 mile west of here, just east of a right-angle turn on Highway 11.)

Facilities: *Sandy Beach 1*: 27 campsites with partial hookups; *Sandy Beach 2*: 34 standard campsites; *both areas*: sites are small+ to medium-sized, with nominal to fair separation; parking surfaces are gravel in Sandy Beach 1, grass in Sandy Beach 2; a bit of additional leveling may be needed; adequate space for large tents; barbecue grills; b-y-o firewood is suggested; water at hookup sites and at central faucets; restrooms with showers; packed gravel driveway in Sandy Beach 1, sand in Sandy Beach 2; gas and groceries and a few other services are available in Jet.

Activities & Attractions: Rockhounding (specifically, hunting for "hourglass" selenite crystals, April to mid-October); hiking; boating; boat launch; fishing; playground.

Natural Features: Located on the north shore of a large bay on the east side of Great Salt Plains Lake; Sandy Beach 1 is on a small knoll away from the shore; Sandy Beach 2 is located right along the shoreline; sites receive light to medium shade/shelter from large hardwoods and evergreens; good lake views at Sandy Beach 2; elevation 1100'.

Season, Fees & Phone: Open all year; please see Appendix for standard Oklahoma state park fees; 14 day limit; park office 405-626-4731.

Camp Notes: This park represents the only place in the world where you can dig for the "hourglass" crystals mentioned above. The delicate crystals can be found as they emerge from the surface, or by deftly digging just beneath the surface of the region's salt flats.

RIVER ROAD
Great Salt Plains State Park

Location: North-central Oklahoma northwest of Enid.

Access: From Oklahoma State Highway 38 at a point 6 miles south of its junction with State Highway 11, 9 miles north of Jet, just on the north end of the river bridge, turn southeast into the campground.

Facilities: 38 assigned campsites with partial hookups, plus a few standard sites; sites are small+, essentially level and closely spaced; parking pads are gravel, mostly medium to long straight-ins; adequate space for large tents on a grassy surface; barbecue grills, plus fireplaces or fire rings; b-y-o firewood is suggested; water at sites and at central faucets; restrooms with showers; holding tank disposal station; paved driveways; gas and groceries and a few other services are available in Jet.

Activities & Attractions: Rockhounding for "hourglass" selenite crystals, April to mid-October; hiking; fishing; boating; boat launch; playground.

Natural Features: Located on a flat along the north bank of the Salt Fork of the Arkansas River, just below the dam on Great Salt Plains Lake; sites are very lightly to lightly shaded by large hardwoods; about one-third of the sites are riverside; views of eroded, colorful bluffs along the river; elevation 1100'.

Season, Fees & Phone: Open all year; reservations accepted for assigned sites; please see Appendix for reservation information and standard Oklahoma state park fees; 14 day limit; park office 405-626-4731.

Camp Notes: Of the pair of state park hookup areas (also see info for Sandy Beach), River Road seems to be the more popular, possibly because of the somewhat better views and perhaps more attractive campsites. The Corps of Engineers also provides a few $4.00 campsites with water, ramadas and vault facilities in the North Spillway area adjacent to River Road. Great Salt Plains Lake is the oldest CoE project in Oklahoma.

Oklahoma 12

BIG BEND
Canton Lake/Corps of Engineers Park

Location: West-central Oklahoma southwest of Enid.

Access: From Oklahoma State Highway 51 at a point 1.8 miles west of Canton and 19 miles east of Seiling, turn north onto a paved, lake access road and travel 4 miles to a "T" intersection; turn east (right) into Big Bend Park and proceed for 0.15 mile to the campground entrance station; a few yards beyond, turn north (left) into the A area, or continue ahead for 0.1 mile to the B area.

Facilities: 141 campsites, most with electrical hookups or partial hookups, in 2 areas; sites are small+ to medium-sized, with nominal to fair separation; most parking pads are paved, basically level, medium-length, straight-ins, and some are extra-wide; adequate space for medium to large tents; ramadas (sun shelters) for many sites; barbecue grills and fire rings; b-y-o firewood is suggested; water at some sites and at central faucets; restrooms with showers; holding tank disposal station; paved driveways; limited+ supplies and services are available in Canton.

Activities & Attractions: Boating; boat launch; fishing (good for catfish, crappie, sand bass, plus walleye and stripers); swimming area; playground.

Natural Features: Located along or above the west shore of Canton Lake, a reservoir on the North Canadian River; sites receive very light to medium shade/shelter from small to large hardwoods and a few evergreens; elevation 1600'.

Season, Fees & Phone: Available all year, with limited services and reduced fees October to April; $8.00 for a standard site, $11.00 for a hookup site; 14 day limit; Canton Lake CoE Project Office (405) 886-2989.

Camp Notes: There are quite a few nice lakeshore sites in both areas; but don't overlook the sites in area A which are up on the hill/bluff that overlooks the shore, and look out across quite a bit of the lake. All things considered, Big Bend gets the nod for best campground on Canton Lake.

Oklahoma 13

CANADIAN
Canton Lake/Corps of Engineers Park

Location: West-central Oklahoma southwest of Enid.

Access: From the junction of Oklahoma State Highway 51 & State Highway 58A (0.8 mile west of Canton, 20 miles east of Seiling), turn north onto Highway 58A and travel north, then northwest, for 1.6 miles; continue northwest on a local access road for 0.25 mile (to a point just past the project office); turn north (right) and proceed 0.4 mile to the campground entrance.

Facilities: 136 campsites, most with electrical hookups or partial hookups, in 2 loops; sites are small+ to medium-sized, with nominal to fair separation; most parking pads are paved, medium-length straight-ins;

some pads may require a little additional leveling; adequate space for medium to large tents; ramadas (sun shelters) for some sites; barbecue grills and fire rings; b-y-o firewood is suggested; water at some sites and at central faucets; restrooms with showers; holding tank disposal station; paved driveways; limited+ supplies and services are available in Canton.

Activities & Attractions: Boating; boat launch and dock; fishing (catfish, crappie, sand bass, walleye, stripers); designated swimming area; playgrounds.

Natural Features: Located on a gentle slope and a flat above the southwest shore of Canton Lake, a flood-control impoundment on the North Canadian River; sites receive very light to medium shade/shelter from large hardwoods and some evergreens; elevation 1600'.

Season, Fees & Phone: Available all year, with limited services and reduced fees October to April; $8.00 for a standard site, $11.00 for a hookup site; 14 day limit; Canton Lake CoE Project Office (405) 886-2989.

Camp Notes: Canadian appears to be the most popular camp spot on the lake. One likely reason is that it's only a few minutes' drive into town. Of the lake's four principal campgrounds, Canadian offers the best possibility of fishing from shore.

LONGDALE
Canton Lake/Corps of Engineers Park

Location: West-central Oklahoma southwest of Enid.

Access: From Oklahoma State Highway 58 at the south edge of the community of Longdale, 7 miles northwest of Canton, turn west onto 7th Street and proceed 2 miles to the campground.

Facilities: 42 campsites; sites are small to medium-sized, with nominal to fair separation; parking pads are hard-surfaced, tolerably level, short to medium-length straight-ins; enough space for medium to large tents; ramadas (sun shelters) for a few sites; barbecue grills and fire rings; some firewood is available for gathering in the area; water at central faucets; vault facilities; paved driveway; gas and groceries are available in Longdale.

Activities & Attractions: Thunder Road Scenic Drive; boating; boat launch and dock; fishing; small playground.

Natural Features: Located on the east shore of Canton Lake, a reservoir on the North Canadian River; sites receive light to medium shade/shelter from large hardwoods; very good lake views from many sites and from the general campground area; bordered by very dense woodland; typically breezy; elevation 1600'.

Season, Fees & Phone: Available all year, with limited services and no fee, October to April; $5.00; 14 day limit; Canton Lake CoE Project Office (405) 886-2989.

Camp Notes: Should you hanker for a place that is even cheaper and more isolated than Longdale, try one of the 15 primitive campsites which are spotted along the nicely shaded, sandy beach in this vicinity. You'll need an "OK" from the project office before camping, and be self-contained and/or self-sufficient, but the reward is your own piece of relatively secluded beachfront property. *Mobility* is the watchword for these edgewater sites, 'cause when the wind picks up and the surf begins to boom.....

SANDY COVE
Canton Lake/Corps of Engineers Park

Location: West-central Oklahoma southwest of Enid.

Access: From the junction of Oklahoma State Highway 58 & State Highway 58A (5 miles northwest of Canton, 2 miles south of Longdale), head west on Highway 58A for 1.2 miles (to the northeast end of the dam); turn north (sharply right) onto a paved local access road and continue for 0.5 mile; swing south (a hard left), then down to the campground entrance.

Facilities: 36 campsites, (consisting of 22 single units, 5 double units, and a 4-site small group area, all of which can be used as single sites if needed), most with electrical hookups; sites are medium-sized, with nominal to good separation; parking pads are paved, mostly medium to long straight-ins; a bit of additional leveling may be required in a number of sites; adequate space for medium to large tents; ramadas (sun shelters) for some sites; barbecue grills and fire rings; a limited amount of firewood may be available for gathering nearby; water at several faucets; restrooms with showers nearby; paved driveways; limited+ supplies and services are available in Canton.

Activities & Attractions: Swimming beach; Thunder Road Scenic Drive; fishing; boating; boat launch.

Natural Features: Located on gently rolling/sloping terrain on the southeast shore of Canton Lake; most sites are quite well sheltered by large hardwoods; elevation 1600'.

Season, Fees & Phone: Available all year, with limited services November to April; $6.00 for a standard site, $9.00 for a partial hookup site; 14 day limit; Canton Lake CoE Project Office (405) 886-2989.

Camp Notes: This is the only campground on the lake which doesn't provide lake views. The campsites are in a nicely wooded spot, but they're on the 'wrong' side of the trees and terrain from the lakeshore.

Oklahoma 16

ROMAN NOSE
Roman Nose State Park

Location: Central Oklahoma northwest of Oklahoma City.

Access: From Oklahoma State Highway 8A at a point 3 miles northwest of the junction of Highway 8A & State Highway 8, 2.5 miles east of the junction of Highway 8A & State Highway 51A north of Watonga, turn north, then almost immediately northeast onto the main campground access road and proceed 0.4 mile to the standard sites or 0.8 mile to the hookup area.

Facilities: 53 campsites, including 35 with partial hookups; (15 additional standard sites are located in 2 small areas adjacent to Highway 8A at the main campground turnoff); sites are small to small+, with minimal to fair separation; parking pads are gravel, mostly short to medium-length straight-ins; a touch of additional leveling may be needed; small to medium-sized tent areas; fireplaces; b-y-o firewood is suggested; water at faucets throughout; restrooms with showers; holding tank disposal station; paved driveways; adequate supplies and services are available in Watonga.

Activities & Attractions: Golf course; swimming pool; tennis court; interpretive programs; fishing; limited boating; boat launch; community building.

Natural Features: Located in a large canyon along the west shore of 80-acre Lake Watonga; a few sites are situated near adjacent, tiny Lake Boecher; sites receive minimal to light-medium shade from large hardwoods and evergreens; bordered by grassy, tree-dotted slopes and rocky outcroppings; elevation 1500'.

Season, Fees & Phone: Open all year; please see Appendix for standard Oklahoma state park fees; 14 day limit; park office (405) 623-4215.

Camp Notes: Its canyon-floor location makes Roman Nose distinctively different from all other Oklahoma state park campgrounds. Simple sites, scenic surroundings. Chief Henry Roman Nose was a Southern Cheyenne whose semi-permanent camp occupied the deep canyon in which the present-day state park is located. If you forgot to b-y-o canvas, you can rent one of several park teepees set up in the campground.

Oklahoma 17

FOSS
Foss State Park

Location: West-central Oklahoma west of Clinton.

Access: From Oklahoma State Highway 73 at a point 0.25 mile west of the junction of Highway 73 with State Highway 44 north of Foss, 12 miles east of the junction of Highway 73 and State Highway 34 north of Elk City, turn north into the park and proceed 0.5 mile to a 4-way intersection; turn west (left) and continue for another 0.5 mile to the campground.

Facilities: 60 campsites, including 40 with partial hookups and 10 with full hookups; sites are small+, with nominal separation; parking pads are gravel/grass, short+ to medium-length straight-ins for partial hookups, or long pull-throughs for full hookups; some pads will require a little additional leveling; generally large, grassy areas for tents; barbecue grills; b-y-o firewood is recommended; water at some sites and at central faucets; restrooms with showers; holding tank disposal station; paved main driveway, gravel sub-drives; gas and groceries in Foss.

Activities & Attractions: Fishing; boat launch nearby; playground.

Natural Features: Located on grassy, gently sloping terrain a short distance from the south shore of Foss Lake; sites are very lightly to lightly shaded by hardwoods; elevation 1700'.

Season, Fees & Phone: Open all year; please see Appendix for standard Oklahoma state park fees; 14 day limit; park office (405) 592-4433.

Camp Notes: Most people come here to enjoy the water sports at this lake on the open, windswept plains. Should the day's gale be too much for your boat (or for you and your shipmates, for that matter), a much more sheltered, water-based alternative is available southeast of here at Crowder Lake State Park, 11 miles south/southeast of Weatherford. Crowder Lake SP has 160 acres of water, 2 acres of land, a half-dozen campsites, and restrooms with solar showers.

Oklahoma 18

RED ROCK CANYON
Red Rock Canyon State Park

Location: South-central Oklahoma west of Oklahoma City.

Access: From U.S. Highway 281/Oklahoma State Highway 8 at the south city limits of Hinton (5 miles south of Interstate 40 Exit 101), turn east into the park entrance and proceed 0.2 mile; check your steering gear and brakes, then descend for another steep, winding 0.2 mile to the canyon floor; the campsites are in 6 principal areas along the next 1.3 miles of park road.

Facilities: 54 campsites, including 49 with partial hookups and 5 with full hookups; (in addition, dozens of standard camp/picnic sites are also available); sites are small, level, with minimal to nominal separation; parking pads are gravel, mostly short to medium-length straight-ins, plus a few long pull-throughs; enough space for medium to large tents in most sites; barbecue grills, fire rings, or fireplaces; a small amount of firewood is available for gathering in the area, b-y-o is recommended; restrooms with showers; paved driveways; limited supplies and services are available in Hinton.

Activities & Attractions: California Road and Rough Horsetail Nature Trails; swimming pool.

Natural Features: Located on the floor of long, narrow Red Rock Canyon; sites are lightly to moderately shaded by large hardwoods, predominantly sugar maples; a small pond has been created on a stream which flows through the length of the canyon; bordered by red sandstone walls; elevation 1200'.

Season, Fees & Phone: Open all year, subject to brief closures during icy periods; please see Appendix for standard Oklahoma state park fees; 14 day limit; park office (405) 542-6344.

Camp Notes: The canyon is noted for its annual spring visits by migrating cliff swallows. Scores of gourd-shaped mud nests created by the so-called "mud-daubers" can be seen bonded to the canyon wall on the west side of the pond.

OKLAHOMA
Southwest

Please refer to the Oklahoma map in the Appendix

Oklahoma 19

FORT COBB: WEST
Fort Cobb State Park

Location: Central Oklahoma southwest of Oklahoma City.

Access: From Oklahoma State Highway 9 at a point 2 miles west of its junction with State Highway 143 north of Fort Cobb, 8 miles east of Carnegie, turn north onto a paved road and head due north for 4 miles; just before the sharp, westerly turn in the road, bear northeast (right) into the campground entrance; area 1 is on the left, just past the entrance; area 2 is ahead then south 0.8 mile.

Facilities: 118 assigned campsites with partial hookups in 2 areas; sites are medium-sized, with nominal to fair separation; parking pads are gravel, respectably level, medium to long straight-ins; small to medium-sized tent spots; barbecue grills or fireplaces; some firewood is available for gathering in the area; water at sites; restrooms with showers; holding tank disposal station; paved driveways; gas and camper supplies, 2 miles south; limited supplies and services are available in Fort Cobb.

Activities & Attractions: Fishing (reportedly good) for crappie, bass, various cats, hybrid stripers, walleye); boating; boat launch; beach.

Natural Features: Located on a point of land on a slope above a bay (area 1) or along the main shoreline (area 2) of Fort Cobb Lake; sites are quite well-sheltered by medium-dense hardwoods and evergreens on a surface of grass and small plants; elevation 1300'.

Season, Fees & Phone: Open all year; reservations accepted; please see Appendix for reservation information and standard Oklahoma state park fees; 14 day limit; park office (405) 643-2249.

Camp Notes: Fort Cobb West is the most out-of-the-way, developed area on the lake. But if this assigned campground proves to be a mite too populated for your preferences, there's always the option of trying-out one of the park's half thousand (give or take a hundred) primitive camping possibilities.

Oklahoma 20

FORT COBB: EAST
Fort Cobb State Park

Location: South-central Oklahoma southwest of Oklahoma City.

Access: From Oklahoma State Highway 146 at a point 4 miles north of Fort Cobb and 6 miles south of Albert, turn west onto a paved local road and proceed 1 mile to a "T" intersection; turn north (right) and drive for 1.9 miles (past the dam and around the north end of the golf course), then southwest (left, since you're heading northwest at this point) to camp areas A, B, C, and D.

Facilities: 89 campsites with partial hookups in 4 areas; sites are small to medium-sized, with nominal separation; parking pads are gravel, short to medium-length straight-ins or long pull-throughs; additional leveling will probably be required in most sites; adequate, though generally sloped, space for large tents; ramadas (sun shelters) for some sites; fireplaces; b-y-o firewood is suggested; water at sites; restrooms with showers; holding tank disposal station; paved driveways; limited supplies and services are available in Fort Cobb.

Activities & Attractions: Golf course, across the bay; swimming beach; fishing for most warm water species; fishing pier; boating; boat launch; marina; playground.

Natural Features: Located on a grassy slope above a large bay on the east side of Fort Cobb Lake; sites receive light to medium shade from large hardwoods, plus a few pines and junipers/cedars; lake views or lake glimpses from most sites; elevation 1300'.

Season, Fees & Phone: Open all year; please see Appendix for standard Oklahoma state park fees; 14 day limit; park office (405) 643-2249.

Camp Notes: The park people say that they take an extra measure of pride in the trees here, and it shows. The landscaping is nicely maintained. (If you happen to pass through the tiny town of Albert, check out the petite post office. It looks more like a Fotomat than a federal facility.)

Oklahoma 21

FORT COBB: GOLF COURSE
Fort Cobb State Park

Location: South-central Oklahoma southwest of Oklahoma City.

Access: From Oklahoma State Highway 146 at a point 4 miles north of Fort Cobb and 6 miles south of Albert, turn west onto a paved local road and proceed 1 mile to a "T" intersection; turn north (right) and drive 1.5 miles (past the dam and around to the northeast side of the golf course); turn southwest (left) onto the golf course road and motor past the pro shop to the campground, on the right.

Facilities: 53 campsites with partial hookups; sites are small to medium-sized, with minimal to nominal separation; parking pads are gravel, short to medium+ straight-ins; a little additional leveling will probably be required in some sites; adequate, generally a bit sloped, space for large tents on a grassy surface; barbecue grills; b-y-o firewood is suggested; water at sites; restrooms with showers; holding tank disposal station nearby; paved driveways; limited supplies and services are available in Fort Cobb.

Activities & Attractions: Fort Cobb State Golf Course; swimming beach; fishing; fishing pier; boating; boat launch; marina.

Natural Features: Located on a hilltop and hillside above a bay on the east shore of Fort Cobb Lake; sites are lightly shaded by large hardwoods, plus a few small pines; good lake views from most sites; elevation 1300'.

Season, Fees & Phone: Open all year; please see Appendix for standard Oklahoma state park fees; 14 day limit; park office (405) 643-2249.

Camp Notes: Fort Cobb's front nine are so-so; but the back nine.....well now, they're another ball game. The bay below the course is one of the biggest water hazards this side of Pebble Beach. The Fort Cobb area lays claim to being the "Crow Capitol of the World". People from all over the globe come here just to shoot crow. Really. That's true. (And, no doubt, some of the duffers who miss their shots on the back nine have to *eat* crow. Ed.)

Oklahoma 22

NORTH SHORE
Quartz Mountain State Park

Location: Southwest Oklahoma north of Altus.

Access: From Oklahoma State Highway 44 at a point 4.5 miles south of Lone Wolf and 5 miles north of the junction of Highway 44 & State Highway 44A, turn west onto a paved access road, cross the railroad tracks, and proceed 1.5 miles to Area 1; or continue northwesterly for another mile to Area 2 (assigned camping). (Note: if the access road isn't signed, look for a paved road which passes between a pair of small, isolated, rocky hills; the road skirts the north side of the larger of the 2 mounds.)

Facilities: 34 campsites with partial hookups in Area 1; 25 assigned campsites with partial hookups in Area 2; sites are small+ to medium-sized, essentially level, with nominal separation; parking surfaces are paved or gravel, mostly medium to long straight-ins; plenty of space for tents; barbecue grills or fireplaces; b-y-o firewood; water at faucets throughout; restrooms with showers; holding tank disposal station; paved driveways; gas and groceries are available in Lone Wolf.

Activities & Attractions: Boating; boat launch; off road vehicle (orv) area (near camp area 2).

Natural Features: Located on the north-east shore of Altus Lake, a reservoir on the North Fork of the Red River; sites receive light-medium shade from large hardwoods on a grassy surface; low, barren-rock hills and mountains loom over the near-level plains; elevation 1500'.

Season, Fees & Phone: Open all year; 14 day limit; reservations accepted for Area 2, May to October; please see Appendix for additional reservation information and standard Oklahoma state park fees; park office (405) 563-2238.

Camp Notes: This region, with its uncharacteristic shapes and colors, could almost be described as a "fantasy land". (The mountains closely resemble those in the Mojave Desert along the Colorado River on the Arizona-California border.) The pinkish domes seemingly rise from the lake's blue waters and from the surrounding plains.

Oklahoma 23

QUARTZ MOUNTAIN
Quartz Mountain State Park

Location: Southwest Oklahoma north of Altus.

Access: From Oklahoma State Highway 44 at a point 2 miles north of its junction with U.S. Highway 283 north of Altus and 10 miles south of Lone Wolf, turn north/northwest onto State Highway 44A and proceed 1.5 miles to a "Y" intersection; bear east (right), then almost immediately left to partial hookup area C, or right into the River Road standard area; or continue east for 0.5 mile to full hookup area A, or 0.7 mile to partial hookup area B.

Facilities: Approximately 85 campsites, including 29 with partial hookups and 20 with full hookups, in 4 areas; (a large group camp is also available sites are small, with nominal separation; parking pads are gravel/earth, medium-length straight-ins in Areas B & C; mostly paved pull-throughs in Area A; pads are reasonably level, except in hookup Area C; enough space for small tents in hookup sites, medium to large tents in standard sites; barbecue grills or fireplaces; ; b-y-o firewood; water at hookup sites and at central faucets; restrooms with showers; holding tank disposal station; paved driveways; camper supplies at the park store (seasonal) and on Route 44A.

Activities & Attractions: Golf course; nature center; scheduled naturalist programs; New Horizon Trail; swimming beaches; swimming pool; boating; boat launches.

Natural Features: Located near the south shore of Altus Lake (Areas A & B) or on slopes above the north bank of a tributary of the North Fork of the Red River (Area C and River Road); sites receive light to light-medium shade from large hardwoods; bordered by low, desert-like, pinkish-tinted mountains; elevation 1500'.

Season, Fees & Phone: Open all year; please see Appendix for standard Oklahoma state park fees; 14 day limit; park office (405) 563-2238.

Camp Notes: All of the camp areas described here are within the main park complex. Good camping is also available at the park's North Shore area (see separate information).

GREAT PLAINS
Great Plains State Park

Location: Southwest Oklahoma northeast of Altus.

Access: From U.S. Highway 183 at a point 1.5 miles north of the small community of Mountain Park, 5 miles north of Snyder and 10 miles south of Roosevelt, turn west onto a paved access road; proceed west for 2 miles, then turn sharply north (right); continue for a remaining total of 2.3 miles north, northwest, then north past the dam, then finally easterly to the campground.

Facilities: 48 campsites with partial hookups; (a number of standard camp/picnic sites are also available); sites are small to small+, with nominal separation; parking pads are gravel, mostly medium to long straight-ins; some pads may require a tad of additional leveling; ample, grassy space for large tents in most sites; barbecue grills; b-y-o firewood; water at sites; restrooms with showers; holding tank disposal station; paved driveways; gas and groceries in Mountain Park and Roosevelt; limited+ supplies and services are available in Snyder.

Activities & Attractions: Fishing for walleye, crappie, bass, wipers and catfish; walleye tournament in spring; boating; boat launches; swimming beaches; nature trail; playground.

Natural Features: Located on a shoreside flat and on a gentle slope above the south-east shore of Tom Steed Lake; campground vegetation consists of tracts of mown grass sprinkled with hardwoods which provide minimal to light shade for most sites; rocky hills and mountains form the backdrop for the campground; elevation 1400'.

Season, Fees & Phone: Open all year; please see Appendix for standard Oklahoma state park fees; 14 day limit; park office (405) 569-2032.

Camp Notes: In a way, the park's name is a misnomer. Although it is indeed on the Great Plains, it really could have been christened after the prominent mountains which dot the sea of grass around the lake. (In fact, the original name for the reservoir was the "Mountain Park Project".) The mountain-plains-lake view from most sites is excellent.

DORIS
Wichita Mountains National Wildlife Refuge

Location: Southwest Oklahoma northwest of Lawton.

Access: From U.S. Highway 62 in the city of Cache, head north on Oklahoma State Highway 115 for 4 miles to the wildlife refuge boundary; continue north for 2 miles, then west (curving around Quanah Parker Lake and past the visitor center turnoff) for an additional 1.7 miles; turn south/southeast (left) for 0.1 mile to the campground. **Alternate Accesses:** From the junction of State Highways 54 & 49, travel east for 13.5 miles; from the junction of Interstate 44 Exit 45 & Highway 49, travel west for 15.5 miles to the campground.)

Facilities: 70 campsites, including 23 with electrical hookups, in 5 loops; (in addition, 20 walk-in sites are also available); sites are small+ to medium-sized, with fair to fairly good separation; parking pads are gravel, medium-length straight-ins; some pads may require a little additional leveling; medium to large tent spots; barbecue grills; a limited amount of firewood is available for gathering; water at central faucets; restrooms with showers; holding tank disposal station; paved driveways; limited+ supplies in Cache.

Activities & Attractions: Buffalo, elk, longhorn, deer, prairie dogs, etc., roaming freely within the refuge; hiking trails; visitor center; limited boating and/or fishing on more than a half-dozen small lakes.

Natural Features: Located on a slightly rolling, wooded slope above the northwest shore of Quanah Parker Lake; sites are very well sheltered/shaded by moderately dense hardwoods; surrounded by the grassy-sloped, rocky-topped Wichita Mountains; elevation 1600'.

Season, Fees & Phone: Open all year; $7.00 for a standard or walk-in site, $10.00 for a hookup site; 10-14 day limit, depending upon the season; Wichita Mountains National Wildlife Refuge Headquarters (405) 429-3222.

Camp Notes: Be sure to obtain a brochure/map at a refuge information station near an entrance in order to determine all the "don'ts" (and the few "do's") for the refuge. This is one of the most forested camps in Western Oklahoma.

KIOWA I

Waurika Lake/Corps of Engineers Park

Location: South-central Oklahoma southeast of Lawton.

Access: From Oklahoma State Highway 5 at a point 1.1 miles southeast of the hamlet of Hastings, turn north onto a paved lake access road and proceed 2 miles; turn east (right) for 0.4 miles to the campground entrance; turn north (left) to one group of sites, or continue ahead for another 0.4 mile to the remaining sites. **Alternate Access:** From Oklahoma State Highway 53 in Corum, travel south on a paved local road for 7 miles; turn east (left) for 1.4 miles to the campground entrance and the campground.

Facilities: 180 campsites with electrical hookups in 2 sections; sites are medium-sized, with fairly good spacing; parking pads are paved, medium to long straight-ins or pull-throughs; a little additional leveling will probably be required; plenty of space for tents; ramadas (sun/partial wind shelters) for many sites; barbecue grills; b-y-o firewood; water at central faucets; restrooms with showers; holding tank disposal station; paved driveways; limited+ supplies and services are available in Temple, 8 miles west.

Activities & Attractions: Fishing; boating; boat launch; swimming beach; large playground; information center.

Natural Features: Located on a large point of land on the west shore of Waurika Lake; campground vegetation consists of about a square mile of grass dotted with a few trees; a number of sites are shoreside; unrestricted lake views from virtually all sites; the lake is encircled by open plains; elevation 1000'.

Season, Fees & Phone: Open all year, with limited services, November to April; $11.00; 14 day limit; Waurika Lake CoE Project Office (405) 228-2111.

Camp Notes: The Natural Features section may seem to provide a stern description of this campground. It certainly is very "plainsy", but it's just as certainly pleasing. The contemporary, wood-and-stone ramadas help decorate the open slopes. (The other 'Kiowa', Kiowa II, is a day use only facility.)

WICHITA RIDGE

Waurika Lake/Corps of Engineers Park

Location: South-central Oklahoma southeast of Lawton.

Access: From Oklahoma State Highway 5 in the hamlet of Hastings, turn north onto a paved lake access road and proceed 4.2 miles; turn east (right) for 0.4 mile to the campground. **Alternate Access:** From Oklahoma State Highway 53 in what remains of Corum, travel south on a paved local road for 5 miles to the campground turnoff. (Note: this area is situated midway between 2 causeways; whether you approach from north or south, you'll know you're close after you've crossed a section of the lake.)

Facilities: 27 campsites; sites are medium+ in size, with fairly good separation; parking pads are paved, medium to long straight-ins; a little additional leveling will be required in most sites; ample space for tents, though it may be sloped; ramadas (sun/partial wind shelters) for a few sites; barbecue grills; b-y-o firewood; water at central faucets; vault facilities; paved driveways; gas and camper supplies, seasonally, 2.5 miles north (toward Corum); limited+ supplies and services are available in Temple, 10 miles southwest.

Activities & Attractions: Fishing; boating; boat launch; Walker Creek Nature Trail, across the lake, 2 miles north.

Natural Features: Located on a ridge on a point of land on the north-west shore of Waurika Lake, a flood-control impoundment on Beaver Creek (a tributary of the Red River); campground vegetation consists of a few small hardwoods on a grassy surface; level plains surround the lake; elevation 1000'.

Season, Fees & Phone: April to November; $5.00; 14 day limit; Waurika Lake CoE Project Office (405) 228-2111.

Camp Notes: Considering all the fish attracters which remain standing at this end of the lake, this should be a productive, cheap fishing camp. The area is also called Wichita Ridge North. A good bargain basement camp.

CHISHOLM TRAIL
Waurika Lake/Corps of Engineers Park

Location: South-central Oklahoma southeast of Lawton.

Access: From Oklahoma State Highway 5 at a point 5 miles east of Hastings, 1 mile east of the turnoff to the project office and 4 miles northwest of Waurika, (at the northeast corner of a sweeping curve in the highway), turn north onto a paved local road and proceed 3.2 miles; turn west (left) onto a paved lake access road and continue for 0.9 mile; turn south (left) into the campground.

Facilities: 94 campsites with electrical hookups; sites are small+ to medium-sized, with fair spacing; parking pads are paved, medium to long straight-ins, plus a number of long pull-throughs; a touch of additional leveling will be required in some sites; tent space galore; ramadas (sun/partial wind shelters) for most sites; barbecue grills; b-y-o firewood; water at several faucets; restrooms with showers; holding tank disposal station; paved driveways; gas and camper supplies nearby; limited+ supplies and services are available in Waurika.

Activities & Attractions: Boat launch; swimming beach; good fishing for crappie, largemouth bass, and wipers; playground.

Natural Features: Located on an almost treeless point on the east shore of Waurika Lake; some sites are situated along a fairly well sheltered bay, a number of others are along the open shore; spacious, open, grassy infield; windswept; elevation 1000'.

Season, Fees & Phone: April to November; $11.00; 14 day limit; Waurika Lake CoE Project Office (405) 228-2111.

Camp Notes: Because of its smaller size and slightly more distant location, Chisholm Trail is usually somewhat quieter than its sister camp, Kiowa I, on the opposite shore. Except for the foregoing minor consideration, they're both fine, Great Plains lake camps.

OKLAHOMA

Northeast

Please refer to the Oklahoma map in the Appendix

SARGE CREEK COVE
Kaw Lake/Corps of Engineers Park

Location: Northern Oklahoma east of Ponca City.

Access: From Oklahoma State Highway 11 at a point 3 miles east of Kaw City, 0.3 mile east of the Kaw Lake Dam, and 8.45 miles west of Shidler, turn south onto a paved access road and proceed 0.2 mile to the campground entrance station and the campground.

Facilities: 51 campsites, many with partial hookups, in 3 loops; sites are small to medium-sized (many are narrow but deep), essentially level, with nominal to good separation; parking pads are gravel, long straight-ins, some are extra wide; some pads, especially in loop B, may require some additional leveling; large, framed-and-gravelled tent pads; ramadas (sun shelters) for some sites; barbecue grills; firewood is usually available for gathering in the area; water at faucets throughout; restrooms with showers; auxiliary vaults; holding tank disposal station; mostly paved driveways, some gravel sub-drives; gas and camper supplies are available in Kaw City.

Activities & Attractions: Boating; boat launch; fishing; playground; amphitheater; designated off road vehicle (orv) area nearby.

Natural Features: Located on the grassy east shore of Kaw Lake, an impoundment on the Arkansas River; campground vegetation consists of tall grass, scattered shade trees and dense stands of hardwoods; some sites have views of the lake and the forested slopes beyond; elevation 1000'.

Season, Fees & Phone: April to November; $9.00 for a standard site, $12.00 for a partial hookup site; 14 day limit; Kaw Lake CoE Project Office (405) 762-5611.

Camp Notes: Sarge Creek campers are many and the campsites are varied. Loop C campsites are mostly situated on an open grassy flat just above the shoreline, while sites in Loops A & B are in or along the edge of a densely wooded area. Sarge Creek is generally kept open later in the season than the other campgrounds on Kaw Lake.

Oklahoma 30

OSAGE COVE
Kaw Lake/Corps of Engineers Park

Location: Northern Oklahoma east of Ponca City.

Access: From U.S. Highway 60 at a point 9.7 miles east of Ponca City and 31 miles west of Pawhuska, turn north onto a paved local road toward Kaw Dam; proceed 0.4 mile, then turn east (right); continue east and north for 2 miles (paved); turn west (left) onto a paved access road for the last 0.6 mile to the campground.

Facilities: 94 campsites, including 20 with electrical hookups, in 4 loops; sites are medium to medium+, with fair to very good separation; parking pads are gravel or paved, pull-offs or straight-ins, ranging from medium to long; many pads may require additional leveling; medium to large tent areas; several sites have ramadas (sun shelters); barbecue grills and fire rings; firewood is available for gathering in the area; water at several faucets; restrooms with showers; holding tank disposal station; paved driveways; camper supplies are available at several locations within 3 miles.

Activities & Attractions: Fishing (crappie and catfish); boating; sailing; boat launch; amphitheater; playground; swimming beach, 2 miles south at Sandy Park.

Natural Features: Located on a forested slope on the southeast shore of Kaw Lake; most sites are ringed with dense, tall hardwoods and undergrowth; some, more open, lakeside sites; other sites away from the shore have lake views through the trees; elevation 1000'.

Season, Fees & Phone: March to November; $8.00 for a standard site, $11.00 for an electrical hookup site; 14 day limit; Kaw Lake CoE Project Office (405) 762-5611.

Camp Notes: Check out the nice, airy lakeside sites if you can cope with a steeeep slope. Some other (also sloped) sites are tucked away in pockets of dense foliage. Still another loop offers more level, lightly forested sites along a protected inlet.

Oklahoma 31

COON CREEK COVE
Kaw Lake/Corps of Engineers Park

Location: Northern Oklahoma east of Ponca City.

Access: From Oklahoma State Highway 11 at a point 5.1 miles west of Kaw City and 6 miles east of the junction of Highway 11 with U.S. Highway 77 (12 miles northeast of the junction of U.S. 77 & U.S. 60 south of Ponca City) turn north onto a paved access road and travel 1 mile; turn east (right) and proceed 2 miles to a "T" intersection; turn north (left) and continue for 0.25 mile to the campground.

Facilities: Approximately 30 campsites, many with partial hookups, a few with electrical-only hookups, in 2 loops; sites are medium-sized, with nominal to fair separation; parking pads are gravel, mostly level, long straight-ins; large, slightly sloped, grassy tent spots; ramadas (sun shelters) for some sites; barbecue grills; firewood is available for gathering in the general vicinity; water at central faucets; restrooms with showers; holding tank disposal station; paved driveways; adequate supplies and services are available in Ponca City.

Activities & Attractions: Boating; sailing; fishing; boat ramp adjacent to the camp area.

Natural Features: Located in a wooded basin on a bluff above the west shore of Kaw Lake; campground vegetation consists of tall grass, and medium-sized planted hardwoods which provide fairly good shade/shelter for most sites; lake views from some sites; a stream flows alongside a number of the sites near the entrance; elevation 1000'.

Season, Fees & Phone: April to September; $9.00 for a standard site, $12.00 for a partial hookup site; 14 day limit; Kaw Lake CoE Project Office (405) 762-5611.

Camp Notes: The facilities here at Coon Creek are less polished than those across the lake at Osage Cove and Sage Creek Cove Campgrounds. Try Coon Creek if the "full" shingle is out at those more popular campgrounds, or if you'd just like a more out-of-the-way spot.

WAH-SHA-SHE: WEST
Wah-Sha-She State Park

Location: Northern Oklahoma north of Bartlesville.

Access: From Oklahoma State Highway 10 at a point 9.3 miles east of the junction of State Highways 10 & 99 and 0.2 mile west of Hulah Dam, turn north onto a paved access road and proceed 0.45 mile to the park entrance and the campground.

Facilities: 56 campsites, including 47 with partial hookups; sites are generally small, with nominal separation; parking pads are gravel, medium-length straight-ins; some pads may require a bit of additional leveling; spacious, basically level, grassy tent areas; barbecue grills and some fire rings; firewood is usually available for gathering in the vicinity; water at faucets throughout; restrooms with showers; holding tank disposal station; paved driveways, gravel sub-drives; gas and groceries are available in Copan, 12 miles east.

Activities & Attractions: Boating; sailing; boat launch; fishing (largemouth bass, white bass, crappie, catfish); designated swimming beach; day use area with shelters.

Natural Features: Located along the south shore of Hulah Lake; campground vegetation consists of mown lawns dotted with small and medium-sized oaks and a few bushes; forested slopes surround the lake; elevation 700'.

Season, Fees & Phone: April to September; please see Appendix for standard Oklahoma state park fees; 14 day limit; park office (918) 532-4627.

Camp Notes: The West unit's campsites are stretched out along both sides of a lakeside roadway. There's some pass-by traffic, balanced by good separation and unrestricted views of the lake from virtually all sites. Another unit of the state park, Wah-Sha-She East, is located on the southeast shore of Hulah Lake near the east end of Hulah Dam. It has ten tent sites, bbq grills, tables, and vaults on a mown, grassy slope near a boat ramp. Both Wah-Sha-She units reportedly fill to capacity on many weekends in early summer.

CANEY BEND
Hulah Lake/Corps of Engineers Park

Location: Northern Oklahoma north of Bartlesville.

Access: From Oklahoma State Highway 10 at a point 7.8 miles east of the junction of State Highway 10 & State Highway 99 and 1.7 miles west of Hulah Dam, turn north onto a paved access road and proceed 0.55 mile to a "T" intersection; swing right and continue for another 0.3 mile to a "Y" intersection, then bear left into the campground.

Facilities: 32 campsites in a complex loop; sites are medium-sized, with fair to very good separation; parking pads are gravel, long straight-ins or long pull-throughs; many pads may require additional leveling; large, grassy tent spots; fire rings or barbecue grills; firewood is available for gathering; water at central faucets; vault facilities; holding tank disposal station; paved main driveway, gravel sub-drives; gas and groceries are available in Copan, 13 miles east.

Activities & Attractions: Boating; boat launch nearby at Hulah Cove; fishing; playground; gravel beach; day use area.

Natural Features: Located on a forested point above the south shore of Hulah Lake; campground vegetation consists of fairly dense, tall oaks and conifers, moderately dense underbrush and mown grass; several sites are adjacent to an open, grassy central 'park'; elevation 700'.

Season, Fees & Phone: April to September; $8.00; 14 day limit; Hulah Lake CoE Project Office (918) 532-4334.

Camp Notes: This facility is reportedly never crowded. There are two additional CoE camping areas on this lake. Skull Creek, on the east shore, is reached from State Highway 10 just east of Hulah Dam, then north for three miles on a gravel road. Damsite has a few campsites on a grassy flat below the dam, on the northeast bank of the Caney River. No fee is charged for camping at either of those two 'basic' facilities.

POST OAK
Copan Lake/Corps of Engineers Park

Location: Northern Oklahoma north of Bartlesville.

Access: From Oklahoma State Highway 10 at a point 5 miles west of the junction of State Highway 10 & U.S. Highway 75, 19 miles east of the junction of State Highway 10 & State Highway 99 and 1.1 miles northwest of Copan Dam, turn east (the east-west highway follows a north-south line in this segment); proceed 0.3 mile to the campground.

Facilities: 17 campsites, most with electrical hookups, in 2 loops; sites are small to medium-sized, level, with nominal to fairly good separation; parking pads are gravel, medium-length straight-ins; spacious, grassy tent areas; fire rings and barbecue grills; some firewood is available for gathering; water at several faucets; restrooms with showers; holding tank disposal station; paved driveways; gas and groceries are available in Copan, 4 miles east.

Activities & Attractions: Boating; boat launches nearby at Osage Plains and Copan Point; fishing (largemouth bass, crappie, catfish, wiper).

Natural Features: Located on a forested bluff above the southwest shore of Copan Lake; campground vegetation consists of mown grass, and medium to tall oaks and hickory trees sheltering most of the campsites; surrounded by fairly dense woodland and tall grass; about half of the sites have fair to good views of the lake through the trees; elevation 700'.

Season, Fees & Phone: April to October; $8.00 for a standard site, $11.00 for an electrical hookup site; 14 day limit; Copan Lake CoE Project Office (918) 532-4334.

Camp Notes: This very good facility shows signs of being underused. Perhaps one reason is because it isn't close enough to the the boat ramps, which are a couple of miles away. There's a good chance that there will be a spot available at this campground even when the more popular Washington Cove, across the lake, is filled to capacity.

WASHINGTON COVE
Copan Lake/Corps of Engineers Park

Location: Northern Oklahoma north of Bartlesville.

Access: From U.S. Highway 75 at a point 9 miles south of the Kansas border and 9 miles north of Dewey, turn west onto Road 7 and proceed 1.25 miles; turn north onto a paved access road to the campground entrance station; continue for 0.5 mile to the campsites. **Alternate Access:** From Oklahoma State Highway 10 at a point 0.8 mile west of its junction with U.S. Highway 75 and 1.3 miles east of Copan Dam, turn north onto a local road and proceed 1.35 miles; turn west (left) onto Road 7 and continue as above.

Facilities: 99 campsites, most with electric hookups; sites are small to medium-sized, with nominal to fairly good separation; parking pads are gravel, medium to long straight-ins; many pads will require additional leveling; medium to large, fairly level, tent spots; fire rings and barbecue grills; firewood is usually available for gathering; water at several faucets; restrooms with showers; holding tank disposal station; paved driveways; gas and groceries are available in Copan.

Activities & Attractions: Boating; fishing (catfish, bass, crappie, and wiper); boat launch nearby at Copan Point.

Natural Features: Located on the densely forested east shore of Copan Lake, an impoundment on Little Caney River; campground vegetation consists of large oaks and other hardwoods, moderately dense undergrowth, and mown grass; sites along the lake are lightly shaded; sites farther up the slope are well shaded; views of the lake and surrounding forested bluffs from some sites; elevation 700'.

Season, Fees & Phone: April to October; $8.00 for a standard site, $11.00 for an electrical hookup site; 14 day limit; Copan Lake CoE Project Office (918) 532-4334.

Camp Notes: The Corps has come up with a fine facility in a good spot here at Washington Cove. Don't get discouraged if you don't find the campsites immediately after you pass the entrance station. They're kind of tucked away amidst all of the greenery.

OSAGE HILLS
Osage Hills State Park

Location: Northern Oklahoma west of Bartlesville.

Access: From U.S. Highway 60 at a point 11 miles west of Bartlesville and 7.8 miles east of the junction of U.S. Highway 60 & Oklahoma State Highway 99, turn south onto the park access road; proceed 2.7 miles, then turn west (right) into the hookup campground; or turn north (another right) and continue for 0.2 mile up a steep paved road to the tent camping area.

Facilities: 21 campsites with partial hookups in the main loop, plus about 15 tent campsites in a second loop; sites are small, with nominal to fair separation; parking pads are paved, mostly medium to long straight-ins or pull-throughs, (pull-offs in the tent loop); many pads will require some additional leveling; medium to large, grassy tent areas, some may be a bit sloped; barbecue grills and fireplaces; b-y-o firewood; water at central faucets; restrooms with showers; holding tank disposal station; paved driveways; complete supplies and services are available in Bartlesville.

Activities & Attractions: Hiking; swimming pool; fishing; limited boating; tennis courts.

Natural Features: Located in the densely forested Osage Hills; sites in the lower (hookup) section are on a mown grass slope shaded by tall oak trees; sites in the upper (tent) section are situated on a tree-dotted grassy flat; Sand Creek and 18-acre Lookout Lake are within the park; elevation 800'.

Season, Fees & Phone: Open all year; please see Appendix for standard Oklahoma state park fees; 14 day limit; park office (918) 336-4141.

Camp Notes: Near the tent area is a picturesque stone lookout structure which offers an outstanding view of the surrounding countryside. The extremely dense hardwood vegetation makes this park an exceptional place to spend some time, particularly during the colorful fall foliage displays.

BIRCH COVE
Birch Lake/Corps of Engineers Park

Location: Northeast Oklahoma northwest of Tulsa.

Access: From Oklahoma State Highway 11 in Barnsdall at the intersection of West Main Street and South 8th, turn south onto South 8th; proceed south for 3.6 miles; turn west (right) onto the Birch Cove access road and continue for 0.7 mile to the park entrance station; the campground is 0.3 mile farther north.

Facilities: 91 campsites with electrical hookups in 4 loops and several strings; sites are small+ to medium-sized, with nominal to good separation; parking pads are hard-surfaced, long straight-ins; many pads may require additional leveling; medium to large spots for tents are grassy, or on a framed gravel surface; some tent areas may be a bit sloped; barbecue grills or firerings; firewood is usually available for gathering in the area; water at several faucets; restrooms with showers; holding tank disposal station; paved driveways; limited supplies and services are available in Barnsdall.

Activities & Attractions: Boating; boat launch; fishing; swimming beach; amphitheater; playground; E-Loh-Gah Nature Trail.

Natural Features: Located on a slope and a ridgetop above the southeast shore of 1100-acre Birch Lake; campground vegetation consists of tall spreading oaks, bushes and tall grass (usually mown within the site); good lake views or lake glimpses from many sites; the lake is encircled by heavily wooded hills; elevation 800'.

Season, Fees & Phone: April to October; $11.00; 14 day limit; Birch Lake CoE Project Office (918) 847-2001.

Camp Notes: Another CoE campground on the northeast corner of the lake is Twin Cove Point. It's in a similar setting, has central water, vault facilities, paved pads and driveways, but no fee.

TALL CHIEF COVE
Skiatook Lake/Corps of Engineers Park

Location: Northeast Oklahoma northeast of Tulsa.

Access: From Oklahoma State Highway 20 at a point 6 miles west of Skiatook and 17 miles east of Hominy, turn south onto the lake access road and travel (past the Skiatook Lake Project Office, across the dam and along the east end of the lake) for 4.9 miles; turn west (left) onto the Tall Chief Cove access road (paved) and proceed 1.3 miles to the campground entrance station; continue ahead for 0.1 mile to the campground.

Facilities: 57 campsites, most with electrical hookups; sites are medium-sized, with fair to fairly good separation; parking pads are gravel, medium-length straight-ins, and most are reasonably level; medium to large areas for tents, some may be slightly sloped; barbecue grills or fire rings; firewood is available for gathering in the area; water at central faucets; restrooms with showers; auxiliary vault facilities; paved driveways; limited+ to adequate supplies and services are available in Skiatook and Hominy.

Activities & Attractions: Boating; boat launch; fishing; swimming beach; Tall Chief Cove self-guiding nature trail.

Natural Features: Located at the southeast end of Skiatook Lake, a 10,000-acre impoundment on Hominy Creek; sites receive light to medium shade/shelter from large hardwoods, tall grass and underbrush; the lake is surrounded by high, densely forested hills; elevation 700'.

Season, Fees & Phone: April to October; $8.00 for a standard site, $11.00 for an electrical hookup site; 14 day limit; Skiatook Lake CoE Project Office (918) 396-2345.

Camp Notes: This may be one of the most underrated, unsung, and undiscovered lakes in the state. The scenery is good (the tree-blanketed hills complement the lake's sparkling blue surface); boating is good (the water is typically very clear); and fishing is good (smallmouth bass in the 5 pound category are fairly common.) Add it all up and it equals a potentially excellent recreational opportunity.

Oklahoma 39

HAWTHORN BLUFF
Oologah Lake/Corps of Engineers Park

Location: Northeast Oklahoma northeast of Tulsa.

Access: From Oklahoma State Highway 88 at a point 1.8 miles east of its junction with U.S. Highway 169 at the south edge of the town of Oologah and 0.3 mile north of Oologah Dam (a few yards north of the Oologah Lake Project Office), turn northeast onto a paved access road and continue for 0.25 mile to the campground.

Facilities: 67 campsites, most with electrical hookups; sites are small+, with nominal to fair separation; parking pads are gravel, medium to long straight-ins or long pull-throughs; many pads may require some additional leveling; large, mostly level, tent spots on a surface of grass or bare earth; barbecue grills and fire rings; firewood is usually available for gathering in the vicinity; water at central faucets; restrooms with showers; holding tank disposal station; paved driveways; gas and groceries are available in Oologah.

Activities & Attractions: Boating; boat launch; fishing; designated swimming beach; Skull Hollow Nature Trail; playground; amphitheater.

Natural Features: Located on a rolling, forested hill above the southwest shore of 30,000-acre Oologah Lake; tall oaks and hickory trees provide ample shade/shelter for many of the sites; some fairly open sites are on tree-dotted lawns close to the lake; several lakeside sites have nice views of a cove; the lake is surrounded by low, forested hills; elevation 700'.

Season, Fees & Phone: April to October; $8.00 for a standard site, $11.00 for an electrical hookup site; 14 day limit; Oologah Lake CoE Project Office (918) 266-2326.

Camp Notes: If Oologah Lake is your target, seriously consider Hawthorn Bluff as *the* place to stay. There's lots to do here, the scenery is great and Hawthorne Bluff *is* easy to get to. (Unless the highway department has been hard at work recently, the other recreation areas on this lake, even those with good facilities, have *rough* access roads.)

Oklahoma 40

BLUE CREEK
Oologah Lake/Corps of Engineers Park

Location: Northeast Oklahoma north of Tulsa.

Access: From Oklahoma State Highway 66 in Foyil (9 miles south of Chelsea, 10 miles northeast of Claremore), turn west onto a paved local access road (signed for Oologah Lake); proceed west across the railroad tracks, swing north, then immediately west again; proceed 2.3 miles west and turn north (right) onto another paved local road; continue north for 0.9 mile, then turn west (left) once again; travel 1.7 miles to the campground entrance station; Loop A is to the left and Loop B is to the right.

Facilities: 61 campsites including many in with electrical hookups Loop A; sites are small to medium-sized, with nominal to fair separation; parking pads in Loop A are paved, long pull-throughs; parking pads in Loop B are gravel, medium to long straight-ins; many pads may require additional leveling; adequate, though slightly sloped, space for large tents; barbecue grills and some fire rings; firewood is sometimes available for gathering, b-y-o is recommended; water at central faucets; restrooms with showers in Loop A, vault facilities in Loop B; paved driveways; gas and groceries are available in Foyil.

Activities & Attractions: Boating; boat ramp; fishing; playground.

Natural Features: Located on a slope above a major bay on the southeast shore of Oologah Lake; sites receive light to medium shade/shelter from hardwoods; bordered by fairly dense woodlands; several unusual geological formations or "mounds" are in the vicinity; elevation 700'.

Season, Fees & Phone: April to September; $6.00 for a standard site in Loop B, $8.00 for a standard site in Loop A, $11.00 for an electrical hookup site; 14 day limit; Oologah Lake CoE Project Office (918) 266-2326.

Camp Notes: If you stay at Blue Creek, you may well be roaming the same hillsides as Will Rogers did. The renowned cowboy-humorist was born in the Verdigris River Valley in 1879.

Oklahoma 41

WALNUT CREEK
Walnut Creek State Park

Location: Northeast Oklahoma west of Tulsa.

Access: From U.S. Highways 64/412 at the exit for South 209th Street West (5 miles west of Sand Springs, 2.7 miles east of the bridge which spans Keystone Lake), head northwest on South 209th St. W. for 14 miles to a point 0.8 mile west of the village of Prue; turn south onto the main park access road and proceed 1.4 miles to the main camping area.

Facilities: 172 campsites, including 88 with electrical or partial hookups; sites are medium-sized, with nominal to fairly good separation; parking pads are gravel/grass, mostly medium to long straight-ins; a few pads may require a little additional leveling; good-sized areas for tents; barbecue grills or fireplaces; b-y-o firewood is suggested; water at partial hookups and at several faucets; central restrooms with showers; vault facilities; holding tank disposal station; paved driveways; gas and groceries are available in Prue.

Activities & Attractions: Boating; boat launches; fishing; swimming beach; playground; day use areas.

Natural Features: Located on 3 points of land on the north shore of the main branch (Arkansas River Arm) of Keystone Lake; sites receive light to medium shade from large hardwoods on grassy flats and gentle slopes; bordered by hilly woodland and prairie; elevation 750'.

Season, Fees & Phone: Open all year; 14 day limit; reservations accepted for 28 assigned partial hookup sites; please see Appendix for additional reservation information and standard Oklahoma state park fees; park office (918) 242-3362.

Camp Notes: The main camp, Area 2, has seven loops, with mostly hookup sites and many standard sites; additional sites are in Area 1, a mile east, and in Area 3, a mile west. Since the campsites are scattered over a couple of square miles in ten loops, there isn't that bursting-at-the-seams feeling here that some parks have. A solid, out-of-the-way place.

Oklahoma 42

APPALACHIA BAY
Keystone Lake/Corps of Engineers Park

Location: Northeast Oklahoma west of Tulsa.

Access: From U.S. Highways 64/412 (Keystone Expressway) at a point 0.3 mile northwest of the bridge which crosses Keystone Lake/Arkansas River, 10 miles northwest of Sand Springs and 8 miles east of the east end of the Cimarron Turnpike, go to the south side of the divided highway and drive northwest on a frontage road for 0.5 mile; turn southwest (left) and proceed 1.2 miles to the park entrance; continue ahead for 0.2 mile, then bear left for a final 0.2 mile to the campground.

Facilities: 18 campsites; sites are small+ to medium-sized, with nominal to fair separation; parking pads are gravel, long straight-ins; a touch of additional leveling may be required in some sites; ample space for large tents; barbecue grills; b-y-o firewood is recommended; water at central faucets; vault facilities; gas and groceries within 1 mile; adequate+ supplies and services are available in Sand Springs.

Activities & Attractions: Boating; boat launch; fishing; swimming beach.

Natural Features: Located at the end of a point on the shore of Keystone Lake (on what was formerly the north bank of the Cimarron River in this spot); sites receive light shade from large hardwoods; elevation 750'.

Season, Fees & Phone: Open all year; $5.00; 14 day limit; Keystone Lake CoE Project Office (918) 864-2239.

Camp Notes: In spring of a typical year, fishing for sand bass in this area is said to be absolutely wild--flip a line, hook a fish. There are some really nice tent sites here. For a site with electricity, you could try Washington Irving Cove South, which is off the north side of the main highway. Washington Irving is on what many campers consider to be one of the prettiest sections of the lake.

Oklahoma 43

NEW MANNFORD
Keystone Lake/Corps of Engineers Park

Location: Northeast Oklahoma west of Tulsa.

Access: From Oklahoma State Highway 51 at the east edge of the city of Mannford, turn north onto a city avenue and proceed 0.6 mile; turn east (right) onto a paved park access road for 0.4 mile to the campground entrance station and the campground.

Facilities: 45 campsites with electrical hookups; sites are medium-sized, most are passably level, with nominal to fair separation; parking pads are gravel, medium to long straight-ins; adequate space for large tents on a grassy surface; barbecue grills; b-y-o firewood is recommended; water at several faucets; restrooms with showers; auxiliary vault facilities; holding tank disposal station; paved main driveways, gravel sub-drives; adequate supplies and services are available in Mannford.

Activities & Attractions: Boating; boat launches; fishing; fishing pier.

Natural Features: Located on a flat and a gentle slope on the shore of Salt Creek Arm, 1 of 3 major arms or branches of Keystone Lake; some sites are quite in the open, others are well-sheltered by large hardwoods; the lake is bordered by wooded hills and bluffs; elevation 750'.

Season, Fees & Phone: Open all year; $11.00; 14 day limit; Keystone Lake CoE Project Office (918) 864-2239.

Camp Notes: The city of Mannford bills itself as the "Striped Bass Capitol of Keystone Lake", so it's no wonder that this park has two boat ramps. This campground is said to be a favorite with senior campers because it's generally somewhat quieter than some other camps on the lake. (The park, which is also known as New Mannford Ramp, has limited day use facilities, and consequently a smaller volume of day-tripper traffic.) Its location on the edge of a sizeable community and all of its attendant services also bolsters its popularity with campers. (Mannford was reborn a quarter-century ago after the original townsite was inundated by the new lake's waters.)

Oklahoma 44

SALT CREEK COVE NORTH
Keystone Lake/Corps of Engineers Park

Location: Northeast Oklahoma west of Tulsa.

Access: From Oklahoma State Highway 51 at a point 2 miles east of Mannford and 12 miles west of Sand Springs, turn north to the park entrance station; continue ahead, left or right to the campsites.

Facilities: 126 campsites, most with electrical hookups, in 3 loops; sites are medium-sized, with nominal to fair separation; parking pads are gravel, medium to very long straight-ins; some pads will require a little additional leveling; large, mostly level areas for tents; barbecue grills; b-y-o firewood is suggested; water at central faucets; restrooms with showers; holding tank disposal station; paved main driveways, gravel sub-drives; adequate supplies and services are available in Mannford.

Activities & Attractions: Boating; boat launches and dock; fishing (good for stripers, also black bass, sand bass, cats, crappie); swimming beach; playground; day use facilities.

Natural Features: Located on a trio of small points at the northwest tip of a major point of land on the Salt Creek Arm on the south side of Keystone Lake; the lake is a 26,000-acre impoundment with several long, slender branches, at the confluence of the Arkansas and Cimarron Rivers; campground vegetation consists of light to medium-dense, large hardwoods and grass; the lake is bordered by well-wooded hills and bluffs; elevation 750'.

Season, Fees & Phone: Open all year; $8.00 for a standard site, $11.00 for an electrical hookup site; 14 day limit; Keystone Lake CoE Project Office (918) 864-2239.

Camp Notes: Lakes established as a consequence of dams built by the CoE often take their names from local communities which receive flood protection from the dam. In this case, however, the former community of Keystone (so called because of its 'key' position at the meeting place of the Cimarron and Arkansas Rivers), was obliterated by the lake which now bears its name.

Oklahoma 45

KEYSTONE
Keystone State Park

Location: Northeast Oklahoma west of Tulsa.

Access: From the junction of Oklahoma State Highway 51 & State Highway 151 (5 miles east of Mannford, 9 miles west of Sand Springs), turn north onto Highway 151 and proceed 0.4 mile; turn west (left) onto the park access road and proceed 0.4 mile to a fork; turn left to Area 1 (partial hookups) or continue ahead to Area 3 (full hookups and standard) & Area 4 (standard). **Alternate Access:** From U.S Highways 64/412 (Keystone Expressway) at the exit for Keystone Dam and Mannford (7 miles west of Sand Springs), turn south onto State Highway 151 and proceed (across Keystone Dam) for 2 miles to the park access road.

Facilities: 136 campsites, including 77 with partial hookups and 25 assigned (reservable) sites with full hookups; sites are small+, with nominal separation; parking pads are mostly gravel (paved in Area 3), medium to long straight-ins; additional leveling will be needed in Area 1; medium to large tent areas; barbecue grills; b-y-o firewood is suggested; water at faucets throughout; restrooms with showers; holding tank disposal station; paved main driveways, some gravel sub-drives; adequate supplies and services are available in Mannford.

Activities & Attractions: Boating; boat launch; fishing; paved, hike/bike trail; playgrounds; central shelters.

Natural Features: Located on a hilly point above a bay on the south shore of Keystone Lake; sites receive minimal to medium shade/shelter from hardwoods on a grassy surface; bordered by wooded hills; elevation 800'.

Season, Fees & Phone: Open all year; reservations accepted for assigned sites; please see Appendix for additional reservation information and standard Oklahoma state park fees; 14 day limit; park office (918) 865-4991.

Camp Notes: Some of the nicer sites are on a tiered slope in Area 1. They all have lake views, and one tier is just a few feet above lake level. There are also some good standard/tent sites in Area 4.

Oklahoma 46

HEYBURN
Heyburn State Park

Location: Northeast Oklahoma southwest of Tulsa.

Access: From Oklahoma State Highway 33 at a point 3 miles east of its junction with State Highway 48 north of Bristow and 13 miles west of Sapulpa, turn south onto a paved park access road and proceed 2.2 miles south, then 1.2 miles east; turn south (right) into the *Sheppard Point* area; or continue east for an additional 0.5 mile, then turn south into the *Rocky Point* (assigned camping) area.

Facilities: *Sheppard Point*: 33 standard campsites; *Rocky Point*: 33 campsites with partial hookups; *both areas*: sites are small, with nominal separation; parking pads are gravel, medium-length straight-ins for hookup sites, pull-offs for standard sites; some pads may require a little additional leveling; adequate space for large tents on a grassy surface; barbecue grills; b-y-o firewood is suggested; water at hookup sites and at central faucets; restrooms with showers; holding tank disposal station; paved main driveways, gravel sub-drives; adequate supplies and services are available in Sapulpa.

Activities & Attractions: Swimming beach; Sheppard Cove Trail; boating; boat launch; playgrounds; central shelter.

Natural Features: Located on a pair of points on the north shore of 3800-acre Heyburn Lake; sites receive light to medium shade/shelter from large hardwoods, plus some pines and junipers/cedars; elevation 800'.

Season, Fees & Phone: Open all year; reservations accepted for assigned sites; please see Appendix for additional reservation information and standard Oklahoma state park fees; 14 day limit; park office (918) 247-6695.

Camp Notes: Picture this: The state park is located on adjacent, dual points on the *north* shore, right? Sheppard Point is deep within the 'grasp' of the 'pincers' of the twin points of Heyburn CoE Park which extend a considerable distance from the *south* shore. Thus you can stand at the tip of Sheppard point and look south, west, east and even *northwest* and *northeast* and still see the lake's south shore!

HEYBURN
Heyburn Lake/Corps of Engineers Park

Location: Northeast Oklahoma southwest of Tulsa.

Access: From Oklahoma State Highway 66 at a point 4 miles southwest of Kellyville and 11 miles northeast of Bristow, turn north onto a paved lake access road and proceed 2 miles north, then west past the dam for another 1.9 miles; turn north (right) to the campground entrance station; continue ahead for 0.1 mile to the campsites.

Facilities: 33 campsites, most with partial hookups; sites are medium-sized, with nominal to fair separation; parking pads are gravel, mostly long straight-ins, plus a few pull-throughs; additional leveling will be needed in about half of the sites; adequate space for medium to large tents; barbecue grills, plus some fire rings; b-y-o firewood is suggested; water at faucets throughout; restrooms with showers; auxiliary vault facilities; holding tank disposal station; paved main driveways, some gravel sub-drives; gas and groceries are available in Kellyville.

Activities & Attractions: Swimming beach; boating; boat launch; fishing; playground; amphitheater; large central shelter; day use area.

Natural Features: Located on a point on the south shore of Heyburn Lake, a 3800-acre impoundment on Polecat Creek; sites receive light to medium shade/shelter from medium to large hardwoods and junipers/cedars; bordered by dense woodland; elevation 800'.

Season, Fees & Phone: Open all year; $8.00 for a standard site, $12.00 for a partial hookup site; 14 day limit; Heyburn Lake CoE Project Office (918) 247-6391.

Camp Notes: Many of the sites here provide excellent vantage points from which to view classic, Oklahoma lake sunsets. Heyburn Lake's other Corps campground, Damsite, also has several lakeview campsites. Damsite is just east of Heyburn Park and has good-sized sites with long, fairly level parking pads, central water, vaults, and no charge for as long as a fortnight.

SPRING RIVER
Spring River State Park

Location: Northeast corner of Oklahoma near the Oklahoma-Kansas-Missouri border.

Access: From Oklahoma State Highway 69A in midtown Quapaw at the corner of Main & 1st Streets (0.2 mile north of the junction of Oklahoma State Highways 69A & 137, 5 miles south of the Kansas-Oklahoma border), drive east on 1st Street for 3.7 miles to the park entrance and the campground.

Facilities: 26 campsites, including 10 with electrical hookups, in a loop and a string; sites are small, with minimal separation; parking pads are gravel, level, short to medium straight-ins or pull-throughs; adequate space for large tents on grass or forest material; barbecue grills; b-y-o firewood is recommended; water at central faucets; vault facilities; paved main driveway, gravel sub-drive; gas and camper supplies in Quapaw.

Activities & Attractions: Canoeing; Spring River Canoe Trail put-in point; fishing; day use area with shelter; sports field.

Natural Features: Located on a forested shelf a few feet above Spring River; tall hardwoods provide light to medium shade/shelter for most sites; river views from some sites; a large, open area of mown grass is adjacent to the campground; elevation 800'.

Season, Fees & Phone: Open all year; please see Appendix for standard Oklahoma state park fees; 14 day limit; park office (918) 542-6969.

Camp Notes: Spring River Park has an atmosphere quite different from most other Oklahoma state parks. Even if you're not planning to paddle down through the tunnel of greenery which envelopes the stream (as quite a few campers do), this is still a pleasant spot to simply sit and ruminate. The wide and typically slow-moving Spring River has a mesmerizing quality.

Oklahoma 49

TWIN BRIDGES
Twin Bridges State Park

Location: Northeast corner of Oklahoma southeast of Miami.

Access: From the junction of U.S. Highway 60 & Oklahoma State Highway 137 (7 miles east of Fairland, 2 miles west of Wyandotte), turn south into Area 1; or proceed north on State Highway 137 for 0.2 mile to the entrances to Area 2 through Area 6 (along both sides of the highway).

Facilities: Approximately 80 campsites, including 62 with electrical hookups; sites are small and closely spaced, or medium-sized with fair spacing; parking pads are gravel, mostly level, medium-length straight-ins and a few medium-length pull-throughs; some pads may require minor additional leveling; generally large, level, tent spots; barbecue grills; b-y-o firewood is recommended; water at several faucets; restrooms with showers; holding tank disposal station; paved driveways; gas and camper supplies are available in Wyandotte.

Activities & Attractions: Boating; fishing; designated swimming beach; playground; central shelters; day use area.

Natural Features: Located on a forested bluff (Areas 2-6) between the Grand (Neosho) River to the west and the Spring River to the east, just north of the confluence of those streams; some sites on the steep 200-foot-high bluff north of Highway 60 overlook one river or the other; other sites (Area 1, off U.S. 60) are within a few yards of the riverbanks; sites are lightly shaded/sheltered by large hardwoods on mown grass; elevation 800'.

Season, Fees & Phone: Open all year; please see Appendix for standard Oklahoma state park fees; 14 day limit; park office (918) 540-2545.

Camp Notes: Campsite surroundings vary considerably at Twin Bridges. Come prepared to look around a little before settling in at a site that's just right for your troop. The park is an excellent vantage point for watching the white pelicans who habitually stop over in April and May and in September and October.

Oklahoma 50

BERNICE
Bernice State Park

Location: Northeast Oklahoma east of Vinita.

Access: From Oklahoma State Highway 85A in the hamlet of Bernice (3 miles east of the junction of State Highways 85A & 85 east of Vinita, 2 miles west of the junction of State Highways 85A & 125), turn south into the campground.

Facilities: 40 campsites, most with electrical hookups; sites are small, with minimal to nominal separation; parking surfaces are gravel or grass, short to medium straight-ins; a few pads may require minor additional leveling; large, level, grassy tent spots; barbecue grills; b-y-o firewood; water at central faucets; restrooms with showers; holding tank disposal station; paved main driveways, gravel sub-drives; gas and camper supplies within 5 miles; virtually complete supplies and services are available in Grove, 14 miles east.

Activities & Attractions: Boating; small boat launch; fishing (largemouth, spotted and white bass, crappie, channel catfish, bluegills and stripers); playground.

Natural Features: Located on the north shore of Grand Lake O' The Cherokees, just east of Horse Creek Cove and west of Monkey Island; campground vegetation consists of mown lawns and scattered, small stands of hardwoods; many sites are beachside; the more sheltered sites are farther from the beach and closer to the highway; elevation 800'.

Season, Fees & Phone: Open all year; please see Appendix for standard Oklahoma state park fees; 14 day limit; park office (918) 786-9447.

Camp Notes: Grand Lake O' The Cherokees has 1300 miles of shoreline, much of which is privately owned. Bernice State Park is one of the relatively few public camping areas on the lake. According to local sources, crappie fishing on Horse Creek Arm, and particularly from the Horse Creek Bridge, attracts innumerable (successful) anglers.

HONEY CREEK
Honey Creek State Park

Location: Northeast Oklahoma east of Vinita.

Access: From U.S. Highway 59/Oklahoma State Highway 10 at a point 1.35 miles south of Grove and 10 miles north of Jay, turn west onto State Park Road and proceed 0.8 mile to the park entrance and the campground.

Facilities: 84 campsites, including 41 with electrical hookups, in 2 loops; sites are small and closely spaced; upper sites are mostly level, while those nearer to the lakeshore are on a fairly steep slope; parking pads are gravel, mostly sloped, short pull-offs at the standard sites, or mostly level medium to long straight-ins in the hookup sites; tent sites are medium to large, grassy and sloped; some barbecue grills and some fire rings; b-y-o firewood; water at several faucets; restrooms with showers; holding tank disposal station; paved main driveways; virtually complete supplies and services are available in Grove.

Activities & Attractions: Boating; sailing; boat launches; fishing (bass, crappie, catfish, stripers); playground; city-operated swimming pool; Har Ber Village museum, reconstructed 19th century settlement, nearby.

Natural Features: Located above the Honey Creek Arm of Grand Lake O' The Cherokees; campground vegetation consists of very tall oaks, other hardwoods and mown grass on the ridgetop; fairly dense tree-and-brush-covered slopes along the lakeshore; most sites are well sheltered; elevation 800'.

Season, Fees & Phone: Open all year; please see Appendix for standard Oklahoma state park fees; 14 day limit; park office (918) 786-9447.

Camp Notes: Because of the many public and privately operated attractions in the Grove area, sites at Honey Creek tend to fill early on holiday weekends. However, reportedly they have "never turned anyone away".

CHEROKEE #1
Cherokee State Park

Location: Northeastern Oklahoma northeast of Tulsa.

Access: From the intersection of Oklahoma State Highway 28 and Broadway Avenue at the east edge of Langley (100 yards west of Pensacola Dam, 0.45 miles east of the junction of Oklahoma State Highways 82 & 28), turn south onto Broadway and follow it south, then east, then south again for 0.9 mile; bear east (left) at a sharp turn in the road and continue for 0.65 mile east and north, then turn northwest (left) off the access road to go down into the campground.

Facilities: 50 campsites, including 18 with electrical hookups; sites are small to medium-sized, essentially level, with minimal to fair separation; parking pads are gravel, medium to long straight-ins; adequate space for large tents on a grassy surface; barbecue grills; b-y-o firewood; water at central faucets; restrooms; holding tank disposal station; paved driveways; limited supplies and services in Langley.

Activities & Attractions: Boating; boat launch; fishing; day use shelter; dam tours in summer.

Natural Features: Located on a riverside flat below Pensacola Dam on the Grand (Neosho) River; campground vegetation consists of mown grass and tall hardwoods which provide medium shade/shelter for most sites; bordered by the main stream on the east and a backwater on the west; a number of sites are streamside; low, wooded bluffs flank the river; elevation 600'.

Season, Fees & Phone: Open all year; please see Appendix for standard Oklahoma state park fees; 14 day limit; park office (918) 435-8086.

Camp Notes: The outlet stream here is a major river with a good, swift current. For those campers who come to fish, (as the majority do), the catch is reportedly very good. And the campground is just that: essentially a fishing camp with a few extras.

CHEROKEE #2 & #3
Cherokee State Park

Location: Northeast Oklahoma northeast of Tulsa.

Access: From the junction of Oklahoma State Highways 82 & State Highway 28 in midtown Langley, proceed east on Oklahoma State Highway 28 (and across Pensacola Dam) for 1.6 miles to Area #2; or travel an additional 0.7 mile to Area #3; turn north into the respective campgrounds.

Facilities: 34 campsites, including 16 with electrical hookups, in the 2 units; sites are small, mostly sloped, with minimal separation; parking pads are gravel, short to medium-length straight-ins or pull-offs; many pads may require additional leveling; adequate, though sloped, space for small tents in Area 2 and medium or large tents in Area 3; barbecue grills or fireplaces; b-y-o firewood is suggested; water at central faucets; restrooms with showers; holding tank disposal station at Area 2; paved driveways; limited supplies and services are available in Langley.

Activities & Attractions: Boating; fishing; playground and swimming beach at Cherokee #2; lighted boat launches; central shelters; day use areas; dam tours during the summer.

Natural Features: Located on forested bluffs above the southwest shore of Grand Lake O' The Cherokees; campground vegetation consists of sparse grass, a little underbrush, and tall hardwoods; many sites have views of the lake through the trees; mile-long Pensacola Dam created Grand Lake and its 1300 miles of shoreline; elevation 700'.

Season, Fees & Phone: Open all year; please see Appendix for standard Oklahoma state park fees; 14 day limit; park office (918) 435-8086.

Camp Notes: Of the five state park units within 3 miles of Pensacola Dam, Cherokee #2 and #3 are the only areas with actual lakefront sites. They are very popular and heavily used.

Oklahoma 54

DISNEY
Disney State Park

Location: Northeast Oklahoma northeast of Tulsa.

Access: From the junction of Oklahoma State Highway 82 & State Highway 28 in Langley, travel east on Oklahoma State Highway 28 (across Pensacola Dam) for 2.5 miles; turn south (right) or north (left) into the camping areas.

Facilities: 22 campsites in 2 sections (15 south and 7 north of the highway); sites are small with minimal separation; parking pads are level, gravel, short to medium-length pull-offs; adequate space for large tents on a grassy surface; barbecue grills or fireplaces; b-y-o firewood is suggested; water at central faucets; restrooms; mostly paved driveways; gas and groceries are available nearby on the highway; limited supplies and services are available in Langley.

Activities & Attractions: Boating; boat launches; fishing; playground.

Natural Features: Located on a grassy, tree-dotted flat 50 yards above the south shore of Grand Lake O' The Cherokees; bordered by forested hills; elevation 700'.

Season, Fees & Phone: Open all year; please see Appendix for standard Oklahoma state park fees; 14 day limit; phone c/o Cherokee State Park (918) 435-8066.

Camp Notes: Camping at Disney puts you within sight and within easy reach of the lake and the boat ramp, but its also along the main highway. For an off-highway camp, check nearby Little Blue State Park, described below.

Oklahoma 55

LITTLE BLUE
Little Blue State Park

Location: Northeast Oklahoma northeast of Tulsa.

Access: From the junction of Oklahoma State Highway 82 & State Highway 28 in Langley, proceed east on Oklahoma State Highway 28 (across the Pensacola Dam) for 2.7 miles; turn south (right) onto a paved local road and proceed south and west for 2 miles down to the campground.

Facilities: 10 campsites; sites are good-sized, with fair separation; parking pads are level, gravel, short to medium-length pull-offs; ample space for large tents on a grassy surface; barbecue grills or fireplaces; b-y-o firewood is suggested; no drinking water in Little Blue (but water is said to be in the works); vault facilities; mostly paved driveways; gas and groceries are available nearby on the highway.

Activities & Attractions: Boating, boat launches, fishing and playground in Disney.

Natural Features: Located on a grassy, tree-dotted, gfently sloping flat along the bank of a small, meandering stream in a small hollow; closely bordered by forested hills; elevation 700'.

Season, Fees & Phone: Open all year; please see Appendix for standard Oklahoma state park fees; 14 day limit; phone c/o Cherokee State Park (918) 435-8066.

Camp Notes: Little Blue is a pretty, woodsy, typically quiet little spot. It's especially good for a camper who is self-contained and/or self-sufficient and who doesn't care to camp within earshot of the main thoroughfare.

Oklahoma 56

SPAVINAW
Spavinaw State Park

Location: Northeast Oklahoma northeast of Tulsa.

Access: From Oklahoma State Highways 20/82 at the southwest edge of the town of Spavinaw and 12 miles northeast of Salina, turn south at either of 2 entrances into the campground; (entrances are 0.4 mile apart near a long 'elbow' curve in the road).

Facilities: 46 campsites, including 26 with partial hookups, in one large area; sites are medium to large, with nominal to fair separation; parking pads are gravel or grass, small to medium-length straight-ins; some pads may require minor additional leveling; adequate space for large tents on a grassy surface; barbecue grills and fireplaces; b-y-o firewood is recommended; water at several faucets; restroom with showers; holding tank disposal station; paved driveways; gas and groceries are available in Spavinaw.

Activities & Attractions: Fishing; playground; central shelter.

Natural Features: Located in a shallow canyon on a grassy, tree-dotted flat just above Spavinaw Creek and just below the Spavinaw Dam spillway (and below Highways 20/82); campground vegetation consists of mown grass and tall hardwoods; views of the creek from many waterfront sites; Spavinaw Lakes are nearby; elevation 600'.

Season, Fees & Phone: Open all year; please see Appendix for standard Oklahoma state park fees; 14 day limit; park office (918) 435-8066.

Camp Notes: Here's a helpful feature: If you buzz by the first park entrance driveway, you'll have a second shot at stepping on the binders before passing the other entrance. This super green place is seasonally crowded with fishermen. Upper Spavinaw State Park is located about 25 miles east near the town of Jay. It has lake access, a popular swimming pool and facilities for picnicking. Camping is reportedly permitted at Upper Spavinaw, but there are very limited facilities and no fee is charged.

Oklahoma 57

SNOWDALE
Snowdale State Park

Location: Northeast Oklahoma east of Tulsa.

Access: From Oklahoma State Highway 20 at a point 2 miles west of the junction of Oklahoma State Highways 20 & 82 in Salina and 8 miles east of Pryor, turn north onto a paved access road; proceed 0.1 mile to the camping area.

Facilities: 37 campsites, including 17 with partial hookups; sites are small to medium+, with nominal to fair separation; parking pads are gravel, medium-length straight-ins or pull-offs for the standard sites, and medium-length straight-ins for the hookup sites; many pads may require minor additional leveling; spacious, grassy tent spots; barbecue grills or fire rings; b-y-o firewood; water at faucets throughout; restrooms with showers; holding tank disposal station; paved driveways; gas and camper supplies nearby on the highway; limited supplies and services are available in Salina.

Activities & Attractions: Boating; boat launch; marina; fishing; swimming beach; playground; picnic shelter; Choteau Museum at nearby Salina State Park.

Natural Features: Located on the gently rolling west shore of Hudson Lake; campground vegetation consists of extensive, mown lawns, dotted by a few small planted hardwoods and flower beds, and bordered by stands of taller hardwoods; some sites are very much in the open, while those along the edge of the park are fairly well shaded; views of the lake and surrounding wooded bluffs from many sites; elevation 600'.

Season, Fees & Phone: Open all year; please see Appendix for standard Oklahoma state park fees; 14 day limit; park office (918) 434-2651.

Camp Notes: The Snowdale facility is definitely a notch or two above the ordinary, and it's located on a very pretty lake. Salina State Park is nearby, on the west edge of the town of Salina. Salina SP has a few tent sites on a large grassy flat, central water and restrooms.

Oklahoma 58

FLAT ROCK CREEK
Fort Gibson Lake/Corps of Engineers Park

Location: Northeast Oklahoma east of Tulsa.

Access: From U.S. Highway 69 at milepost 170 (8 miles south of Chouteau, 8 miles north of Wagoner), turn east onto a paved access road (signed for Flat Rock Creek Access Area) and proceed 2 miles; turn south (right) and go another 2 miles; turn west (right again) and continue for 0.7 mile to the campground entrance station and the campground.

Facilities: 46 campsites, including many with electrical hookups, in 2 loops; sites are small to medium-sized, with nominal to fair separation; parking pads are gravel or paved, medium to long straight-ins; some pads may require a bit of additional leveling; adequate space for large tents on a grass or earth surface; barbecue grills and some fire rings; b-y-o firewood; water at central faucets; restrooms with showers; holding tank disposal station; paved driveways; adequate supplies and services are available in Wagoner.

Activities & Attractions: Boating; boat launches; fishing (black bass, white bass, crappie, catfish).

Natural Features: Located on a grassy slope on a bay on the west shore of Fort Gibson Lake; campground vegetation consists of mown lawns and tall hardwoods providing moderate shade/shelter throughout; most sites have views of the lake through the trees; Blue Bill Point is visible across the bay to the west; the lake is ringed by low, forested hills; elevation 600'.

Season, Fees & Phone: March to October; $8.00 for a standard site, $11.00 for an electrical hookup site; 14 day limit; Fort Gibson Lake CoE Project Office (918) 687-2167.

Camp Notes: Because the campsites at Flat Rock Creek are built in a terraced arrangement, virtually every camper can enjoy some sort of a lake view. It'd be hard to beat this spot--pleasant environment, very good facilities, far enough off the main road to be tranquil, but close enough to be conveniently easy to get to.

Oklahoma 59

BLUE BILL POINT
Fort Gibson Lake/Corps of Engineers Park

Location: Northeast Oklahoma east of Tulsa.

Access: From U.S. Highway 69 at milepost 167 +.5 (10 miles south of Chouteau, 6 miles north of Wagoner), turn east onto a local access road; proceed 0.9 mile, turn north (left) and continue north for 1.2 miles, then turn east (right) again; proceed 0.8 mile (the road jogs toward the south after about 0.4 mile) to the campground.

Facilities: 43 campsites, including 34 with electrical hookups; sites are small to medium-sized, with nominal to fair separation; parking pads are paved, basically level, medium to long straight-ins; adequate space for large tents on a grassy surface; barbecue grills and fire rings; b-y-o firewood; water at several faucets; restrooms with showers; holding tank disposal station; paved driveways; gas and groceries near Highway 69; adequate supplies and services are available in Wagoner.

Activities & Attractions: Boating; boat launch; fishing (black bass, catfish, white bass, crappie).

Natural Features: Located on a tree-dotted, grassy flat along a bay on the west shore of 19,000-acre Fort Gibson Lake; campground vegetation consists of mown grass and medium to tall hardwoods providing moderate to generous shade in all sites; most sites have views of the lake through the trees; the lake is ringed by low, forested hills; cranes, herons and other protected waterfowl frequent the area; elevation 600'.

Season, Fees & Phone: March to October; $8.00 for a standard site, $11.00 for an electrical hookup site; 14 day limit; Fort Gibson Lake CoE Project Office (918) 687-2167.

Camp Notes: Blue Bill Point and Flat Rock Creek (see separate description) are a pair of campgrounds with very similar settings and facilities. Campers who like to watch sunrises may prefer Blue Bill Point, while those who'd rather watch the setting sun may favor Flat Rock Creek. Either way you look at it, these are nice camps.

ROCKY POINT
Fort Gibson Lake/Corps of Engineers Park

Location: Northeast Oklahoma east of Tulsa.

Access: From U.S. Highway 69 at milepost 166 +.5 (11 miles south of Chouteau, 5 miles north of Wagoner), turn east onto a local access road and proceed 3 miles; turn north (left) and continue for 1 mile to the campground.

Facilities: 71 campsites, including 64 with electrical hookups, in 2 loops; sites are small to medium-sized, with nominal to fair separation; most parking pads are paved, medium to long straight-ins; many pads may require additional leveling; adequate space for large tents on a grassy surface; barbecue grills; b-y-o firewood; water at several faucets; restrooms with showers; holding tank disposal station; paved driveways; adequate supplies and services are available in Wagoner.

Activities & Attractions: Fishing; boating; boat ramps; central shelter; designated swimming beach.

Natural Features: Located on a pair of points of land extending into a bay along the west shore of Fort Gibson Lake; campground vegetation varies from mown lawns and scattered hardwoods in the lower numbered section to mown lawns and fairly dense stands of hardwoods in the sites with higher numbers; most sites have lake views; several sites also have nice views of the nearby Cookson Hills; elevation 600'.

Season, Fees & Phone: March to October; $8.00 for a standard site, $11.00 for an electrical hookup site; 14 day limit; Fort Gibson Lake CoE Project Office (918) 687-2167.

Camp Notes: Rocky Point is one of a trio of very nice CoE campgrounds in this area. Just across the bay are Blue Bill Point and Flat Rock Creek. Several features set Rocky Point apart from the other two: Rocky Point is situated on a bluff, it has a number of relatively unsheltered sites, it has a swimming beach, and its access road is considerably wider. (This last item could be important to someone pulling a particularly large outfit).

AFTON LANDING
Arkansas River System/Corps of Engineers Park

Location: Eastern Oklahoma southeast of Tulsa.

Access: From Oklahoma State Highway 51 at a point 5.2 miles west of Wagoner, 9 miles east of Coweta, and 0.1 mile east of the Verdigris River Bridge, turn south onto a paved access road; (the access road actually angles sharply toward the west/southwest, so it'll be a very sharp right turn if you're approaching from the west); proceed 1 mile to the campground.

Facilities: 22 campsites, most with electrical hookups, in 2 loops; sites are small, with nominal separation; parking pads are paved, medium to long straight-ins; many pads may require a little additional leveling; adequate space for large tents on a grassy surface, but they may be a bit sloped; barbecue grills and fire rings; firewood is often available for gathering in the area; water at central faucets; restrooms with showers; holding tank disposal station; paved driveways; adequate supplies and services in Wagoner.

Activities & Attractions: Fishing; boating; boat launch; central shelter; access to the 60-mile-long Jean-Pierre Choteau National Recreation Hiking Trail.

Natural Features: Located on a flat above the north bank of the Verdigris River; sites are situated along the river or around an open field of tall grass; sites are lightly shaded by large hardwoods; some sites have river views; elevation 600'.

Season, Fees & Phone: March to October; $8.00 for a standard site, $11.00 for an electrical hookup site; 14 day limit; phone c/o Fort Gibson Lake CoE Project Office (918) 687-2167.

Camp Notes: The setting and atmosphere at this CoE campground are different from most other CoE camps in the region: Afton Landing is situated along a riverbank rather than a lakeshore. It is one in a series of camp areas on a navigation system of locks and dams along the tributaries of the Arkansas River.

TAYLOR FERRY SOUTH
Fort Gibson Lake/Corps of Engineers Park

Location: Eastern Oklahoma southeast of Tulsa.

Access: From Oklahoma State Highway 51 at a point 6.8 miles east of the junction of Oklahoma State Highways 51 & 16 in Wagoner, 7 miles west of Hulbert, and 1.1 miles west of the bridge which spans Fort Gibson Lake, turn south onto a paved access road; proceed 0.35 mile and turn east (left); continue for 0.8 mile to the campground entrance station and the campground.

Facilities: 102 campsites, including 96 with electrical hookups, in 2 loops; sites are generally small, with minimal to nominal separation; parking pads are paved, medium to long straight-ins; many pads may require additional leveling; tent areas are large, grassy, and mostly sloped; barbecue grills plus some fire rings; b-y-o firewood is recommended; water at faucets throughout; restrooms with showers; holding tank disposal station; paved driveways; adequate supplies and services are available in Wagoner.

Activities & Attractions: Boating; fishing; boat launch; large day use area across the highway at Taylor Ferry North.

Natural Features: Located on sloping terrain around a cove on the west shore of 19,000-acre Fort Gibson Lake, an impoundment on the Grand (Neosho) River; campground vegetation consists of mown grass and moderately dense, medium to tall hardwoods; the lake is surrounded by a fairly dense hardwood forest; most sites have lake views; elevation 600'.

Season, Fees & Phone: March to October; $8.00 for a standard site, $11.00 for an electrical hookup site; 14 day limit; Fort Gibson Lake CoE Project Office (918) 687-2167.

Camp Notes: There are some variations in these sites depending upon where they're situated. Sites toward the top of the slope are more level than those closer to the shore, and sites north of the cove are less sheltered than those toward the south end of the campground. All things considered, though, this is a good camp.

Oklahoma 63

SEQUOYAH BAY
Sequoyah Bay State Park

Location: Eastern Oklahoma southeast of Tulsa.

Access: From Oklahoma State Highway 16 at a point 7 miles south of Wagoner and 4 miles northwest of Okay, turn east onto a paved access road; travel east for 4 miles to the park entrance; assigned camping (Loop A) is to the left and unassigned camping is straight ahead. **Alternate Access:** From midtown Okay at the junction of State Highways 16 & 251A, proceed north and east on Highway 251A for 1 mile; turn north (left) for 2 miles; turn east (right) and go 1.5 miles to the park.

Facilities: 175 campsites, including 61 with partial hookups, in 5 loops; sites are small to medium-sized, with nominal to fair separation; parking pads are gravel, short pull-offs for standard sites or short to medium straight-ins for hookup sites; many may require additional leveling; large grassy tent spots, may be sloped; barbecue grills; b-y-o firewood; water at several faucets; restrooms with showers; holding tank disposal station; paved driveways; adequate supplies and services are available in Wagoner.

Activities & Attractions: Boating; boat launch; fishing; sheltered fishing dock; designated swimming area; playground; tennis courts; day use shelters.

Natural Features: Located on grassy slopes on the west shore of Fort Gibson Lake; most sites have light to medium shade; the park contains acres of mown lawns and stands of hardwoods; many sites have views of the lake and the surrounding forested hills; elevation 600'.

Season, Fees & Phone: Open all year; reservations accepted for assigned sites; please see Appendix for additional reservation information and standard Oklahoma state park fees; 14 day limit; park office (918) 683-0878.

Camp Notes: This is a *nice* park. Note that there are *two* state parks on Fort Gibson Lake: Sequoyah *Bay* State Park (this one), and Sequoyah State Park (see separate listing.)

Oklahoma 64

SEQUOYAH
Sequoyah State Park

Location: Eastern Oklahoma southeast of Tulsa.

Access: From Oklahoma State Highway 51 at a point 8 miles east of Wagoner, 6 miles west of Hulbert and 0.9 mile east of the bridge across Fort Gibson Lake, turn south onto the park road; all camp loops are situated east or west of the main park road, within 3 miles of the highway.

Facilities: 304 campsites, including 136 with partial hookups and 28 with full hookups, in 7 loops; sites are mostly small and closely spaced; most parking pads are gravel, straight-ins or pull-offs; many pads may require additional leveling; tent areas vary from small to large, grass or earth surface, and many are sloped; fire rings; b-y-o firewood is recommended; water at faucets throughout; restrooms with showers; laundry facility; holdng tank disposal station; paved main park roads; gravel driveways; adequate supplies and services are available in Wagoner.

Natural Features: Located on a densely forested peninsula on the east shore of Fort Gibson Lake; campground vegetation in some loops consists of tall conifers and hardwoods with sparse grass; other loops are situated on tree-dotted grassy slopes; light to moderate shelter/ shade; many sites have lake views; elevation 600'.

Activities & Attractions: Boating; boat launch; fishing; swimming beach; playground; hiking, fitness and nature trails; tennis courts; golf course; nature center; shelters in day use areas.

Season, Fees & Phone: Open all year; reservations accepted for assigned sites; please see Appendix for additional reservation information and standard Oklahoma state park fees; 14 day limit; park office (918) 772-2046.

Camp Notes: Because the campsites, features, attractions and activities at this park are so extensive and varied, it would be a good idea to first check at the park office for a map and information on how to find your way around this complex community. The park is named for Sequoyah, inventor of the Cherokee alphabet, who lived not far from here in Sallisaw.

Oklahoma 65

WILDWOOD
Fort Gibson Lake/Corps of Engineers Park

Location: Eastern Oklahoma southeast of Tulsa.

Access: From Oklahoma State Highway 80 at a point 5.2 miles southwest of the junction of State Highways 80 & 51 in Hulbert, 15 miles north of the town of Fort Gibson, and 16 miles northeast of Okay, turn north into the campground. (This section of Highway 80 may well be the twistiest, hilliest road in all of Oklahoma!)

Facilities: 30 campsites, most with partial hookups; sites are medium+ in size, with nominal to fair separation; parking pads are paved, mostly level, long straight-ins or very long pull-throughs; spacious, grassy tent spots, but some may be slightly sloped; barbecue grills; b-y-o firewood is recommended; water at faucets throughout; restrooms with showers; holding tank disposal station; paved driveways; limited supplies and services are available in Hulbert.

Activities & Attractions: Boating; boat launch; fishing; adjacent picnic areas, east of the campground.

Natural Features: Located on a tree-dotted, grassy bluff overlooking the south-east shore of Fort Gibson Lake; campground vegetation consists of mown lawns and scattered hardwoods; many sites are situated right on the edge of the bluff and have great views of the lake; the lake is ringed by forested hills; elevation 600'.

Season, Fees & Phone: March to October; $9.00 for a standard site, $12.00 for a partial hookup site; 14 day limit; Fort Gibson Lake CoE Project Office (918) 687-2167.

Camp Notes: Wildwood Campground is really a pleasant, sequestered spot--removed from the major hustle and bustle of the lake. Damsite is another nearby campground. It is, on the other hand, closer to the hub of the area's activity. It's about 10 miles west of Wildwood, off Highway 251A on the west bank of the Grand (Neosho) River and just below Fort Gibson Dam. There are 47 small, well-sheltered sites at Damsite with electrical hookups, bbq's, restrooms, showers, central water and an applicable price tag.

Oklahoma 66

CHEROKEE LANDING
Cherokee Landing State Park

Location: Eastern Oklahoma southeast of Muskogee.

Access: From Oklahoma State Highway 82 at a point 13 miles south of Tahlequah, 5 miles north of Cookson and 0.2 mile west of the bridge across the Illinois River, turn south onto a paved access road and proceed 0.3 mile to the park and the campground.

Facilities: 84 campsites, most with partial hookups, in 4 loops; sites are small to medium-sized, with nominal to fair separation; parking pads are gravel, medium to long straight-ins; some pads may require a touch of additional leveling; spacious, level, grassy areas for tents; barbecue grills or fire rings; b-y-o firewood; water at faucets nearly throughout; restrooms with showers; holding tank disposal station; paved driveways; gas and groceries are available at numerous small stores along the highway.

Activities & Attractions: Boating; boat launch; fishing; playground; designated swimming beach; day use area with sports field.

Natural Features: Located on a long, narrow point at the northeast end of Tenkiller Lake; campground vegetation consists of expanses of mown lawns dotted with small to medium-sized hardwoods and a few small pines; lake views from most sites; forested hills and mountains surround the lake; elevation 700'.

Season, Fees & Phone: Open all year; please see Appendix for standard Oklahoma state park fees; 14 day limit; park office (918) 457-5716.

Camp Notes: Cherokee Landing compares very favorably with the other state facility, Tenkiller State Park, at the opposite end of the lake about 10 miles south of here. Cherokee Landing may not offer as many activities, or as wide a selection of campsite types, but there is more room to roam here, and usually fewer campers and day-trippers to bump into. While Tenkiller SP has a 'natural' appearance, Cherokee Landing has more of a white-glove-and-tweezers, manicured look. Good camping here.

Oklahoma 67

PETTIT BAY
Tenkiller Lake/Corps of Engineers Park

Location: Eastern Oklahoma southeast of Muskogee.

Access: From Oklahoma State Highway 82 at the east edge of the small community of Keyes (9 miles south of Tahlequah, 10 miles northwest of Cookson, 5 miles northwest of the Illinois River bridge at the north end of Tenkiller Lake), turn south onto Indian Road; proceed 1.9 miles south, then turn east (left) onto a paved access road; continue east for 1.5 miles, then turn south (right) for 0.2 mile to the campground entrance station; Area 1 is to the right and Area 2 is to the left. (Note: Keyes isn't depicted on many maps, but it's there allright!)

Facilities: 98 campsites, about half with electrical hookups, in 2 loops; sites are small to large, with nominal to fairly good separation; parking pads vary from short, gravel straight-ins to long, paved pull-throughs; most parking pads are reasonably level (considering the terrain); some large, level, grassy tent spots, plus a few framed tent pads; fire rings and/or barbecue grills; some firewood is usually available for gathering; water at several faucets; restrooms with showers; holding tank disposal station; paved driveways; gas and groceries+ are available in Keyes.

Activities & Attractions: Boating; fishing; boat launch; designated swimming beach; day use shelters.

Natural Features: Located on the top and sides of a forested hill above Pettit Bay on the west shore of Tenkiller Lake; campground vegetation consists of tall grass, light to medium-dense hardwoods and a few conifers; several lakeside sites have good views of the islands, lake, and surrounding hills; elevation 700'.

Season, Fees & Phone: Open all year; $8.00 for a standard site, $11.00 for an electrical hookup site; 14 day limit; Tenkiller Lake CoE Project Office (918) 487-5252.

Camp Notes: Reportedly, before its remodeling, Pettit Bay wasn't popular enough to be open all year long. The improvements will probably make it a busier place.

Oklahoma 68

COOKSON BEND
Tenkiller Lake/Corps of Engineers Park

Location: Eastern Oklahoma southeast of Muskogee.

Access: From Oklahoma State Highways 100/82 in Cookson, (15 miles north of Vian, 19 miles south of Tahlequah), turn west onto a paved access road and proceed 2.15 miles to the campground entrance station and the campsites.

Facilities: 129 campsites, many with electrical hookups, in several areas; sites are small to small+, with fairly good separation; parking pads are mostly gravel, medium to long straight-ins, plus a few paved pull-throughs; most pads are tolerably level (considering the slope); medium to large, framed-and-gravelled tent pads; barbecue grills plus some fire rings; b-y-o firewood is recommended; water at central faucets; restrooms with showers; holding tank disposal station; paved driveways; gas and groceries are available in Cookson.

Activities & Attractions: Boating; sailing; boat launch; fishing; scuba diving; swimming area.

Natural Features: Located on the top and sides of several forested hills on a point on the east shore of Tenkiller Lake, a 13-mile-long, mile-wide impoundment on the Illinois River; campground vegetation consists of mown grass, and short to tall hardwoods which provide light to moderate shade/shelter for most sites; many sites have good views of the lake and of the rocky bluffs across the lake to the west; elevation 700'.

Season, Fees & Phone: Open all year; $8.00 for a standard site, $11.00 for an electrical hookup site; 14 day limit; Tenkiller Lake CoE Project Office (918) 487-5252.

Camp Notes: On the whole, site separation is a bit more generous here than at the neighboring camps to the south, Chicken Creek and Snake Creek Cove. A considerable amount of CCC-vintage rockwork adds an element of charm to this campground.

Oklahoma 69

CHICKEN CREEK
Tenkiller Lake/Corps of Engineers Park

Location: Eastern Oklahoma southeast of Muskogee.

Access: From Oklahoma State Highways 100/82 at a point 14 miles northeast of Gore and 3 miles south of Cookson, turn west onto a paved access road; continue west, north, and west again as the road winds for 1.9 miles to the campground.

Facilities: 101 campsites, including 59 with electrical hookups, in several clusters; sites are small to medium-sized, with nominal to fair separation; parking pads are gravel, medium to long straight-ins; some pads may require additional leveling; adequate space for medium to large tents on a grassy surface; barbecue grills; b-y-o firewood is recommended; water at central faucets; restrooms with showers; holding tank disposal station; paved driveways; gas and groceries are available in Cookson.

Activities & Attractions: Boating; boat launch; fishing; scuba diving; designated swimming beach.

Natural Features: Located on a forested slope on the east shore of Tenkiller Lake, about midway between the north and south ends of the lake; campground vegetation consists of short to tall hardwoods scattered across acres of mown grass; most sites are moderately shaded/sheltered; sites are built in a tiered arrangement on the hillside so many have views of the lake and surrounding forested hills; elevation 700'.

Season, Fees & Phone: Open all year; $8.00 for a standard site, $11.00 for an electrical hookup site; 14 day limit; Tenkiller Lake CoE Project Office (918) 487-5252.

Camp Notes: Because the total 130-mile shoreline of Tenkiller Lake is publicly owned, the entire lake area may be explored by boat or by foot (where accessible). It would be easy to occupy one of these sites for an entire 14 days, and explore a fresh stretch of shoreline each new day.

Oklahoma 70

SNAKE CREEK COVE
Tenkiller Lake/Corps of Engineers Park

Location: Eastern Oklahoma southeast of Muskogee.

Access: From Oklahoma State Highways 100/82 at a point 11.5 miles northeast of Gore, 5.5 miles south of Cookson, and 0.35 miles north of the Cherokee-Sequoyah County Line, turn west onto a paved access road; proceed 0.5 mile to a 3-way fork; bear right and continue 0.5 mile farther to the campground.

Facilities: 112 campsites, including 90 with electrical hookups, in 2 loops; sites are small to medium-sized, with nominal to fair separation; parking pads are gravel, medium to long straight-ins or pull-throughs; many pads may require additional leveling; adequate space for medium to large tents; barbecue grills; b-y-o firewood is recommended; water at central faucets; restrooms with showers; holding tank disposal station; paved driveways; gas and groceries are available in Cookson.

Activities & Attractions: Boating; boat launch; fishing; scuba diving; grassy swimming beach; playground; day use shelter; 1.5-mile Buzzard Roost Nature Trail nearby at Cato Creek Landing.

Natural Features: Located on a forested slope overlooking a narrow bay on the southeast shore of Tenkiller Lake; campground vegetation consists of mown lawns and tall hardwoods; Tenkiller Lake is a long, narrow lake on the Illinois River, with typically clear waters and mild weather; a favorite stopover for migratory waterfowl; ringed by forested hills and mountains; elevation 700'.

Season, Fees & Phone: Open all year; $8.00 for a standard site, $11.00 for an electrical hookup site; 14 day limit; Tenkiller Lake CoE Project Office (918) 487-5252.

Camp Notes: Overall, Snake Creek Cove Campground has a "neat as a pin" environment. It is reportedly especially popular with families who enjoy the large swimming areas and playground facilities.

TENKILLER
Tenkiller State Park

Location: Eastern Oklahoma southeast of Musgogee.

Access: From Oklahoma State Highway 100 at a point 8 miles northeast of Gore and 9 miles south of Cookson, turn north into the park; Loops B thru E are straight ahead and Loops F thru J are to the right, all within 3 miles.

Facilities: 240 campsites, including 51 with partial hookups and 36 with full hookups, in 10 loops; sites vary from small with nominal separation, to medium with very good separation; most parking pads are gravel, medium to long pull-throughs or straight-ins; some pads will require additional leveling; adequate space for large tents, mainly in Loops B, C, D, and E; barbecue grills or fire rings; b-y-o firewood; restrooms with showers; holding tank disposal station; paved driveways; gas and groceries are available nearby on the highway.

Activities & Attractions: Boating; sailing; boat launch; fishing; swimming pool; scuba diving; playground.

Natural Features: Located on the south shore of Tenkiller Lake; most sites are situated along either side of a long cove, and amid limestone cliffs; campground vegetation varies from mown, treeless slopes in the southwest corner, to densely forested, rocky areas north of the cove; long, narrow Tenkiller Lake, on the Illinois River, is bordered by the Cookson Hills and several mountain peaks; many lakeside sites; elevation 700'.

Season, Fees & Phone: Open all year; reservations accepted for assigned sites; please see Appendix for additional reservation information and standard Oklahoma state park fees; 14 day limit; park office (918) 489-5643.

Camp Notes: There is just about every conceivable campsite variation imaginable at Tenkiller State Park: Loop J is perched high atop a tree-dotted hill, Loop I is on a densely forested slope, and Loop D is on a grassy lakeside slope. Loops B, C, E, F, G & H also have their own unique qualities. There's a site to please every preference.

STRAYHORN LANDING
Tenkiller Lake/Corps of Engineers Park

Location: Eastern Oklahoma southeast of Muskogee.

Access: From Oklahoma State Highway 10A at a point 1.85 miles north of the junction of State Highways 10A & 100, 12 miles east of Braggs and 7 miles northeast of Gore, turn east onto a paved access road and proceed 0.9 mile to the campground.

Facilities: 50 campsites, most with electrical hookups; sites are small, with minimal to nominal separation; parking pads are gravel, fairly level, medium-length straight-ins; adequate space for small tents on a grassy or gravel surface; barbecue grills; b-y-o firewood is suggested; water at several faucets; restrooms with showers; holding tank disposal station; paved driveways; gas and groceries in Braggs; limited supplies and services are available in Gore.

Activities & Attractions: Boating; sailing; boat launch; scuba diving; fishing; small swimming beach; exceptional views from an overlook just west of the dam--of the lake, the islands, and the surrounding green hills and mountains.

Natural Features: Located on a forested ridge on a peninsula on the southwest corner of Tenkiller Lake; campground vegetation consists of mown grass, a few cedars, and medium to large hardwoods; some sites are near-lakeside, on a shelf about 30 feet above the water; the lake is ringed by the well-forested Cookson Hills and several prominent peaks; 13,000-acre Tenkiller Lake is typically very clear and blue; elevation 700'.

Season, Fees & Phone: Open all year; $8.00 for a standard site, $11.00 for an electrical hookup site; 14 day limit; Tenkiller Lake CoE Project Office (918) 487-5252.

Camp Notes: Tenkiller Lake boasts at least ten major public camp areas. This is one of several CoE campgrounds on Tenkiller that stays open year 'round. The tenants of Strayhorn Landing, who are usually senior campers, reportedly like it so well they often stay "the limit".

ARROWHEAD POINT
Arkansas River System/Corps of Engineers Park

Location: Eastern Oklahoma southeast of Muskogee.

Access: From Oklahoma State Highway 10 at a point 3 miles south of Braggs, 15 miles south of the junction of State Highway 10 & U.S. Highway 62 east of Muskogee, and 9 miles north of Gore, turn west onto a gravel access road; proceed 1 mile, then turn south (left) and continue for 2 more miles; turn east (left again) for a final 0.1 mile (roadway becomes paved) to the park entrance station and the campground. (Note: Access to this camp is on a narrow, gravel/dirt road which could be tricky under inclement conditions.)

Facilities: 30 campsites in 2 loops; sites are small+ to medium-sized, with minimal to fairly good separation; parking pads are paved, medium to long straight-ins; many pads may require additional leveling; adequate space for medium to large tents; barbecue grills or fire rings; firewood is generally available for gathering in the vicinity; water at central faucets; restrooms with showers; holding tank disposal station; paved driveways; gas and groceries are available in Braggs.

Activities & Attractions: Boating; boat launch; fishing.

Natural Features: Located on a grassy, hardwood-blanketed hill overlooking the east bank of the Arkansas River; campground vegetation consists of mown grass, light underbrush, and short to medium-tall hardwoods which provide light to moderate shade/shelter for most sites; dense forest surrounds the camp area; several riverside sites; elevation 500'.

Season, Fees & Phone: Open all year; $8.00; 14 day limit; park manager's office (918) 489-5541 or Webbers Falls Lock and Dam CoE Project Office (918) 464-2631.

Camp Notes: A threesome of CoE camps on the west bank of the Arkansas River are accessible from U.S. 64 between Muskogee and I-40: Hopewell Park, Spaniard Creek and Brewers Bend are reportedly very popular when the fishing is good. Legend has it that Merle Haggard put the finishing touches to "Okie From Muskogee" while camping and catfishing right here at Arrowhead Point.

GREENLEAF
Greenleaf State Park

Location: Eastern Oklahoma southeast of Muskogee.

Access: From Oklahoma State Highway 10 at a point 3.2 miles south of Braggs, 15 miles south of the junction of Oklahoma State Highway 10 & U.S. Highway 62 east of Muskogee and 9 miles north of Gore, turn east onto a paved access road and continue for 0.7 mile to the park entrance; campsites are situated along or near the next 0.3 mile of park road.

Facilities: 139 campsites, including 63 with partial hookups and 24 with full hookups, in 5 loops; sites are small to medium-sized, with nominal to fair separation; most parking pads are gravel (some are paved), medium to long straight-ins for hookup sites, or grass pull-offs for standard sites; many pads may require additional leveling; large, grassy, but mostly sloped, tent spots; barbecue grills and/or fire rings; b-y-o firewood is suggested; water at several faucets; restrooms with showers; holding tank disposal station; paved main driveways; gas and groceries are available in Braggs.

Activities & Attractions: Boating; boat launch; fishing; sheltered fishing pier; swimming pool; designated swimming beach on the lake; hiking trail; day use shelters.

Natural Features: Located on grassy, tree-dotted hills/slopes bordering 930-acre Greenleaf Lake; campground vegetation consists of acres of mown lawns and medium-sized hardwoods; most sites are moderately shaded; views of the lake and surrounding forested hills from many sites; elevation 500'.

Season, Fees & Phone: Open all year; reservations accepted for assigned sites; please see Appendix for additional reservation information and standard Oklahoma state park fees; 14 day limit; park office (918) 487-5196.

Camp Notes: Greenleaf, a large park on a small lake, is a nice change of pace from the other recreation areas in eastern Oklahoma, many of which are small parks on the shores of large lakes. As comparatively small as the lake is, the hiking trail that circumnavigates it is a full 20 miles long.

BRUSHY CREEK
Sallisaw State Park

Location: Eastern Oklahoma north of Sallisaw.

Access: From downtown Sallisaw at the intersection of U.S. Highways 59 & 64 (Cherokee Avenue) and Maple Street, turn north onto Maple Street (the Marble City Highway) and travel northerly for 6.5 miles; turn southwest (left) onto a paved access road and proceed 1 mile to the campground.

Facilities: 28 campsites, about half with partial hookups; sites are small to medium-sized, with minimal separation; parking pads are mostly gravel (some have a small, concrete rectangular section), medium-length straight-ins; several pads may require minor additional leveling; large, mostly sloped, grassy tent spots; barbecue grills; b-y-o firewood is recommended; water at several faucets; restrooms with showers; holding tank disposal station; paved driveways; adequate supplies and services are available in Sallisaw.

Activities & Attractions: Boating; boat launch and dock; fishing; grassy swimming beach; playground; volleyball court; day use shelter.

Natural Features: Located on a grassy slope along the east shore of Brushy Lake, a small, picturesque impoundment on Sallisaw Creek; campground vegetation consists of mown grass dotted with hardwoods which provide light to medium shade/shelter; many sites have lake views; the lake is ringed by densely forested hills; elevation 600'.

Season, Fees & Phone: Open all year; please see Appendix for standard Oklahoma state park fees; 14 day limit; park office (918)-775-2091.

Camp Notes: Brushy Creek is also known as the Brushy Lake Unit of Sallisaw State Park. It is the more 'comfortable' unit of the two-unit Sallisaw State Park. The other area, Sallisaw Creek, is four miles west of Sallisaw off U.S. 64. It has about 20 camp/picnic sites, bbq's and restrooms along its namesake stream.

APPLEGATE COVE
Robert S. Kerr Lake/Corps of Engineers Park

Location: Eastern Oklahoma south of Sallisaw.

Access: From U.S. Highway 59 at a point 7.3 miles south of Interstate 40 Exit 308 for Sallisaw, 0.6 mile north of Kerr Dam, turn west onto a paved local road; proceed west 1.9 miles to a fork; bear left and continue for 0.5 mile to the campground.

Facilities: 27 campsites, including many with electrical hookups, in 2 loops; sites are small+ to medium+ in size, with nominal to fair separation; most parking pads are paved, medium-length straight-ins; some pads may require minor additional leveling; tent spots are mostly large and level; barbecue grills or fireplaces; firewood is usually available for gathering in the vicinity; water at a central faucet; vault facilities; holding tank disposal station; paved driveways; gas and groceries along U.S. 59; adequate supplies and services are available in Sallisaw.

Activities & Attractions: Boating; boat launches and docks; fishing; day use area; U.S. Coast Guard facility, adjacent; visitor center at lock and dam site.

Natural Features: Located on a grassy flat along a cove on the north-east shore near the east end of Robert S. Kerr Lake; campground vegetation consists of mown grass and stands of hardwoods; many sites have expansive views west across the lake to the rest of its low, forested shoreline; some sites are situated around an open meadow and others are in areas of quite dense shade/shelter; elevation 500'.

Season, Fees & Phone: March to November; $6.00 for a standard site, $9.00 for an electrical hookup site; 14 day limit; Robert S. Kerr Lake CoE Project Office (918) 775-4475.

Camp Notes: Some elaborate CCC-style rockwork sets this campground apart from the ordinary small Corps camp. (Maybe *you* can figure out what the *Coast Guard* is doing next door--a half-thousand miles inland. Ed.)

SHORT MOUNTAIN COVE
Robert S. Kerr Lake/Corps of Engineers Park

Location: Eastern Oklahoma south of Sallisaw.

Access: From U.S. Highway 59 at a point 2.5 miles south of Kerr Dam, 11 miles south of Interstate 40 Exit 308 for Sallisaw, and 4 miles north of the junction of U.S. 59 & Oklahoma State Highway 9, turn west onto a paved local road; proceed west for 1.1 miles; turn north (right) and continue for 0.15 mile to a "T" intersection; turn east (right) and continue for 0.7 mile east, north and then west to the campground. (Note: a left turn at the "T" intersection will take you to Cowlington Point (see below.)

Facilities: 49 campsites, including many with electrical hookups, in 2 loops; sites are small+ to medium-sized. with fair to good separation; parking pads are paved, mostly level, medium to long straight-ins or long pull-throughs; tent spots are large and level, with a grass/earth surface; assorted fire appliances; firewood is usually available for gathering; water at a hand pump; vault facilities; paved driveways; gas and groceries are available on Highway 59.

Activities & Attractions: Boating; boat launch; fishing; nature trail; day use area with shelter; visitor center at the locks.

Natural Features: Located on a gentle slope on a point of land on the southeast shore of Robert S. Kerr Reservoir; campground vegetation consists of grass and clusters of hardwoods; some lakeside sites; low, wooded terrain around most of the lake, except wooded hills to the east; elevation 500'.

Season, Fees & Phone: March to November; $6.00 for a standard site, $9.00 for an electrical hookup site; 14 day limit; Robert S. Kerr Lake CoE Project Office (918) 775-4475.

Camp Notes: Another area CoE facility near here is Cowlington Point Campground. It's located 2 miles west of Short Mountain Cove, has 25 similar campsites, water at a hand pump, vault facilities and the same fee structure. Short Mountain Cove may be preferred by many campers because it's a little closer to more of the lake's attractions.

Oklahoma 78

INDIAN POINT
Little River State Park

Location: Central Oklahoma in east Norman.

Access: From Interstate 40 Exit 166 for Choctaw Road in the southeast corner of Oklahoma City, travel due south for 11.3 miles on Choctaw Road/East 120th Avenue (Choctaw becomes East 120th at the Norman city limit); turn east (right) onto Alameda Street and proceed 1 mile to the park entrance; turn south (right) into Area C; or continue east, then north, for 1.5 miles to Areas A & B. **Alternate Access:** From Interstate 35 Exit 108 in the southwest corner of Norman, drive east on Oklahoma State Highway 9 for 10 miles to 84th Avenue; turn north onto 84th Avenue for 2 miles to Alameda Street; head east on Alameda Street for 4 miles to the park entrance.

Facilities: 79 campsites, including 56 with electrical hookups; sites are small+ to medium-sized, with nominal to fair separation; parking pads are gravel, mostly short to medium-length straight-ins; a little additional leveling may be required in some sites; medium to large areas for tents; diverse fire facilities; b-y-o firewood is suggested; water at faucets throughout; restrooms with showers; holding tank disposal station; paved driveways; gas and groceries are available 6 miles north on Choctaw Road.

Activities & Attractions: Swimming beach; boating; boat launch; sailboat launch; fishing; archery range; nature trail.

Natural Features: Located on sloping terrain on a point near the north shore of Thunderbird Lake, a 6000-acre reservoir on Little River and its tributaries; sites receive medium shade from large hardwoods; elevation 1100'.

Season, Fees & Phone: Open all year; please see Appendix for standard Oklahoma state park fees; 14 day limit; park office (405) 364-7634.

Camp Notes: Each of Little River State Park's four principal areas has its individual merits (also see information for Clear Bay, Little Axe and Post Oak). But Indian Point seems to offer just a wee bit more than the others.

Oklahoma 79

CLEAR BAY
Little River State Park

Location: Central Oklahoma in southeast Norman.

Access: From Oklahoma State Highway 9 at its intersection with 142nd Avenue SE in Norman (14.5 miles east of Interstate 35 Exit 108 for the University of Oklahoma, 4.5 miles west of Norman's east city limit, turn northwest into the park entrance and proceed 0.8 mile to a 3-way intersection; continue ahead for 0.1 mile to Area 1; or turn north (right) for 0.2 mile, then northwest (left) for a final 0.1 mile to Area 2.

Facilities: Approximately 100 campsites, including 71 with electrical or partial hookups; sites are small+, with nominal to fair separation; parking pads are gravel, short to medium-length straight-ins, plus a few long pull-throughs; additional leveling will probably be required in many sites; adequate space for large tents, may be sloped; barbecue grills or fire rings; b-y-o firewood; water at partial hookup sites and at several faucets; restrooms with showers; holding tank disposal station; paved driveways; camper supplies at the park store, near the highway; gas and groceries are available at several points along Highway 9.

Activities & Attractions: Boating; boat launch; fishing; swimming beach; hiking trail.

Natural Features: Located on the top and sides of hills above the south shore of 6000-acre Thunderbird Lake, at the juncture of the Clear Creek Arm with the main body of the lake; sites receive light to medium shade from large hardwoods on a surface of sparse grass; elevation 1100'.

Season, Fees & Phone: Open all year; please see Appendix for standard Oklahoma state park fees; 14 day limit; park office (405) 364-7634.

Camp Notes: Only some of the park's Area 2 campsites have any sort of lake view, but Area 1's sites seem to be slightly higher and a little breezier. Area 1 may experience a little more day traffic.

Oklahoma 80

LITTLE AXE
Little River State Park

Location: Central Oklahoma in east Norman.

Access: From Oklahoma State Highway 9 at a point 17 miles east of Interstate 35 Exit 108 for the University of Oklahoma and 1.8 miles west of Norman's east city limit, turn north onto Little Axe Drive and proceed 0.6 mile north, then jog 0.05 mile westerly to a "T" intersection; continue west (left) for 0.6 mile to the park entrance station, then another 0.6 mile to the campsites.

Facilities: 77 assigned campsites, including about one-third with electrical hookups; sites are small to small+, reasonably level, with nominal to fair separation; parking pads are gravel, short pull-offs or medium-length straight-ins; adequate space for large tents; barbecue grills or fireplaces; b-y-o firewood; water at several faucets; restrooms with showers; holding tank disposal station; paved driveways; gas and groceries are available at several points along Highway 9.

Activities & Attractions: Boating; boat launch; swimming beach.

Natural Features: Located along the shore at the tip of a point at the east end of Thunderbird Lake; sites are moderately shaded by large hardwoods; elevation 1100'.

Season, Fees & Phone: April to October; reservations accepted; please see Appendix for additional reservation information and standard Oklahoma state park fees; 14 day limit; park office (405) 364-7634.

Camp Notes: Of the pair of campgrounds in this vicinity (also see Post Oak), only Little Axe has lake access and lake views. Both areas have their individual merits.

Oklahoma 81

POST OAK
Little River State Park

Location: Central Oklahoma in east Norman.

Access: From Oklahoma State Highway 9 at a point 17 miles east of Interstate 35 Exit 108 for the University of Oklahoma and 1.8 miles west of Norman's east city limit, turn north onto Little Axe Drive and proceed 0.6 mile north, then jog 0.05 mile westerly to a "T" intersection; continue north (right) at the "T" on 156th Avenue NE and proceed 0.6 mile; turn west onto Rock Creek Drive and continue west/southwest for 0.5 mile to the park entrance station and the campground.

Facilities: 22 assigned campsites with partial hookups; sites are small to small+, most are tolerably level, with nominal to fair separation; parking pads are gravel, medium to long straight-ins; adequate space for large tents; barbecue grills or fireplaces; b-y-o firewood; water at sites and at several faucets; restrooms with showers; holding tank disposal station; paved driveways; gas and groceries are available at several points along Highway 9.

Activities & Attractions: Boating; boat launch; swimming beach.

Natural Features: Located on a ridgetop above the shore at the 'base' of a point at the east end of Thunderbird Lake; sites are moderately shaded by large hardwoods; elevation 1100'.

Season, Fees & Phone: April to October; reservations accepted; please see Appendix for additional reservation information and standard Oklahoma state park fees; 14 day limit; park office (405) 364-7634.

Camp Notes: Post Oak probably should get the honors for quietest and most comfortable state park campground on the lake. Pleasantly wooded surroundings here.

Oklahoma 82

OKMULGEE
Okmulgee State Park

Location: Eastern Oklahoma northwest of Henryetta.

Access: From midtown Okmulgee at the junction of U.S. Highway 75 & Oklahoma State Highway 56, turn west onto Highway 56 and proceed 6.4 miles; bear left onto a paved access road and continue for 1.1 miles to Area 3, 1.5 miles to Area 2 or 2.7 miles to Area 1.

Facilities: 92 campsites, including 42 with partial hookups; sites in Area 1 are small, with very little separation; sites in Areas 2 and 3 are medium-sized, with nominal to fair separation; parking pads mostly gravel, medium-length straight-ins in Area 1, medium to long straight-ins in Area 2 and pull-offs in Area 3; many pads will require additional leveling; tent spots are small in Area 1, large in Areas 2 and 3; assorted fire facilities; b-y-o firewood is recommended; water at several faucets; restrooms with showers; holding tank disposal station; paved driveways; complete supplies and services are available in Okmulgee.

Activities & Attractions: Boating; fishing (primarily catfish); nature trail; swimming beach; playground; day use areas.

Natural Features: Located along the east shore of Okmulgee Lake, a medium-sized reservoir on the Deep Fork of the Canadian River; Area 1 is situated on a tree-dotted, mown grass bluff, Area 2 is on a forested flat, and Area 3 is on a fairly open grassy lakeside slope; views of the lake from most sites; long, narrow Okmulgee Lake is surrounded by densely forested, low hills; elevation 700'.

Season, Fees & Phone: Open all year; reservations accepted for assigned sites; please see Appendix for additional reservation information and standard Oklahoma state park fees; 14 day limit; park office (918) 756-1471.

Camp Notes: Area 1 tends to become a bit congested during peak seasons. There are some excellent tent sites in Area 2. Area 3 attracts many boaters and tenters. This is a *nice* park.

Oklahoma 83

GENTRY CREEK COVE
Eufaula Lake/Corps of Engineers Park

Location: Eastern Oklahoma east of Henryetta.

Access: From U.S. Highway 266 at a point 2.1 miles west of the junction of U.S. 266 & Oklahoma State Highway 72, 8.7 miles west of Checotah and 18 miles east of Henryetta, turn south onto a paved access road; proceed 0.7 mile to a fork; bear right and continue for 0.3 mile to the west loop; or bear left and continue for 0.6 mile to the east loop.

Facilities: 40 campsites, about half with electrical hookups; sites are small to medium-sized, with minimal to fair separation; parking pads are paved, short to long straight-ins, plus a few very long pull-throughs; many pads may require some additional leveling; tent spots are generously sized, slightly sloped, and grassy; barbecue grills and fire rings; firewood is usually available for gathering; water at central faucets; restrooms with showers (in the west loop) plus auxiliary vaults; holding tank disposal station; paved driveways; adequate supplies and services are available in Checotah.

Activities & Attractions: Boating; boat launch; fishing (bass, crappie, catfish and walleye).

Natural Features: Located on small hillocks on a point at the northern tip of Eufaula Lake; campground vegetation consists of mown grass, patches of tall grass, and dense stands of hardwoods and conifers; many lakeside sites; a small pond is located behind some sites; the campground is bordered by dense woodland; low forested hills encircle most of Eufaula Lake's 600-mile-long shoreline; elevation 600'.

Season, Fees & Phone: April to October; $8.00 for a standard site, $11.00 for an electrical hookup site; 14 day limit; Eufaula Lake CoE Project Office (918) 799-5843.

Camp Notes: Gentry Creek Cove is a well-groomed, out-of-the-way spot. This is the lake's only camping area that's north of Interstate 40. It is perhaps best suited to campers with a moderately high level of self-containment.

Oklahoma 84

FOUNTAINHEAD
Fountainhead State Park

Location: Eastern Oklahoma east of Henryetta.

Access: From Oklahoma State Highway 150 at a point 4 miles south of Interstate 40 Exit 259 and 2 miles northwest of the junction of U.S. Highway 69 & Oklahoma State Highway 150 north of Eufaula, turn into any of 4 separate entrances to the camp areas; (the park stretches along both sides of Highway 150 for 3 miles.)

Facilities: 166 campsites, including 50 with partial hookups (Area 2) and 33 with full hookups (Area 4); sites vary from small to medium (Area 2) to large (Area 4), with minimal to good separation; parking pads for standard sites are pull-offs; parking pads for partial hookup sites are gravel, slightly sloped, medium to long straight-ins; parking pads for full hookup sites are paved, long straight-ins or very long pull-throughs; adequate space for large tents on a grass or earth surface; barbecue grills and some fire rings; b-y-o firewood is recommended; water at several faucets; restrooms with showers; holding tank disposal station; paved main driveways, gravel sub-drives; adequate supplies and services are available in Eufaula.

Activities & Attractions: Boating; fishing; nature center; interpretive trail; hiking trail; longhorn and elk exhibit; bird sanctuary.

Natural Features: Located on a peninsula on the northwest shore of Eufaula Lake, between the lake's North Canadian and Deep Fork Arms; sites receive light to medium shade/shelter from large hardwoods; a few sites have lake views; bordered by dense woods; elevation 600'.

Season, Fees & Phone: Open all year; reservations accepted for assigned sites; please see Appendix for additional reservation information and standard Oklahoma state park fees; 14 day limit; park office (918) 689-5311.

Camp Notes: Fountainhead offers quite a variety of sites. It would be enlightening to look around before checking in.

Oklahoma 85

BELLE STARR
Eufaula Lake/Corps of Engineers Park

Location: Eastern Oklahoma east of Henryetta.

Access: From the junction of U.S. Highway 69 & Oklahoma State Highway 150 (7 miles south of Interstate 40, 6 miles north of Eufaula), turn east onto Texanna Road; travel 1.9 miles, then turn south (right) onto Belle Starr Road; proceed 1.3 miles, then turn east (left) onto a paved access road and go 0.6 mile to *Belle Starr North*; or continue for another 0.7 miles, then turn east (left) to the *Belle Starr South* campground entrance station and the campground.

Facilities: *Belle Starr South*: 110 campsites with electrical hookups; sites are medium to large, with fair to good separation; parking pads are paved, medium to long straight-ins or long to very long pull-throughs; some pads may require minor additional leveling; spacious, mostly level, grassy or sandy tent areas; barbecue grills; b-y-o firewood is recommended; water at several faucets; restrooms with showers; holding tank disposal station; paved driveways; *Belle Starr North*: 12 basic campsites and vault facilities; adequate supplies and services are available in Eufaula.

Activities & Attractions: Boating; fishing (crappie, catfish, sand bass in this locale); playground; swimming beach; Dogwood Nature Trail; day use shelter.

Natural Features: Located on points of land on the north shore of Eufaula Lake; campground vegetation consists of expanses of mown grass and fairly dense stands of hardwoods; most sites have views of the lake and low mountains to the east; Eufaula Lake is ringed by tree-blanketed hills and mountains; elevation 600'.

Season, Fees & Phone: April to October; $5.00 in the North unit, $11.00 in the South unit; 14 day limit; Eufaula Lake CoE Project Office (918) 799-5843.

Camp Notes: If you're particularly attached to your watercraft, you'll appreciate the fact that at Belle Starr South you may be able to beach your boat right next to your tent or camper.

PORUM LANDING
Eufaula Lake/Corps of Engineers Park

Location: Eastern Oklahoma east of Henryetta.

Access: From Oklahoma State Highway 2 in Porum (9 miles south of Interstate 40 and 2 miles north of the junction of State Highways 2 & 71), travel west on Texanna Road for 5.2 miles; turn south (left) onto a paved access road and continue for 0.25 mile to the campground entrance and the campsites. **Alternate Access:** From the junction of U.S. Highway 69 & Oklahoma State Highway 150 (7 miles south of Interstate 40, 6 miles north of Eufaula), turn east onto Texanna Road; head easterly for 13.5 miles; turn south (right) and continue as above.

Facilities: 53 campsites, including 45 with electrical hookups; sites are small to medium-sized, with nominal to good separation; parking pads are paved, medium to long straight-ins; some pads may require additional leveling; space for medium to large tents; barbecue grills or fire rings; b-y-o firewood is suggested; water at faucets throughout; restrooms with showers; holding tank disposal station; paved driveways; gas and groceries are available nearby, on Texanna Road in the hamlet of Porum Landing.

Activities & Attractions: Boating; boat launch and dock; fishing; designated swimming beach; day use area with shelter.

Natural Features: Located on a grassy, tree-dotted slope on a small, protected bay on the northeast shore of Eufaula Lake; campground vegetation consists of mown grass and medium-height hardwoods and conifers; most sites are lakeside or have views through the trees of the bay and local hills; elevation 600'.

Season, Fees & Phone: March to November; $8.00 for a standard site, $11.00 for an electrical hookup site; 14 day limit; Eufaula Lake CoE Project Office (918) 799-5843.

Camp Notes: A distinctive feature at Porum Landing is the well-sheltered bay. The main part of the lake is readily accessible, yet a boat could probably find a safe harbor here in virtually any weather.

DAMSITE SOUTH
Eufaula Lake/Corps of Engineers Park

Location: Eastern Oklahoma southeast of Henryetta.

Access: From Oklahoma State Highway 71 at a point 5 miles north of the junction of State Highways 71 & 9 near Enterprise, 6 miles southwest of the junction of Oklahoma State Highways 2 & 71 just south of the town of Porum, and 0.45 mile south of Eufaula Dam, turn west onto a paved access road; proceed 0.15 mile to a fork; continue straight ahead to the west loop, or take the right fork to the east loop.

Facilities: 57 campsites, including about 30 with electrical hookups; sites are small+ to medium-sized, with fair to very good separation; parking pads are paved, medium to long straight-ins; most pads will require some additional leveling; tent areas are large, grassy and slightly sloped; barbecue grills and fire rings; b-y-o firewood is suggested; water at central faucets; restrooms with showers; holding tank disposal station; paved driveways; gas and groceries are available nearby on Highway 71.

Activities & Attractions: Boating; boat launch; fishing; Terrapin Nature Trail; designated swimming beach; day use area with shelter.

Natural Features: Located near the northeast end of Eufaula Lake, on a small point on the south shore; vegetation consists of acres of pine-dotted grass, plus fairly dense stands of hardwoods; many sites are lakeside or within a few yards of the lake; views across the lake to pink cliffs and forested hills; el. 600'.

Season, Fees & Phone: April to October; $8.00 for a standard site, $11.00 for an electrical hookup site; 14 day limit; Eufaula Lake CoE Project Office (918) 799-5843.

Camp Notes: This campground is said to be popular with families because of the nice swimming beach and the nature trail. Another campground in the vicinity is Damsite East. It has five sites and is located north and east of the dam on a grassy shelf above the Canadian River.

BROOKEN COVE
Eufaula Lake/Corps of Engineers Park

Location: Eastern Oklahoma southeast Henryetta.

Access: From Oklahoma State Highway 71 at a point 3 miles north of the junction of State Highways 71 & 9 near Enterprise, 8 miles southwest of the junction of State Highways 71 & 2 south of the town of Porum and 2.25 miles south of Eufaula Dam, turn west onto a paved access road; proceed 1.5 miles west and then north to a "T" intersection; turn southwest (left) and continue for 0.5 mile to the campground entrance station and the campsites.

Facilities: 62 campsites, many with electrical hookups, in 2 loops; sites are small+ to medium-sized, with nominal to fair separation; parking pads are paved, medium to long straight-ins, plus some long pull-throughs; many pads may require additional leveling; most tent spots are large, grassy, and slightly sloped; barbecue grills and some fire rings; b-y-o firewood is suggested; water at central faucets; restrooms with showers; holding tank disposal station; paved driveways; gas and groceries are available along Highway 71.

Activities & Attractions: Boating; boat launches and docks; fishing; playground; swimming beach; day use shelter.

Natural Features: Located on a slope on the south shore near the northeast end of Eufaula Lake; campground vegetation consists of tree-dotted mown lawns and stands of hardwoods; some sites have been cut into the moderately steep slope; good views of the lake to the north, of Brooken Cove to the west and of long, forested Brooken Mountain to the southwest; elevation 600'.

Season, Fees & Phone: April to October; $8.00 for a standard site, $11.00 for an electrical hookup site; 14 day limit; Eufaula Lake CoE Project Office (918) 799-5843.

Camp Notes: Access to this very nice campground is less than easy to explain because the roads go everywhichaway in this region. It might be good to pack a compass and extra food, water and fuel--and good luck!

Oklahoma 89

HIGHWAY 9 LANDING
Eufaula Lake/Corps of Engineers Park

Location: Eastern Oklahoma southeast of Henryetta.

Access: From Oklahoma State Highway 9 at a point 7 miles west of the junction of Oklahoma State Highways 9 & 71 and 8 miles east of Eufaula (and U.S. Highway 69), turn north into the *North* Unit or south into the *South* Unit; **Additional Access:** From State Highway 9 at a point 0.5 mile east of the turnoffs to the North and south Units, turn off the south side of the highway into the *East Unit*.

Facilities: *North & South Units*: 73 campsites, including 67 with electrical hookups; sites are small to medium-sized, with minimal to nominal separation; parking pads are paved, medium to very long straight-ins; tent areas are mostly grassy, large and sloped; barbecue grills and fire rings; b-y-o firewood is suggested; water at central faucets; restrooms with showers; holding tank disposal station; paved driveways; *East Unit*: 9 campsites, including a few with electrical hookups, paved parking pads, water at central faucets, vault facilities; adequate supplies and services are available in Eufaula.

Activities & Attractions: Boating; boat launch and docks; fishing; designated swimming beach; playground; ball diamond; day use area.

Natural Features: Located on the top and sides of several small, forested ridges on the east shore of the Longtown Arm of Eufaula Lake; campground vegetation consists of mown grass and scattered pines and hardwoods; views across the bay from many sites; bordered by dense forest; elevation 600'.

Season, Fees & Phone: April to October; $8.00 for a standard site, $11.00 for an electrical hookup site; 14 day limit; Eufaula Lake CoE Project Office (918) 799-5843.

Camp Notes: The irregular terrain here brought about some interesting campsites. Some sites are virtually perched atop the forested ridge, while others are so close to the shoreline that they have been submerged during periods of high water.

Oklahoma 90

ARROWHEAD
Arrowhead State Park

Location: Eastern Oklahoma northeast of McAlester.

Access: From U.S. Highway 69 at milepost 12 +.7 in Canadian (10 miles south of Eufaula, 20 miles north of McAlester), turn east onto a park loop road for 0.2 mile to a fork; the left fork will follow the north edge of the park for 3 miles to Area 4; the right fork will follow the south edge for 1.3 miles to Area 1, 3.3 miles to Area 2, and 4 miles to Area 3.

Facilities: 214 campsites, including 65 with partial hookups and 20 with full hookups, in 4 major areas; sites vary from small and closely spaced to medium-sized and fairly well separated; parking pads in Area 1's full hookup sites are grass, long parallel pull-throughs; pads for partial hookup sites are mostly gravel, medium-length straight-ins; pull-along standard site parking; many large, level, grassy tent spots (also a few framed tent pads); barbecue grills or fire rings; b-y-o firewood is suggested; water at central faucets; restrooms with showers; holding tank disposal station; paved driveways; gas and groceries are available in Canadian.

Activities & Attractions: Boating; boat launches; fishing; swimming beach; Outlaw Hiking Trail; golf course.

Natural Features: Located on the top and sides of a hill on a peninsula on the west shore of Eufaula Lake; Area 1 is on a grassy flat bordered by dense forest, Areas 2 & 3 are on a roadside/lakeside shaded slope; Area 4 is on a forested ridgetop; elevation 600'-700'.

Season, Fees & Phone: Open all year; reservations accepted for assigned sites; please see Appendix for additional reservation information and standard Oklahoma state park fees; 14 day limit; park office (918) 339-2204.

Camp Notes: The most exceptional feature of this park is the unusually good vantage point which provides extraordinary views of Eufaula Lake and the Canadian River Valley.

Oklahoma 91

CROWDER POINT
Eufaula Lake/Corps of Engineers Park

Location: Eastern Oklahoma northeast of McAlester.

Access: From U.S. Highway 69 at milepost 7 +.9 (15 miles south of Eufaula, 2.5 miles south of Crowder, 15 miles north of McAlester), turn east onto Rock Creek Road, then turn immediately north (left) onto a paved access road and continue for 0.5 mile to the camp area; sites are situated along a 0.7 mile stretch off of the main campground driveway.

Facilities: 21 campsites; sites are small to medium-sized, with nominal to very good separation; parking pads are mostly paved, short to medium-length straight-ins, plus a few gravel pull-offs; several pads will require minor additional leveling; tent spots are generally small to medium-sized, a bit lumpy, on earth/forest material; some sites include rock retaining walls and pads to make the sites more level; fire rings; firewood is usually available for gathering; water at several faucets; restrooms; holding tank disposal station; paved main driveways; gravel sub-drives; gas and groceries are available in Crowder.

Activities & Attractions: Boating; boat launches; day use shelter.

Natural Features: Located on a forested point above the west shore of Eufaula Lake; campground vegetation consists of sparse grass, moderate undergrowth and tall conifers and hardwoods; some sites out on the point offer good views of the lake and some offshore islands; elevation 600'.

Season, Fees & Phone: April to October; $8.00; 14 day limit; Eufaula Lake CoE Project Office (918) 799-5843.

Camp Notes: Crowder Point Campground is located within a few hundred feet of a major four-lane highway. It could serve well as a convenient highwayside stop, especially for a camper-boater.

OKLAHOMA
Southeast
Please refer to the Oklahoma map in the Appendix

Oklahoma 92

ROBBERS CAVE: WEST
Robbers Cave State Park

Location: Southeast Oklahoma east of McAlester.

Access: From Oklahoma State Highway 2 at a point 5.5 miles northwest of Wilburton and 16 miles south of Quinton, turn west into the *Lake Carlton* area; or turn west, then swing south and go 0.8 mile (parallel to the highway) to the *Deep Ford* area; or turn west and go north for 0.75 mile to the *Equestrian* camp.

Facilities: *Lake Carlton* and *Deep Ford*: a total of 40 standard sites; *Equestrian* area: 25 campsites with partial hookups, plus a few standard sites; all areas: sites vary from small and close together to medium-sized and well separated; parking pads are earth/gravel, short straight-ins or pull-offs in Lake Carlton and Deep Ford, long straight-ins in the equstrian area; adequate space for medium to large tents; fire rings or fireplaces; b-y-o firewood is suggested; water at hookup sites and at several faucets; restrooms with showers; holding tank disposal station; paved driveways; adequate supplies and services are available in Wilburton.

Activities & Attractions: Nature Center; hiking trails; 25 miles of equestrian trails; fishing; boating; beach; swimming pool; tours of Robbers Cave; amphitheater.

Natural Features: Located in the San Bois Mountains; Carlton and Deep Ford are on a grassy, tree-dotted flats on the shore of small lakes; the equestrian camp is on a forested flat; 3 lakes are located in the park; elevation 700'.

Season, Fees & Phone: Open all year; please see Appendix for standard Oklahoma state park fees; 14 day limit; park office (918) 465-2565.

Camp Notes: The park's amphitheater, on Lake Carlton's shore, is not your garden-variety campfire circle. It is uncommonly large for a state park, and can accommodate up to 1200 people. Over the years, the amphitheater has been the site of numerous weddings, revivals, films, and performances.

Oklahoma 93

ROBBERS CAVE: EAST
Robbers Cave State Park

Location: Southeast Oklahoma east of McAlester.

Access: From Oklahoma State Highway 2 at a point 5.5 miles northwest of Wilburton and 16 miles south of Quinton, turn east and proceed 0.45 mile up to to the *Old Circle* and *Whispering Pines* loops.

Facilities: *Whispering Pines*: 15 campsites with full hookups plus a few standard campsites; *Old Circle*: 15 campsites with partial hookups; *both areas*: sites are small to medium-sized, with nominal to good separation; sites in Old Circle are well separated but not very level; sites in Whispering Pines are fairly level but not very spacious; parking pads are earth/gravel, short to long straight-ins or pull-offs; adequate space for medium sized tents, but the space may be slightly sloped; fire rings or fireplaces; b-y-o firewood is suggested; water at sites; restrooms with showers; holding tank disposal station; gravel driveways; adequate supplies and services are available in Wilburton.

Activities & Attractions: Nature Center; hiking trails; 25 miles of equestrian trails; fishing for crappie, bass and catfish; boating; beach; swimming pool; tours of Robbers Cave; amphitheater; hunting in season.

Natural Features: Located on an open forested hillside in the San Bois Mountains; sites receive light-medium shelter from tall pines and hardwoods; elevation 800'.

Season, Fees & Phone: Open all year; reservations accepted for assigned sites; please see Appendix for additional reservation information and standard Oklahoma state park fees; 14 day limit; park office (918) 465-2565.

Camp Notes: Robbers Cave itself is a massive sandstone lair with a secret exit that made it a favorite hideout for the bad guys (and gals) of the Old West. Popularly included on the grotto's guest register are Jesse and Frank James, the Younger Brothers, and a local girl who made the headlines, Belle Starr.

Oklahoma 94

VICTOR
Lake Wister State Park

Location: Southeast Oklahoma southwest of Poteau.

Access: From U.S. Highway 270 at a point 2.3 miles southeast of Wister, 8 miles southwest of Poteau and 0.4 mile north of Wister Dam, turn west onto LeFlore County Road 138 (paved); travel west 5.2 miles; turn south (left) and continue for 0.4 mile to the campground.

Facilities: 61 campsites, including 44 with full hookups; sites are small, essentially level, with nominal separation; parking pads are gravel, short to medium-length straight-ins; small, grassy tent areas; fire rings, plus a few fireplaces and barbecue grills; b-y-o firewood is recommended; water at faucets throughout; restrooms with showers; holding tank disposal station; paved driveways; limited supplies and services are available in Wister.

Activities & Attractions: Fishing (reportedly very good for bluegill, sand bass, channel catfish, and walleye); boating; boat launch at nearby Wards Landing; playground; basketball court; day use area with shelter.

Natural Features: Located on a grassy bluff above the north shore of 4000-acre Wister Lake; campground vegetation consists of mown grass in the camp area, tall grass in the surrounding area, and a string of hardwoods along the bluff edge; 'fish attracters' (partly submerged tree stumps) are conspicuous; the lake is ringed by forested hills and mountains; elevation 500'.

Season, Fees & Phone: Open all year; reservations accepted for assigned sites; please see Appendix for additional reservation information and standard Oklahoma state park fees; 14 day limit; park office (918) 655-7756.

Camp Notes: From the campsites at Victor, there are some terrific views of the lake and the Ouachita Mountains to the south. There are some other nice campsites in the park located at small camp areas on Quarry Isle (which is actually a peninsula), at lake level, and at Damsite, below the dam along the Poteau River.

Oklahoma 95

WARDS LANDING
Lake Wister State Park

Location: Southeast Oklahoma southwest of Poteau.

Access: From U.S. Highway 270 at a point 2.3 miles southeast of Wister, 8 miles southwest of Poteau and 0.4 mile north of Wister Dam, turn west onto LeFlore County Road 138 (paved); proceed west for 3.2 miles; turn north (right) into the campground.

Facilities: 28 campsites, including 15 with partial hookups; sites are small, with nominal to fair separation; parking pads are gravel, short to medium-length straight-ins or medium to long pull-offs; minor additional leveling may be necessary at some sites; adequate, grassy spaces for large tents; fireplaces; firewood may be available for gathering, b-y-o to be sure; water at several faucets; restrooms with showers; holding tank disposal station nearby; paved driveways; limited supplies and services are available in Wister.

Activities & Attractions: Boating; boat launch across the highway; fishing for bluegill, sand bass, channel catfish, and walleye; swimming beach nearby; playground; Lone Star Nature Trail; historic site of Lone Star School.

Natural Features: Located on a forested slope above the north shore of Wister Lake; campground vegetation consists of mown grass surrounded by a dense forest of hardwoods and some conifers; most sites are situated along the perimeter of a clearing at the edge of the forest; the lake is within a short walk of the campground; elevation 500'.

Season, Fees & Phone: Open all year; please see Appendix for standard Oklahoma state park fees; 14 day limit; park office (918) 655-7756.

Camp Notes: The sites at Wards Landing have no actual lake views, but they are situated in a very pleasant glen, within a short walk of the lake. Across the roadway is an Area 2 'Wilderness Campground' which has 20 or so tent sites on a steep forested slope, restrooms with showers, no fire facilities and a small fee.

Oklahoma 96

CEDAR LAKE
Ouachita National Forest

Location: Southeast Oklahoma south of Poteau.

Access: From U.S. Highway 59 at a point 5.3 miles south of Hodgen, 10 miles south of Heavener and 9 miles north of the junction of U.S. Highway 59 & Oklahoma State Highway 1, turn west onto Holson Valley Road/Forest Road 5 (paved) and proceed west 2.8 miles; turn north (right) onto Forest Road 269 (paved) and continue for 0.7 mile to a fork; the North Shore camp is 0.7 mile straight ahead and the South Shore camp is 0.8 mile to the west (left).

Facilities: 88 campsites, including 4 with electrical hookups, in 3 loops; sites are small to medium-sized, with minimal to fairly good separation; parking pads are paved, short to medium-length straight-ins; many pads may require additional leveling; framed-and-gravelled tent pads, adequate for medium to large tents; fire rings and some fireplaces; firewood is usually available for gathering; water at central faucets; restrooms with showers; holding tank disposal station; paved driveways; limited supplies and services are available in Heavener.

Activities & Attractions: Hiking trails; Old Pine Interpretive Trail; swimming beaches; limited boating (7.5 hp motors); fishing; equestrian trails and camp loop; amphitheater; Talimena Scenic Drive nearby.

Natural Features: Located on the east and south shores of 90-acre Cedar Lake in the densely forested Ouachita Mountains; sites are all fairly well sheltered in a forest of hardwoods and conifers; elevation 800'.

Season, Fees & Phone: Open all year; $6.00 for a standard site, $8.00 for an electrical hookup site; 14 day limit; Choctaw Ranger District, Heavener, (918) 653-2991.

Camp Notes: Cedar Lake is one of the better national forest camps in the West. Heck, considering the paved pads and access roads, showers, hookups, and the superscenic lakeside setting, it ranks up there with the best of 'em.

Oklahoma 97

WINDING STAIR
Ouachita National Forest

Location: Southeast Oklahoma south of Poteau.

Access: From Oklahoma State Highway 1 (Talimena Scenic Drive) at a point 26 miles east of Talihina and 2 miles west of the junction of Oklahoma State Highway 1 & U.S. Highway 59 north of Big Cedar, turn north onto a paved access road; proceed north for 0.15 mile, then swing west (left) into the campground.

Facilities: 27 campsites; sites are small to medium-sized, with nominal to fairly good separation; parking pads are hard-surfaced, fairly level, medium to long straight-ins; spacious tent spots on a surface of forest material or on framed-and-gravelled pads; assorted fire facilities; firewood is usually available for gathering; water at central faucets; restrooms; paved driveway; gas and camper supplies are available in Big Cedar, 7 miles south.

Activities & Attractions: Emerald Vista, adjacent; Ouachita National Recreation Trail; Robert S. Kerr Arboretum and Nature Center located 5 miles east.

Natural Features: Located (some might say 'perched'), high atop Winding Stair Mountain in the Ouachita Mountains; campground vegetation consists of tall hardwoods and conifers, light undergrowth, and sparse grass; views, from nearby, of the Poteau River Valley to the north; elevation 1900'.

Season, Fees & Phone: May to September (possibly at other times, but with no water and no fee); $6.00; 14 day limit; Kiamichi Ranger District, Talihina, (918) 567-2466.

Camp Notes: If you didn't know you were in Oklahoma, this spot could lead you to believe that you were in the dense forests of the Oregon Cascades. There is an extraordinary 180° panorama to be admired from a few feet away at Emerald Vista. The name, Emerald, comes from the intense color of the mountains and hills in the Poteau Valley. Fall foliage is a knockout!

Oklahoma 98

BILLY CREEK
Ouachita National Forest

Location: Southeast Oklahoma south of Poteau.

Access: From Oklahoma State Highway 63 at a point 5.8 miles west of Big Cedar and 19 miles east of Talihina, turn northeast onto Forest Road 6022 (paved, should be signed for Billy Creek Campground); proceed 0.25 mile, then turn north (left) and go north for 0.55 mile to the end of the pavement; continue northerly on gravel for another 0.25 mile to a fork; bear right (the left fork would take you 9 miles to Talimena Scenic Drive); continue for 0.65 mile to another fork; bear left and continue for a final 0.2 mile to the campground.

Facilities: 12 campsites in a loop and a string; sites are small to medium+ in size, with nominal to good separation; parking pads are gravel, medium to long straight-ins; some pads may require minor additional leveling; adequate space for large tents on a surface of forest material or framed-and-gravelled tent pads; fireplaces or fire rings; firewood is usually available for gathering; water at central faucets; vault facilities; gravel driveways; gas and camper supplies on Highway 63.

Activities & Attractions: Hiking; Billy Creek Trail connects to the Ouachita National Recreation Trail; 4wd road from Highway 63 to Highway 1 (Talimena Scenic Drive); adjacent picnic area.

Natural Features: Located on a forested shelf above Billy Creek; campground vegetation consists of tall hardwoods and conifers, with areas of grass and light underbrush; about half of the sites overlook the stream; timber 'stairs' have been built into the bank of the creek to provide a walkway from the sites down to the creek, about 20 feet below; elevation 800'.

Season, Fees & Phone: May to September; $5.00; 14 day limit; Kiamichi Ranger District, Talihina, (918) 567-2466.

Camp Notes: This is really an ideal spot to get away from the madding crowd. Call it 'reachably remote'. You should be able to pick your way up the campground during daylight hours in sunlight without incident. At night or in the rain, though, be especially watchful for all of the turns and forks and small signs pointing the way to the this little hideout.

Oklahoma 99

TALIMENA
Talimena State Park

Location: Southeast Oklahoma southwest of Poteau.

Access: From Oklahoma State Highway 1 at a point 6 miles east of Talihina and 1.5 miles south of the junction of U.S. Highway 271 & Oklahoma State Highway 1 (Talimena Scenic Drive), turn east into the park; tent sites are straight ahead, the hookup area is on the right.

Facilities: 12 campsites, including 7 with partial hookups; sites are small and closely spaced; parking pads are grass, short to medium-length straight-ins for the hookup sites, pull-offs for the tent sites; most pads are reasonably level (considering the terrain); adequate space for large tents on mown lawns or on framed-and-gravelled pads; barbecue grills and/or fire rings; b-y-o firewood is recommended; water at several faucets; holding tank disposal station; paved driveways; limited supplies and services (including terrific 'burgers and 'fries) are available in Talihina.

Activities & Attractions: Westernmost point on the Ouachita National Recreational Trail, a 175-mile-long hiking trail that winds through these densely forested mountains; westernmost point of the 54-mile-long Talimena Scenic Drive is 1.5 mile north of here at the junction of Highways 271 & 1; playground; day use area with shelter.

Natural Features: Located on the west slope of the forested Ouachita Mountains; campground vegetation consists of mown lawns ringed by trees in the hookup area, and open forest in the tent area; elevation 800'.

Season, Fees & Phone: Open all year; please see Appendix for standard Oklahoma state park fees; 14 day limit; park office (918) 567-2052.

Camp Notes: Talimena, with only 20-acres, is one of the smallest state parks in Oklahoma with camping. It's a favorite trailhead for Ouachita National Recreation Trail users. (Incidentally, the name of the mountains is pronounced something like "*Wash*-taw".)

Oklahoma 100

POTATO HILLS
Sardis Lake/Corps of Engineers Park

Location: Southeast Oklahoma southeast of McAlester.

Access: From Oklahoma State Highway 2 at a point 5 miles north of Clayton, 3.35 miles north of the junction of U.S. Highway 271 and Oklahoma State Highway 2, 25 miles south of Wilburton, turn west onto the Potato Hills Central access road and proceed 0.05 mile to the campground entrance station; turn south (left) for 0.3 mile to Area A, or continue ahead for 0.2 mile to Areas B, C, and D.

Facilities: 94 campsites with partial hookups; sites are small to medium-sized, with nominal to fair separation; parking pads are gravel, medium to long straight-ins; sites in Loop D may require additional leveling; adequate space for medium-sized tents on a grass/forest material surface; barbecue grills or fire rings; some firewood may be available for gathering in the vicinity; water at faucets throughout; restrooms with showers; holding tank disposal station; paved driveways; limited supplies and services are available in Clayton.

Activities & Attractions: Boating; boat launch nearby at Potato Hills South; fishing (bass, crappie, channel catfish and sunfish); designated swimming beach at Potato Hills South; day use area and shelter; ball diamond; Lost Buffalo Interpretive Trail.

Natural Features: Located on a forested flat on the east shore of Sardis Lake, in a wide valley surrounded by densely forested mountains and hills; campground vegetation consists of medium tall hardwoods, light underbrush and trimmed grass; the 14,000-acre lake has a low shoreline coated with grass and trees; elevation 600'.

Season, Fees & Phone: April to October; $11.00; 14 day limit; Sardis Lake CoE Project Office (918) 569-4131.

Camp Notes: Potato Hills is a top-notch facility in a terrific setting. A lot of campers say that it's tough to surrender their spot when the magic 14 days has expired.

Oklahoma 101

CLAYTON LAKE
Clayton Lake State Park

Location: Southeast Oklahoma southeast of McAlester.

Access: From U.S. Highway 271 at a point 4.4 miles south of Clayton and 33 miles northeast of Antlers, turn west into the park; turn immediately south (left) and continue for 0.2 mile to the south area or continue west (straight ahead) then north (right) to the north area.

Facilities: 64 campsites, including some with electrical hookups; sites are small to medium-sized, with minimal to nominal separation; parking pads are gravel, short to medium-length straight-ins; many pads may require additional leveling; adequate, generally sloped, space for large tents on a surface of grass or forest material; barbecue grills or fire rings; firewood may be available for gathering; water at several faucets; restrooms with showers; holding tank disposal station; paved driveways; limited supplies and services are available in Clayton.

Activities & Attractions: Fishing (channel catfish, crappie); limited boating (10 mph); boat launch; swimming beach; hiking trail; playgrounds; day use area with shelters.

Natural Features: Located on a forested slope on the east shore of 95-acre Clayton Lake; campground vegetation consists of medium to tall trees, light underbrush and some areas of mown grass; a few sites have good lake views, most sites have glimpses of the lake through the trees; closely bordered by forested hills; elevation 600'.

Season, Fees & Phone: Open all year; reservations accepted for assigned sites; please see Appendix for additional reservation information and standard Oklahoma state park fees; ; 14 day limit; park office (918) 569-7981.

Camp Notes: The best sites in the park may very well be those on a grassy hill above the lake just south of a small creek ford. There is a comfy, backwoods atmosphere in this park nestled in the foothills of the Kiamichi Mountains.

Oklahoma 102

THE POINT
Chickasaw National Recreation Area

Location: South-central Oklahoma north of Ardmore.

Access: From Oklahoma State Highway 7 at a point 3 miles west of Sulphur, 7 miles east of Davis, and 10 miles east of I-35 Exit 55, turn south onto Charles F. Cooper Drive and travel 5 miles; turn northeast (left) onto a paved access road and proceed 0.8 mile to the campground.

Facilities: 52 campsites; sites are small to medium-sized, with nominal to fairly good separation; most parking pads are gravel, short straight-ins, plus some long pull-throughs; most pads will require some additional leveling; large areas for tents, many are fairly level; fireplaces or fire rings; b-y-o firewood is suggested; water at central faucets; restrooms, plus auxiliary vault facilities; paved driveways; adequate to adequate+ supplies and services are available in Davis and Sulphur.

Activities & Attractions: Boating; boat launch nearby; fishing.

Natural Features: Located on a hill on a major point of land which extends southward from the north shore of Lake of the Arbuckles; the point divides 2 main arms of the lake (Guy Sandy Creek inlet and Rock Creek inlet); the campground overlooks the west shore of Rock Creek Arm (the farther east of the pair of arms); sites receive medium shade/shelter from large hardwoods and junipers/cedars, plus some underbrush; the lake is bordered by densely forested, low hills; elevation 900'.

Season, Fees & Phone: Open all year; $6.00; 14 day limit; Chickasaw National Recreation Area Headquarters, Sulfur, (405) 622-2824.

Camp Notes: Another campground in this recreation area which merits consideration is Guy Sandy. It can be reached from Oklahoma 7 at a point 6 miles west of Sulphur and 7 miles east of I-35, then by traveling south on a paved road for 3.5 miles. It has 40 sites on a hill above the west shore of Guy Sandy Creek Arm, drinking water and vaults. Near the campground is an excellent, well-sheltered boat launch and dock facility.

ROCK CREEK
Chickasaw National Recreation Area

Location: South-central Oklahoma north of Ardmore.

Access: From U.S. Highway 177 on the south edge of downtown Sulphur, (0.05 mile south of the Travertine Creek bridge), turn west onto a paved access road and proceed 1.3 miles to the campground. (Special Note: From I-35 Exit 55, take Oklahoma State Highway 7 to 12th Street on the west side of Sulphur, then south to the campground.)

Facilities: 106 campsites; sites are small+ to medium-sized, the majority are acceptably level, with fair to fairly good separation; parking pads are paved/packed gravel, mostly medium to long pull-throughs, plus some medium-length straight-ins; large areas for tents; fireplaces; b-y-o firewood is suggested; water at several faucets; restrooms; holding tank disposal station; paved driveways; adequate+ supplies and services are available in Sulphur.

Activities & Attractions: Travertine Nature Center, 2 miles east, has exhibits, films and programs; mineral springs; spacious, adjacent day use facilities; fishing on small Veterans Lake, south of the campground; boating, boat launches, and fishing on Lake of the Arbuckles, accessible from several points within the recreation area, 7 to 10 miles southwest.

Natural Features: Located on a large flat along Rock Creek (most sites) and on a hill above the stream (about one-fourth of the sites); campground vegetation consists of moderately dense hardwoods and some junipers/cedars; elevation 900'.

Season, Fees & Phone: Open all year; $6.00; 14 day limit; Chickasaw National Recreation Area Headquarters, Sulfur, (405) 622-2824.

Camp Notes: Rock Creek is probably the best of the campgrounds in Chickasaw NRA. Although it is certainly a good camp, it is still only average among all of the campgrounds in Oklahoma. A similar comment might be made for the national recreation area as a whole. While the region's scenery is undeniably pleasant, there are literally dozens of other areas in this fine state which surpass it.

COLD SPRINGS
Chickasaw National Recreation Area

Location: South-central Oklahoma north of Ardmore.

Access: From U.S. Highway 177 on the south edge of downtown Sulphur, (just at the south end of the Travertine Creek bridge), turn east onto a paved park road and proceed 0.7 mile; turn north (left) into the campground.

Facilities: 64 campsites; sites are small to medium-sized, with nominal to fair separation; parking pads are gravel, short straight-ins; a touch of additional leveling may be needed in some sites; generally adequate space for large tents, may be a little sloped; fireplaces; b-y-o firewood is suggested; water at several faucets; restrooms; paved driveways; adequate+ supplies and services are available within walking distance in Sulphur.

Activities & Attractions: Exhibits, films, self-guiding nature trails, also guided nature walks (summer weekends), at the Travertine Nature Center, 1 mile east.

Natural Features: Located on gently sloping terrain several yards above the north bank of Travertine Creek; campground vegetation consists of moderately dense, large hardwoods, a few junipers/cedars and some underbrush; surrounded by very dense vegetation; elevation 900'.

Season, Fees & Phone: May to September; $6.00; 14 day limit; Chickasaw National Recreation Area Headquarters, Sulfur, (405) 622-2824.

Camp Notes: Although this isn't really a streamside campground, you may be able to *hear* the small creek flowing by, as long as local traffic cooperates. Downtown Sulphur is just a few brush-busting yards north of the campground, and there's plenty of movement on the road to and from the highway and the nature center. (The camp is so conveniently close to town, there's a good chance that, if you get tired of eating beans and wienies, you could call a pizza place to deliver a Large Supreme to your campsite. If you want to rent a video to accompany the pizza, they're available too; but since there are no hookups here, you'll have to plug your vcr into a current bush. Ed.)

BUCKHORN
Chickasaw National Recreation Area

Location: South-central Oklahoma north of Ardmore.

Access: From U.S. Highway 177 at a point 10 miles north of its junction with Oklahoma State Highway 53 east of Gene Autry, 0.5 mile north of the Buckhorn Creek bridge, and 5 miles south of Sulphur, turn west onto a paved lake access road and travel 2.3 miles; turn south (left) into a pair of loops, or continue ahead for another 0.2 mile, then turn south again into the remaining loops.

Facilities: 171 campsites, including a number of park n' walk units; sites vary from small to medium+, with nominal to fairly good separation; parking pads are gravel, short to medium-length straight-ins, pull-offs or pull-throughs; additional leveling will be required in most sites; adequate space for medium to large tents, though generally sloped; fireplaces; some firewood is available for gathering in the general area; water at central faucets; restrooms; holding tank disposal station nearby; paved driveways; ranger station nearby; adequate+ supplies and services are available in Sulphur.

Activities & Attractions: Boating; boat launch; fishing; short hiking trail; amphitheater; exhibits, films, self-guiding nature trails, also guided nature walks (weekends), at the Travertine Nature Center, on the south edge of Sulphur, 1.5 miles east of U.S. 177.

Natural Features: Located on hilly, forested terrain above the southeast shore of Lake of the Arbuckles; most sites are well shaded/sheltered by medium to tall hardwoods and some junipers/cedars; the lake is bordered by wooded hills; elevation 900'.

Season, Fees & Phone: Open all year; $6.00; 14 day limit; Chickasaw National Recreation Area Headquarters, Sulfur, (405) 622-2824.

Camp Notes: Of the nra's trio of campgrounds which are accessible from U.S. 177, this is the only one with lake access. It also is the largest campground in the recreation area.

DUKES FOREST
Lake Murray State Park

Location: South-central Oklahoma south of Ardmore.

Access: From Interstate 35 Exit 24 for Lake Murray State Park, travel east on Oklahoma State Highway 77S for 2.3 miles to the park entrance; turn north (left) and proceed 3 miles; turn east (right) for 0.2 mile to the campground. **Alternate Access:** From U.S. Highway 70 at a point 3 miles east of I-35 Exit 29, turn south onto State Highway 77 for 3 miles to the campground turnoff.

Facilities: 34 assigned, partial hookup sites, plus a number of standard/tent sites; sites are small+ to medium-sized, with fair to good separation; parking pads are gravel, mostly medium to long straight-ins; a little additional leveling may be required in many sites; adequate space for large tents; fireplaces; b-y-o firewood; water at faucets throughout; restrooms with showers; holding tank disposal station; paved driveways; camper supplies at the park store, 2 miles south.

Activities & Attractions: Playground; central shelter; swimming, golf course, hiking trails, nature trails, boating, fishing, horse stables, within 3 miles.

Natural Features: Located on a hill/bluff top above the west shore of Lake Murray; sites are moderately shaded/sheltered by medium to tall hardwoods and some junipers/cedars; elevation 800'.

Season, Fees & Phone: March to November; reservations accepted for assigned sites; please see Appendix for additional reservation information and standard Oklahoma state park fees; 14 day limit; park office (405) 223-4044.

Camp Notes: The park's only reservable campsites are those in this campground (also called just plain "Duke"). It is also the only campground which doesn't offer direct lake access or lake views. However, those items are offset to an extent by what is possibly the best forest environment of any camp in the park.

ELEPHANT ROCK & TIPPS POINT
Lake Murray State Park

Location: South-central Oklahoma south of Ardmore.

Access: From Interstate 35 Exit 24 for Lake Murray State Park, head east on Oklahoma State Highway 77S for 2.3 miles to the park entrance; turn north (left) for 1.1 miles; turn east (right) onto a paved access road and proceed 0.25 mile, then turn northeast (left) for 1 mile to *Elephant Rock* or continue ahead for another 0.2 mile, then bear southeast (right) for 0.25 mile to *Tipps Point*. **Alternate Access:** From U.S. Highway 70 at a point 3 miles east of I-35 Exit 29 and 20 miles west of Madill, turn south onto State Highway 77 and proceed 2 miles to the campground access road.

Facilities: *Elephant Rock*: 50 campsites with full hookups; *Tipps Point*: 35 campsites with partial hookups; *both camps*: a number of standard sites are also available; sites are very small to small+, acceptably level, with minimal separation; parking pads are gravel, short straight-ins, or medium to medium+ pull-offs or pull-throughs; adequate space for small to medium-sized tents; fireplaces; b-y-o firewood; water at faucets throughout; restrooms with showers; holding tank disposal station in Elephant Rock; paved main driveways, gravel sub-drives; camper supplies at the park store, 1 mile south; complete supplies and services are available in Ardmore.

Activities & Attractions: Buckhorn Hiking Trail from Tipps Point; boating; boat launches; fishing.

Natural Features: Located on the west shore of 6000-acre Lake Murray; sites are lightly to moderately shaded/sheltered, primarily by hardwoods; elevation 800'.

Season, Fees & Phone: Open all year; please see Appendix for standard Oklahoma state park fees; 14 day limit; park office (405) 223-4044.

Camp Notes: Elephant Rock has some lakeside sites, but the main hookup loop is on a very lightly shaded flat within walking distance of the lake. Tipps Point, on the other hand, has several snug, but scenic, surfside sites situated on a short strip on the the south side of the point.

BUZZARD ROOST
Lake Murray State Park

Location: South-central Oklahoma south of Ardmore.

Access: From Interstate 35 Exit 24, travel east on Oklahoma State Highway 77S for 2.3 miles to the park entrance; turn south and continue on Highway 77S for an additional mile; turn southeast (left) onto the campground access road and proceed 0.4 mile to the campground.

Facilities: Approximately 50 campsites, including 30 sites with partial hookups; sites are small to small+, about half are level, with minimal to nominal separation; parking pads are gravel, mostly short to medium-length straight-ins; large areas for tents; a number of sites have framed tent pads; fireplaces; b-y-o firewood; water at hookup sites and at central faucets; restrooms with showers; holding tank disposal station; paved driveways; camper supplies at the park store, 1 mile north; complete supplies and services are available in Ardmore, 6 miles north.

Activities & Attractions: Fishing; boating; marina; golf course nearby; Tucker Tower Nature Center, 2 miles south, has a museum, offers nature/history programs spring through fall; hiking trails throughout the park.

Natural Features: Located on a flat and a slope along a small point of land on the west shore of Lake Murray, 6000-acre impoundment; sites receive light to medium shade/shelter from large hardwoods; the lake is surrounded by low, wooded hills; elevation 800'.

Season, Fees & Phone: March to November; please see Appendix for standard Oklahoma state park fees; 14 day limit; park office (405) 223-4044.

Camp Notes: This appears to be an especially popular spot for tent camping. Although a number of sites have bay views, there aren't any really superior lake views. It's just a nice place to camp.

MARIETTA LANDING
Lake Murray State Park

Location: South-central Oklahoma southeast of Ardmore.

Access: From Interstate 35 Exit 24, head east on Oklahoma State Highway 77 for 2.3 miles to the park entrance; turn south onto Oklahoma State Highway 77s and proceed 5.6 miles south and southeast to a point just past the dam; turn north (left) into the campground. **Alternate Access:** From U.S. Highway 70 at a point 8 miles east of I-35 Exit 29 and 15 miles west of Madill, turn south onto Oklahoma State Highway 77S and travel 8.3 miles (along the east shore of the lake) to the campground turnoff.

Facilities: 39 campsites, including 30 with partial hookups, in 2 loops; sites are small+ to medium-sized, with nominal to fairly good separation; parking pads are gravel, mostly medium to long straight-ins; additional leveling will probably be needed in most sites; medium to large areas for tents; barbecue grills; b-y-o firewood; water at hookup sites and at central faucets; restrooms with showers; holding tank disposal station; paved or gravel driveways; complete supplies and services are available in Ardmore, 10 miles north.

Activities & Attractions: Boating; boat launch; fishing; central shelter.

Natural Features: Located on a short bluff along the shore of a long, slender bay at the southeast corner of Lake Murray; most sites are well-sheltered/shaded by medium to tall hardwoods and a few junipers/cedars; elevation 800'.

Season, Fees & Phone: Open all year; please see Appendix for standard Oklahoma state park fees; 14 day limit; park office (405) 223-4044.

Camp Notes: Lake Murray has some of the clearest, bluest water you'll find in this region. (It's almost exclusively spring-fed.) A really attractive lake.

ROCK TOWER
Lake Murray State Park

Location: South-central Oklahoma southeast of Ardmore.

Access: From U.S. Highway 70 at a point 8 miles east of I-35 Exit 29 and 15 miles west of Madill, turn south onto Oklahoma State Highway 77S and travel 4.2 miles; turn southwest (right) onto a paved access road and proceed 0.5 mile to the campground.

Facilities: 38 campsites, including 26 with full hookups, in 2 loops; sites are medium-sized, with nominal to fair separation; parking pads are gravel, short, extra wide straight-ins for standard sites, medium to long pull-throughs or straight-ins for hookup sites; hookup site pads will require additional leveling; large, level, grassy tent areas in standard sites, sloped in hookup units; fire rings or barbecue grills; b-y-o firewood; water at faucets throughout; restrooms with showers; gravel driveways; complete supplies and services are available in Ardmore, 10 miles north.

Activities & Attractions: Tower (about 3 stories high) of native rock built by the CCC in the 1930's; boating; small boat launch; fishing; fishing pier.

Natural Features: Located on a grassy hilltop (standard sites) and on a hillside (hookup sites) on the middle-east shore of Lake Murray; sites receive light to medium shade from large hardwoods and junipers/cedars; elevation 800'.

Season, Fees & Phone: March to November; please see Appendix for standard Oklahoma state park fees; 14 day limit; park office (405) 223-4044.

Camp Notes: The square-based, pyramid-topped tower is certainly a curiosity. It and another tower on the west shore were constructed by the good ol' CCC when it built the lake and its trimmings. If you choose one of the standard sites, you can admire it close-up, because it's right in the middle of the camp loop.

MARTINS LANDING
Lake Murray State Park

Location: South-central Oklahoma southeast of Ardmore.

Access: From U.S. Highway 70 at a point 8 miles east of I-35 Exit 29 and 15 miles west of Madill, turn south onto Oklahoma State Highway 77S and proceed 2.8 miles; turn northwest (right) into the campground.

Facilities: Approximately 60 campsites, including 31 with electrical hookups, in 2 areas; sites are small to medium-sized with minimal to nominal separation; parking pads are gravel, medium to long, straight-ins for hookup sites, and pull-offs for standard sites; adequate space for large tents on a grassy slope; barbecue grills; b-y-o firewood; water at several faucets; restrooms with showers; paved driveways; complete supplies and services are available in Ardmore, 10 miles north.

Activities & Attractions: Boating; boat launch and dock; fishing; sandy swimming beach; central shelter; day use area; orv area nearby, north of the campground.

Natural Features: Located on a tree-dotted, grassy slope on the east shore of Lake Murray; campground vegetation consists of medium to tall junipers/cedars, oaks and other hardwoods; reeds grow along much of the shoreline; light to medium shade/shelter throughout; elevation 800'.

Season, Fees & Phone: March to November; please see Appendix for standard Oklahoma state park fees; 14 day limit; park office (405) 223-4044.

Camp Notes: There are some really nice tent spots in this campground. They're virtually lakeside, on a grassy slope, and provide a beautiful view of the 6000-acre blue lake ringed by forested hills. Martins Landing is the campground least likely to be busy even when the rest of the park, most of which is on the west shore, is overwhelmed by enthusiastic recreationers.

Oklahoma 112

CANEY BEND
Lake Texoma/Corps of Engineers Park

Location: South-central Oklahoma west of Durant.

Access: From Oklahoma State Highway 32 on the west edge of Kingston, 0.05 mile west of the junction of State Highway 32 & U.S. Highway 70, turn south onto Donehoo Street; proceed 3.6 miles, then turn east onto East Lasiter; continue east and south for 2.2 miles (gravel for 2 miles) to the park entrance station; hookup campsites are to the left and standard sites are to the right.

Facilities: 52 campsites, including 42 with electrical hookups, in 2 loops; sites are small, with minimal to fair separation; parking pads are gravel, medium to long straight-ins; many pads will require additional leveling; adequate space for medium to large tents, but they may be sloped; fireplaces or barbecue grills; firewood is usually available for gathering in the general area; water at several faucets; restrooms with showers; holding tank disposal station; paved driveways; limited supplies and services are available in Kingston.

Activities & Attractions: Boating; boat launch; fishing (stripers, white bass, crappie, catfish).

Natural Features: Located on a forested slope on a small point above a well-sheltered bay on the north shore of Lake Texoma; most sites are lightly to moderately shaded by medium to tall hardwoods; lake views from many sites; elevation 600'.

Season, Fees & Phone: April to November; $8.00 for a standard site, $9.00 for a standard site with water, $11.00 for an electrical hookup site; 14 day limit; Lake Texoma CoE Project Office (214) 465-4990.

Camp Notes: This is a very popular spot with the locals (perhaps because it's not the easiest place for the rest of us to find). This appears to be an excellent spot for boater-campers. The well-protected small bay below the campground is located off of a larger bay/arm which in turn is right off of the main body of the lake.

Oklahoma 113

BUNCOMBE CREEK
Lake Texoma/Corps of Engineers Park

Location: South-central Oklahoma southeast of Ardmore.

Access: From U.S. Highway 377 in the village of Willis (1.3 miles north of Oklahoma-Texas border at the Red River bridge and 12 miles southwest of Kingston), turn east onto a paved local road; proceed east for 1.55 miles (only the first 0.3 mile is paved) to the park entrance; Loop A is to the left, Loop B is straight ahead and Loops C & D are to the right.

Facilities: 56 campsites in 4 loops; sites are small to medium-sized, with nominal to fair separation; parking pads are gravel, short to medium-length straight-ins; many pads may require additional leveling; adequate space for large tents on a grassy surface; barbecue grills or firerings; firewood is usually available for gathering; water at central faucets; vault facilities in Loops A & B, restrooms with showers in Loops C & D; holding tank disposal station; paved driveways; gas and groceries are available in Willis.

Activities & Attractions: Boating; boat launch; fishing; day use.

Natural Features: Located on the west shore of the Buncombe Creek Arm of Lake Texoma; campground vegetation consists of sparse grass, medium to tall conifers, oaks and other hardwoods; sites in Loop A are scattered over a grassy slope, those in Loop B are on a tree-dotted, sloped point, and those in Loop C are in more dense forest; Lake Texoma, 10th largest lake in the U.S., has a shoreline of 580 miles; some waterfront sites; elev. 600'.

Season, Fees & Phone: April to September; $8.00; 14 day limit; Lake Texoma CoE Project Office (214) 465-4990.

Camp Notes: Buncombe is more like a remote riverside camp than a Texoma lakeside campground. The views across the 'arm' reveal nary a building nor dock to contradict the illusion.

Oklahoma 114

ROOSTER CREEK
Lake Texoma State Park

Location: South-central Oklahoma west of Durant.

Access: From U.S. Highway 70 at a point 0.3 mile west of the Roosevelt Memorial Bridge over Lake Texoma and 4.3 miles east of Kingston, turn south onto the park road; proceed 0.1 mile to a fork; bear right and continue for 0.6 mile, 0.8 mile, or 1 mile to the three camp areas; (the first 2 camp areas are just before and after a bridge over Rooster Creek.)

Facilities: 97 campsites with partial hookups, 66 sites with full hookups, plus dozens of standard sites; sites are small to medium-sized, with nominal to fair separation; parking pads are grass/gravel, mostly level, medium to long pull-throughs, straight-ins or whatevers; some very nice spots for large tents along a cove; barbecue grills; b-y-o firewood is recommended; water at faucets throughout; restrooms with showers; holding tank disposal station; paved main driveway, gravel sub-drives; limited supplies and services are available in Kingston.

Activities & Attractions: Boating; fishing; hiking trail; swimming beach; golf course; equestrian trails; go-cart track; airport.

Natural Features: Located on grassy hills above the north shore of Lake Texoma; campground vegetation consists of acres of mown grass and stands of hardwoods; some sites are unsheltered and others are in medium shade/shelter; some sites have bay views; elevation 700'.

Season, Fees & Phone: Open all year; please see Appendix for standard Oklahoma state park fees; 14 day limit; park office (405) 564-2566.

Camp Notes: Many recreationers come to Texoma State Park to enjoy its many and varied activities and to spend the night in its many and varied habitats--from basic tent camping spots to lodge accomodations. (A 3000' paved airstrip is an additional convenience item you don't find next door to just every campground.)

Oklahoma 115

CATFISH BAY
Lake Texoma State Park

Location: South-central Oklahoma west of Durant.

Access: From U.S. Highway 70 at a point 0.3 mile west of the Roosevelt Memorial Bridge over Lake Texoma and 4.3 miles east of Kingston, turn south onto the park road; proceed 0.1 mile to a fork; bear east (left) and continue for 0.6 mile to another fork; bear left again for 0.05 mile to the campground; hookups are to the right, most standard sites are to the left.

Facilities: 117 sites with partial hookups, 20 sites with full hookups, plus dozens of standard sites; sites are small, with minimal to nominal separation; parking pads are grass/gravel, medium to long pull-throughs or straight-ins; many pads may require additional leveling; adequate space for medium to large tents, some spots are sloped; barbecue grills for some sites; b-y-o firewood is recommended; water at faucets throughout; restrooms with showers; holding tank disposal station; paved main driveway, gravel sub-drives; limited supplies and services are available in Kingston.

Activities & Attractions: Boating; fishing; playground; golf course; volleyball courts; go-cart track; in-park airport.

Natural Features: Located on a slope above a cove on the north shore of Lake Texoma; campground vegetation consists of medium to tall hardwoods and mown grass in the standard area, and sparse grass and a few scattered trees in the hookup area; some sites have views of the bay; elevation 700'.

Season, Fees & Phone: Open all year; reservations accepted May to September; please see Appendix for additional reservation information and standard Oklahoma state park fees; 14 day limit; park office (405) 564-2566.

Camp Notes: Catfish Bay is famous for great fishing and its periodic bass tournaments. Campers here don't seem to mind being a little congested at times. Nearby Rooster Creek Campground offers a bit more elbow room but not as many sites that are close to the water's edge.

JOHNSON CREEK
Lake Texoma/Corps of Engineers Park

Location: South-central Oklahoma west of Durant.

Access: From U.S. Highway 70 at a point just east of the Roosevelt Memorial bridge across Lake Texoma and 10 miles west of Durant, turn north onto a paved access road and proceed 0.2 mile to the park entrance station and the campground.

Facilities: 54 campsites, many with partial hookups; sites are small to medium-sized, with minimal to fair separation; parking pads are gravel, long to very long straight-ins; many pads may require additional leveling; adequate, though possibly sloped, space for medium to large tents; fire rings; firewood is usually available for gathering in the vicinity; water at faucets throughout; restrooms with showers; holding tank disposal station; paved driveways, gravel sub-drives; adequate supplies and services are available in Durant.

Activities & Attractions: Boating; boat launch; fishing; nature trail; day use area with shelter.

Natural Features: Located on a forested slope on the east shore of Lake Texoma; some sites are lakeside, others are on a short hill above the shoreline; campground vegetation consists of mown grass and scattered medium to tall hardwoods; most sites have lakeviews; elevation 600'.

Season, Fees & Phone: April to November; $8.00 for a standard site, $9.00 for a standard site with water, $12.00 for a partial hookup site; 14 day limit; Lake Texoma CoE Project Office (214) 465-4990.

Camp Notes: This is one of the most easily accessible campgrounds on the lake. Trophy camper-fishermen can munch on this morsel of info: Johnson Creek is just five miles from Cumberland Cove, the site of a world record catch. A 118½ pound blue catfish was hooked on a four-inch sunfish and landed in Cumberland Cove.

WILLOW SPRINGS
Lake Texoma/Corps of Engineers Park

Location: South-central Oklahoma west of Durant.

Access: From U.S. Highway 70 at a point just east of the Roosevelt Memorial bridge over Lake Texoma and 10 miles west of Durant, turn south onto a pved local road and proceed 1 mile to a fork; bear right to the hookup area; or continue south (straight ahead) for 0.55 mile to the end of the point, then turn right to most of the standard sites.

Facilities: 27 campsites, including 13 with electrical hookups, in 2 areas; sites are fairly good-sized, with nominal to fair separation; parking pads are gravel, medium to long straight-ins or pull-throughs; additional leveling may be required in some sites; adequate space for large tents on a grassy surface; fire rings; firewood is usually available for gathering in the surrounding area; water at central faucets; restroom with showers near the hookup sites, vault facilities at the south end of the park; holding tank disposal station; paved main driveways, gravel sub-drives; gas and groceries are available within a mile.

Activities & Attractions: Boating; boat launch; fishing; day use area with shelter.

Natural Features: Located on a grassy point on the east shore of Lake Texoma; sites are situated on a grassy, tree-dotted lakeside flat and slope; the campground is bordered by a forest of medium tall trees and dense underbrush; good lake views from most sites; elevation 600'.

Season, Fees & Phone: May to September; $8.00 for a standard site, $11.00 for an electrical hookup site; 14 day limit; Lake Texoma CoE Project Office (214) 465-4990.

Camp Notes: The characteristics of Willow Springs Campground which distinguish it from other CoE areas on Lake Texoma are the openness of the terrain and vegetation, and the excellent tenting opportunities.

LAKESIDE
Lake Texoma/Corps of Engineers Park

Location: South-central Oklahoma southwest of Durant.

Access: From U.S. Highway 70 at a point 9 miles west of Durant and 1 mile east of the Roosevelt Memorial bridge which spans Lake Texoma, turn south onto Streetman Road; proceed 4 miles to the campground entrance station; sites are to the right just beyond the entrance, or straight ahead then around to the left.

Facilities: 93 campsites, including many with partial hookups, in 3 loops; (plans call for adding 60 more campsites); sites are small to medium-sized, with minimal to nominal separation; parking pads are gravel, level, medium to long straight-ins; adequate space for medium to large tents on grass or framed tent pads; fire rings and barbecue grills; b-y-o firewood is recommended; water at faucets throughout; restrooms with showers; holding tank disposal station; paved driveways; gas and groceries at several stops along U.S. 70; adequate supplies and services are available in Durant.

Activities & Attractions: Boating; boat launches; fishing; equestrian/hiking trail to Platter Flats Campground.

Natural Features: Located on grassy, tree-dotted gently rolling terrain on a point on the east shore of Lake Texoma; willows, oaks and other hardwoods are scattered across acres of mown grass; most sites are lakeside or have views of the lake; elevation 600'.

Season, Fees & Phone: April to October; $8.00 for a standard site, $9.00 for a standard site with water, $11.00 for an electrical hookup site, $12.00 for a partial hookup site; 14 day limit; Lake Texoma CoE Project Office (214) 465-4990.

Camp Notes: Lake Texoma is especially noted for its striped bass fishing, and Lakeside would make an excellent headquarters for launching your efforts for same.

Oklahoma 119

PLATTER FLATS
Lake Texoma/Corps of Engineers Park

Location: South-central Oklahoma southwest of Durant.

Access: From U.S. Highway 70 at a point 6 miles west of Durant, 4 miles east of the Roosevelt Memorial bridge across Lake Texoma, turn south onto a paved access road and proceed 5 miles; turn west (right) and continue on a curving road for 3 miles, then turn north (right) to the campground entrance station. **Alternate Access:** From U.S. Highways 69 & 75 in Calera, follow a paved local road west for 2.5 miles to Platter; turn north and continue north, then west, for 5 miles to the campground.

Facilities: 83 campsites, including 42 with partial hookups (more hookups are planned), in 2 loops; sites are small to medium-sized, with nominal separation; parking pads are gravel, medium to long straight-ins; some pads may require minor additional leveling; adequate space for large tents; fire rings, plus some barbecue grills; firewood is usually available for gathering; water at faucets throughout; restrooms with showers; holding tank disposal station; paved or gravel driveways; gas and groceries in Platter; adequate supplies and services are available in Durant.

Activities & Attractions: Boating; boat launches; fishing; equestrian/hiking trail to Lakeside Campground.

Natural Features: Located above a bay on the east shore of Lake Texoma; some sites are on a tree-dotted grassy point and others are on a forested slope above the bay; sites receive light to medium shade/shelter from hardwoods; many sites are lakeside or have lake glimpses through the trees; elevation 600'.

Season, Fees & Phone: March to November; $8.00 for a standard site, $9.00 for a standard site with water; $12.00 for a partial hookup site; 14 day limit; Lake Texoma CoE Project Office (214) 465-4990.

Camp Notes: In addition to having some excellent campspots, Platter Flats has a reputation for having the 'best' (i.e., easiest-to-use) boat ramp on the lake.

Oklahoma 120

BURNS RUN
Lake Texoma/Corps of Engineers Park

Location: South-central Oklahoma southwest of Durant.

Access: From Oklahoma State Highway 75A on the west edge of the community of Cartwright at a large, triangular traffic median (just north of Dennison Dam, 6 miles north of Denison Texas and 3 miles west of the junction of Highway 75A & U.S. Highway 69, proceed west for 0.5 mile to a fork; Burns Run East is to the left; or continue for 1.3 miles west, then turn south (left) for another mile toward Burns Run West.

Facilities: 200 campsites, including many with electrical hookups; sites are small to medium-sized, with nominal separation; parking pads are gravel, medium to very long straight-ins; some pads may require minor additional leveling; medium to large tent spots; barbecue grills; b-y-o firewood is recommended; water at faucets throughout; restrooms with showers; holding tank disposal station; paved driveways; gas and groceries in Cartwright and nearby Colbert; adequate+ supplies and services are available in Denison.

Activities & Attractions: Boating; boat launches; fishing; playground; basketball court; designated swimming beach; day use areas with picnic shelters.

Natural Features: Located on a peninsula on a sheltered bay on the southeast shore of Lake Texoma; sites receive very light to medium shade/shelter from large hardwoods; the lake is bordered by forested hills; elevation 600'.

Season, Fees & Phone: April to November; $9.00 for a standard site, $11.00 for a partial hookup site; 14 day limit; Lake Texoma CoE Project Office (214) 465-4990.

Camp Notes: Of the two Burns Run units, Burns Run West has more sites and is closer to the main body of the lake; Burns Run East has a more sheltered boating environment, it's closer to the main highway, and it's available for camping during more months of the year.

BOGGY DEPOT
Boggy Depot State Park

Location: South-central Oklahoma north of Durant.

Access: From Oklahoma State Highway 7 at a point 6.4 miles east of Wapanucka, 10 miles west of Atoka, and just west of the bridge over Clear Boggy Creek, turn south onto a paved local road; proceed south, east, south, then east into the park for a total of 3.5 miles; turn south (right) to the hookup section or continue east to the standard sites.

Facilities: 93 campsites, including 10 with electrical hookups and 6 with full hookups; sites are small to medium-sized, essentially level, with minimal to fair separation; parking pads are paved, long pull-throughs for the full hookup sites, earth/gravel medium straight-ins or pull-offs for other sites; ample space for large tents; barbecue grills and fire rings; firewood may be available for gathering in the area; water at several faucets; restrooms with showers; holding tank disposal station; paved driveways; limited supplies and services are available in Wapanucka.

Activities & Attractions: Interpretive display; fishing (white bass, catfish and perch); day use area.

Natural Features: Located in a hardwood grove and an adjacent meadow; campground vegetation in the hookup area consists of tall oaks and sparse grass; standard sites in the east portion of the park are situated on a tree-dotted grassy flat; light to medium shade/shelter for most sites; small lake in the park; elevation 600'.

Season, Fees & Phone: Open all year; please see Appendix for standard Oklahoma state park fees; 14 day limit; park office (405) 889-5625.

Camp Notes: The historical significance of Boggy Depot dates back to the 1840's when it was an important supply point for troops and pioneers. It was also a stop on the Butterfield overland mail route which ran from St. Louis to San Francisco. In it's own present-day right, this is a simple, very pleasant camp stop.

KIAMICHI
Hugo Lake/Corps of Engineers Park

Location: Southeast Oklahoma east of Hugo.

Access: From U.S. Highway 70 at a point 6.8 miles east of the junction of U.S. Highways 271 & 70 in Hugo and 2.5 miles west of Sawyer, turn north onto Armadillo Road and proceed 0.75 mile to the park entrance station; continue for 0.5 mile, then turn west (left) onto Hickory Road; continue west to the 4 camp areas: for 0.7 mile to Ivy, 1.1 miles to Juniper, 1.7 miles to Maple and 2.3 miles to Quail.

Facilities: 105 campsites, including 90 with electrical hookups; sites are small to medium-sized, with minimal to nominal separation; parking pads are gravel, medium to long straight-ins; many pads may require additional leveling; some adequate spaces for large tents (especially good in the Quail area); barbecue grills and/or fire rings; b-y-o firewood is suggested; water at central faucets; restrooms with showers; holding tank disposal station; paved driveways; adequate supplies and services are available in Hugo.

Activities & Attractions: Boating; boat launch; fishing; playground; designated swimming beach; nature trail.

Natural Features: Located on the grassy, tree-dotted south shore of Hugo Lake; campground vegetation consists of mown grass, and small to medium-height hardwoods which provide light to medium shelter/shade for most sites; the 13,000-acre lake has a low, grass/tree-covered shoreline; elevation 400'.

Season, Fees & Phone: Open all year; $8.00 for a standard site, $11.00 for an electrical hookup site, $13.00 for a 'prime' electrical hookup site; 14 day limit; Hugo Lake CoE Project Office (405) 326-3345.

Camp Notes: Some of the nicest, roomiest sites are in the Nettle subloop, off Maple Road. Kiamichi is a top contender for the 'steepest boat ramp ever built' distinction. (Set the emergency brake and hang on tight to your bow line!)

Oklahoma 123

VIRGIL POINT
Hugo Lake/Corps of Engineers Park

Location: Southeast Oklahoma east of Hugo.

Access: From U.S. Highway 70 at a point 10 miles east of Hugo, 1 mile east of the bridge/dam over the Kiamichi River, and 6 miles west of Fort Towson, turn north onto Oklahoma State Highway 147; head north for 2.6 miles; turn west (left) onto the park access road and proceed 1 mile to the entrance station; continue for 0.1 mile to a fork in the road; camp Area B is to the north (right), and camp Areas C & D are to the south (left).

Facilities: 52 sites with electrical hookups, in 3 areas; most sites are small, with minimal to fair separation; parking pads are gravel, medium to long straight-ins; many pads may require additional leveling; adequate space, though slightly sloped, for medium to large tents on a grassy surface; some ramadas (sun shelters); barbecue grills or fire rings; firewood is usually available for gathering in the vicinity; water at central faucets; restrooms with showers; supplemental vaults; holding tank disposal station; paved driveways; gas and groceries are available in Sawyer, 3 miles south.

Activities & Attractions: Boating; boat launch; fishing for largemouth, spotted and white bass, crappie, channel and flathead catfish, bluegill and other sunfish, buffalo, carp, and drum--what a menagerie!.

Natural Features: Located on a bay on the southeast shore of Hugo Lake; sites receive light to light-medium shade/shelter from short to medium-height hardwoods; many sites are shoreside; the lake is ringed by a low, grassy, tree-dotted shoreline; elevation 400'.

Season, Fees & Phone: March to November; $11.00; 14 day limit; Hugo Lake CoE Project Office (405) 326-3345.

Camp Notes: This is probably the best choice for camping on Hugo Lake: the scenery seems to be a bit better, the vegetation is a little neater, and there's more likely to be a fresh breeze off the lake.

Oklahoma 124

RAYMOND GARY
Raymond Gary State Park

Location: Southeast Oklahoma east of Hugo.

Access: From U.S. Highway 70 at a point 0.6 mile east of Fort Towson and 10 miles west of Valliant, turn south onto Oklahoma State Highway 209 and proceed 1.6 miles to the park entrance; continue for a few hundred feet to a "Y" intersection; the hookup area is to the left and most of the tent sites are to the right.

Facilities: 37 campsites, including 10 with full hookups, in 4 areas; sites are small, with minimal separation; parking pads in the hookup loop are gravel/grass, level, medium to long straight-ins; parking pads in the standard area are gravel, short straight-ins or pull-offs; adequate space for large tents on a grassy slope; barbecue grills and a few fireplaces; b-y-o firewood is recommended; water at several faucets; restrooms with showers; paved driveways; gas and groceries are available in Fort Towson.

Activities & Attractions: Fishing; playground; paved bike/hike path along the shoreline; Fort Towson Historical Park, 3 miles north; day use area with shelters.

Natural Features: Located on a grassy slope and on a ridge above the east shore of 400-acre Raymond Gary Lake on the Kiamichi River, just above the Kiamichi's confluence with the Red River; the long narrow lake is bordered by low hills; campground vegetation consists of mown grass and scattered hardwoods; many tent sites are lakeside; hookup sites are perched atop the ridge with glimpses of the lake through the trees; elevation 400'.

Season, Fees & Phone: Open all year; please see Appendix for standard Oklahoma state park fees; 14 day limit; park office (405) 873-2307.

Camp Notes: There are two small tent areas worth checking out, one just below the dam with six sites, and one on a shelf above the lake with four sites. This park, with its expanses of mown grass and the hike/bike path, has a hint of an urban park atmosphere.

Oklahoma 125

PINE CREEK
Pine Creek State Park

Location: Southeast Oklahoma northeast of Hugo.

Access: From Oklahoma State Highway 3 at a point 26 miles east of Antlers, 4.5 miles west of the Little River/Pine Creek Lake crossing, and 31 miles west of Broken Bow, turn north onto a paved access road; travel 5 miles north and east to the park (the road curves twice toward the east in this 5 mile stretch); camping is to the right and to the left.

Facilities: 24 campsites in 2 loops; sites are small to large with nominal to fairly good separation; parking areas are grass/gravel, medium-length straight-ins or any-which-way-you-cans; additional leveling will probably be needed in many sites; some spacious, grassy tent sites, but they may be a bit sloped; barbecue grills and fire rings; firewood may be available for gathering in the surrounding area, b-y-o to be sure; water at central faucets; restrooms; holding tank disposal station; paved driveways; gas and groceries are available along the main highway.

Activities & Attractions: Boating; boat launch; fishing; playground; day use area with shelters; hiking in an adjacent state natural area.

Natural Features: Located on a grassy flat along a wide spot on Little River (the north arm of Pine Creek Lake); some sites are situated in a stand of hardwoods and some are located out on a grassy point bordered by Little River to the east and Turkey Creek to the west; elevation 400'.

Season, Fees & Phone: Open all year; please see Appendix for standard Oklahoma state park fees; 14 day limit; park office (405) 876-3298.

Camp Notes: Pine Creek State Park is also known as Turkey Creek Landing. The park is right along a low shoreline subject to flooding. A number of campers potentially can moor their watercraft right at their site.

Oklahoma 126

LITTLE RIVER
Pine Creek Lake/Corps of Engineers Park

Location: Southeast Oklahoma northeast of Hugo.

Access: From Oklahoma State Highway 3 at a point 29 miles east of Antlers, 1.7 miles west of the Little River/Pine Creek Lake crossing, and 28 miles west of Broken Bow, turn south onto a paved access road and proceed 1 mile to a fork; Loops B, C & D are to the north (left) and Loops E through H are straight ahead.

Facilities: 88 sites, including 41 with electrical hookups and a few with partial hookups, in 7 loops; sites are small to medium-sized, with nominal to fair separation; parking pads are gravel, medium to long straight-ins; many pads may require some additional leveling; adequate space for large tents on a grassy surface; barbecue grills or fire rings; firewood is usually available for gathering; water at several faucets; restrooms with showers; holding tank disposal station; paved driveways; gas and groceries are available along Highway 3.

Activities & Attractions: Boating; boat launch; fishing (largemouth bass, crappie, catfish); nature trail; designated swimming beach; playground; day use area with shelter.

Natural Features: Located on a rolling, wooded slope on the northwest shore of Pine Creek Lake just north of Rock Creek; hardwoods and a few pine trees dot the grassy slopes; vegetation in the south area is more dense than in the north area; the lake is ringed by low, well-wooded hills; elevation 400'.

Season, Fees & Phone: March to December; $8.00 for a standard site, $11.00 for an electrical hookup site, $12.00 for a partial hookup site; 14 day limit; phone c/o Hugo Lake CoE Project Office (405) 326-3345.

Camp Notes: This is a very nice just-off-highway stop. It's also within a half-hour's drive of the Indian Nation Turnpike, which gives it reasonably easy access from places like Oklahoma City and Tulsa, and yet it has an almost totally remote atmosphere. Reportedly, "the fishing is pretty good" here.

Oklahoma 127

CARSON CREEK
Hochatown State Park

Location: Southeast Oklahoma north of Idabel.

Access: From U.S. Highway 259 at a point 9 miles north of Broken Bow and 29 miles south of Smithville, turn east onto a park road and proceed 2.5 miles to a fork; turn south (right) to hookup areas 2 & 3 or follow signs to tent areas F, G & H.

Facilities: 83 campsites, including 12 with electrical hookups, 6 with partial hookups, and 10 with full hookups; sites are small to medium-sized, with minimal to nominal separation; parking pads are gravel, medium to long straight-ins for the hookup sites and however-you-may for the tent sites; many pads may require additional leveling; adequate, but rocky, spots for large tents; barbecue grills or fire rings; firewood is usually available for gathering; water at hookups sites and at central faucets; restrooms with showers; auxiliary vaults; holding tank disposal station; paved driveways; gas and groceries are available along Highway 259.

Activities & Attractions: Boating; 3 boat launches; bass fishing; hiking trails; playground; golf in the park's nearby Cedar Creek area.

Natural Features: Located on forested slopes above and along the southwest shore of Broken Bow Lake; vegetation consists of tall hardwoods and conifers, sparse grass, and a little underbrush; elevation 600'.

Season, Fees & Phone: Open all year; please see Appendix for standard Oklahoma state park fees; 14 day limit; park office (405) 494-6452.

Camp Notes: It is possible to take the hiking trail from the campgrounds northward for a couple of miles to the park's golf course, if you're into that sort of thing. Originally the pair of Hochatown units and adjacent Beavers Bend State Park were all part of the same operation. But the huge area became so popular and developed that it was split into two separate entities. Justifyably so. The lakeshore atmosphere in Hochatown is distinctively different from the forested, riverside environment in Beavers Bend.

Oklahoma 128

STEVENS GAP
Hochatown State Park

Location: Southeast Oklahoma north of Idabel.

Access: From U.S. Highway 259 at a point 8.4 miles north of Broken Bow and 29.6 miles south of Smithville, turn east onto a park road and proceed 1.7 miles; turn south (right) to hookup area 1 or follow signs to tent areas A-E.

Facilities: 80 campsites, including 7 with partial hookups, and 13 with full hookups; sites are small to medium-sized, with minimal to nominal separation; parking pads are gravel, medium to long straight-ins for the hookup sites and random parking for standard tent sites; many pads may require additional leveling; adequate areas for large tents; barbecue grills or fire rings; firewood is usually available for gathering in the area; water at hookups and at central faucets; restrooms with showers; auxiliary vaults; holding tank disposal station; paved driveways; gas and groceries are available along Highway 259.

Activities & Attractions: Boating; 3 boat launches; fishing; fish cleaning station; hiking; designated swimming beach; playground.

Natural Features: Located on forested slopes above and along the southwest shore of Broken Bow Lake; vegetation consists of tall hardwoods and conifers, sparse grass, and a little underbrush; the 14,000-acre lake is dotted with wooded islands and surrounded by tree-blanketed hills; elevation 600'.

Season, Fees & Phone: Open all year; please see Appendix for standard Oklahoma state park fees; 14 day limit; park office (405) 494-6452.

Camp Notes: Some of the standard/tent sites at Hochatown have terrific views of this superscenic lake.

BEAVERS BEND
Beavers Bend State Park

Location: Southeast Oklahoma north of Idabel.

Access: From U.S. Highway 259 at a point 5 miles north of Broken Bow and 33 miles south of Smithville, turn east onto State Highway 259A; proceed 4 miles to a fork in the road; Areas A-C (mostly hookups) are to the south (right) and Loops D-H (mostly standard sites) are to the north (left). (Note that State Highway 259A, a park loop road, also joins U.S. Highway 259 at a point 7 miles north of Broken Bow.)

Facilities: 163 campsites, including 110 with partial hookups; hookup sites are small, with nominal separation; standard sites are small to medium-sized, with nominal to fair separation; parking pads are mostly gravel (some paved pads in the hookup section), mostly short to medium straight-ins; some pads may require minor additional leveling; some spacious tent spots, especially in Loop G; assorted fire facilities; b-y-o firewood is recommended; water at faucets throughout; restrooms with showers; holding tank disposal station; paved driveways; adequate supplies and services are available in Broken Bow.

Activities & Attractions: Trout fishing on Mountain Fork, bassing on the lake; hiking; nature trail; nature center; Forest Heritage Center (museum); riverside swimming beach; playground; tennis and volleyball courts; canoeing and floating.

Natural Features: Located on a forested flat on the west bank of Mountain Fork River below Broken Bow Dam; sites receive light to medium shade/shelter from tall cedars and hardwoods; some riverside sites; elevation 500'.

Season, Fees & Phone: Open all year; reservations accepted for assigned sites; please see Appendix for additional reservation information and standard Oklahoma state park fees; 14 day limit; park office (405) 494-6300.

Camp Notes: Beavers Bend State Park is one of the finest camp spots in this remote corner of Oklahoma. The park offers just about every type of outdoor activity you could possibly imagine (plus one or two that aren't on standard checklists. Included are the usual pursuits of swimming, fishing, and boating. But the roll call to action also lists miniature golf, hayrides, bumper boating and "party barges" for rent (no kidding). It seems the good word has spread near and far because there are usually plenty of Lone Star license plates to be seen here.

Jackcamping and Backpacking in the West's Parks and Forests

In addition to camping in established campgrounds, as do the majority of visitors, thousands of campers opt for simpler places to spend a night or a week or more in the West's magnificent parks and forests.

Jackcamping

"Jackcamping", "roadsiding", "dispersed camping", or "siwashing" are several of the assorted terms describing the simplest type of camp there is: just pulling a vehicle a few yards off the main drag, or heading up a gravel or dirt forest road to an out-of-the-way spot which looks good to you. Sometimes, especially when the "Campground Full" plank is hung out to dry in front of all the nearby public campgrounds, or there *aren't* any nearby public campgrounds, it might be the only way to travel.

From what we can determine "jackcamping" is an extension of the Medieval English slang word "jacke", meaning "common", "serviceable" or "ordinary". The explanations of "roadsiding" and "dispersed camping" are self-evident. "Siwashing" is an old term from the Southwest. It apparently refers to the practice of cowboys and other travelers making a late camp by just hunkering-down in an *arroyo* or 'dry wash'. After hobbling your horse, the saddle is propped-up against the *side* of the *wash*, (hence *si'wash* or *siwash*), forming a leather 'recliner' of sorts in which to pass the night out of the wind and cold. It may not be the most comfortable way to spend the night, but by two or three a.m. you get used to the smell of the saddle anyway.

As a general rule-of-thumb, jackcamping isn't allowed in local, state and national parks. In those areas, you'll have to stay in established campgrounds or sign-up for a backcountry site.

However, jackcamping is *usually* permitted anywhere on the millions of road-accessible acres of national forest and BLM-managed federal public lands, subject to a few exceptions. In some high-traffic areas it's not allowed, and roadside signs are *usually* posted telling you so. ("Camp Only in Designated Campgrounds" signs are becoming more common with each passing year.) In certain high fire risk zones or during the general fire season it may not be permitted. For the majority of areas in which jackcamping is legal, small campfires, suitably sized and contained, are ordinarily OK. All of the rules of good manners, trash-removal, and hygiene which apply to camping anywhere, regardless of location, are enforced. (Would *you* want to camp where someone else had left their "sign"?) For off-highway travel, the "Shovel, Axe and Bucket" rule is usually in effect (see below).

Since you don't want the law coming down on you for an unintentional impropriety, it's highly advisable to stop in or call a local Forest Service ranger station or BLM office to determine the status of jackcamping in your region of choice, plus any special requirements (spark arrestors, the length of the shovel needed under the "Shovel, Axe and Bucket" rule, campfires, stay limit, etc.) Local ranchers who have leased grazing rights on federal lands are sensitive about their livestock sharing the meadows and rangelands with campers. So it's probably best to jackcamp in "open" areas, thus avoiding leaseholder vs taxpayer rights confrontations altogether. (Legalities notwithstanding, the barrel of a 12-gauge or an '06 looks especially awesome when it's poked inside your tent at midnight.) Be sure to get the name of the individual in the local public office who provided the information "just in case".

If you're reasonably self-sufficient or self-contained, jackcamping can save you *beaucoups* bucks--perhaps hundreds of dollars--over a lifetime of camping. (We know.)

Backpacking

Take all of the open acres readily available to jackcampers, then multiply that figure by a factor of 100,000 (or thereabouts) and you'll have some idea of the wilderness and near-wilderness camping opportunities that are only accessible to backpackers (or horsepackers).

Backpackers usually invest a lot of time, and usually a lot of money, into their preferred camping method, and perhaps rightfully so (timewise, anyway).

Planning an overnight or week-long foot trip into the boondocks is half the work (and half the fun too!). Hours, days, even *weeks*, can be spent pouring over highway maps, topographic maps, public lands/BLM maps, and forest maps looking for likely places to pack into. (We know!)

Backpacking in Western National Forests

To be editorially above-board about this: Of all the possible federal and state recreation areas, your best opportunities for backpack camping are in the national forest wilderness, primitive, and wild areas. Prime backpacking areas in most state parks and many national park units are measured in acres or perhaps square miles; but the back country in the national forests is measured in tens and hundreds and thousands of square miles. Here's where planning really becomes fun.

Backpacking in Western National and State Parks

Finding a backpack campsite in the West's *parks* is relatively straightforward: much of the work has been done for you by the park people. Many state and national parks which are large enough to provide opportunities for backcountry travel have established backcountry camps which are the *only* places to camp out in the toolies. Yes, that indeed restricts your overnight choices to a few small areas in many cases; but you can still enjoy walking through and looking at the rest of the back country.

Throughout this series, designated backpack campsites and other backpacking opportunities are occasionally mentioned in conjunction with nearby established campgrounds.

Backpacking in Southwest Plains National Forests

A couple million acres of beautiful backcountry can be explored in Texas and Oklahoma National Forests, and you probably couldn't go wrong in selecting any national forest wilderness or primitive area. The best places? In Texas, the Big Thicket comes first to mind. It's a place where you can still lose yourself in solitude (and in other ways, to boot.) In southeast Oklahoma, 40 miles of the Ouachita National National Recreation Trail passes through beautiful mountain forest from near Talihina to the Arkansas border, then continues for another 130 miles to Little Rock, Arkansas. The Jean Pierre Chouteau Trail follows 60 miles of the Verdigris River from Catoosa, near Tulsa, to the confluence of the Verdigris and Arkansas Rivers near Fort Gibson. There are a half dozen public camp/picnic areas along the route.

Backpacking in Southwest Plains National Parks

Although backpacking opportunities are generally more limited in Southwest Plains National Parks than they area in regions farther west, there are still some good to outstanding areas to get away from everything and everybody.

You won't find many national parks in the lower 48 with more room to roam than *Big Bend* and *Guadalupe Mountains* National Parks, and *Padre Island* National Seashore. Each national park unit lists an unspecified "limited" number of hike-in backcountry campsites in "various locations" throughout the parks. A permit is needed for backcountry camping in all the foregoing areas.

Backcountry information and 'regs' are subject to change. Therefore we suggest that you use the Phone information in the text to contact your selected park's headquarters and ask for the "backcountry office" or "backcountry ranger" to initialize your trip planning. In virtually every case, they'll be able to provide detailed information and maps--at no charge, or at most a couple of bucks for first-rate maps. The majority of the backcountry people are enthusiastic boondockers themselves, and they'll generally provide sound, albeit conservative, suggestions. Let's face it: they don't want to have to bail anybody out of a tough spot by extracting them on foot, in a dusty green government-issue jeep, a helicopter--or by what they call at Grand Canyon an "emergency mule drag-out". (Try living that one down when you get home, dude!)

Backpacking in Southwest Plains State Parks

In Texas, *Enchanted Rock* and *Hill Country* State Natural Areas are the obvious choices (see information in the Texas text). Several other state parks (also noted in the text) have smaller, walk-in or backpack areas. In Oklahoma, be sure to check out the 15-mile trail around long, slender Greenleaf Lake in Greenleaf State Park. The trail is said to have been designed with overnight trips as its principal purpose.

Boat Camping in Southwest Plains National Parks

Big Bend National Park lists again lists a "limited" number of boat-in/float-in camps along the Rio Grande. *Padre Island* National Seashore indicates that boat-in camping is available along the Gulf Coast and on Laguna Madre Island in all areas that are not posted as being off limits. *Lake Meredith* and *Amistad* Recreation Areas also offer an unspecified "limited" number of boat-in camps along the shores of their lakes.

At the risk of demagoguery: We can vouch that it really pays to start planning months in advance for a backcountry trip. Besides, planning is half the fun.

Creative Camping

In their most elementary forms, outdoor recreation in general, and camping in particular, require very little in the way of extensive planning or highly specialized and sophisticated equipment. A stout knife, some matches, a few blankets, a free road map, a water jug, and a big sack of p.b. & j. sandwiches, all tossed onto the seat of an old beater pickup, will get you started on the way to a lifetime of outdoor adventures.

Idyllic and nostalgic as that scenario may seem, most of the individuals reading this *Double Eagle™* Guide (and those *writing* it) probably desire (and deserve) at least a few granules of comfort sprinkled over their tent or around their rv.

There are enough books already on the market or in libraries which will provide you with plenty of advice on *how* to camp. One of the oldest and best is the *Fieldbook*, published by the Boy Scouts of America. Really. It is a widely accepted, profusely illustrated (not to mention comparatively inexpensive) outdoor reference which has few true rivals. It presents plenty of information on setting up camp, first aid, safety, woodlore, flora and fauna identification, weather, and a host of other items. Although recreational vehicle camping isn't specifically covered in detail, many of the general camping principles it does cover apply equally well to rv's.

So rather than re-invent the wheel, we've concentrated your hard-earned *dinero* into finding out *where* to camp. However, there are still a few items that aren't widely known which might be of interest to you, or which bear repeating, so we've included them in the following paragraphs.

Resourcefulness. When putting together your equipment, it's both challenging and a lot of fun to make the ordinary stuff you have around the house, especially in the kitchen, do double duty. Offer an "early retirement" to servicable utensils, pans, plastic cups, etc. to a "gear box".

Resource-fullness. Empty plastic peanut butter jars, pancake syrup and milk jugs, ketchup bottles, also aluminum pie plates and styrofoam trays, can be washed, re-labeled and used again. (The syrup jugs, with their handles and pop-up spouts, make terrific "canteens" for kids.) The lightweight, break-resistant plastic stuff is more practical on a camping trip than glass containers, anyway. *El Cheapo* plastic shopping bags, which have become *de rigueur* in supermarkets, can be saved and re-used to hold travel litter and campground trash. When they're full, tie them tightly closed using the "handles". In the words of a college-age camper from Holland while he was refilling a plastic, two-liter soft drink bottle at the single water faucet in a desert national park campground: "Why waste?".

Redundancy. Whether you're camping in a tent, pickup, van, boat, motorhome or fifth-wheel trailer, it pays to think and plan like a backpacker. Can you make-do with fewer changes of clothes for a short weekend trip? How about getting-by with half as much diet cola, and drink more cool, campground spring water instead? Do you really *need* that third curling iron? Real backpackers (like the guy who trimmed the margins off his maps) are relentless in their quest for the light load.

Water. No matter where you travel, *always* carry a couple of gallons of drinking water. Campground water sources may be out of order (e.g., someone broke the handle off the hydrant or the well went dry), and you probably won't want to fool around with boiling lake or stream water. (Because of the possibility of encountering the widespread "beaver fever" (*Giardia*) parasite and other diseases in lakes and streams, if treated or tested H_2O isn't available, boil the surface water for a full five minutes.)

Juice. If you're a tent or small vehicle camper who normally doesn't need electrical hookups, carry a hotplate, coffee pot, or hair dryer when traveling in regions where hookup campsites are available. The trend in public campground management is toward charging the full rate for a hookup site whether or not you have an rv, even though there are no standard sites available for you to occupy. In many popular state parks and Corps of Engineers recreation areas, hookup sites far outnumber standard sites. At least you'll have some use for the juice.

Fire. Charcoal lighter fluid makes a good "starter" for campfires, and is especially handy if the wood is damp. In a pinch, that spare bottle of motor oil in the trunk can be pressed into service for the same purpose. Let two ounces soak in for several minutes. Practice the same safety precautions you would use in lighting a home barbecue so you can keep your curly locks and eyebrows from being scorched by the flames. Obviously use extreme caution--and don't even *think* about using gasoline. A really handy option to using wood is to carry a couple of synthetic "fire logs". The sawdust-and-paraffin logs are made from byproducts of the lumber and petroleum industries and burn about three hours in the outdoors. The fire logs can also be used to start and maintain a regular campfire if the locally gathered firewood is wet.

Mosquitoes. The winged demons aren't usually mentioned in the text because you just have to *expect* them almost anywhere except perhaps in the dryest desert areas. Soggy times, like late spring and early summer, are the worst times. If you're one of us who's always the first to be strafed by the local mosquito squadron, keep plenty of anti-aircraft ammo on hand. The most versatile skin stuff is the spray-on variety. Spray it all over your clothes to keep the varmints from poking their proboscis through the seat of your jeans. A room spray comes in handy for blasting any bugs which might have infiltrated your tent or rv. Fortunately, in most areas the peak of the mosquito season lasts only a couple of weeks, and you can enjoy yourself the rest of the time. Autumn camping is great!

Plants. Poison ivy, oak and sumac can be found in many wooded regions throughout the West. Avoid off-trail brush-busting or brushing up against trailside vegetation with bare skin. Oleander, those beautifully flowering bushes planted in campgrounds all over the Western Sunbelt are toxic, so keep your pets and your kids from nibbling on them. Likewise, in the desert regions, steer plenty clear of cholla cactus. The Indians call it the "jumping cactus" with good reason.

Snakes. Anywhere you go in the Southwest, expect to find snakes, so place your hands and feet and sother vital parts accordingly. (Recently, one of the publishers inadvertently poked her zoom lens to within a yard of a coiled rattler's snout. The photographer's anxieties were vocally, albeit shakily, expressed; the level of stress which the incident induced on the snake is unknown.)

Creepy-crawlers. In arid Desert Southwest regions, watch for scorpions and other ground-based critters. In the Southwest Plains, tarantulas make their appearances in spring and fall, but the fuzzy arachnids will leave you alone if you reciprocate.

Bumps in the night. When you retire for the night, put all your valuables, especially your cooler, inside your vehicle to protect them against campground burglars and bruins. While camping at Canyon Campground in Yellowstone National Park more than two decades ago, a pair of young brothers unwittingly left their stocked cooler out on the picnic table so they had more room to sleep inside their ancient station wagon. Sometime after midnight, they were awakened by a clatter in the darkness behind the wagon. After they had groggily dressed and crept out to investigate, the sleepy siblings discovered that a bear had broken into their impenetrable ice chest. Taking inventory, the dauntless duo determined that the brazen backwoods *bandito* had wolfed-down three pounds of baked chicken breasts, a meatloaf, one pound of pineapple cottage cheese, four quarters of margarine, and had bitten into two cans of Bud-- presumably to wash it all down. The soft drinks were untouched. (We dined sumptuously on Spam and pork 'n beans for the rest of the trip. Ed.)

Timing. Try staying an hour ahead of everyone else. While traveling in Pacific Time, set your clock to Mountain Time; when in the mountains, keep your timepiece ticking on Central Time. That way you'll naturally set up camp an hour earlier, and likewise break camp an hour prior to other travelers. You would be amazed at how much that 60 minutes will do for campsite availability in the late afternoon, or for restrooms, showers, uncrowded roads and sightseeing in the morning.

Horsepower. Your camping vehicle will lose about four percent of its power for each 1000' gain in altitude above sea level (unless it's turbocharged). Keep that in mind in relation to the "pack like a backpacker" item mentioned previously. You might also keep it in mind when you embark on a foot trip. The factory-original human machine loses about the same amount of efficiency at higher elevations.

Reptile repellant. Here's a sensitive subject. With the rise in crimes perpetrated against travelers and campers in the nation's parks and forests and on its highways and byways, it's become increasingly common for legitimate campers to pack a 'heater'--the type that's measured by caliber or gauge, not in volts and amps. To quote a respected Wyoming peace officer: "Half the pickups and campers in Wyoming and Montana have a .45 automatic under the seat or a 12-gauge pump behind the bunk". If personal safety is a concern to you, check all applicable laws, get competent instruction, practice a lot, and join the NRA.

Vaporhavens. Be skeptical when you scan highway and forest maps and see hundreds of little symbols which indicate the locations of alleged campsites; or when you glance through listings published by governmental agencies or promotional interests. A high percentage of those 'recreation areas' are as vaporous as the mist rising from a warm lake into chilled autumn air. Many, many of the listed spots are actually picnic areas, fishing access sites, and even highway rest stops; dozens of camps are ill-maintained remnants of their former greatness, located at the end of rocky jeep trails; many others no longer exist; still others *never* existed, but are merely a mapmaker's or planner's notion of where a campground *might* or *should* be. In summation: Make certain that a campground exists and what it offers before you embark on 20 miles of washboard gravel travel in the never-ending quest for your own personal Eden.

We hope the foregoing items, and information throughout this series, help you conserve your own valuable time, money, fuel and other irreplaceable resources. ***Good Camping !***

172

Appendix

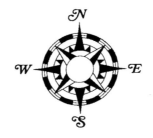

Texas

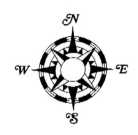

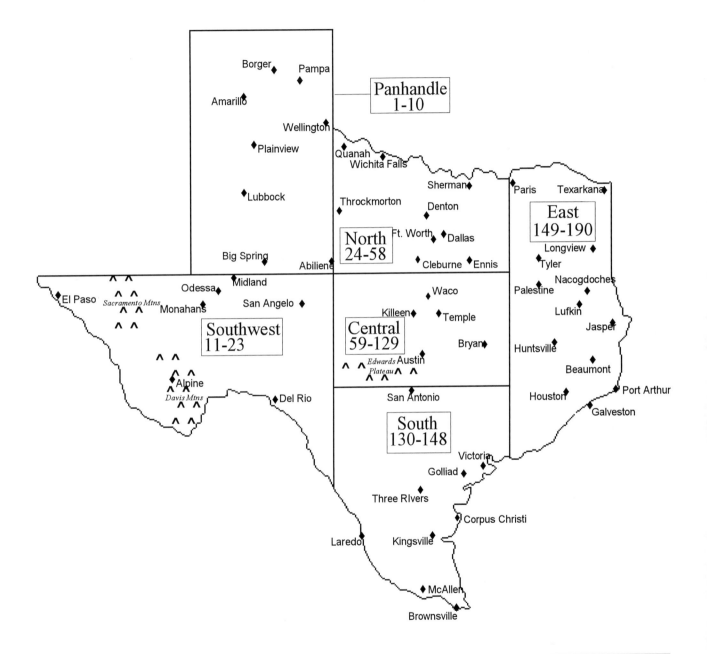

Borger Pampa

Panhandle
1-10

Amarillo

Wellington

Plainview Quanah
Wichita Falls

Sherman

Lubbock Throckmorton Denton

North
24-58 Ft. Worth Dallas

Paris Texarkana

East
149-190

Big Spring Cleburne Ennis Longview
Abilene Tyler

Midland Nacogdoches
Odessa Waco Palestine

El Paso Sacramento Mtns San Angelo Killeen Temple Lufkin
Monahans Jasper

Southwest
11-23 Central
59-129 Bryan Huntsville

Beaumont

Edwards Austin
Plateau Houston Port Arthur
Alpine Galveston
Davis Mtns Del Rio San Antonio

South
130-148

Victoria

Golliad

Three RIvers

Corpus Christi

Laredo Kingsville

McAllen

Brownsville

Oklahoma

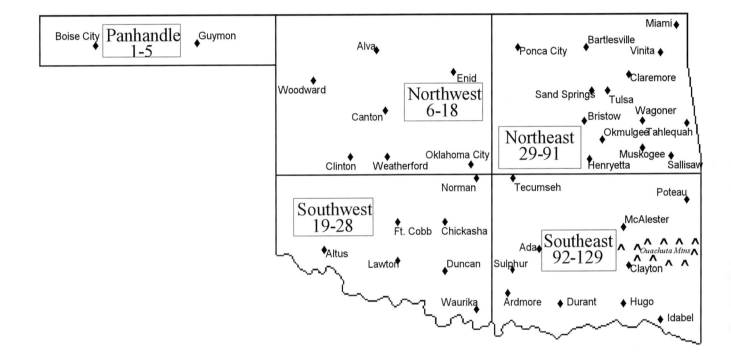

Boise City ◆ **Panhandle 1-5** ◆ Guymon

Alva ◆

Enid ◆

Woodward ◆

Northwest 6-18

Canton ◆

Ponca City ◆

Miami ◆

Bartlesville ◆

Vinita ◆

Claremore ◆

Sand Springs ◆ Tulsa

Wagoner ◆

Bristow ◆

Northeast 29-91

Okmulgee Tahlequah ◆

Clinton ◆ Weatherford ◆

Oklahoma City ◆

Muskogee ◆

Henryetta ◆ Sallisaw

Norman ◆

Tecumseh ◆

Poteau ◆

Southwest 19-28

Ft. Cobb ◆ Chickasha ◆

McAlester ◆

Ada ◆ **Southeast 92-129** ^ ^ ^ ^ ^

Altus ◆

Lawton ◆ Duncan ◆

Sulphur ◆ *Ouachuta Mtns* ^

Clayton ◆ ^

Waurika ◆

Ardmore ◆ Durant ◆ Hugo ◆

Idabel ◆

SOUTHWEST PLAINS STANDARD STATE PARK FEES

Texas

Camping fees for Texas state parks are set by individual park managers within guidelines established by the state parks department. According to official statements issuded by the Texas Parks and WIldlife Department: "The park managers know their customers, the demand, and the competition betters than anyone and are best able to meet their customers' needs and determine the appropriate fees."

Consequently, a broad range of fees, organized into a half dozen major categories, is in effect within the park system. *Changes may be expected at any time.*

The following is a digest of the complex fee structure:

Park entry	$3.00-$6.00
Primitive campsite	$4.00-$8.00
Standard campsite (water)	$6.00-$12.00
Partial hookup campsite (water, electricity)	$9.00-$15.00
Full hookup campsite (water, electricity, sewer)	$10.00-$16.00
Screened shelters	$15.00-$25.00

In general, expect campsite fees toward the upper end of the spectrum in popular parks close to large metro areas, or parks with unique natural appeal.

Certain parks, especially the types mentioned in the foregoing paragraph, also have additional fees for so-called 'premium' campsites. Seasonal rates are in effect in some parks as well.

Weekly and monthy discount camping rates are available in several dozen parks.

It is recommended that you call your selected park a few days prior to arrival to determine the exact campsite fees you'll be charged. (As of this printing, credit cards are not accepted in payment for camping.)

Oklahoma

Primitive ("unimproved") campsite	$6.00
Tent campsite (water)	$6.00
Partial hookup (water, electricity "semi-modern") campsite	$10.00
Full hookup (water, electricity, sewer "modern") campsite	$13.00
Add for "assigned" sites	$1.00
Group campsites	$175.00-$225.00 min.

Note: Annual park entry permits, offering substantial savings for frequent park users, are available in both states.

Please remember that all fees are subject to change without notice.

SOUTHWEST PLAINS CAMPSITE RESERVATIONS

Southwest Plains State Parks

Reservations may be made for certain individual and group campsites in Texas and Oklahoma state parks, as noted in the text. As a general rule-of-thumb, reservations for holiday weekends should be initiated at least several weeks in advance.

Texas state park reservations may be made by calling a Central Reservations Center in Austin Monday through Friday from 8:00 a.m. to 5:00 p.m., Central Time, **(512) 389-8900**.

Oklahoma state park reservations must be made directly with the park office of the state park area in which the campground is located. Reservations are accepted Monday through Friday from 8 a.m. to 5 p.m., Central Time. (Telephone reservations, the most common type, may be made using the *Phone* information in the text.)

Oklahoma reservations may be made by telephone, in writing, or in person. A fee equal to the amount of the first night's campsite fee is required at the time the reservation is made. Telephone reservations will be valid for five (5) days, pending the receipt of the fee. If the fee isn't received within the five day period, the telephone reservation is cancelled. The advance fees will be refunded if the accepted reservation is cancelled at least 72 hours prior to the scheduled arrival date; otherwise, the fee is forfeited.

Campsite assignments are made according to the type requested (tent or rv), but specific sites can't be reserved. Reservation requests for adjoining sites are accommodated, if possible. When making a reservation, be prepared to tell park personnel about the major camping equipment you plan to use, (size and number of tents, type and length of rv, additional vehicles, boat trailers, etc.). Be generous in your estimate.

Additional information may be obtained from the state parks department headquarters:

Texas Parks and Wildlife Department, Austin, TX
(800) 792-1112 or (512) 389-4890

Oklahoma Tourism & Recreation Department, Oklahoma City, OK
(800) 652-6552 or (405) 521-2409

Southwest Plains National Forests and National Parks

The *USDA Forest Service* and the *National Park Service* have also established reservation systems which affect hundreds of national forest campgrounds and certain national park areas nationwide. *At present*, national forest and national park campgrounds in the Southwest Plains are *not* included in the reservation systems. However, continuous changes can be expected as campgrounds with reservable sites are added or removed from the lists. For current information about campgrounds with reservable sites you may call (toll-free):

For *national forest* campgrounds: 800-280-CAMP   (800-280-2267)

For *national park* campgrounds: 800-365-CAMP   (800-365-2267)

Reservations for certain other campgrounds in the Southwest Plains *may* be obtainable directly from the public agency responsible for the camping area, as indicated in the text.

Please remember that all reservation information is subject to change without notice.

INDEX

Important Note:

In the following listing, the number to the right of the campground name refers to the Key Number in boldface in the upper left corner of each campground description in the text.

(E.G. **Texas 30** is **Abilene**. The number does *not* indicate the page number; page numbers are printed in the text only as secondary references.)

* A thumbnail description of a campground marked with an asterisk is found in the *Camp Notes* section of the principal numbered campground.

TEXAS

OKLAHOMA